THE TOWN OF STAMFORD

(28) CHURCH OF ALL SAINTS, from south.

ROYAL COMMISSION ON HISTORICAL MONUMENTS
ENGLAND

An Inventory of
Historical Monuments

THE TOWN
OF
STAMFORD

LONDON · HER MAJESTY'S STATIONERY OFFICE

TABLE OF CONTENTS

FOREWORD

William Stukeley, the 18th-century antiquary, described Stamford as 'the most elegant town upon the great northern road', and few will disagree with this judgement today. As the site of a river-crossing by one of the great trackways of prehistoric England, as one of the Five Boroughs established under the Danelaw, as a thriving centre in the medieval period, and as a town with Georgian buildings of high architectural quality, Stamford has for long provided material for historians of varying interests. However, a complete inventory of the archaeological remains and the standing buildings has been lacking and it was this deficiency which prompted the Commissioners to choose Stamford as the subject for the present volume. The work was carried out by the staff of the Cambridge office of the Commission. As expected, the investigation of such an historic town revealed a large number of early buildings hidden behind later street-fronts, and it is hoped that by providing a full list of these structures a picture of the extent of Stamford during the medieval and the immediate post medieval periods will be presented. At the same time attention has been paid to the stylistic development of the Classical architecture of the 18th and early 19th centuries. To all who value the retention of early buildings, whether for historical or aesthetic reasons, it is gratifying to note that Stamford has suffered less than many ancient towns. Nevertheless the threat to town buildings is particularly real and it is hoped that this inventory will be of use to those bodies, whether public or private, who are concerned with matters of planning.

The Commissioners have expressed in the *Report* their thanks for the help which the staff has received from local historians, owners of houses and shops, and many others, and I would like to endorse these words of gratitude.

In accordance with the Commission's practice no major monument has been included in the Inventory which has not been inspected and the account of it checked by one of my fellow Commissioners. Thanks are particularly due to Professor M. W. Barley, Mr. H. M. Colvin, Dr. C. A. R. Radford, Sir John Summerson and Dr. A. J. Taylor in this connection. However, any corrections to the Inventory would be welcomed.

I would draw attention to the fact that the record cards may be consulted by accredited persons who give written notice of their intention to the Secretary of the Commission. Copies of photographs may be bought on application to the National Monuments Record.

ADEANE
Chairman

COMMISSIONERS

The Right Honourable the Lord Adeane, P.C., G.C.B., G.C.V.O. (*Chairman*)

Her Majesty's Lieutenant of Lincolnshire (*ex officio*)

Henry Clifford Darby, Esq., O.B.E.

Courtenay Arthur Ralegh Radford, Esq.

Howard Montagu Colvin, Esq., C.B.E.

William Francis Grimes, Esq., C.B.E.

Maurice Willmore Barley, Esq.

Sheppard Sunderland Frere, Esq.

Richard John Copland Atkinson, Esq.

Sir John Betjeman, C.B.E.

Harold McCarter Taylor, Esq., C.B.E.

George Zarnecki, Esq., C.B.E.

John Kenneth Sinclair St Joseph, Esq., O.B.E.

Arnold Joseph Taylor, Esq., C.B.E.

Paul Ashbee, Esq.

Arthur Richard Dufty, Esq., C.B.E.

Secretary

Robert William McDowall, Esq., O.B.E.

ROYAL COMMISSION ON THE ANCIENT AND HISTORICAL MONUMENTS AND CONSTRUCTIONS OF ENGLAND

Report to The Queen's Most Excellent Majesty

MAY IT PLEASE YOUR MAJESTY

We, the undersigned Commissioners, appointed to make an Inventory of the Ancient and Historical Monuments and Constructions connected with or illustrative of the contemporary culture, civilization and conditions of life of the people of England, excluding Monmouthshire, from the earliest times to the year 1714, and such further Monuments and Constructions subsequent to that year as may seem in our discretion to be worthy of mention therein, and to specify those which seem most worthy of preservation, do humbly submit to Your Majesty the following Report, being the thirty-fourth Report on the work of the Commission since its first appointment.

2. We have pleasure in reporting the completion of our recording of the monuments in the town of Stamford.

3. Following our usual practice we have prepared an illustrated Inventory of the monuments, which will be issued as a non-Parliamentary publication entitled *The Town of Stamford*. As in recent Inventories accompanying Reports, the Commissioners have adopted the terminal date of 1850 generally for the monuments described in the Inventory though exercising discretion where reference to later monuments seemed desirable.

4. The methods adopted in previous Inventories of describing monuments have been broadly followed, but an attempt has been made to reduce the length of the descriptions where possible.

5. The descriptions of the major monuments in Stamford have been referred to the appropriate specialists and to a number of owners, and we are satisfied that no significant standing monument dating from between earliest times and 1850 has been omitted.

6. Our special thanks are due to incumbents and churchwardens and to owners and occupiers who have allowed access by our staff to the monuments in their charge. We are particularly indebted to The Trustees of the Burghley Estate Trust, the Most Honourable the Marquess of Exeter and his agent, Mr. J. C. P. Langton, for granting ready access to the Burghley Estate documents, and likewise to the Town Clerk, the staff at the Stamford Library, the Lincolnshire Archives Offices, the Northamptonshire Record Office, and the officers of the Stamford Archaeological Society, for permission to study documents and drawings in their charge. We wish to place on record our indebtedness to local historians, especially: Dr. E. C. Till, who most generously placed at the Commission's disposal his transcriptions of documents relating to property-ownership and other matters pertaining to our work; Miss Christine Mahany, B.Sc., who provided constant information of current archaeological discoveries, and Dr. Alan Rogers whose publications on the history of the town have proved of great value. We are also grateful for the specialized information given by Mr. Richard Marks concerning ancient glass.

7. The town of Stamford has survived to a large degree undamaged by incongruous modern intrusions. The tallest buildings are still the church towers, so preserving a traditional sky-line which is becoming an increasingly rare feature of our towns. The modern by-pass road and the introduction of vehicle-free precincts have allowed the town's ancient buildings to be seen to better advantage than hitherto. Although a great number of houses have remained without recent alteration, several have been mutilated by their conversion into shops and the introduction of discordant shopfronts; it is hoped that further destruction of this nature will be prevented.

8. We humbly submit to your Majesty's notice the following recommendations for the preservation of monuments in Stamford. In view of the historical and architectural value of Stamford as a whole we believe that the entire area which constituted the medieval town should be regarded with special consideration for conservation purposes. Within that area, certain streets have either buildings of outstanding merit or contain groups of buildings where any destruction would reflect adversely on the whole; individual monuments, with the exception of churches, have therefore not been enumerated. The following early parish churches lie within the medieval town and are especially worthy of preservation:

(28) ALL SAINTS, 13th and 15th century.

(29) ST. GEORGE, 13th to 17th century; medieval glass and 18th-century monuments.

(30) ST. JOHN BAPTIST, 15th century; medieval glass.

(31) ST. MARTIN, 15th century; medieval glass and post-Reformation monuments.

(33) ST. MARY, 13th to 15th century; late medieval ceiling of chapel.

(54) THE FORMER PARISH CHURCH OF ST. PAUL, now Stamford School chapel, 12th and 13th century.

The preservation of the following streets or groups of streets is thought to be of paramount importance:

The area which incorporates ST. GEORGE'S SQUARE, ST. MARY'S STREET (E. half in particular), ST. MARY'S PLACE and ST. MARY'S HILL; several buildings date from the medieval period but the character of the area is given by the large number of buildings of the 18th and early 19th centuries designed in the Classical style, many being of outstanding quality.

BARN HILL, running into ALL SAINT'S PLACE; some houses are medieval but most are of the 18th and early 19th centuries and have impressive facades.

BROAD STREET, one of the principal streets of the town, containing a large number of buildings of varying dates; retention as a group is recommended.

HIGH STREET, a notable street with large houses on the N. side, dating mostly from the 18th century.

IRONMONGER STREET, a linking street with 18th-century buildings on each side worthy of group conservation; several of them have early 19th-century shopfronts.

ST. PAUL'S STREET (W. half), containing many ancient houses, the earliest dating from the 13th century; the street now presents a mainly 17th-century appearance.

HIGH STREET ST. MARTINS, this wide approach road to the town has an 18th-century character with many houses of architectural merit; some houses incorporate extensive medieval remains.

Four monuments standing outside the medieval town are especially worthy of preservation:

(46) GATEWAY OF FRANCISCAN PRIORY, late 14th century.

(47) ST. LEONARD'S PRIORY, 12th-century church and other remains.

(288) RUTLAND TERRACE, first half of 19th century.

(427) ROCK HOUSE, first half of 19th century.

With the exception of St. Leonard's Priory, the areas and buildings listed above are contained within the present Stamford Conservation Area.

9. We further recommend that should any earthwork included in the Inventory be threatened with damage or destruction it should be investigated archaeologically in advance. In particular we would call attention to the importance of Stamford in the pre-Conquest and immediately post-Conquest ages. Little is known about the Danish, Anglo-Saxon and later medieval fortifications, all of which lay within the area covered by the present volume. We would urge that no opportunity of investigating these monuments should be overlooked, even where recent development has obliterated all surface indications.

10. In compiling the foregoing recommendations our criteria have been architectural or archaeological importance, not only locally but nationally, and the degree of loss to the nation that would result from destruction, bearing in mind the extent to which the monuments are illustrative of the contemporary culture, civilization and conditions of life of the people of England, as required by Your Majesty's Warrant. We have not taken into account any attendant circumstances, such as the cost of maintenance, usefulness for present-day purpose, or problems of preservation.

11. We desire to express our acknowledgement of the good work accomplished by our executive staff in the preparation of this Inventory, in particular Mr. S. D. T. Spittle (editorial); Mr. R. F. Taylor, Mr. D. A. H. Richmond and Mrs. S. E. Ault (architectural investigation); Mr. C. C. Taylor (earthworks investigation); Dr. B. E. A. Jones (documentary research); Mr. P. N. Hammond and Mr. R. Beeton (draughtsmanship); Mr. R. Braybrook (photography), and Mr. J. N. Hampton (air photography). Mr. A. P. Baggs and Mr. C. A. Hartridge participated in the architectural investigation but resigned before its completion.

12. We desire to add that our Secretary and General Editor, Mr. R. W. McDowall, O.B.E., M.A., F.S.A., has afforded us constant assistance.

13. The next Inventory to be prepared by our Cambridge staff will be of the historical architecture in the north-east of Northamptonshire. This will proceed concurrently with the recording of the earthworks and other archaeological sites in that county, of which the first Inventory, *Archaeological Sites in North-East Northamptonshire*, was published in 1975.

Signed:

ADEANE (*Chairman*)
ANCASTER
H. C. DARBY
C. A. RALEGH RADFORD
H. M. COLVIN
A. J. TAYLOR
W. F. GRIMES
M. W. BARLEY

S. S. FRERE
R. J. C. ATKINSON
JOHN BETJEMAN
H. M. TAYLOR
G. ZARNECKI
J. K. S. ST JOSEPH
PAUL ASHBEE
A. R. DUFTY
R. W. McDOWALL (*Secretary*)

ABBREVIATIONS

ABBREVIATIONS AND SHORTENED TITLES OF WORKS OF
REFERENCE

Arch. J.	Archaeological Journal.
BM	British Museum.
Blore	T. Blore, An Account of the Public Schools, Hospitals and other Charitable Foundations in the Borough of Stamford (1813).
Bodl.	Bodleian Library, Oxford.
Burton	G. Burton, Chronology of Stamford (1846).
Butcher	R. Butcher, Survey and Antiquities of the Town of Stamford (1646). References in the text are to the edition published as an appendix to Peck's Academia Tertia Anglicana (1727).
Cal. Chart.	Calendar of Charter Rolls.
Cal. Close	Calendar of Close Rolls.
Cal. Inq. Misc.	Calendar of Inquisitions Miscellaneous.
Cal. Pat.	Calendar of Patent Rolls.
CUAP	Cambridge University Air Photograph (Copyright reserved).
Designs	W. Stukeley, Designs of Stanford Antiquitys, 1735. MS held by Stamford Archaeological Society.
Drakard	J. Drakard, History of Stamford (1822).
Ex. MS.	Exeter manuscripts at Burghley House.
Exeter Day Books	in Burghley Estate Office, Stamford.
Gent's Mag.	Gentleman's Magazine.
Gunnis	R. Gunnis, Dictionary of British Sculptors 1660–1851 (1953).
HMC	Royal Commission on Historical Manuscripts.
Harrod	W. Harrod, Antiquities of Stamford and St. Martin's (1785).
Knipe's map	Plan of the Borough of Stamford by James Knipe. Surveyed 1833 and published 1834. BM Map Room 3425 (1).
LAO	Lincolnshire Archives Office.
LRS	Lincolnshire Record Society.
M–S	M. Stevenson, A list of Monumental Brasses in the British Isles; followed by Roman numeral referring to brass as listed therein.
Margary	I. D. Margary, Roman Roads in Britain (1967).
Med. Arch.	Medieval Archaeology.
Mercury	Lincoln, Rutland and Stamford Mercury.
NMR	National Monuments Record.
NRO	Northamptonshire Record Office.
Nattes' drawings	Drawings by J. C. Nattes in possession of Mrs Peart, Stamford.
OS	Ordnance Survey.
PRO	Public Record Office.
Peck	F. Peck, Academia Tertia Anglicana (1727).
RCHM	Royal Commission on Historical Monuments (England).
Rogers	The Making of Stamford (1965), ed. A. Rogers.
Rot. Hund.	Rotuli Hundredorum, Record Commission (1818).
Stamford Report 1	A. Rogers, The Medieval Buildings of Stamford, Stamford Survey Group Report (1970).
Stamford Report 2	J. Hartley and A. Rogers, The Religious Foundations of Medieval Stamford, Stamford Survey Group Report (1974).
Stanfordia Illustrata	W. Stukeley, Stanfordia Illustrata, Vols i and ii, 1735 and 1736; Corpus Christi College Library, Cambridge, nos. 619 and 618.
Survey of 1845	Survey of wastes and encroachments in the Manor of Stamford, by Cuming and Hall; in Stamford Town Hall.
Twopeny	Drawings by W. Twopeny in BM Prints and Drawings. Reference numbers given in text.
VCH	The Victoria History of the Counties of England.
Wing	J. Wing, Geodaetes Practicus Redivivus (1700).

EDITORIAL NOTES

1. Monuments, numbered throughout the Inventory in a single sequence, are grouped in various categories as shown in the Table of Contents. Houses are listed numerically under their streets which are arranged in alphabetical order.

2. Fig. 1 shows the boundary of the present borough, the map in the end-pocket illustrates the central area where most of the monuments are concentrated, and separate maps within the text indicate the location of monuments in the streets (Figs. 70, 85, 86, 100, 111, 138, 143, 169, 187, 201, 206, 209).

3. Constructions since 1850 have usually been termed 'modern' unless their character warrants a description and a more precise dating.

4. Churches are normally described in the order E. to W. and N. to S., repetitive features such as arcades and windows being numbered in the same order. Dates in the descriptions of memorials are those of the deaths of the persons commemorated, as recorded; surnames in brackets are maiden names. Proper names are recorded as they appear on the memorials or other objects but otherwise the normally accepted spelling has been adopted. Church plate is of silver unless otherwise described.

5. The plans are either hatched to indicate dates of construction or are shown in black for original walls and in outline for later walls.

6. For monuments not readily orientated to a cardinal point a conventional N. point has sometimes been assumed. Plans of houses are shown with the street at the bottom.

7. Unless otherwise described, roof coverings are of stone slates.

8. The class references in the accounts of certain houses are designed to avoid repetitive descriptions; the classes are explained in the Sectional Preface (see Houses and Fig. 7).

9. The description of all heraldry before 1600 is included in the accounts of the relevant monuments; subsequent heraldry is treated selectively.

10. A glossary of archaeological and architectural terms at the end of the volume contains only those terms which are used in the inventory and for which an insufficient definition is given in the Concise Oxford Dictionary, 4th ed. (1951), reprinted with revised *addenda* (1954).

LIST OF ILLUSTRATIONS

(The prefixed numerals in brackets refer to the monument numbers in the text)

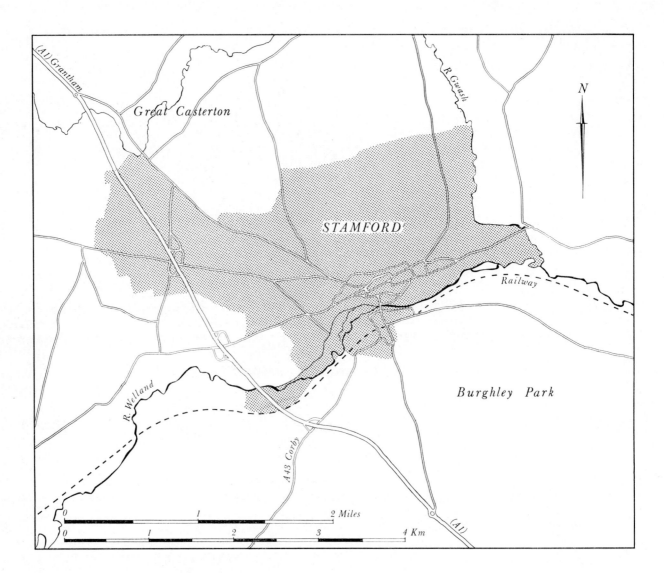

Fig. 1   Map showing the extent of the borough of Stamford. Area covered by Inventory.

THE TOWN OF STAMFORD

SECTIONAL PREFACE

TOPOGRAPHICAL HISTORY OF STAMFORD
(Figs. 1, 2 and 4)

STAMFORD is a small town in the S.W. corner of Lincolnshire, 11 miles N.W. of Peterborough. It lies mainly on the N. bank of the River Welland at the lowest reasonable crossing-place, and where the flood-plain is at its narrowest for several miles in either direction. To the E. the flood-plain widens progressively until the fenland is reached after about 7 miles. The next medieval bridge upstream, between Ketton and Collyweston, is approached on one side by a long stretch of road liable to flooding. At Stamford itself the land rises fairly steeply in several terraces to about 200 ft. OD. Over most of the surrounding area the rock is Lincolnshire Limestone, which forms a gently rolling plateau dissected by several stream and river valleys. The largest of these is the River Gwash which flows into the Welland to the E. of the town, and forms its boundary in that direction. Further W. the plateau is cut by a valley which runs in a south-easterly direction on the line of Casterton Road and Scotgate; it then turns S. into the W. side of the present Red Lion Square to join the Welland near the S. end of Castle Dyke. This, the Scotgate valley, is of particular significance in the siting of Stamford (Fig. 2).

Although Stamford lies in the area where the prehistoric line of communication known as the Jurassic Way crosses the Welland Valley (W. F. Grimes in A. Rogers (ed.) *The Making of Stamford* (1965), 1–14) there is no evidence for prehistoric occupation within the borough despite ample evidence of occupation in the surrounding area, especially on the lower Welland gravels. The Roman Ermine Street between Casterton and Water Newton crossed the Welland half a mile upstream from the narrowest point of the flood-plain, at a point where easy gradients of the valley sides create a good crossing-place. The extent of Roman occupation in the area is not easy to define but a tessellated pavement was found near St. Mary's Hill in 1839 (1) and possible cremation urns appear to have been discovered in the 18th century in High Street and Barn Hill (2–3); more recently further casual discoveries have been made (4). However, the history of Stamford as a settlement appears to begin in the post-Roman period, and much of the early development of the town can only be learnt from the evidence provided by the topography of the present town, supplemented by the small amount of historical and archaeological material available.

The first attempt to interpret Stamford's topographical history was made in the early 18th century by William Stukeley, then incumbent of All Saints'. He believed that he could discern the outlines of 'Hengist's camp', of Roman type, to the W. of Red Lion Square, the axial Via Praetoria on the line of St. Peter's Street, and the site of the forum where St. Peter's church stood (Fig. 3). Although the tactical importance of the Scotgate valley and Castle Hill was appreciated, the fact that the land falls away steeply on the S. of St. Peter's Street was ignored. Stukeley's interpretation persisted into the 19th century, and Knipe's map of 1833 marks a headland in the open fields N.W. of Rutland Terrace as the W. boundary of a supposed Roman camp.

In more recent times, Hoskins has postulated a ford a few yards E. of the present bridge, the approach roads to which had been diverted in the Middle Ages (W. G. Hoskins, *Local History in England* (1972), 98–9); this would imply an original settlement around St. Mary's church. This suggestion, however, finds little support in the present topography of the town. More recently the recognition of the probable site of

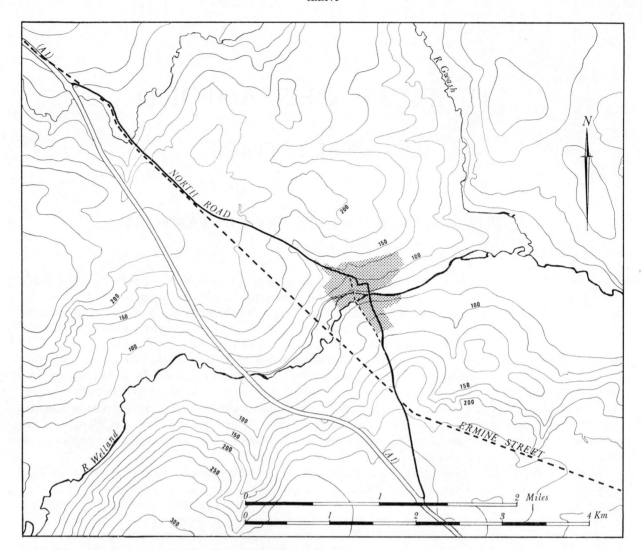

Fig. 2 Medieval Stamford in its physical setting showing N.–S. roads.

the Danish burh in the area bounded by Broad Street, St. George's Street, St. Mary's Street and Red Lion Square, and the complementary identification of the S. part of St. Martin's as the Saxon burh (C. Mahany, *The Archaeology of Stamford* (1969), 4–6) have given a more satisfactory basis on which to build an interpretation of Stamford's physical growth. The account given below differs in several respects from previous interpretations.

During the Roman period the principal settlement near Stamford was that at Casterton (P. Corder, *Roman Town at Great Casterton* (1951–61)), and this site appears to have been occupied by Saxons until the 6th century. The pattern of Anglo-Saxon settlement in the Stamford area, as revealed by place-names and village sites, involved two types of site. To the S. of the Welland there is a series of villages and village-sites set well back from the river, either on the valley-side or on the summit of the plateau, the settlements being from one to two miles apart. Near Stamford there are Collyweston, Easton, Wothorpe, Burghley, Pilsgate and Barnack, with Bainton further E. on the fen edge. To the N. of the Welland is a similar series of settlements also between one and two miles apart, but situated close to the river. Ketton is on the small River Chater, followed by Tinwell, Uffington, Tallington and West Deeping. Stamford fits into this regular sequence between Tinwell and Uffington. There is thus good reason to believe that long before the Danish burh was established in 877 there was a Saxon settlement in the area of the present town. The two poorly recorded discoveries of Anglo-Saxon date do not indicate the location of this settlement (7).

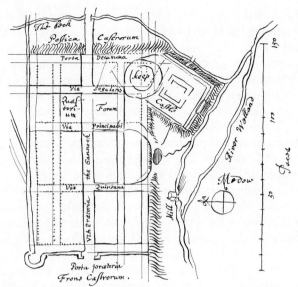

Fig. 3   Copy of drawing by W. Stukeley
of supposed camp of Roman pattern.

An examination of ancient parish boundaries in the area helps to clarify the relationship between Stamford and its neighbouring settlements. To the S. of the Welland the parishes are mainly elongated strips of land stretching back from the river. The single exception, Barnack, was probably formed by merging the two pre-Conquest settlements of Barnack and Pilsgate. The parishes of St. Martin's Within and St. Martin's Without were originally one, and contained the vanished settlement of Burghley which was probably the original settlement in the parish and took its name from the Saxon burh. Stamford Baron or St. Martin's Within, is an intrusion into both the pattern of parishes and the pattern of Saxon estates and settlements.

To the N. of the Welland the arrangement of parish boundaries is less regular owing partly to physical features such as the River Gwash, and partly to later alterations to the boundaries. The interlocking boundaries of Great and Little Casterton, as well as their place-names, suggest that they once formed a single unit, while Tickencote may have been split off from Tinwell. Stamford itself appears to have gained the land to the W. of Ermine Street from Tinwell, a parish which has every appearance of having been encroached upon. Without this land beyond Ermine Street, Stamford would have had the same rectangular shape that is more usual for the parishes N. of the Welland.

Another interpretation is possible. Stamford appears in some respects to be the medieval successor of Roman Casterton, and in Domesday Book an area called Portland and described under Great Casterton seems to have been the W. part of Stamford. The line of the Great Casterton–Ryhall parish boundary is continued southwards within Stamford by the medieval parish boundary separating All Saints' and St. Paul's. Further S. the boundary between St. Michael's and St. Mary's on the W. and St. George's on the E. is not exactly on this alignment. It could then be suggested, but not demonstrated, that Stamford derives its territory from Tinwell, Casterton and Ryhall.

The position of the early Saxon settlement on the N. bank of the Welland cannot be located closely. The medieval North Road running through the town from S. to N. took a tortuous and implausible route. After crossing the Welland at the present bridge it first turned W. into St. Mary's Street, then N. into St. John's Street, and turned again in Red Lion Square to Scotgate. The most probable explanation for this awkward route is that the road was diverted from an earlier line to one which had to recognize an existing pattern of man-made topographical features, and indeed this route skirts the S.W. corner of the Danish burh. The original line of the medieval North Road must be sought elsewhere.

The most suitable site for a ford is probably a few yards upstream from the medieval bridge. Here the flood-plain is just wide enough for the river to follow a shallow course, and the approach on either side is an easy descent. At this point the river and mill-stream are now crossed by the George and Lammas bridges respectively. Both foot-bridges, now rebuilt, are recorded in the 17th century but are of earlier origin. They are linked by a modern causeway following the line of an early pathway, the maintenance of which has long been the concern of the town council. The medieval North Road S. of St. Martin's is aligned on this crossing; just S. of the occupied area it bends to the E. but the alignment, after a gap, is picked up and continued to the crossing by Wothorpe Road. On the N. side the route would have continued along Castle Dyke and then climbed onto the limestone plateau through the valley along the modern Scotgate, ultimately joining Ermine Street just S. of Casterton. The George and Lammas bridges, therefore, mark what is on topographical evidence the most probable position of the first Saxon river-crossing.

If the identification of this crossing is correct, then the original Saxon settlement would have been near the mouth of the stream, now culverted, flowing down Scotgate and Castle Dyke. The centre of the settlement is likely to be indicated by its church. In this area there are two churches, St. Peter's and All Saints' with dedications that may denote early foundation; both are recorded in Domesday as being in Portland, under Great Casterton. The two parishes are now united and their original boundaries unknown except in the S. extremity where Mallory Lane is recorded as being the boundary in 1299 (Peck IX, 34). Mallory Lane is on the line of the culverted stream, suggesting that the boundary may have run along the line of this stream, and thence along the Great North Road. All Saints' may perhaps be regarded as the earlier on the evidence of it having been split into two parts by a narrow strip of St. Paul's parish, although Stukeley believed St. Peter's to be the older parish on account of its extent (Stanfordia Illustrata I, 24).

The size and importance of this settlement is unknown, but its position at a crossing of a navigable river must have given it advantages over its neighbours. This advantage was seized upon by the Danes in the 9th century when they fortified Stamford and made it one of the Five Boroughs in this part of the Danelaw. The Anglo-Saxon Chronicle records that in 877 the Danish army shared half of Mercia among themselves. They established several political and military centres, each having an army whose members were settled in the surrounding area. Stamford was one of these and the burh, mentioned in 918, was doubtless established about 877.

This Danish burh (8) lay immediately E. of the Saxon village, on a terrace overlooking both the original settlement and the Welland. The main axial road of the burh would have been the present High Street on the line of an existing E.-W. routeway which ran along the N. side of the Welland valley. The S. side of the burh was probably on the crest of the scarp of the main Welland valley; the W. side was against the E. edge of the present Red Lion Square where the land slopes gently away, as it does on the E. where the boundary is marked by St. George's Street. The N. boundary was along the S. side of Broad Street, carefully acknowledging the tactical difficulties of the sloping site.

A possible expansion of settlement dating from some time after the Danish conquest is represented by the medieval parish of St. Clement, later united with that of St. John and now with All Saints'. This parish, bisected by the later medieval walls, was a roughly rectangular area on either side of Scotgate, immediately N.W. of the original Saxon settlement. The church is not recorded before 1223, but the dedication to St. Clement suggests an early origin for both the church and the extension of settlement along the Scotgate valley.

The Danish military occupation of Stamford lasted for 40 years, until Edward the Elder in 918 'went with the army to Stamford and ordered the burh on the south side of the river to be built, and all the people who belonged to the more northern burh submitted to him, and sought to have him as their lord' (Anglo-Saxon Chronicle, under 920 AD, quoted from English Historical Documents I. (1955), 198). Only topographical evidence remains to indicate the position of this Saxon burh (9) (Fig. 4). Stukeley's suggestion that it lay on the site of the later St. Michael's Nunnery is not supported by any evidence now visible (Stanfordia Illustrata II, 60). The most probable site is the area in St. Martin's, on the first terrace above the Welland, bounded on the N. by the steep drop to the flood-plain, on the E. by Park Lane, and on the S. by Pinfold Lane and the modern borough boundary. On the W. the line is less well-defined, but continued on the alignment of Pinfold Lane, a little E. of Wothorpe Road. The straight section of High Street St. Martins would then have been the axial road, as High Street was in the Danish burh. The deflection of the

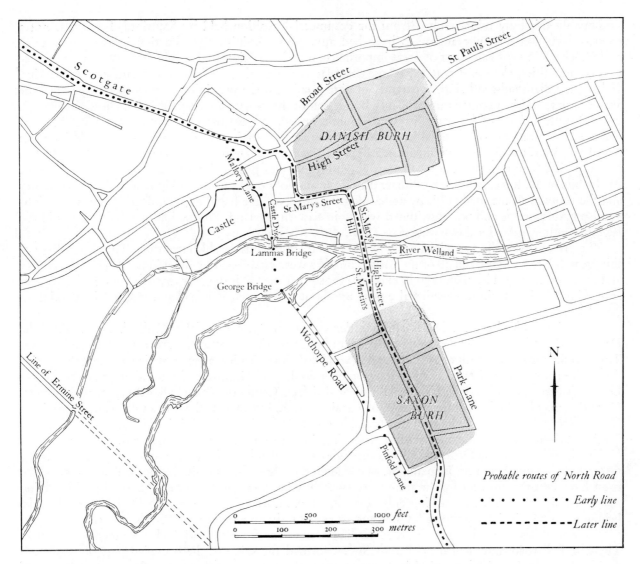

Fig. 4   Map showing Danish Burh (8) and Saxon Burh (9), and lines of North Road.

main road just S. of the Saxon burh, from the alignment leading towards Wothorpe Road and the river crossing, to the axis of the Saxon burh, indicates how the burh was laid out alongside the North Road rather than across it, a feature shared with the Danish burh.

The Danish and Saxon burhs faced each other across the narrowest part of the Welland valley, where the flood-plain is only 100 yards wide and the river flows between high banks which provide a suitable site for a bridge. When the bridge was first built is not known, but it was in existence by 1086, and probably much earlier. As soon as the Saxon burh was built the North Road was diverted to run along its axial road; at its N. end it turned slightly E. to the bridge. On the N. of the river the road ran straight up the scarp along St. Mary's Hill, and then turned W. along St. Mary's Street, skirting but not entering the Danish burh (Fig. 4).

During the 40 years of Danish overlordship Stamford, as one of the Five Boroughs, had obviously been of great importance, and in the following years of Saxon rule this importance was retained. There are several indications of prosperity during the late Saxon period. From about 979 to the 12th century there was a mint functioning in the town. The large number of moneyers, and the number of dies which were used, both point to an output exceeded only by the large towns of London, York, Winchester and Lincoln.

Presumably this busy mint resulted from the commercial position held by Stamford, for it was not a county-town and does not appear to have had any great administrative function in the post-Danish period. The Mid Lent Fair, later of great importance, may have originated at this time. We know of only two commodities, cloth and pottery, whose manufacture and sale contributed to Stamford's prosperity. Haberget, a diamond-twill cloth apparently of high quality, was a prestigious export to Europe until the 13th century, and its manufacture probably began before the Norman Conquest (*Med. Arch.* XIII (1969), 148–66). Other cloths of lesser quality were doubtless produced; by the 13th century the word Stanfort had come to mean a good material irrespective of its place of origin, but the name may not derive from Stamford as has usually been assumed (A. L. Poole, *From Domesday Book to Magna Carta*, 86). In the late Saxon period Stamford was one of the few English centres of production of glazed pottery with a fine, hard white body. It is easy to over-estimate the significance of pottery because of its relative indestructibility and the consequent use made of it by archaeologists; however like haberget, Stamford Ware was a high-quality luxury article and was distributed widely in Eastern England. Production may have begun in the late 9th century, using local estuarine clays (*Med. Arch.* XIII (1969), 95).

The prosperity of the town in the late Saxon period led to considerable expansion. The chronology of this growth is not certain, but all of the parish churches were established by the middle of the 12th century and many of them had by then been in existence for some time. This suggests that the town had grown to approximately its maximum medieval extent by about 1100, even if it had not reached its maximum population.

Expansion took place on all sides of the settlement on the N. bank of the Welland. To the E. of the Danish burh settlement extended along the road leading from the E. entrance, now called St. Paul's Street. This was the medieval parish of St. Paul, and beyond lay Holy Trinity, a parish which was largely outside the 13th-century wall-circuit. Further development took place immediately S., along the present St. Leonard's Street, associated with the parish of St. Michael Cornstall. The medieval name of this street, Cornstall, may imply the former existence of a grain market. Just outside the S.E. angle of the burgh is St. George's church, and a small knot of streets and houses forming its parish. It is in this area to the E. of the Danish burh that most of the known kilns producing Stamford pottery have been found.

The land between the Danish burh and the river was probably built upon at an early date. St. Mary's Street and the churches of St. John and St. Mary lie on the edge of the Danish burh, the defences of which must have become obsolete by the time these two churches were built. Both have small parishes lying mainly outside the burh, encroaching only along its edge. St. Mary's Hill was probably laid out when the bridge was built; it rises up the valley side and stops abruptly on meeting St. Mary's Street.

Settlement also spread along the road leading westwards from the original Saxon village towards Tinwell. This road, now called St. Peter's Street, formed the spine of the occupied part of St. Peter's parish. Beyond this parish lay that of St. Mary Bynnewerk, whose church was described as 'extra burgum' in 1157. Whatever the precise meaning of the phrase, it reflects the relatively late date of settlement at the W. end of St. Peter's Street. When the town walls were built on their present line in the 13th century, St. Mary Bynnewerk, as its name indicates, was within their circuit.

Early extension along the line of the North Road would have been a natural development. The parish of St. Clement, which incorporated most of Scotgate, appears to represent such expansion. Perhaps for tactical reasons most of the parish was left outside the town walls in the 13th century. Broad Street lies immediately N. of the Danish burh, and its shape and width suggest that it may have begun as a market place. To the S. of the Welland the road from Easton, which joined the old North Road just outside the Saxon burh, was extended along a tortuous course, now Church Lane and Church Street, to meet the new High Street St. Martins which had been extended N. when the bridge was built (Plate 3). Settlement also extended eastwards along the bank of the Welland; its street, formerly known as Estebythewater and now as Water Street, is probably coterminous with the former parish of All Saints by the Bridge. This riverside suburb may have arisen in response to the need for wharfage downstream from the bridge.

By 1086 Domesday Book records some 412 houses in the five wards of Stamford N. of the Welland; the population of the sixth ward, St. Martin's, is not indicated. St. Martin's, though always regarded as part of the borough, was administratively in Northamptonshire and belonged to the Abbey of Peterborough. The Domesday figures suggest that by then Stamford was approaching the size of the 13th-century walled town. Between 1066 and 1086 a castle was built at Stamford, displacing five houses. It commanded the pre-Danish crossing and was also on the most easily defensible site in terms of 11th-century military techniques. The small number of houses displaced is perhaps partly explained by the sloping site which was not well-suited to domestic occupation. The extent to which the town was defended at this early date is not known, but the fact that it withstood two sieges in the Anarchy of the 12th century and only fell to the third siege suggests that there was a defensible circuit. The stone town walls of which fragments remain probably date from the period of murage grants in the 13th century. The first of these grants was in 1261 and the last in 1352 (H. Turner, *Town Defences in England and Wales* (1971), 238; *Cal. Pat.*).

During the 12th and 13th centuries six religious houses were founded in Stamford. All of them were established on the periphery of the town, although one extended its site by purchasing occupied houses. The Priory of St. Leonard was founded as a cell of Durham in the early 12th century; in origin it seems to be associated with the need for a convenient base from which to administer estates in the area. The house stands remote from the town, on the edge of the river valley. St. Michael's Nunnery which followed in the middle of the century was sited just beyond the occupied area of St. Martin's parish.

The Mendicant Orders lost no time in establishing themselves in Stamford. The Franciscans arrived by 1230, acquiring a site on the E. edge of the town next to the parish of Holy Trinity; by 1241 the Dominicans had a house just outside the town in St. George's parish, and shortly afterwards the Carmelites were given a small site between the two other friaries. This site was gradually extended by purchase into the parish of Holy Trinity. The Friars of the Sack had a house in Stamford but the order was suppressed in 1274, and in 1341 the site was given to the Austin Friars. It lay immediately outside the town on the W. The siting of these religious houses on the edge of the town underlines other evidence for the size of Stamford in the 13th century by which time the town had reached its greatest extent.

During the Middle Ages the commercial functions of Stamford appear to have been distributed widely over the town. Red Lion Square and St. Mary's Hill were important shopping areas in the 12th and 13th centuries. Most documentary references to both shops and undercrofts relate to these streets and to High Street St. Martins. References to Jews also suggest that they were mainly living within a short distance of Red Lion Square; they had a synagogue (PRO, SC 11/426) but its site is unknown. The importance of High Street in the 13th century is not easy to demonstrate, but it had a market and a conduit by the later Middle Ages. Surviving or recorded domestic buildings of this date are widely distributed and although their continued existence is due to factors operating at a later date, their quality indicates that wealth was not closely confined to one quarter of the town. However, some activities were localized. Pottery kilns appear to have been limited to the E. part of the town, and names such as Butcher Row (PRO, SC 11/422) and Street of Fishmongers (PRO, C 41/174) indicate groups of tradesmen dealing in similar commodities.

Markets were held in Red Lion Square where the temporary stalls became rebuilt as permanent shops, in High Street where the stalls acquired a permanent cover by the 18th century, in Barn Hill until 1781, in St. Mary's Place after 1481, and perhaps at an early date in St. Leonard's Street whose medieval name, Cornstall, suggests a specialized market. Stamford Baron was always in a subsidiary position but had an economic life of its own, shops being recorded in the 13th century.

Stamford's prosperity in the 13th century was due mainly to its position on the Welland, close to the fenland producing cattle, horses and hemp, to the limestone uplands producing sheep and grain, and to the Northamptonshire forest producing cattle and sheep. The local sheep, noted for their long fleece, gave wool of very good quality which commanded a high price. Stamford acted as a collecting-centre for this wool, some of which was woven in the town into luxury cloth such as haberget, but most was sent down the Welland to Boston whence it was exported to Flanders. Some wool went to France through King's Lynn, and in return woad was imported to dye the locally-woven cloth (*Rot. Hund.* i, 353, 357; *Revue du Nord* 25 (1953), 89 ff.). Stamford probably acted also as a collecting-centre for grain which in the Middle Ages was transported by river wherever possible. Grain and livestock markets continued to be of importance into the 19th century.

The surviving churches are evidence of the prosperity of the town in the 13th century. All Saints' was built on an ambitious scale with much decorative enrichment, St. Mary's was rebuilt with a splendid tower, and St. George's and St. Paul's retain work of the period; St. Michael's had fragments remaining after later rebuilding. Only St. Paul's retains any earlier masonry, all other Romanesque work having been

xlii

swept away in later periods of rebuilding. By contrast parts of several houses of the 12th and 13th centuries remain, bearing witness to the wealth of the town at that time.

During this period of prosperity the townsmen gradually increased their influence in the government of Stamford. In 1202 a charter was secured changing the date of the weekly market from Sunday to Monday, and the town had its ancient liberties confirmed. A commune was granted in 1257 along with trading privileges, and in 1313 this was enhanced by the right to elect a burgess as alderman to rule the commune. Full borough status and freedom from the control of the lord of the manor was not obtained until 1462 (Rogers, 42).

In the early 14th century the Gilbertines had a hall in Stamford where advanced teaching took place, and St. Leonard's Priory may have had some scholastic functions. These institutions were apparently of relatively little influence but in 1334 they were joined by a number of northern students from Oxford. The choice of Stamford for this short-lived secession may have been due as much to geographical factors as scholastic (VCH *Lincs.*, 428).

By the 14th century the centres of the English wool and cloth trade were moving away from the old areas of importance, such as Lincolnshire, to new regions such as East Anglia, where the manufacture of worsteds was increasing. Although local wool remained a major element in the economy of the area, there was clearly a decline in prosperity. Stamford and Lincoln, both inland towns, had derived much of their importance from their roles as local centres of the wool trade. During the 15th century Lincoln suffered a serious economic decline that Stamford appears to have avoided. The activities of the Browne family, merchants of the Staple, based on Calais, show that considerable personal wealth was still to be gained from collecting and dealing in wool during the 15th century. In the later 15th century the largest occupational group on the council was the drapers and mercers, forming 20 per cent of the whole (Rogers in Everitt, *Perspectives in English Urban History* (1973), 32); other textile-working trades represent a further 10 per cent, with an equal percentage of leatherworkers.

The population of Stamford was apparently declining by the beginning of the 15th century. The incomes of the churches had begun to fall, partly owing to a changing pattern of piety, but partly resulting from a contraction of the town. The parish of St. Michael Cornstall, always poor, had been merged with St. George's as early as 1309, and St. Leonard's Street, probably the nucleus of the parish, has remained a relatively poor area. By 1428 Holy Trinity church, whose parish had been encroached upon by the Carmelite Friary, appears to have been taken over by a guild fraternity who changed the dedication to St. Stephen. In this way the demolition of the church was delayed until 1556, when the parish was merged with St. Michael's. All Saints' by the Bridge was amalgamated with St. Martin's in 1434, and St. Mary Bynnewerk parish with St. Peter's in 1462. All these parishes were on the periphery of the town, and none was large or rich. The first half of the 16th century saw the disappearance of a further four parishes, all a little nearer the centre of Stamford. St. Andrew's was merged with St. Michael's in 1546, St. Paul's with St. George's by 1548, St. Clement's with St. John's in 1553, and St. Peter's with All Saints' by 1560.

The churches which survived these redundancies, however, show that Stamford remained a relatively rich town. St. John's and St. Martin's were entirely rebuilt and All Saints', St. Mary's and St. George's were all extensively rebuilt in the middle and second half of the 15th century. Much of this work, of very high quality, bears witness to continued prosperity, even if at a lower level than hitherto. A charter granting borough status was obtained in 1462 and in 1481 this was supplemented by a second charter granting a market whose profits were to belong to the townsmen, not the lord of the manor. The Browne family was exceptional in its wealth, enabling it to build a hospital and rebuild the greater part of All Saints' church; the contemporary baker William Hikham completed the guild chapel at St. Mary's; in the following century one citizen handsomely endowed a school in 1532 and another rebuilt the Town Hall in 1558. Surviving domestic buildings, though much altered, also give the same impression of a thriving community.

The sack of Stamford by the Lancastrian army in 1461 played only a small part in the gradual decline of the town. The deserted house sites, reported by Leland some 80 years later and ascribed to the Lancastrian attack, are equally likely to have been the result of a shrinking population. Although there is little direct evidence of decline before the 15th century it was certainly taking place by the middle of that century. In 1574 unemployment and poverty caused the council to require that townsmen should be given employment in preference to strangers; later in the century the town had difficulty in raising money to pay taxes, and in 1624 was described as a 'poor decayed town'.

About the beginning of the 17th century the population of Stamford appears to have begun a steady increase which, though checked in the early 18th century, continued until the 19th century. Stamford had always been a thriving market serving the nearby widely differing areas of fen and upland, and it had long been a major stage on the Great North Road. These functions had been supplemented in the Middle Ages by industry, which had subsequently declined. During the 17th century both industry and transport were improved. The main trades were based on locally-produced materials, especially wool, hemp and leather. Attempts to introduce canvas manufacture in the 1560s failed. The malting industry, based on local grain and river transport, revived later in the 17th century and was to become of great importance. Efforts to revive trade by improving navigation began in 1570 but the canal to Deeping (27) was not opened until the 1660s. This allowed Stamford to play a greater part in the distribution of grain, imported timber and, later, coal. Road travel was improved by the introduction of long-distance coach services.

As population increased derelict sites in the town were again built on. In 1600 the E. side of Gas Street had consisted of gardens where houses had formerly stood; by the middle of the century these gardens, in one of the poorer areas of Stamford, again had houses on them (Blore, 285–90). The number of stone-masons, recorded when they became freemen, increased greatly, and this is reflected in a change in the buildings of the town. Timber framing went out of fashion and use; those who could afford it refronted their houses in stone, and those who could not covered the exposed woodwork with laths and plaster. Although the face of the town changed, no new streets were laid out. The old pattern persisted, the area of the medieval town proving large enough for current needs.

It is difficult to define the areas of commercial prosperity in the 17th century. The large inns generally follow the line of the Great North Road. The George (239) was rebuilt at the beginning of the century; the Bull (352) and the George and Angel (350) almost adjoined in St. Mary's Street, and the Red Lion (278) stood near All Saints' church. The Blue Bell in High Street (240–244) though rebuilt shortly before 1595, seems to have been declining, but the importance of High Street is demonstrated by the buildings that were put up at the end of the century. Water Street, Scotgate, St. Leonard's Street, and to a lesser extent St. Peter's Street were of little social or economic consequence; St. Paul's Street appears by contrast to have enjoyed a quiet prosperity.

By the 18th century the commercial centre of Stamford was clearly the High Street and Red Lion Square. Streets of a socially high class were Barn Hill, St. George's Square, the S. half of High Street St. Martins, and to a lesser degree Broad Street. St. George's Square and the E. end of St. Mary's Street benefited from the building first of the Assembly Room and later of the Theatre. During this century, the new Town Hall and the building operations of the 9th Earl of Exeter radically altered and improved St. Mary's Hill and the N. end of St. Mary's Street, and gave them a fashionable quality which was soon marred by the introduction of shops.

Stamford's importance as a market town and social and economic centre for the surrounding area increased during the 18th century. Besides merchants dealing in local produce and imported coal and timber, and manufacturers including tanners and maltsters, there was a wide range of professional men such as apothecaries and solicitors. Ironmongers and cabinet makers occur in numbers, some being of more than average competence. Among the cabinet makers, Benjamin Tipping and Henry Tatam did work for the Earls of Exeter (*Country Life*, 3 May 1973; 29 Aug. 1974). The town's position as a centre for social life is reflected in several new institutions, for example in a theatre, originally in Broad Street, and in regular assemblies. Horse racing on Wittering Heath began before 1619; a new course was laid out at Easton about 1717 and an annual three-day meeting established which became an important social event. The present stand, in Wothorpe, now in Cambridgeshire, was built in 1766 (Fig. 5).

The 18th century saw a complete change in the physical appearance of Stamford. Affluence, fashion and the presence of good building stone nearby resulted in the wholesale refronting or rebuilding of houses in the current style. In almost every case both workmanship and design were by men living and working in Stamford, and these same craftsmen also worked in the surrounding area. John Sutton in 1670 built the shell of Lyndon Hall, Rutland; George Portwood in 1737 designed the tower of Witham-on-the-Hill church, Lincolnshire; and William Legg designed alterations to Casewick Hall, Lincolnshire, in 1785. The products of Stamford's monumental masons are also found over a wide area.

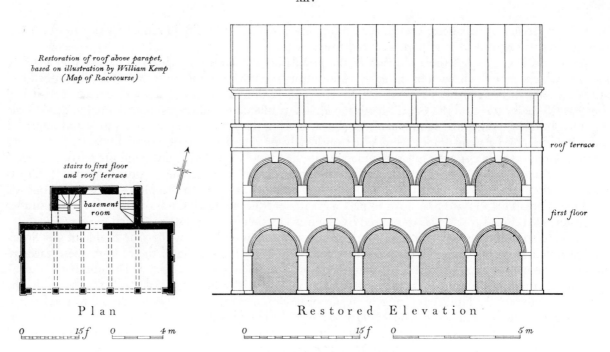

*Restoration of roof above parapet,
based on illustration by William Kemp
(Map of Racecourse)*

*stairs to first floor
and roof terrace*

*basement
room*

roof terrace

first floor

P l a n

R e s t o r e d   E l e v a t i o n

0   15 f   0   4 m

0   15 f   0   5 m

Fig. 5   Stamford Racecourse at Wothorpe. Reconstruction of 18th-century grandstand.

As Stamford's population continued to increase, the town gradually filled the area within the medieval walls. The site of 24 St. Mary's Street (358) was an open space with a ruined barn on it as late as 1753, but had been built upon by 1779. In about 1749 a row of cottages was built in the garden behind 3 St. Leonard's Street (316), other space not being available. Expansion beyond the medieval walls was hardly possible, for the open fields remained unenclosed until 1875. Immediately outside the walls and encircling the town was a narrow belt of manorial waste used mainly for grazing; there were also several ancient enclosures, one of which was a bowling green. Encroachment before 1800 was rare. In 1771 Robert Hunt built an iron foundry on the fields near the present North Street Chapel (39), but there was relatively little other building.

Only after about 1810 were cottages built in large numbers on the peripheral waste; by 1828 there were about 100 cottage encroachments, and the Survey of 1845 lists 380 houses, apart from a miscellany of carthouses, hovels and sheds. A group of cottages, sheds and yards, called New Town, covered an enclosure just beyond Scotgate, beginning some time in the 1820s. Rutland Terrace was built on a bowling green to the W. of St. Peter's Street and was the only row of fashionable houses to be built on a new site in the early 19th century. Most of the encroachments were on the N. side of the town where the closely-built houses rapidly earned a dubious reputation. Part of the area of Tenter Meadows had been used for the gas works opened in 1825 (452) and more houses and workshops were built nearby in subsequent years. In 1840 a new estate was laid out on the site of Blackfriars; it was not included in the 1845 survey of encroachments. Its history is instructive for although the N. part, intended for small houses, was built over fairly rapidly, the S. part, intended for large houses, was used instead as private gardens by the richer townspeople. Pressure on space within the town took two forms; one was for building-sites, which led to houses being built on former gardens, the other for pleasure-gardens to replace those lost to housing. Despite this, several large gardens remained in the town.

Enclosure of St. Martin's parish took place in 1796. Burghley Park was immediately extended to reach the Great North Road and the occupied area of the town, thus preventing expansion in that direction. The park was surrounded by a wall, and the Burghley Lodges were built in 1799. Land on the W., formerly St. Michael's Nunnery precinct, was also owned by the Cecils, and not made available for building. All new houses in St. Martin's were therefore confined to Water Street and the area around Church Street. Two alterations to the road pattern were made at enclosure in 1796. Barnack Road was laid out, replacing the earlier road from Burghley Lane, and the road to Easton was diverted from Church Street and Church Lane so that it ran directly into High Street St. Martins. On the N. side of the Welland the enclosure of Stamford open fields was held up mainly because the second Marquess of Exeter wished to gain as his freehold the encroachments on the waste around the edge of the town and also to acquire as much land as possible, mainly common land, in the open fields, before allowing enclosure to take place (S. Elliott in *Lincs. History and Archaeology* I.4 (1969), 23 ff; *Agr. Hist. Review* 20 (1972), 155 ff).

After enclosure in 1875 Stamford expanded over the fields to the N. The Freehold Land Society's estate was an important early development, though most building was in the hands of private speculators. That part of the town within the line of the medieval walls has undergone relatively little alteration in the present century. Some new building has taken place on garden plots, a number of buildings have been replaced, and one or two buildings of quality have been undeservedly demolished (189) or needlessly vandalized (188). Internal alterations for commercial enterprises have formed the major changes, and few noteworthy buildings have been put up since the death of the architect Edward Browning. The early 19th-century cottages around the periphery of the medieval town have been almost totally demolished, removing a social problem and also providing space for an encircling road which does little damage to the fabric of the medieval town. The Great North Road was diverted to a new route to the W. of the town in 1961.

ECCLESIASTICAL BUILDINGS

Five medieval parish churches remain in Stamford and in Stamford Baron (All Saints, St. George, St. John Baptist, St. Martin, and St. Mary); another, St. Paul's, is now non-parochial. There are also four Nonconformist churches dating from before 1850 and a Roman Catholic church of later date, which has been included in the Inventory in view of its decorative quality.

Four churches are recorded in Domesday Book but only St. Peter's, which stood close to the post-Conquest castle, and All Saints' are specifically named. Twelfth-century documents show that the following churches were by then also in existence: St. Andrew, Holy Trinity, St. Michael the Great, St. Michael Cornstall, St. Mary at the Bridge, St. Mary Bynnewerk, and St. Paul. Of these former churches, St. Michael the Less or Cornstall was demolished in the 14th century, St. Paul's was partly pulled down, and the remainder were destroyed in the 15th century and later; one (St. Michael the Great) was totally rebuilt in the 19th century. The earliest references to the churches of St. Clement and St. John Baptist are in the early 13th century. The documentary history of these churches has been the subject of recent study (Stamford Report 2) and their sites have been generally identified (map in end-pocket).

The earliest surviving structure is that of St. Paul's church, the S. wall of which may be dated to the early years of the 12th century (Plate 6). With the exception of some quoins at All Saints' it is the only non-monastic work of the Norman period to remain *in situ*; some displaced fragments survive at St. John's. However, at St. Leonard's Priory part of the standing nave arcade was completed in the mid 12th century; the piers are characteristically drum-like with capitals having re-entrant angles (Plate 7). Apsidal terminations to the presbytery and N. transept, revealed by recent excavation, are presumably also mid 12th-century (Fig. 39).

In the 13th century many of the earlier churches were rebuilt, often with much elaboration. Of the six medieval churches that survive, four were partially or totally rebuilt in the early part of the century, and much work of this period remains; at the other two churches (St. John's and St. Martin's) there are structural features in the 15th-century fabric which indicate former churches, perhaps also belonging to the 13th century. Architectural fragments recorded from St. Michael's also suggest the building of an arcade at this time (Drawing by Twopeny, 1834; 290 d.13, p. 59). The use of blind arcading for the enrichment of external walls was characteristic of the period. At All Saints' in *c.* 1230, the lower stages of the walls were decorated with a continuous band of arcading (Plate 11), and at St. Mary's the W. tower was embellished with tier upon tier of blind arches of varying sizes and designs (Plates 10, 12). Judging from the relative heights of the external wall-arcading and the nave arcade at All Saints', the upper stages of the aisle wall, which was replaced in the 15th century, may have comprised groups of lancets rising into small gables thereby giving a serrated skyline to the side wall; wall-arcading was allowed to continue uninterrupted round the projections for a stair against the S. aisle wall and round a square turret at the S.W. corner; the stair served an upper compartment in the turret and was perhaps originally open to the aisle. Buttresses remained shallow, in the 12th-century tradition, and are often no more than part-octagonal pilasters. The W. doors of St. Mary's and St. Leonard's priory church, illustrate the development of arches and mouldings during the transitional period of the late 12th and early 13th centuries (Plate 9). Internally, piers with detached shafts, annulets, water-holding bases and stiff-leaf capitals follow the standard forms; bases with a less pronounced profile indicate a date late in the category, for example at St. George's. Capitals have ornament ranging from vestigial leaf decoration at St. Leonard's to standard stiff-leaf forms exemplified at All Saints', St. Mary's and St. Paul's (Plates 8, 9). Late in the century, capitals are simplified to a plain cove beneath a crowning moulding (e.g. All Saints', N. arcade).

Redundant weathercourses on the E. faces of W. towers in St. John's, St. Martin's and St. Mary's provide direct evidence of the character, and to some extent the date, of the naves with which they were formerly associated. They are often the only indication of the sequence of rebuilding in later periods. In most cases the weathercourses imply that the towers were built, or rebuilt, against older naves that have been subsequently rebuilt. At St. Mary's there are two roof-weathercourses at different pitches, one presumably associated with a 12th-century nave, the other with a nave of the 13th century (Plate 14). The weathercourse at St. Martin's (Plate 20) returns on the N. and S. of the tower showing that the aisles continued westward in the early period as they still do although rebuilt in the 15th century. The N.W. tower of St. John's retains a weathercourse which indicates the eaves-height of the former nave; a low-pitched weathercourse over the aisle roof strangely does not relate to the present aisle roof of the Perpendicular period.

Building activity during the 14th century does not appear to have been extensive, but during the first half of the century a former aisle at St. Mary's was replaced by a wide chapel (Plate 15), and a stone spire was added to the 13th-century tower. The dominant feature in the chapel is an enriched tomb recess, incorporating in its design a window in the back wall (Plate 16). The spire sits somewhat heavily on the early tower, but is enriched with sculpture of particular elegance (Plate 16). The 14th-century reuse of early round piers and bases in the nave arcade at St. George's, together with octagonal pier-drums, produced a bizarre result scarcely justifying the economy (Plate 14).

The general rebuilding and alteration of early churches during the second half of the 15th century have long been regarded as the consequences of Stamford's devastation in 1461 by Lancastrian forces after the Battle of Wakefield. Leland writing some 80 years later said that the town had not then been fully repaired (*Itinerary* (1907–10) vol. 4, 88–90). However, the effects of the sack may have been exaggerated at least in connection with the churches. One 15th-century church, St. John's, was almost certainly rebuilt about ten years before the Battle of Wakefield as testified by a reference to dated glass which in part remains (Peck, XIV, 35–7). At St. Martin's the body of the early church appears to have remained standing when the west tower was rebuilt, probably in the middle of the 15th century. At St. George's too, the chancel was apparently completed before the town's occupation in about 1461; a bequest from Sir William Bruges, who died in March 1450, suggests that the work was by then substantially complete. These activities imply a degree of church building immediately before the Lancastrian advance, the effects of which may have fallen more on domestic buildings than ecclesiastical. Two churches were certainly rebuilt after the town's occupation (All Saints' and St. Mary's), and the stimulus may well have come as much from the thriving economic conditions of the time, as illustrated by the affluence of the Browne family, as from a necessity to carry out repairs resulting from deliberate damage during the troubles.

The plans of the late medieval churches generally followed those of their 13th-century predecessors with variations limited to large porches and substantial rood-stair turrets. Elevations and architectural details are somewhat uniform in design. Some masons' marks noted in churches of this period are illustrated on Fig. 6. Mouldings conform to a standard pattern with piers and arches having hollow-chamfered and wave mouldings, and semicircular shafts with separate bases and capitals forming the inner order. Uniformity in design of towers is demonstrated at St. John's and St. Martin's, both of which may be dated

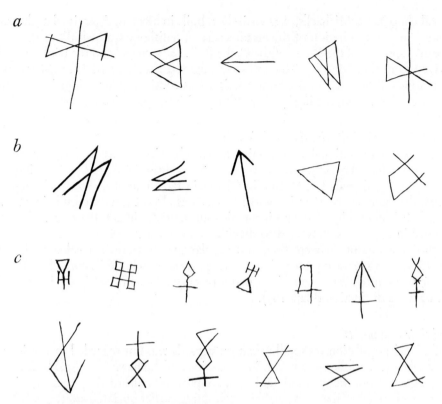

Fig. 6 Masons' marks in churches.
a.(28) All Saints, tower; b.(30) St. John Baptist; c.(31) St. Martin.

on separate evidence to the middle of the 15th century (Plate 26); a large belfry window of two lights with the mullion rising to the apex is characteristic. The tower at All Saints' is slightly more elaborate, having areas of blind panelling, and is further embellished by a tall spire. Elaboration in design relied less on sculpture than on architecturally-derived decoration such as bands of cusped panelling (Plate 19). For example, the sculptured corbels in the nave of St. Martin's were probably afterthoughts and detract from the simple elegance of the arcade. Likewise, carved corbels terminating the tower vault at All Saints' are whimsies scarcely discernible from the ground; the vault is primarily enriched with blind panels, each with a cusped head (Plate 18). A similar vault was added to the 13th-century tower of St. Mary's, and the same decoration was used to ornament door jambs and heads, e.g. the vestry door of All Saints' (Plate 19). An element of fantasy was occasionally introduced to relieve the rigidity of the Perpendicular architecture: the north porch at All Saints' is conceived as a miniature castle, and buttresses at the same church are perversely placed beneath the parapet gutter-outlets resulting in an ingenious method for the disposal of rain-water through gargoyles on the lower part of the buttress (Plate 17). Incorporated in the architectural composition of the tower of All Saints' is a stone clock dial, set within a window-like opening (Plate 19). This rarity may be compared with one, also of the late 15th century, at Raunds church, Northamptonshire, which is set internally in the tower arch; two others are on the tower of Conington church, Huntingdonshire. With the exception of that at Browne's Hospital piscinae of this period are notably plain, and sedilia are without canopies.

The special purpose of the late 15th-century chapel attached to Browne's Hospital has led to a building of individual proportions. By continuing the roof height of the two-storey range on the west, and reducing its length by a western cross passage beneath a gallery, the interior presents a noble and lofty appearance in spite of the subsequent loss of a large east window (Plate 66).

An example of 17th-century Gothic survival has been recorded. At St. George's, where the W. tower was apparently rebuilt with a peculiarly oblong plan, the Gothic style was preserved for some pointed-headed openings (Plate 27).

One medieval church, St. Michael's, was entirely rebuilt in 1835-6. A revived 13th-century style was chosen specifically 'in exact imitation of the architecture of Salisbury Cathedral'. In the event, the E. end of the nave broadly reproduced the E. end of the Cathedral's Lady chapel and the triple arched porches were apparently derived from those on the Cathedral's west front (Plates 27, 28). A 13th-century style was also preferred for the tower although a 14th-century design was considered (drawings in church). The interior has no such medieval derivation, having greater affinity with the galleried halls of other denominations.

Nonconformist and Roman Catholic churches and chapels
Apart from a small Congregational community nonconformity seems to have made relatively little progress in Stamford before the early 19th century. Consequently there are few buildings of before 1850, and these have been much altered. The Methodist Chapel in Barn Hill of *c.* 1803 has been gutted and partly rebuilt (Plate 29); the later one of 1834 in North Street was almost totally rebuilt in 1901. The Congregationalists rebuilt their chapel in 1819, and it remains substantially intact (Plate 29). The Baptist chapel in Bath Row, opened in 1835, was converted to dwellings shortly after 1846.

Roman Catholics in Stamford were few, and regular masses were first celebrated at a house in All Saints' Street in 1815. By 1826 the congregation was large enough to build its own chapel, enlarged in 1833, and in 1864 the present church was opened in Broad Street (35). Its belfry, designed in a Continental Gothic vein, is a work of some distinction (Plate 163).

Churchyards and their monuments
The pressure of a large population on small urban graveyards was not regarded as a serious problem until the 19th century when townsfolk were becoming conscious of the hazards to health. St. Martin's was the first parish to acquire new burying ground, taking the opportunity afforded by enclosure in 1796. The new St. Michael's church included a catacomb partly for rehousing earlier burials from the old church, and partly for the use of the richer few who might be buried within the new building. In 1849 All Saints' acquired a catacomb, built by Robert Woolston for £50, which being capable of holding 100 to 120 coffins, was expected to remain in use for about two years. The municipal cemetery was only created in 1855.

The decoration of churchyard monuments generally follows the pattern of development seen elsewhere in the country, but weathering has made many of the epitaphs illegible. Most headstones are in local oolite and date from after 1780. There are some in Swithland slate which date from after 1767, and several in Welsh slate, first used in the early part of the 19th century but mainly after 1840. Many headstones were apparently carved in Stamford as shown by those which bear signatures. All the exceptions were in imported materials: three by Hibbitt of Colsterworth, and one by T. Smith of Grantham, all in Swithland slate, and one in Welsh slate to Daniel Lambert by Pollard and Shenton of Leicester, Lambert's home town.

Fittings
Among ecclesiastical fittings, medieval glass in the churches of St. George, St. John and St. Martin, and in Browne's Hospital, is of particular importance. This mostly belongs to the middle and to the second half of the 15th century and is contemporary with the architecture although only a small amount is *in situ.* That which has remained in its original setting has however afforded valuable evidence for the dating of the architecture. For example, the heraldic panels in St. Martin's church, which relate to a sequence of bishops, establish the time-span for the rebuilding of the church, and confirm the evidence of heraldry carved in the masonry, which might otherwise be suspected as antiquarianism. Also, an 18th-century record of former inscriptions on glass in St. John's (Peck XIV, 35-7), referring to the provision of glass, has provided a close date for the completion of the N. aisle, at least, of that church. Unfortunately no documents survive to show conclusively that this and other 15th-century glass was the product of the important Stamford workshop of glaziers but it was probably the source of it. Evidence for the workshop is limited to the last quarter of the 15th century, but its activity doubtless covered a longer span. A detailed study of this and associated glass is currently in preparation (R. Marks, *Corpus Vitrearum Medii aevi*), and will include a stylistic analysis beyond the scope of this inventory. The best-preserved or otherwise important glass is illustrated on Plates 34-39.

Other medieval fittings, although of individual merit, do not fall into particular categories warranting discussion; reference to each type may be found in the Index. The more notable are the ceiling of the N. chapel in St. Mary's, the brasses in All Saints', the wooden screens in St. John's and Browne's Hospital, the clockface on the tower of All Saints' and the tomb probably of Sir David Phillips (d. 1506) in St. Mary's.

With the exception of monuments, post Reformation fittings are few. Some rarities and curiosities of this period include the 17th-century commemorative brass panel to the bellfounder Toby Norris, composed of letters from bell-inscription dies; the 17th-century wall-painting in All Saints' listing penalties for misuse of the bells; the early 18th-century altar frontal and pulpit cloth in St. John's. A number of bells dating from the 17th century are by the Norris family, bellfounders of Stamford.

Outstanding among the monuments in churches are the three Cecil monuments in St. Martin's (1, 4 and 5) and the Cust monument in St. George's (5). These are of metropolitan quality. Wall monuments of the 18th and early 19th centuries are mostly of simple design. A large number are signed by local masons particularly in the later period (see Index: Sculptors and Monumental Masons); in 1725 George Portwood, principally known for architectural work in the town, charged 1½d. a letter for cutting and blacking (Ex. MS, 21/24).

Restorations during the mid 19th century led to the repewing of most churches, and although the pews are of competent workmanship, the effect is rather ponderous. The architect principally engaged in this work was Edward Browning of Stamford (1816–1882). The altar frontal in St. Mary's installed under J. D. Sedding's direction in 1890 is a notable example of gilded metalwork in relief.

Guilds

Some ten medieval guilds are recorded in Stamford, associated with seven of the parish churches. They varied greatly in wealth and influence, the three in St. Martin's parish being of little importance. Both of the guilds in St. Mary's parish were wealthy and one, St. Mary's, developed into the later borough corporation. These guilds have left scarcely any architectural evidence of their existence. The chapel of Corpus Christi guild in St. Mary's church (33), the elaboration of which was partly due to private munificence, is the only chapel to survive, unless the S.E. chapel in All Saints' was used by the guild of that name. The large room, known as the Audit Room, at Browne's Hospital may have been used for guild rather than almshouse purposes, and the undercroft in No. 4 St. Mary's Place (342) is almost certainly a remaining fragment of the guildhall of Corpus Christi.

SECULAR BUILDINGS

HOUSES

The different plan-forms found in Stamford have been classified (see Fig. 7) in order to help the reader to comprehend the range and development of houses in the town. This classification is deliberately broad, concentrating on general aspects of planning, and is not intended to have an application outside Stamford. Houses built before 1450 are usually too fragmentary to be included. Some houses fall outside the classification, either because only single examples exist or because of idiosyncratic design; others have been so altered that their original form cannot readily be determined. The classification can be summarized as follows:

Class 1. House having an open hall, and a storeyed end-bay roofed (a) in line or (b) as a cross wing.
Class 2. Storeyed house with hall and service rooms, the stack on the rear wall of the main room.
Class 3. Main range and cross-wing house, two storeys throughout.
Class 4. Two-room storeyed house, roofed at right-angles to the street.
Class 5. Two-room storeyed house, the front roofed parallel to the street, the rear wing at right-angles.
Class 6. Two-room storeyed house with stack at one gable end.
Class 7. Two-room storeyed house with entrance-passage behind the chimney stack.
Class 8. Internal-stack house with (a) two or (b) three rooms in line.
Class 9. Double-pile house, the stair rising (a) centrally in the rear half or (b) to one side.
Class 10. House with two rooms flanking a central entrance, the stacks usually in the gables.
Class 11. House with central entrance, the third room in a rear wing; the stairs are (a) in the body of the house or (b) in an angle-turret.
Class 12. Two-room house with rear wing, the stairs in the main range.
Class 13. Two-room house with central stairs, (a) without or (b) with an entrance-hall.
Class 14. Two-room house with stairs at side, (a) without or (b) with an entrance-hall.
Class 15. Single-room house.

Fragmentary remains of several houses of the 12th and early 13th centuries survive in Stamford and others are known from early 19th-century drawings (Plate 61). The plain chamfered half-round arch continued in use into the early 13th century in this area, making precise dating difficult; for convenience such houses are referred to as belonging to the 12th century (Fig. 8).

Three houses have vestiges of what must have been ground-floor undercrofts. The evidence survives in the form of arcades, formerly open, of one or more bays and at right-angles to the street. In each building the evidence points to the absence of a vault, in which case the floor above would have been of timber. Two of these houses possibly had almost square plans. No. 10 St. Mary's Hill (336) appears to have had a two-bay arcade, and a length of about 35 ft.; the surviving 12th-century doorway of high quality to the N., and the evidence of further arcading to the S., suggest that the house occupied the site of 9 and 10, which have a combined width of 40 ft. In the late Middle Ages the N. half of this house was rebuilt as a range at right-angles to the street, perhaps reflecting the original roof arrangement. No. 9 St. Mary's Street (347) has a two-and-a-half bay arcade indicating a building 37 ft. deep, while the houses now adjoining, which might occupy the site of the original one, have a combined frontage of 42 ft. In both these houses the living accommodation must have been on the first floor. These large square houses of the 12th century have so far not been recognized in many other towns. Contemporaneous houses of similar size are Moyses Hall, Bury St. Edmunds; Norman House, Western Shore, Southampton; Jew's House and Aaron's House, Lincoln. The two examples from Lincoln are in ranges parallel to the street, whereas the two Stamford buildings, like Moyses Hall and the later Gysors Hall, Boston, appear to have been roofed at right-angles to the street. Aaron's House at Lincoln also differed in having a ground-floor open hall, whereas all the other buildings appear to have had the hall on the first floor.

The third house with a ground-floor undercroft, 17 St. George's Square (297), belongs to the 13th century. It differed from the others in being parallel to the street, 21 ft. wide overall and of uncertain length; with buttresses, string-course and eaves cornices, and a two-light window, it was clearly a house of high

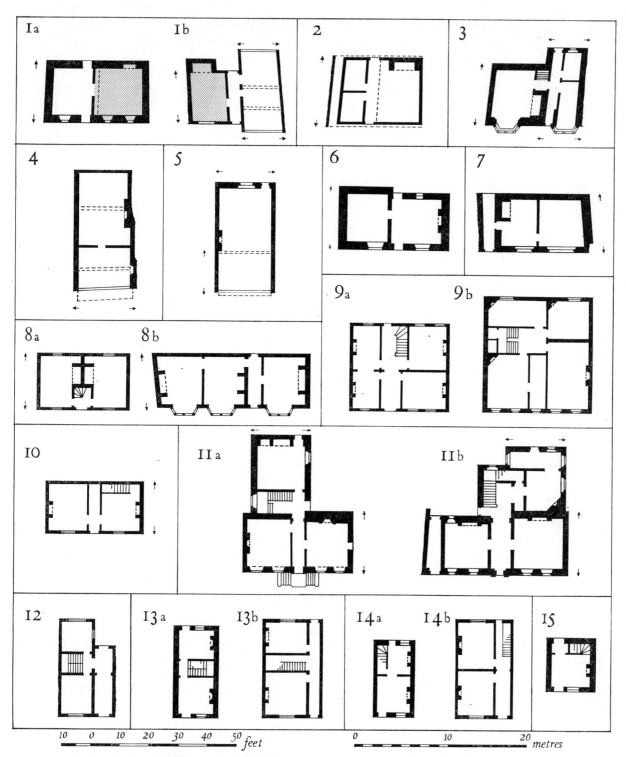

Fig. 7 CLASSIFICATION OF HOUSE TYPES.

The diagrams are based on plans of houses listed below, but later alterations have been omitted. Compartments shown with a stippled background denote halls open to the roof; small arrows indicate gables or hips of roofs.

1a.(103) 16 Barn Hill; 1b.(415) 35–36 St. Peter's Street; 2.(368) 40 St. Mary's Street; 3.(375) 12 St. Paul's Street; 4.(353) 17 St. Mary's Street; 5.(348) 10 St. Mary's Street; 6.(212) 23 High Street St. Martins; 7.(395) 7 St. Peter's Hill; 8a.(224) 41 High Street St. Martins; 8b.(224) 39–40 High Street St. Martins; 9a.(288) 8 Rutland Terrace; 9b.(246) 10 Ironmonger Street (first floor); 10.(242) 3 Ironmonger Street; 11a.(72) 3 All Saints' Place; 11b.(100) 13 Barn Hill; 12.(317) 4 St. Leonard's Street; 13a.(322) 18 St. Leonard's Street; 13b.(288) 17 Rutland Terrace; 14a.(117) 8 Belton Street; 14b.(288) 4 Rutland Terrace; 15.(171) 6 Gas Street.

quality (Plate 61). An arch perhaps from a similar undercroft is rebuilt near 53 High Street St. Martins (232) and another was recorded as having been found in 1818 at the E. end of the S. side of St. Leonard's Street (*Mercury*, 12 May 1893). No. 15 St. Peter's Street (405), which appears to have a late 12th-century origin though almost totally rebuilt, is also parallel to the street but nothing can be said of its plan save that it was one room deep. The Horns Inn on the site of 12 Broad Street was a 44-ft.-wide building consisting of a single range parallel to the street, and having a near-central 12th-century doorway (Twopeny 290/b.1, No. 489); it was demolished in the late 19th century. The Ram Inn, 27 High Street St. Martins, before demolition in 1876, was also a single range about 40 ft. wide and parallel to the street; Buckler shows that it had a 12th-century doorway, 5 ft. wide and about 9 ft. high, near the centre of the elevation (Plate 61; BM Add. MS 24434 No. 79). The size of the opening invites comparison with that at St. Mary's Guild, Lincoln, which is similarly very large; this building has a ground-floor undercroft and apparently a first-floor hall.

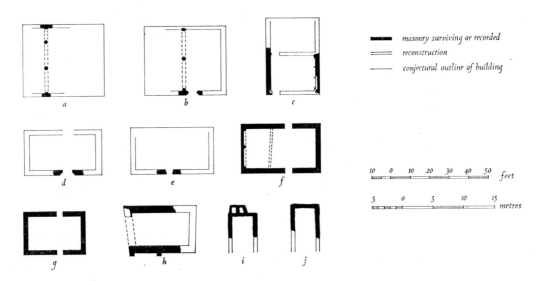

Fig. 8 Plans of 12th and 13th-century houses.
a.(347) 9 St. Mary's Street; b.(336) 10 St. Mary's Hill; c.(338) 13 St. Mary's Hill;
d. 27 High Street St. Martins (demolished); e. 12 Broad Street (demolished);
f.(379) 16–17 St. Paul's Street; g.(378) 15 St. Paul's Street; h.(297) 17 St. George's Square;
i.(16) former house in Water Street; j.(16) former house in Water Street.

No. 13 St. Mary's Hill (338) dates from the 13th century and retains an undercroft with original entrance and flanking windows, suggesting use as a shop. The undercroft is partly below ground level, and vaulted; the openings to the street are offset to the N. perhaps implying that the entrance to the house above was to the S. of the elevation. The building above was of two storeys and contained two rooms on plan, at right-angles to the street; communication between the rooms was apparently at the S. end. The ground-floor rooms were low, so the main rooms would have been on the first floor. The two 13th-century houses in St. Paul's Street (Nos. 14, 16–17) are the earliest survivors in Stamford to have had for certain ground-floor halls. No. 16–17 (379) had an open hall at the W. end, and perhaps a storeyed service and solar end to the E., though only the W. wall of the hall with its high quality blind arcading survives in recognizable form (Fig. 193; Plate 60). No. 14 (377) appears to have been similar, with its hall to the E. and with blind arcading, but here the hall also had an aisle (Plate 62). A third house formerly existed in Water Street, and was drawn in the 19th century by Twopeny (Plate 61; Twopeny 290/b. 2, pp. 42, 43). It had an open hall lit by traceried two-light windows, and was presumably entered by opposed doors. These houses would have conformed to class 1 (see p. liii).

No substantial remains of houses of the 14th century are now recognizable. The roof of an open hall at 25 High Street St. Martins (216) could be as early as the 14th century, but the surviving part tells us little of the building except that it lay parallel to the street; presumably it resembled the later two-cell houses of class I in the town. Houses built at right-angles to the street are now rare and are not easily interpreted. Most of the remaining houses of the 15th and 16th centuries consist of two units parallel to the street; sometimes one unit is built as a cross wing. The surviving houses were all of relatively high social class, and in the better ones accommodation was doubtless supplemented by additional buildings behind. Nos. 11-12 St. Mary's Street (349) has a courtyard at the back, though the ranges that surround it are now post-medieval. One proper courtyard-house survives, apart from fragments of inns, although the early 16th-century range behind 6 Barn Hill (95) must almost certainly have belonged to such a house. This courtyard-house, 69 High Street St. Martins (238), consists of three ranges, one of which contained an open hall. The plan is not clear, and it is possible to interpret it as two separate houses or tenements. The W. range had an open hall and a storeyed cross wing, separated by two passages with a chamber above; the E. range may have consisted on plan of two rooms also separated by an entrance.

A feature found in several houses of the 16th and 17th centuries is an entry at one side, usually 3 to 5 ft. wide, providing access to the rear of the premises independent of the house. These entries are particularly associated with urban houses, where a continuous frontage is an obstacle to access to the yard behind. In class 2 houses the entry can be at the hall end, as 9 St. Mary's Hill (335), or at the service end as 40 St. Mary's Street (368), while in class 4 houses it is of necessity at the end opposite to the cross wing, as at 20 High Street St. Martins (210). Goldsmiths Lane passes through such an entry at 33 Broad Street, a building which also has a carriage-entry, a much larger type of access which is now rare in Stamford and is today mainly associated with inns (as 33 Broad Street (144), 25 High Street St. Martins (216), 19 St. Mary's Street (355)). In the 16th and 17th centuries the word 'entry' was generally applied to internal passages, but was also used for foot-passages, for example in the list of fittings of Richard Snowden's house in 1582 (Ex. MS, 33/11) where the street end was closed by a gate with a wicket. They may also appear in probate inventories e.g. LAO 1641/17 (of 1641); 163/27 (of 1665); 182/351 (of 1667). The usefulness of entries has meant that many have survived to the present day. Despite remodelling they still exist at 31 Broad Street (141) and 34 St. Peter's Street (414). In some large houses of the 18th century side passages gave rise to some ingenious attempts to disguise an embarrassing asymmetry. Those at 19 St. George's Square (299) and Brazenose House (383) have gone, but they survive as monuments (100), (301) and (376).

Several 17th-century probate inventories of large houses and inns record 'gatehouses', for example in 1683 (LAO, 183/237). These presumably refer to the wide carriage-entries such as that at 19 St. Mary's Street (355); the Bull Inn (352) had one opening on to St. Mary's Street and a 'back gate' leading towards High Street. The first known reference to gatehouses is in the early 14th century, when a large tenement in Water Street is said to have had a solar at one end and a great gate at the other (PRO, E 315/37 no. 20). Several houses away from the centre of the town managed to obtain a rear access, often by a postern and entry as at Torkington House (417). No. 12 St. Paul's Street (375) is known to have had a rear access to its stables, and this was probably also necessary for the Norris' bell-founding business.

Class 1. Before 1500 most houses in Stamford had open halls, and were built in stone or timber-frame. The basic medieval plan is typified by 17 Broad Street (135), with an open hall at one end and a two-storey section at the other, all under a single roof and parallel to the street. This plan, class I, is seen at 11-12 St. Mary's Street (349), where the storeyed service and solar end was rebuilt in ornate timber-frame in the late Middle Ages (Plate 70). At 16 Barn Hill (103), a 15th-century vicarage, the solar projects beyond the passage into the hall, where it is carried on a beam, an arrangement intended to give extra space at first-floor level on a restricted site (Fig. 82). One house, 21 All Saints' Street (82), was originally open to the roof throughout. No. 40 St. Mary's Street (368) dating from *c.* 1500 has a formal passage defined by walls, and two service rooms at the lower end. This house shares with 56 High Street (192) the curious feature of an asymmetrical roof, the first floor construction of (368) resembling a single-aisled hall (Fig. 185).

Open-hall houses in Stamford appear rarely to have had cross wings. At 28 St. Mary's Street (362) the storeyed end is roofed as a cross wing, though it does not project beyond the walls of the main range. No. 35 St. Peter's Street (415) has a full cross wing, and perhaps the W. range of 69 High Street St. Martins (238) could also be included. It is not clear whether 25 High Street St. Martins (216) had a cross wing before the 16th century. The large stone house formerly standing W. of monument (281), called Peterborough Hall by Stukeley when he made a partially conjectural drawing (Designs, 73; Plate 70), had an open hall and cross wing.

Class 2. There is no evidence among the surviving houses in Stamford for open halls being built after *c.* 1500. During the 16th and 17th centuries most of the existing open halls were floored over. Houses built during the 16th century in general followed the earlier plans, differing mainly in being storeyed throughout (class 2), but a larger proportion of these new houses had a cross wing (class 3). These houses are almost invariably of timber-frame. The chimney stack which heats the hall is generally on the rear wall, as at 8 and 9 St. Mary's Hill (334, 335), 9 St. George's Square (294) and 12 Water Street (442); exceptionally at 11 St. George's Street (304) it is placed on the front wall.

Class 3. The range and cross wing houses of class 3 often have their passage within the cross wing, as at 51 High Street (189) and 10–11 St. Paul's Street (374). The stack, generally against the rear wall, is sometimes placed between hall and cross wing so that it could heat both rooms, as at 20 High Street St. Martin's (210), 6 St. Peter's Hill (394) and 3 Austin Friars Lane (84). At 12 St. Paul's Street (375) it backs onto the cross passage. Both class 2 and 3 houses, being storeyed, may have a continuous jetty, as originally at 7 St. Paul's Street (372), 51 High Street (189) and 11–12 High Street (177).

During the 16th century class 1 houses were converted to classes 2 or 3 by the insertion of a floor in the open hall. No. 20 St. Mary's Street (356) was floored in the 15th century, and 16 Barn Hill (103) as late as the 17th century. Similar houses to classes 1 and 2 are found at Burford, Oxfordshire, where there are even fewer cross wings than at Stamford. Class 1 houses may be compared with Bull Cottage, Witney Street, and class 2 houses with the Highway Hotel, High Street (M. Laithwaite in *Perspectives in English Urban History* (1973) ed. Everett, 76, 78).

Class 4. All the houses so far discussed have relatively wide frontages. Houses built on narrower plots in the late and post-medieval periods were one room wide and of different plan. Two houses in Water Street (16) dating from the 13th century are known only from excavations (C. Mahany, *Archaeology of Stamford* (1969), 13–16); built at right-angles to the street, they had cellars and, at the rear, privies. Surviving houses of this class are hard to interpret in their present state. Nos. 17 and 18 St. Mary's Street (353, 354), both single ranges at right-angles to the street and probably of two-room plan originally, are houses which belong to this class; no. 18 has a crown-post roof over the back room.

Class 5. A more complex form, probably of higher social standing, is also found. These houses generally appear to have had two rooms on plan. The front is roofed parallel to the street, and behind is a wing which may occupy the full width of the house. The largest example is 56 High Street (192), which resembles a class 2 house with contemporary rear wing. The front range, however, is not very wide and possibly consisted of one room with a passage on the W.; the whole house therefore would have been of two-room plan. No. 20 St. Mary's Street (356) also seems to have consisted of a jettied range of single-room plan parallel to the street, and a rear wing of similar size; no. 10 St. Mary's Street (348), probably dating from the 17th century, has the plain rectangular form of class 4 but at present has two roofs at right-angles as in class 5, to which it should technically belong. At 5 St. Leonard's Street (318) the wing is also as wide as the front range; this too is an early 17th-century house. No. 14 High Street (178) has had its earlier part demolished, but appears to have conformed to class 5, with a rear wing containing a large stack. The 16th-century structure at 10 High Street (176) could be the rear wing of a large house of this class.

Only one early house, 9 St. Mary's Street (347), has two ranges lying parallel to the street. The original arrangement on the ground floor is not now recoverable, but the first floor had a single room in each range. Medieval double-pile urban houses generally had an open hall in the rear range, e.g. 20 and 40 Jordan Well, Coventry, and Tackleys Inn, Oxford (*Med. Arch.* VI–VII (1962–3), 221, 217). This Stamford house, storeyed throughout like 5 Pottergate, Lincoln, represents a further development of that plan, but it incorporates part of a large 12th-century house which may have affected its form.

There was a change in the plan-types of new houses in about 1600. Although the basic form of a two-cell structure parallel to the street remained the same, internal planning was altered. A few houses of class 2 were built, perhaps including 11–12 High Street, and also class 3, including 7–9 Red Lion Street (285), but they are early and could even date from the late 16th century. Classes 4 and 5 also continued in restricted use.

Class 6. The first major change to take place *c.* 1600 was the abandonment of the lateral stack, hitherto used almost exclusively, in favour of axially-placed stacks, generally at one gable end of the house. The earliest internal stacks are those already noticed in class 3 houses such as 20 High Street St. Martin's (210) and 7–9 Red Lion Street (285), and also the possibly inserted stack at 12 St. Paul's Street (375) and 3 St. Peter's Street (398). The gable stack at 21 All Saints' Street (82) is exceptional.

The class 2 house developed naturally into class 6 by transferring the stack position to the gable wall of the main room. Entrance was still gained by a near-central doorway which could lead to a lobby, as at 26 Austin Street (91) of 1706, or to a central passage as at 30 St. Peter's Street (411) of *c.* 1650 and 1 Ironmonger Street (240) of the late 17th century. The stair could be in a separate compartment at the service end, as at the two last-mentioned houses, or beside the stack as at 30 St. Peter's Street.

Class 7. A less common plan has the stack backing onto a passage at the end of the building. The stack thereby becomes internal, the passage being not an entry but an integral part of the house and its only access. No. 7 St. Peter's Hill (395), built just after 1600, is the earliest example in Stamford; no. 23 St. George's Street (308) dates from about the middle of the 17th century. This plan-form, though nowhere common, has a wide distribution, being found as far distant as Sherborne (RCHM, *Dorset* I, Sherborne (60, 71, 99)) and at 27 High Street, Uppingham, Rutland.

Class 8. Axially-placed chimney stacks are characteristically placed internally in 17th-century rural houses but in Stamford they are usually built at gable-ends. Consequently two and three-cell houses with internal stacks have been grouped as a single class. Two-cell houses of this form (class 8a) originated in the early 17th century, and usually have lobby entrances and stairs against the stack (RCHM, *Cambs.* I and II, class I; H. M. Colvin in *Studies in Building History* ed. Jope (1961), 223). At 45 High Street St. Martins (227) the stack is built against the rear wall. This type of house remained common in Stamford until the middle of the 19th century, by which time it was only used for small dwellings. Three-cell houses (class 8b) are essentially rural buildings and their appearance in a town is noteworthy. Two are in St. Leonard's Street (319, 320); both are early and of timber-frame.

The end of the 17th century saw several fundamental changes in domestic planning in Stamford. A heightened sense of symmetry in external design had its counterpart in internal planning, and coupled with new ideas of room-use, culminated in the houses of the Augustan Age.

Class 9. The double-pile house developed in the late 16th century as a gentry-house, used at first for buildings such as Red Hall, Bourne, Lincs., of the early 17th century. This type of house, class 9, first appeared in towns about the middle of the 17th century, and in Stamford the earliest example is 19 St. George's Square (299), completed in 1674. Typically the stairs rise in the centre of the back range, and the entrance is directly into one room, the hall. The kitchen occupied the rest of the front range, and there seems to have been a principal withdrawing room at the front of the house on the first floor. In the early 18th century this plan was used for a pair of semi-detached houses of very high quality, at 66–67 High Street St. Martins (237). Brazenose House of 1723 (383) has a separate entrance-hall dividing the two front rooms, and this developed form is also seen at 20 St. George's Square (300). At Brazenose the kitchen is in a front room, but at 20 St. George's Square and also Barn Hill House (96) of 1699 a fall in ground level made it possible to put the kitchen in a basement.

In the 18th century a variation is found, which may be called class 9b, where the stairs rise on one side of the house between front and rear rooms. The earliest examples, 9–10 Ironmonger Street (246) and 18–19 High Street (180), have lost their original ground-floor arrangement, but 46 High Street St. Martins (228), built *c.* 1830, remains intact. This plan was always associated with large houses and remained in use into the 19th century (RCHM, *Cambs.* I and II, where it is Class U).

Class 10. The early post-medieval house represented by class 2, and in the 17th century by class 6, remained in use until the end of the 17th century at least. One of the latest examples, 1 Ironmonger Street (240), illustrates how this class 6 plan could be adapted to resemble a symmetrically-fronted house. Houses of class 10 (class T of RCHM *Cambs.* I and II) first appear in English towns about the beginning of the 17th century, and have two rooms flanking an entrance passage. Gable stacks are common but not universal. A symmetrical plan and elevation is normal, but the earliest examples in Stamford tend to be asymmetrical, as 11 Broad Street (132), perhaps indicating that locally the type developed from class 6. Houses of class 10 appear in Stamford and other nearby towns in the early 18th century, as in Oundle (RCHM, *Monuments Threatened or Destroyed*, p. 51), and only become common in the early 19th century.

Three further houses should be discussed at this point. All follow the same plan, although one (184) was converted from an older house. They are two rooms deep and six bays, or three rooms, wide and were built in the first half of the 18th century. On the ground floor a passage divides each house unequally, and in each case this also marks the division of the house into two dissimilar tenements, the larger of class 9 and the smaller of class 13. At 9–10 Ironmonger Street (246) the deeds show that this was the original arrangement, and that the owner lived in the larger house. The first-floor planning and fittings at 18–19 and 25–26 High Street (180, 184) indicate the same arrangement. Similar pairs are found in other towns, e.g. Witham, Essex (*Post-Med. Arch.* 6 (1972), 18).

The basic arrangement of two rooms flanking an entrance was not adequate for a large house in the 18th century, unless service accommodation was located elsewhere. At Austin House and 12 Austin Street (85, 87) it is provided in the ample basement, a device made possible by the fall in land. Basements of the metropolitan type were not common in Stamford, but some examples are found along the edge of the scarp above the flood-plain where a drop in level already existed. The usual expedient was to provide services in a rear wing.

Class 11. The provision of a rear wing produces a separate house-type, class 11. The stairs, instead of being in the body of the house, are either in the wing or in a turret in the entrant angle. Staircases in the rear wing probably occur first, as at 3 All Saints' Place (72) of the very early 18th century, but the arrangement of a turret in the angle of range and wing is convenient and occurs for example at 13 Barn Hill (100) of 1740. Houses of this class were always of high social standing and are usually of a good standard of architectural design. Several houses originally of this class have been altered in subsequent years. No. 18 St. George's Square was completely replanned and partly rebuilt in the early 19th century, and about the same time 21 St. George's Square was even more drastically altered, the rear wing being replaced by a second range parallel to the street (see below *Alterations*).

Class 12. An L-shaped house, smaller than class 11, developed during the 18th century and forms class 12. In plan the main range contains only one room, with an entrance-hall along one side opening out to a stair which rises behind the room. Service and other rooms are in a rear wing, reached usually from the stair hall. This plan, related to the standard terrace houses of the period, occurs in Stamford for houses of good social standing. It first appeared after 1750 in houses such as 25 St. Mary's Street and 13 Maiden Lane (359), and continued in use into the early 19th century.

During the 18th century two new house-plans appear, related to both metropolitan and provincial terrace houses. Two rooms deep and one room wide, they are entered at one end of the elevation.

Class 13. These houses were usually roofed parallel to the street. The first of this type to be found in Stamford, class 13, has its stair rising between the front and rear rooms. Occasionally it is found as a non-parlour house (class 13a) where the front room is entered directly from the street, but in Stamford most surviving examples are parlour houses (class 13b) where an entrance-hall separates the front room from the circulation of the house. Although the plan is found in other towns in the late 17th century, e.g. Taunton (Taylor, *Post-Med. Arch.* 8 (1974)) and Knighton (Woodfield, *Trans. Radnor Soc.* (1974)), it does not occur in Stamford until the early 18th century when it is used for semi-detached and terraced groups of high architectural pretension. Three such houses form 8–10 High Street St. Martins (206) and three houses of this class are paired with class 9 houses in grandiose semi-detached pairs (180, 184, 246). This type reappears in the early 19th century when it is used for terraced houses such as those in Adelaide Street. The problem of lighting the staircase of these houses was overcome in Adelaide Street (114) by continuing the stair well into the roof, where it is lit by a dormer window.

Class 14. The most common small house plan, class 14, has its stair in the rear corner of the house, opposite the main entrance, and in its simplest form is a non-parlour house entered directly into the front room (14a). At a higher social level there is a parlour and a hallway (class 14b). This plan-type makes a later appearance in Stamford than class 13, but both were adopted for the bulk of middle-class housing in Stamford in the early 19th century. Both classes 13 and 14 were used in Rutland Terrace (288) and class 14 was used for high-quality developments such as Rock Terrace (426).

Class 15. The small single-room house of class 15 existed from the earliest times but being of low social status only the 19th-century examples have, in general, survived to the present day. These were the houses of the labouring classes, and requiring little land were built on the encroachments around the edge of the town, such as North Street, along with small class 13 and 14 houses. This plan was also used for the small tenements built in back yards in the 18th and early 19th centuries, for example the 18th-century row behind 3 St. Leonard's Street (316). Some newel stairs winding alongside the chimney stack are to be found in Stamford houses of the 17th and 18th century, for example 26 St. George's Street (309), but in the 19th century most stairs rose along one wall. In a few exceptional cases this plan seems to have been used for larger buildings of importance, e.g. 1 St. George's Square dating from the early 18th century. Nos. 15, 16, and 17 High Street (179) must have had service wings originally but appear now to belong to this class.

Contemporary description of houses and their rooms
After *c.* 1600 contemporary descriptions of houses give a better understanding of how they were used. It is not possible to apply to these descriptions the same classification devised for standing buildings, and interpretation is further hampered by the incompleteness, for various reasons, of many descriptions. During the 17th century every house described in probate inventories had a main living room, called the hall, and most had a parlour. A few houses had two parlours, and some had three or more especially in the late 17th century. The main store room was called the buttery and is specifically mentioned in every house before 1681. After that date it was replaced, in name at least, by a pantry, although this room-name, first appearing in 1677, is only found in a quarter of all inventories. Before 1684 kitchens are named at about half the houses described, but their position is not clear; they become more common after 1700. The number of chambers recorded increased from an average of about two to each house in the first half of the 17th century to about three in the second half, the range increasing from between one and four to between two and five. Most buildings with more than five chambers were inns. Before 1684 about half of the inventories record shops, though their function and position in the building varies, several clearly being work-shops in the yard behind the house. A characteristic two-room house with an entry at one end, presumably belonging to class 2, 6 or 7, was that of George Barlow; in 1689 it had a hall, parlour and entry each with a chamber over (LAO, 188/404). Another two-room house, which may have been of class 2, 4, 5, 6, 7, 8 or 10, was occupied by John Neale; in 1738 it had a house (main living room) and 'other room', a best chamber and 'other chamber', garret and cellar (LAO, 210/115).

During the 18th century changes occurred in both the houses and the surviving descriptions. Inventories decrease in numbers towards the middle of the century, as newspaper advertisements increase. Advertisements generally describe larger houses of fairly high social standing, while inventories mainly apply to the lower strata of society; inventories attached to wills proved in the Prerogative Court of Canterbury, which would correct the imbalance, are not yet available. As may be expected, the terminology of advertisements is more up-to-date than that of the inventories and this also reflects the relatively modernized condition of those houses. Similarly the conservative terminology of the inventories is also partly an indication of the slow rate at which new ideas penetrated down the social scale. The smaller houses described in the inventories prior to 1763 have a hall and parlour, usually a kitchen, sometimes a pantry, and two or three chambers, rarely more. The advertised houses, after 1733, are similar in accommodation, though with more chambers. Instead of a hall and parlour they have two parlours usually of equal status, and after 1773 one of these is sometimes called a dining room or drawing room. The change from hall to parlour probably implies the presence of a separate entrance lobby or hall as opposed to direct access to the room from the street.

Evidence for first-floor reception rooms is found only after 1770, though they clearly existed earlier (e.g. (299)). Where shops occupied much of the ground floor, living accommodation was commonly displaced upwards; Mrs. Taylor's shop in High Street in 1806 had a shop and kitchen, with dining room and bedroom above (*Mercury* 5 Sept.). Larger houses, not necessarily with shops, often had a drawing or even dining room on the first floor. An example of the changes in room-use between the 17th and 18th centuries is 12 St. Paul's Street (375) which was described in 1626 as containing hall, parlour, hall chamber, shop chamber, parlour chamber, kitchen chamber, kitchen and buttery as well as a workhouse and hay barn (LAO, 131/443). By 1742 a change in emphasis of room-use resulted in the house being described as having two parlours, a wainscotted hall, kitchen, larders, pantry, cellar, and six chambers, closets and a garret; outside there was a paved yard and a garden (*Mercury*, 2 Dec. 1742). An advertisement in 1786 described it as having three good parlours, kitchen, cellaring, three genteel bedchambers with closets and three good servants rooms. The garden now had a stable besides outhouses such as a brewhouse and wash house (*Mercury*, 1 Dec. 1786).

A class 10 house, 16 All Saints' Place (74), was described in 1793 as having a parlour, kitchen, pantry and scullery on the ground floor, and two chambers and a dressing-room on each of the upper floors (*Mercury*, 15 July). By 1817 one of the first-floor rooms was being used as a drawing room, with two parlours on the ground floor (*Mercury*, 10 Oct.). A smaller house of the same plan (169) had in 1822 a kitchen, a parlour, and two sleeping rooms above (*Mercury*, 3 May). No. 21 St. George's Square was probably a class 11 house before the rear section was rebuilt; in 1773 it had its kitchen, cellars and brewhouse in the basement, two parlours and a dining room on the first ground floor, and three chambers above (*Mercury*, 5 Aug.). A more characteristic arrangement is that of an unidentified house with two parlours and a kitchen on the ground floor, a drawing room and two chambers above, and three garrets in the roof (*Mercury*, 13 Sept. 1781). No description of a class 12 house has been identified, but 49 Broad Street (148) which resembles this plan had in 1792 a large dining parlour and kitchen on the ground floor, a drawing room and two lodging rooms on the first floor, and four further lodging rooms in the attic (*Mercury*, 2 Mar.).

The earliest bathroom and water-closet are those recorded at 23 St. Mary's Street (358) in 1814, the house of a wealthy merchant. Vale House (250) had a shower bath by 1823 (*Mercury*, 5 Aug. 1814, 5 Sept. 1823). Houses were sometimes subdivided temporarily by forming a unit for letting; in such cases the kitchen, a room not easily improvised, was always shared. An early example is an unidentified house in High Street, where in 1778 the apartment had four lodging rooms and use of the kitchen (*Mercury*, 8 Oct.).

Alterations

The process of modernizing houses to meet current needs and concepts is a continuous one, and the main trends in Stamford may be briefly examined. The most common alteration during the later Middle Ages was to floor over an open hall to give a two-storeyed building. In this way class 1 houses were converted to class 2 or 3 in the course of the 16th century, and probably some open halls remained to be floored over in the 17th century. This was done at 28 St. Mary's Street (362) in the 16th century, and at 25 High Street St. Martins (216) about the same time (Plate 71). A further modification of class 2 and 6 houses was made, often during the 18th century, which converted them from sub-medieval houses, entered directly into the main living room, to more convenient class 10 houses with rooms protected from the door by an entrance hall. This modernization is well documented at 23 High Street St. Martins (212) where a lease specifies the insertion of a new wall and removal of the stairs to a more convenient position (Ex. MS, 88/52). By providing a new stack in the former service room and perhaps moving the original hall fireplace to a new position on the other gable, houses of classes 1, 2 and 6 could easily be converted and almost completely disguised.

The simplest and most usual way of enlarging houses in Stamford was to add a rear wing. This was done at 55 High Street (191), at 12 St. Paul's Street (375) in *c*. 1600, and, later in the 17th century, at 40 St. Mary's Street (368). Commonly the wing was added behind the hall only, as at 12 St. Paul's Street, a class 3 house. The reason for this is clear for an addition to a cross wing would mean the exclusion of light from the rear room of the cross wing. Presumably the same reason would apply to those class 2 houses where there were two service rooms. Nos. 11–12 St. Mary's Street (349) and 35–36 St. Peter's Street (415) have the same improvement. Enlargement by building detached blocks, as happened in some other parts of England, is rare in Stamford where a rear wing along one side of the plot was the normal method of extending a house.

The other method of enlargement employed in Stamford in the 17th century and later was to build a rear range parallel to the front range, doubling the depth of the house. Nos. 11–12 High Street (177) was a class 2 house enlarged in this way probably early in the 17th century. This can be seen in the 19th-century alterations at 21 St. George's Square, where the final plan is almost that of a class 10 house. Houses of class 10 and 11 were sometimes enlarged and given more spacious accommodation by a process that also destroyed the symmetry of the elevation, and produced a plan similar to class 9. The central entrance hall and one flanking room were thrown into one; the main doorway was moved to the nearest window-opening of the other room which in turn became a spacious entrance hall (Fig. 149). This also necessitated the rearrangement of the back parts of the house. Most examples seem to date from the early 19th century, such as 38

High Street St. Martins (223) and 18 St. George's Square (298) (Plate 113). No. 15 Broad Street (134) was probably altered during the middle of the century.

Only rarely does extra accommodation appear to have been gained by heightening, except by raising the front wall of an attic or first floor to improve head room, as at 1 Broad Street (126) and 17 Barn Hill (104). Generally an increase in height accompanied almost total rebuilding, as happened at 54–55 High Street (191) and 25–26 High Street (184). The principal exception is 19 High Street St. Martins (209), though the amount of internal reconstruction appears to have been more than originally envisaged (Ex. MS, 88/51).

As fashions changed and the fabric of houses came to need refurbishing, buildings were modified externally to conform to new canons of taste. Stone-mullioned windows often had one or more mullions removed to give a larger glazed area, and in the 18th and 19th centuries sash windows were inserted in place of the older types. The walls of timber-framed houses were commonly encased or replaced in stone. Sometimes this only involved replacing the lower stage, beneath a jetty or bressummer, as at 20 High Street St. Martins (210) and 35–36 St. Peter's Street (415). Usually the walls were built against the line of the outer face of the original frame, necessitating an extension of the roof; the resulting change in pitch two feet from the eaves is often the only indication of a timber-framed origin for an otherwise stone building. At 35–36 St. Peter's Street the front wall was, exceptionally, built internally thereby reducing floor space inside the house. In 1747 John Burton leased a house at the N.E. corner of Castle Street with a covenant to spend £50 on repairs, including building the 'outward walls' in stone (Hall Books 3, 162).

Cellars

Many houses in Stamford have cellars, but as most are devoid of architectural detail it is almost impossible to know their date. Several medieval structures may have escaped recognition because of the lack of datable features. Nos. 1–2 Castle Street (153) illustrates the problem, for none of its visible detail is easily dated, but is almost certainly of late medieval date.

Documentary references show that cellars were being built by the 13th century; the earliest one recorded was 12½ ft. by 15 ft. (PRO, E 315/44, p. 39). The Hundred Rolls record no less than five new cellars constructed in the third quarter of the 13th century. Richard of Wardale built a cellar in St. Mary's parish about 1267, approached by steps occupying an area 8 ft. wide and 4 ft. long in the street. John Plouman, in the same parish, had his cellar steps next to his house door. About 1257 Gilbert of Cestreton, a wool merchant, built three cellars with external steps opposite the W. gable of All Saints' Church; the building may have been a terrace forming part of a speculative enterprise (*Rot. Hund.* 351b, 352a).

Three vaulted undercrofts of the 13th century survive, one of which (1 St. Mary's Place (340)) is only a fragment. A fourth example is known from excavations (16). That at 24 High Street St. Martins (214) is a simple rectangular vaulted structure without any original openings. At 13 St. Mary's Hill (338) the undercroft is two bays wide and was originally at least three bays long. The entry from the street is preserved almost intact, and suggests that the undercroft was used as a shop. The later undercroft at 23 High Street (183) may have served a similar function (Plates 58–60).

The 15th-century vaulted undercroft at 4 St. Mary's Place (342), also entered from the street, may have been below a guildhall. A former undercroft at the Bull Inn (352) seen by Stukeley in 1746 had eight vaulting ribs meeting at a central boss shield (3 *dolphins salient*) and had two blocked windows on the S., street, front (Surtees Soc. 76 (1883), p. 339). The undercroft below 69 High Street St. Martins (238) could not be examined; the building above is of *c*. 1500.

Cellars covered by beam-and-joist floors are difficult to date, but were common in the 18th and 19th centuries. The better-class cellars, however, have elliptical vaults. Their side walls are commonly coursed rubble, but the vault itself is of well-cut ashlar. They occur at the very beginning of the 18th century (e.g. the cellars below the Theatre (60) and 18–19 High Street (180)) and continue until well into the early 19th century. That at 46 High Street St. Martins is of brick and dates from *c*. 1830 (228).

Almshouses

The earliest surviving almshouse building in Stamford is Browne's Hospital (48), established and built in 1475; the plan is derived from earlier medieval hospitals which had a single large room with cubicles for the inmates along the sides, and a chapel projecting from one end. At Browne's Hospital the main block includes the chapel but otherwise is of two storeys, with cubicles in a low poorly-lit ground-floor room. The first floor is occupied by the Audit Room, known as the Great Chamber in the 17th century (inventory of 1677 in hospital archives). The magnificence of this room invites speculation as to whether it was intended to have a public use. Comparison may be made with buildings such as St. Saviour's Hospital, Wells, built shortly after 1424 by Bishop Bubwith's executors, with a hall used as a town hall at the W. end (J. Parker, *Architectural Antiquities of the City of Wells* (1866), 69–70). In 1731 the small rooms were furnished with a bed, a shelf, a candlestick and extinguisher; by 1766 most had acquired a second shelf and a cupboard (inventories in hospital archives).

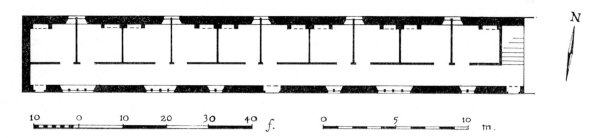

Fig. 9 (49) Lord Burghley's Hospital. Reconstruction of plan of range of *c.* 1616.

Lord Burghley's Hospital (49) is a rehabilitation of an older decayed establishment; the new range of lodgings probably built in 1616 survives much altered. Originally there was on the ground floor a long corridor with ten rooms opening off it (Fig. 9). This feature of an internal passage giving access to the rooms is found only occasionally in almshouses, a nearby example being the Maison Dieu at Melton Mowbray, Leicestershire, of 1640. An open cloister, such as those of the 16th and 18th centuries at Abingdon, is more common. The upper floor at Burghley Hospital is a semi-attic, and was presumably used as a long gallery for indoor exercise.

All the remaining buildings follow the normal post-medieval pattern of single-room lodgings each entered from outside. Two, Fryer's and Truesdale's Hospitals (50, 53), share the distinction of having been designed by Basevi, while Snowden's (52) was designed by Pierce, a local man. Corporation Buildings (422), a municipal scheme for housing the poor of the town in 1795, was a double row of single-room dwellings. Williamson's Almshouse (398) was established in 1762 in an existing house, extra rooms being provided in a narrow wing built on the back; the plan resembled a pair of houses and each inmate may have had two rooms.

Hopkins' Almshouse (51) is of two storeys, with access to the first-floor rooms from an open terrace at the rear, an arrangement recalling that at Cobbs Well, Fowey, of *c.* 1700 (RCHM, *Monuments Threatened or Destroyed* (1963), p. 28). St. Peter's Callis, rebuilt in 1863, was in the early 19th century a building with lodgings on two storeys, the upper reached by an external stone staircase and a covered timber gallery on the rear or S. elevation (Stamford Report 2, 53).

Most of the almshouses were rebuilt in the early 19th century in the revived Gothic style; Hopkins' Almshouse of *c.* 1770 was the earliest in this style which was perhaps chosen in this instance because of the proximity of the medieval town gate which was destroyed at the time the almshouses were built.

INNS AND PUBLIC HOUSES

Standing on the Great North Road half-way between London and York, Stamford had a large number of inns from the Middle Ages onwards. A 'great inn called Kyngesin' is mentioned in 1388 (*Cal. Inq. Misc.* v. (1387–93) no. 93) probably in St. Mary's Hill. The Angel, later George and Angel, 13–14 St. Mary's Street (350), is mentioned in 1458 (Peck XIV, 47) and was part of the endowment of Browne's Hospital.

The Blue Bell (243) was rebuilt shortly before 1595, but within a hundred years had declined greatly and was subdivided into small tenements. All the earlier inns were built with courtyards which survive to a greater or lesser degree at the George (239), George and Angel (350), Blue Bell (243), Black Bull (352), Eagle and Child (355); smaller hostelries simply had a yard behind the street frontage, as at the Bull and Swan (216), and Coach and Horses (209), with stables and other outbuildings arranged informally. A large entry for the passage of wheeled vehicles was an essential feature of the larger inns.

Of the early inns, only the George remains (239). Built in the early 17th century, it consists of four rooms flanking an open entrance passage, and two stair turrets at the rear. The ground-floor rooms included a kitchen and a dining room; on the upper floors were lodging rooms but the circulation system is not easily reconstructed. Probably an access linked the stair turrets across the W. front, and the E. rooms were reached by short passages leading from it (Fig. 132). Galleried ranges of uncertain date flanked the yard, and were replaced in the 18th century. The new N. range had lodging rooms reached from a central stair and apparently by a corridor along the rear wall.

The Black Bull was almost completely rebuilt as the Stamford Hotel in 1810 (352), but inventories allow the arrangement of rooms to be reconstructed (LAO, 116/173 (of 1614); 131/407 (of 1626); 36/501 (of 1630); 17/115 (of 1674)). The lodgings were on two storeys, in pairs on either side of staircases; possibly there was no gallery. The Stamford Hotel was not originally an inn but a centre of social and political activity, and only became a commercial concern in 1828.

Built in the mid 18th century, the former Globe, 8 High Street (174), has recently been gutted. It is known to have had a bar, kitchen and large dining room on the ground floor, and 14 bedrooms on the two upper floors, reached from the staircase by a long passage (*Mercury*, 21 July 1768). Smaller hostelries of the late 18th and early 19th centuries resemble the more substantial small houses of the period. The Salutation (16 All Saints' Street (80), late 18th-century) and Coach and Horses (19 High Street St. Martins (209), partially rebuilt 1798) are basically class 9 houses. The Salutation had a bar and two tap rooms on one side of the hallway and private rooms on the other, with bedrooms on the first floor (1845 Survey, Browne's Hospital Archives). Public houses and ale houses were usually dwelling houses which, like the Carpenter's Arms (54 St. Leonard's Street (326)) had one front parlour converted into a public bar. The house of Sarah Kidington, victualler, contained in 1738 a great room with closets, presumably drinking booths (LAO, 210/30). The Balloon (6 Blackfriars Street (125)) is an example of a building intended from the start to be a public house; it had a parlour and a bar at the front, a kitchen behind, and dining-room and bedrooms on the upper floors (*Mercury*, 28 Dec. 1827).

SHOPS

The first documentary reference to a shop in Stamford is in the early 13th century (PRO, E 315/44, p. 39). Like many of the shops described in medieval documents, this was a small building consisting of a cellar, a shop and a solar and is similar to one mentioned later in St. Martin's parish (PRO, E 315/32, p. 21). A building lease in 1434 of an empty plot in St. Mary's parish specifies no more than a shop with a solar above (PRO, E 315/31, p. 3). A larger building is described in a draft building lease of 1484, as having a hall, shop, two chambers, and a kitchen at the back (Ex. MS, 53/4).

The most important medieval shop to survive is the undercroft at 13 St. Mary's Hill (338), which has steps leading down from street level through a door flanked by windows into a part-underground vaulted room of high quality. The remaining undercrofts include two (23 High Street (183) and 4 St. Mary's Place (342)) which have doors leading to the street; in 23 High Street, this may have originally been the only access. Both of these could have served as shops although that at 4 St. Mary's Place was beneath a guildhall. Other undercrofts and cellars referred to in medieval documents (see *Cellars*, above) may also have been shops. As early as the Middle Ages buildings in Stamford were subdivided into shops and tenements in separate occupation. Some time before 1362 John Absolom gave the guild of St. Mary a cellar beneath Peter Wisbech's solar (PRO, C 41/174; *Cal. Pat.* 1361–4, 227). Four shops below one solar, apparently in Red Lion Square, were clearly all separately occupied in 1235. (*Cal. Chart.* 1226–57, p. 205).

In the 17th and 18th centuries most shops were simply one room on the ground floor of a house, distinguished by a more generous provision of windows. At 14 and 15 High Street (178, 179) window-openings on the ground floor had a rebate and a hollow-moulding; occupying the full width of the tenement, they had low sills, and lintels almost at ceiling level. No. 55 High Street (191) had windows with low sills and ovolo-moulded jambs which also appear to have occupied the full width of the room (Fig. 110). Similar ovolo-moulded jambs with sills 2½ ft. above floor-level were observed at both 18 and 19 High Street (180) of *c.* 1720.

In 1775 the plans for rebuilding 15 St. Mary's Street (351) (Fig. 173) show the shop as a heated room with two closely-placed windows. A similar arrangement of two windows, but here apparently separated by a door, formerly existed in the E. room of 1 Red Lion Street (283), built in 1793. Perhaps the early 18th-century High Street shops had several closely-placed windows in this fashion. The front room of 25 Broad Street (139) was apparently designed for use as a shop or office, with a central door flanked by windows, and a separate side entrance to the house (Fig. 95). The interiors of all early shops have been altered, but an inventory made in 1721 of fittings in the house in High Street leased by John Spencer, mercer, included in the shop two sashes (i.e. removable windows), counters, drawers, wainscot and the inner door (LAO, LD 40/52).

During the 19th century shops in the centre of the town grew progressively larger, and began to encroach deeper into the building. The drapery shop built by Edward Thorpe at 3 High Street *c.* 1823 had a shop and counting house occupying the whole ground floor and a three-storey warehouse behind, the living quarters being mainly above the shop (172) (Fig. 101). The two modest shops at 50–51 Broad Street (149) have a small front room for a shop and a larger living room behind. No. 6 Ironmonger Street (244) is a larger building with a shop fitted with cupboards on the ground floor, and a kitchen behind, the remainder of the living accommodation being on the upper floor. At 21 High Street (182) the shop was probably confined to the S. room before 1836 when the present shop front was installed (*Mercury*, 17 Feb. 1815, 6 May 1836) and the shop extended to occupy the whole of the ground floor.

In the late 18th and early 19th century several shop fronts of impressive design were put up. That at 18–19 High Street (180), perhaps installed by the chemist Mills, was the most splendid before its recent mutilation; it consisted of a series of fluted Corinthian columns supporting an entablature (Plate 93). No. 4 St. Mary's Street (344) and 7 High Street (173) are two accomplished examples of shop-design of the early 19th century with shallow bowed windows (Plates 138, 139). The design of 7 High Street resembles some of the plates in *Designs for Shop Fronts* (1792) by I. and J. Taylor. Less elaborate designs were made in the economical Doric or Tuscan styles, as at 25–26 High Street (184), and 21 High Street (1836) (182). Fronts of even more simple design have moulded pilaster strips in place of engaged columns, as at 28–29 High Street (185). Of the later fronts, 9 Ironmonger Street (246) and 13–14 St. Mary's Street (350) of *c.* 1849 are noteworthy. The bow window of 31 Broad Street (141) of 1848 projects ten inches, the maximum allowed under the Stamford Improvement Act.

Offices

In the 18th century offices were frequently no more than a convenient room set aside in a private house. Such domestic counting houses are still in use today and involve no special planning; a room entered from near the front door is all that was required. The strong-room and adjoining two rooms at Torkington House, St. Peter's Street (417), approached from a side-door under the carriage-entry, were probably offices for James and John Torkington, attorneys, in the early 19th century.

The earliest building which can be identified as an office is 24 St. Mary's Street (358), built by James Bellaers, merchant, next to his house, sometime before 1779. There were two ground-floor rooms, the front one with a central entrance; the first floor was used as an extension to the house. Immediately after 1827 T. H. Jackson, an attorney, built an office at 21 St. Mary's Street (357) adjoining his house. Again there were two rooms on the ground floor, and a small strong-room behind. The wine cellar below was separately entered and sublet. The mid 19th-century office at 15 Barn Hill (102) is also of two-room plan with a strong-room below the stairs (Fig. 81).

Wharves and warehouses

The Welland, though not a river of impressive size, must have been navigable as far as Stamford during the entire medieval period, even if only by the comparatively small boats that were in use at that time. In the

13th century wool was being exported from Stamford mainly through Boston (*Rot. Hund.* I. 353, 357) and it was presumably the better river connection that favoured that town against King's Lynn. By the 16th century navigation was impossible, the townsmen alleging that watermills up-stream from Deeping were the main obstacles (Act of 13 Eliz. I). During the early 17th century a canal 9½ miles long was dug to by-pass this stretch of the Welland (27). By the early 19th century traffic along the canal was by means of gangs of up to four lighters, each lighter of between 7 and 14 tons burden. The total load for a gang was 36 to 42 tons and the journey from Boston took up to four days (Drakard, 393).

The obstruction created by Stamford Bridge caused wharves to be confined to the banks on the downstream side. In 1756 Henry Ward made a quay on the N. bank of the Welland E. of the bridge (Court Rolls), and this is the only warehouse which remains today (450); others formerly existed on the N. side of Water Street where *c.* 1740 James Bellaers was landing coal and sending grain and malt down river (deeds, 16 Water Street). In 1731 Alderman Collington was importing Scandinavian timber and clay from the Isle of Wight (*Mercury*, 5 Aug.) and Drakard records that coal and timbers were the main items of trade in 1822 (Drakard, 393).

In 1840 the new plan for Blackfriars Estate included a wharf to the E. of Brownlow Street, but it was not built. River trade was superseded by the opening of the railway in 1846; coal was being brought from Peterborough by the following February (*Mercury*, 12 Feb. 1847), and the canal finally ceased to carry traffic in 1863.

INDUSTRIAL BUILDINGS

Two watermills dating from the 17th century survive in the town; they are rectangular structures with water wheels at the ends (65, 66). Only the base of one windmill was recorded (67).

There are few other industrial buildings in the town, and they generally date from the early 19th century. Stamford's importance as a marketing centre for agricultural products is reflected in the early growth of a flourishing brewing and malting industry. Most of the brewery buildings have been rebuilt but maltings are still a prominent element in the town's architecture. Dating from the 19th century, they are of rubble construction with small windows and heavily-constructed floors, and most are in St. Martin's parish.

Several attempts were made to establish silk throwsting in Stamford. Of the buildings erected for this, known as 'spinning schools', only that of George Gouger remains but greatly altered (143). Part of a brass foundry of *c.* 1843 survives at Broad Street (138).

The number of apothecaries in the 19th century is an indication of Stamford's local status; the business at 2 Red Lion Square (278) has been in existence for 250 years. Thomas Mills was one of the more important chemists, and his apothecary's workshop survived until recently behind 19 High Street (180).

MARKETS

In the Middle Ages markets in Stamford were held in the open, both in the streets and in Red Lion Square. The booths in the latter became progressively more permanent until they were rebuilt as proper small shops with rooms above; these encroachments were removed in the late 18th century. The market in High Street had a covered building, rebuilt in 1751 as a roofed space with open sides (Nattes' drawing of 1804); other traders had stalls against the adjacent buildings. It was demolished in 1808 when a new shambles and market were built (61) to designs by W. D. Legg (Fig. 60). A covered corn exchange was built in 1839 to replace an open market in Broad Street (Plate 66), but this was only used until 1859 when it was replaced by a closed hall on the opposite side of Broad Street. An open Buttermarket was built in Red Lion Square in 1861 to designs by Edward Browning, and still survives.

GARDENS

The larger town gardens have been altered or subdivided, and those of *c.* 1840–50 on the Blackfriars site are now abandoned. The Castle site was terraced for gardens but they too have gone. William Stukeley had a large garden at 9 Barn Hill (97) with prospect mound, temples, obelisk and summer house, of which only the early 17th-century gateway, remodelled as a great alcove, remains. His collection of medieval sculptured masonry, one of several to adorn 18th-century Stamford gardens, has, like its fellows, been dispersed. (See also S. Piggott, *William Stukeley*, 141, 151.)

Barn Hill House (96) retains part of a formal garden, overlooked by a classical summer house (Plate 104). The surviving formal features at the garden of Vale House (250), consisting of a terrace and a bridge spanning the mill leat, are now incorporated in an informal setting (Plate 150).

Several large houses retain in their gardens terraces which lie on the line of the town wall, probably incorporating part of it. In each case the terrace faces the garden and has a parapet on the external 'wall' face. That at 38 St. Peter's Street (417) may date in its present form from *c.* 1840; the terrace at 3 Broad Street (128) incorporates early masonry, and its parapet was refurbished in 1721, probably by George Denshire. At 14 Barn Hill (101) and 18–19 Broad Street (136) the terrace was raised over a loggia which faced the garden. A wooden loggia was built in a similar commanding position at 8 Rutland Terrace in about 1830 (288).

BUILDING MATERIALS AND CONSTRUCTION

Stone

The outcrop of Jurassic rock running from Yorkshire to Somerset provides some of England's finest building stone. Stamford lies on this outcrop, within 4 miles of the quarries at Barnack and Ketton, and 7 miles from Clipsham; it is unlikely that much stone was carried to the town from a greater distance before the 19th century. Most of the building stone used in the town came from the Lincolnshire Limestone beds of the Inferior Oolite; mainly oolites, they range from even-textured stones to coarse shelly ragstones.

Within and immediately around Stamford the Lincolnshire Limestone produces an oolite suitable for general building purposes, some beds yielding stone of a very high quality; this is known as Stamford stone. Both during and after the Middle Ages this stone was usually won by digging pits rather than by horizontal quarrying. Archaeological excavation has revealed many quarry-pits within the town and castle, dating from the 12th century and earlier. They are up to 30 ft. across, and when exhausted were immediately filled in. As late as 1764 Edward Sharpe, a mason, had a stone pit behind his house in Barn Hill (Court Roll). Most Stamford stone, however, must have come from pits in the open fields. Around 1270 Master Reginald of the hospital of St. Thomas on the Bridge had a quarry in the open fields which he extended into the highway; this encroachment was 40 ft. long and 8 ft. wide (*Rot. Hund.* I. 352). Pits in Pingle Field are mentioned in 1725 and 1839 (*Mercury*, 5 Apr. 1839) and a 'newly opened freestone pit' was advertised in 1822 (*Mercury*, 31 May). In 1785 the 9th Earl of Exeter had paid £2. 12. 6. for 'filling up and levelling stone pits in Stamford fields' (Exeter Day Books), and in 1843 the 2nd Marquess made payments for 'filling up a stone quarry and bringing half an acre into cultivation' (Ex. MS, 47/31/10). South of the Welland in St. Martin's parish Robert Hames had won stone before 1796 from a 4¾-acre field at TF 036069; when the workhouse was later built on the site the infilled quarry was found to be 30 ft. deep (NRO, St. Martin's Enclosure Award; *Mercury*, 4 Mar. 1836).

The quarry at Rock House must date from the Middle Ages and further quarries are visible at the ends of the gardens on both sides of Scotgate. The Rock House quarry may be that called St. Clement Delves in 1619 when a pinfold was made in it (Hall Book 1 fo. 329); it had probably fallen into disuse some time before 1466, for in that year a quarry in Scotgate was declared to be a public dunghill or rubbish-tip (Hall Books 1 fo. 7). In 1699 the top of this quarry was protected by a fence (Court Rolls, October 1699). Another medieval quarry existed further E., called St. Michael's Delves; it had fallen out of use by 1617 (Hall Books 1 fo. 324 v). By the mid 19th century the main quarries within the town were those on the boundary with Casterton, producing a high quality oolite from the lower beds of the Upper Lincolnshire Limestone. A coralline bed in the Upper Lincolnshire Limestone was called Stamford Marble; being very crystalline it takes a high polish, and was used in the 18th and early 19th centuries for chimney-pieces (Judd, *Geology of Rutland* (1875), 162). It was also used for the stairs of the Stamford Hotel (352).

The relatively coarse bedding and jointing of Stamford stone meant that it was possible to raise large blocks of stone, though the method of quarrying by pits must have also produced much rubble and waste. Not surprisingly, therefore, the major part of the masonry in Stamford is of coursed rubble. The locally-quarried freestone blocks were sometimes large. In 1807 blocks averaging 3 ft. long cost 2s. 1d. a ft. cube (Browne's Hospital Records, draft specification). This freestone was used for quoins and dressings, particularly for the flush dressings fashionable in the second half of the 18th century and the early 19th century. Gandy originally intended using it for all the quoins and chimneys of the Infirmary (62) in 1826 (correspondence, in hospital).

Quarrying appears to have been done mainly by masons, several of whom had their own quarries. In 1624 Robert Spademan provided stone for the repairs to the tower of St. John's church carried out by Valentine Hall (Vestry Book). During the 18th century the Earls of Exeter raised stone from their own quarries to provide materials for building; in 1761 William Shaw was being paid for this work, and in the 1780s John Pearson was digging in the Earl's quarries at Wothorpe. This stone would have been made available to other masons, such as those employed by George Betts to rebuild 19 High Street St. Martins (209) in c. 1798. William Legg also provided stone for masons, as he did for the buildings in St. Mary's Street (367) in 1791 (Exeter Day Books). George Portwood too quarried stone; in 1721 a large iron hammer was stolen from his freestone quarry (Mercury, 24 Aug.). Before 1796 Robert Hames had a quarry at St. Martins, and he opened a new quarry at Ketton in 1807 (Mercury, 10 July). When John Hames became bankrupt in 1794, the sale included 'stone in the solid rock ready bared', besides 'stone in the log, ashlin ready wrought and ashlin and jambs in the rough' (Mercury, 22 Aug.).

The medieval quarries at Barnack were worked, as at Stamford, by means of pits, excavating downwards rather than horizontally (Beresford and St Joseph, Medieval England (1958), 232). The stone produced was a hard shelly limestone from the upper part of the Upper Lincolnshire Limestone. It was generally used as rectangular blocks, but sometimes large blocks and slabs were made into coffins, coffin-slabs and architectural features such as tympana (Butler, Arch. J. (1964), 111f). Shelly limestone of Barnack type was widely used in the 12th, 13th and 14th centuries, not only in Stamford but over much of eastern England whither it was carried by water. By the 18th century it was used only for inferior purposes; in 1825 hard Barnack stone was used to surface the Great North Road (Mercury, 10 June).

During the Middle Ages Purbeck marble was imported to Stamford for slabs for brasses, and also for the font at All Saints' church. A white Purbeck marble was used for the slabs for some brasses in the same church (brasses (1)). Relatively little of the comparable stone from Alwalton, only 10 miles away, seems to have been used in the town. After about the middle of the 14th century the hard shelly Barnack rag was superseded by an oolite with shell fragments, probably also from the upper beds of the Upper Lincolnshire Limestone. This stone continued in use for major buildings and dressings until the end of the 16th century. Clipsham stone is of similar texture; one of the earliest examples of its use is an inscribed panel of shortly after 1380 (189).

At the end of the Middle Ages the shelly stone from the Upper Lincolnshire Limestone gave way in popularity to more even-grained oolites mainly from the lower sections of this Limestone. The most notable source was Ketton, where the quarries provided much of the freestone and ashlar used in post-medieval Stamford. Some of the Stamford masons had interests at Ketton; Robert Hames had a quarry there and the Hibbins family is found in both places in the 18th and 19th centuries. Slabs of Ketton were used for paving, and thicker slabs, called half-paces, were used as hearth-stones and cost 6d. a foot at the George Hotel (239) in 1725 (Ex. MS, 51/21/24). Probably most of the 18th-century tombstones are in Ketton stone. Among major buildings, Ketton was used at the Infirmary (62) in 1826, and at the Institution (59) in 1842. In 1807 blocks 3 ft. long cost 3s. 2d. per foot cube (Browne's Hospital).

The quarries at Little Casterton were opened on a large scale in 1834, and their working extended into the borough. The quarries at TF 013082 are now filled and built over. The first quarry was owned by Francis Simpson of Stamford (Mercury, 13 June 1834) and a second was opened in 1845 by Clement Brand (Mercury, 9 May). The stone is a fine even-textured oolite, and came out in large blocks. Other limestone differing little in its essential qualities from Stamford stone was obtained from adjacent parishes from time to time, but was not of great importance. In the late 18th century William Willamott dug stone for the Earl of Exeter on Wothorpe Warren (Exeter Day Books, 1771 onwards) where in 1774 he built and operated a lime kiln; in 1778 John Pearson also dug stone there. Wothorpe stone and lime were used for refacing and enlarging 19 High Street St. Martins (209) in 1797 (Ex. MS, 88/51). Ryhall and Easton stones are also mentioned in the early 19th century.

A distinctive fissile sandy limestone known as Pindle was dug at Wittering in the early 19th century from the same beds that produced Collyweston slate. The slabs of this fine and hard stone are seldom more than 2 ins. thick, and give a pleasant texture to the wall surface. The large number of courses meant extra expense in both lime and labour; in 1826 Gandy estimated that ordinary pindle walling cost 7s. 6d. to 8s. 6d. a yard as opposed to 4s. 6d. for Ryhall, an ordinary rubble stone (Infirmary records). Consequently it is rarely found. The first occurrence is at 21 St. Mary's Street (357), shortly after 1827. Edward Browning put it to good decorative use on the buildings flanking the bridge in 1849, and Gandy used it at the Infirmary. In 1844 the Marquess of Exeter was paying Thomas Roffe for raising the stone from pits at the rate of 6d. a yard (Burghley Account Book).

Ancaster stone, from the lower beds of the Upper Lincolnshire Limestone, was perhaps little used before the 19th century. It was the facing-stone for Rutland Terrace in 1830 (288). Later in the century, Bramley Falls stone was brought from Yorkshire for the Town Bridge (64).

Masonry techniques

Almost all masonry walling in Stamford is of coursed rubble. The stones vary from being very roughly dressed to being carefully squared and accurately shaped blocks. In the post-medieval period freestone quoins and dressings are found on all but the poorer buildings where wooden lintels and angles without quoins are normal.

From the late 17th century the better houses are faced in ashlar. Where the construction can be determined this ashlar is composed of slabs sometimes no more than 4 ins. thick, laid on the face of a rubble wall. In 1726 George Portwood charged 2d. a foot for such ashlar stone, but 'parapetting ashlar', where blocks alone formed a true ashlar wall, and hence about a foot thick, cost 6d. a foot (Ex. MS, 51/21/24). Significantly John Pearson in 1775 made no difference in labour charges for building in rubble or ashlar, both being priced at 1s. a yard (Ex. MS, 89/24). Chamfered quoins cost 2s. a foot in 1725 and rubble walling 2s. 6d. a yard in 1726 (Ex. MS, 51/21/24).

In about the middle of the 18th century a distinct masonry style arose, using flush freestone dressings for doors, windows and quoins (Plate 121). Arranged alternately, these quoins were used to give a deliberate decorative effect in the best work, and sometimes the lintels were continued as a band of ashlar from one window to the next. This style was relatively economical and continued in use until the mid 19th century.

Several rubble-built houses are now plastered, and resemble ashlar-faced buildings. The details of some other houses show that they too were formerly rendered. Clearly in many cases, such as 34 High Street St. Martins (219), this rendering was intended to conceal the scars of altered openings in an older building. This house was presumably rendered in the early 19th century when it was replanned. No. 28 St. Mary's Street (362) was formerly rendered, obscuring a variety of archaeological details; the plastering of other buildings may also cover unsightly scars (255, 294).

Exposed wooden lintels are relatively rare features, most buildings having flat or nearly flat arches made up of three or more stones. During the 17th century mullioned windows were constructed with mullions supporting what are in effect stone lintels, any timberwork being internal and concealed. In the 17th century and earlier, door heads were made of single stones or two stones meeting in the centre.

Where heavy floor beams require maximum bearing, especially in warehouses and maltings, their outer ends are almost on the external wall face. These beam-ends are covered by a slab of stone slate, which protects the beams, makes the wall flush, and disguises the construction.

Bricks

The earliest brick buildings in Stamford were built in the middle of the 18th century and were of good quality; however, brick was not widely used before the early 19th century. The first brickmaker of whom we have information is John Newark, who began operations in St. Martins, at TF 03350620 in 1754 (Ex. MS, 77/10/3), perhaps using Upper Lias Clays; he also made pantiles, 'flat tiles', and 'garden pots' (*Mercury*, 4 June 1767). Newark was probably succeeded by John Charlesworth, but the kilns closed after the expiry of Newark's original lease in 1776 or 1777 (Stamford Baron Court Rolls, 1776). Charlesworth continued in business until his death in 1781, and his widow was still burning bricks, but N. of the river, in 1788 (Court Rolls).

Later, brick production was based on Emlyns Closes near the present Recreation Ground, in the open fields and also on the Lings, an area of common pasture now the Williamson Cliff Brickworks. In 1779 Charlesworth was digging clay from the Upper Estuarine beds on the Lings (Court Rolls; at TF 018079). George Neale's 1½ acre brick yard near Emlyns Closes passed in 1825 to William Smith (*Mercury*, 25 Mar., 4 Nov.); in 1845 a nearby claypit of ¾ acre had become a garden as agricultural use was clearly no longer possible; in that year Robert Woolston had a 2¾ acre brickfield in the same area (Survey of 1845). Woolston probably began brickmaking in *c*. 1842 (*Mercury*, 8 Jan. 1864). The 18th-century bricks were fired to a red colour; during the early 19th century an orange-red or yellow-red was normal, probably the result of the use of the Upper Estuarine clays from the N. of the town.

Coade stone was used for a monument of 1800 in St. John's church, and the statue of Justice on the Stamford Hotel (352) may also be of this material. In 1858 Blashfield opened his terracotta works in Stamford (451) employing some of Coade's moulds. He used clay from Poole, Wakerley, and Uffington, and Lower Estuarine clays from St. Martin's; the business finally closed down in 1875. Several buildings in Stamford are decorated with his terracotta ((185) by 1876; Scotgate Inn in 1871) and others with an inferior ware which was made by John Lumby in the years following 1861.

Timber framing

The surviving timber-framed buildings in Stamford, in so far as they can be examined, exhibit little variety in constructional technique. From the late 15th to the early 17th centuries the usual style of framing was close-studding with studs about 6 ins. wide set at 12 to 18-inch centres. The earliest dated example is in Browne's Hospital of 1475, and the latest may be the rear range of 11–12 High Street (177), built in the early 17th century. Braces in timber-framed walls are always from the post down to the sill, and are set internally to avoid interrupting the external pattern of parallel studs, as at 9 St. Mary's Street (347). Such braces are rarely recorded, probably because they are hidden behind plaster. In some houses the gables have raking studs on either side of a central stud. The rear block of 10 High Street (176) has a single pair of such raking studs, while the N. gables of 25 High Street St. Martins (216) have two pairs. This style of framing the tops of gables was also seen in Lincoln in the late 15th and early 16th centuries, but in Stamford it was probably more usual to have only vertical studs, as at 10 St. Mary's Hill (336). Storeyed houses are commonly jettied.

The one exceptional building is 6–7 Red Lion Square (280) where the frame consists of a series of slightly curved parallel braces, with only occasional studs or posts; these braces form a herringbone pattern. This building is not closely datable but may belong to the late 15th century; its unusual construction may perhaps be accounted for in part by its exceptional character, for whatever its function it was a large and important building (Fig. 139).

A small amount of timber-framed building was carried out in the late 17th and 18th centuries. Slender timbers generally of imported softwood, used as studs at about 2 ft. intervals, form a frame which is not infilled but plastered on both faces. The upper floor of the rear wing of 5 Ironmonger Street (243) dates from the early 18th century, and is jettied; a smaller projecting section at 25 St. Mary's Street (359) dates from *c*. 1766.

The types of infilling of timber-frame show little variation. Among surviving buildings the commonest method was to slip stone slates into grooves between the studs and to cover both sides with hard plaster. This technique can be demonstrated at Browne's Hospital of 1475, 68 High Street St. Martins (238), 10 High Street (176), and 40 St. Mary's Street (368). An alternative method was simply to fill the spaces with panels of hard plaster held in place by pegs set at about 18-inch intervals in the sides of the studs. At 6–7 Red Lion Square (280) these panels are formed of small stones set in plaster, which received a further coat of plaster on each face and a final, thin and very hard, external rendering. In all of these methods both faces of the timbers were generally left exposed.

Frames of the 17th and 18th centuries were completely covered with plaster on laths, and many earlier buildings were doubtless similarly rendered at this time. The surface of the plaster was roughened by impressing it with a tool such as a trowel-blade. At 9 St. Mary's Street (347) the gable has a scalloped border resembling a barge-board. Decorative pargeting is rare.

Roof construction

Probably the earliest surviving roof-structure is the fragment, perhaps of the late 13th century, at 16–17 St. Paul's Street (379). The tiebeam is arch-braced, and channelled for passing-braces which, along with a crown post, have been mostly removed. The arch-braces are of almost square section and are not jointed but face-pegged to both tie beam and wall post. Face pegging is an early technique, occurring locally at Lincoln in c. 1290 (*Arch. J.* 131 (1975)).

Dating from later in the Middle Ages are several roofs each of which has members of uniform scantling. The earliest is probably the hall roof at 25 High Street St. Martins (216), consisting of pairs of rafters each with a collar; the timbers are square in section, and no evidence for a longitudinal purlin could be seen. Typologically later is the smoke-blackened roof at 34 St. Peter's Street (414), where only every third pair of rafters has a collar. In this house purlins lie in the angle between rafter and collar; such clasped purlins later became a frequent feature of Stamford roof carpentry. The roof of 21 All Saints' Street (82) may be a little later still; here the bays are wider, the hall being of only two bays, and there are in addition windbraces between principals and purlins. Over the S. range of 69 High Street St. Martins (238) is a similar roof of c. 1500 with bays of normal width; here the principals had the refinement of a diminution in depth above the clasped purlin, seen also at 6 Barn Hill (95) in the 16th century (Plate 77), and at 10 High Street (176). The roof of 40 St. Mary's Street (368) of similar date, has undiminished principals. Clasped purlins occur in Lincoln from the third quarter of the 15th century onwards (*Arch. J.* 131 (1975)).

Crown-post roofs are now uncommon in Stamford. The most ornate is that at 16 Barn Hill (103), where the crown post is braced to both collar-purlin and tiebeam. That at 6–7 Red Lion Square (280) is of high quality but quite plain, as is the mutilated roof at 35–36 St. Peter's Street (415). The roof over 18 St. Mary's Street (354) (Plate 76) has ogival braces and probably belongs to a lower level in the social scale. Dating is difficult but these survivals probably all date from the late 15th or perhaps early 16th centuries.

Roofs in Stamford during the 16th and 17th centuries appear mainly to have been of simple construction, with windbraces going out of use during the 16th century. Purlins are frequently clasped by the collar against the principals. During the first half of the 18th century, beginning perhaps just before 1700 but continuing no later than c. 1745, several roofs were built with principals having curved feet. No crucks were identified, but these roofs are related to raised or upper crucks. The earliest of these roofs include 54–55 High Street (191), and the building behind 14 High Street (178) (Fig. 104); later examples are 3 All Saints' Place (72) and 24 St. Mary's Street (358); no. 13 Barn Hill (100) is dated 1740 and 35 High Street St. Martins (220) is of similar date and design. In some of these roofs the purlins instead of being canted to the pitch are set square. At 1 Red Lion Square (277) square-set purlins possibly date from the late 17th century, but most are found in 18th-century buildings; the latest examples are those of the early 19th century at 1–3 St. John's Street (311). Frequently, as at 13 Barn Hill (100) of 1740, and at 54–55 High Street (191), they are associated with principals with curved feet, and form the lower tier of purlins at the level of the curve; the upper tiers of purlins are canted normally. These purlins are tenoned into the sides of the principals, and some are tusk-tenoned; this technique is known to have been used in the late 18th century by Mrs. Pilkington (S. range of the George Hotel (239), 1791; nos. 1–2 St. Mary's Hill (331), 1792) and may have been a speciality of the firm.

Roofing materials

Stone slates were obtained from a bed of fissile sandy limestone near the base of the Lower Lincolnshire Limestone, the main source for Stamford being the workings at Collyweston and Easton-on-the-Hill, Northamptonshire (RCHM, *Northants.* I, Collyweston (11)). These slates were employed in Stamford during the Middle Ages (see Castle (10)), the first documentary reference to their use being for the repair of houses in 1389 (Durham Priory Account Rolls). They were also used for most new buildings in the town during the 18th and early 19th centuries; only after 1850 were they largely replaced in popularity by Welsh slates and pantiles. It is not clear at what date thatch ceased to be used for new buildings. Council Orders such as that of May 1676 which required that all new houses within the town should be tiled or slated, and that existing buildings be so covered within three years (Hall Book 2, 73), must have been partly ignored, for as late as 1835 the Marquess of Exeter was having houses in St. George's Street rethatched (Burghley Estate Office, Accounts). Slating was measured by the rod of 36 square yards; in 1700 slates cost

12s. to 14s. a thousand at the pit, and this number would cover almost one rod. In 1700 the cost of slating a rod of roof was £2 (Wing, 269), and this is what John Burton charged in 1775 (Ex. MS, 89/24); Wing priced labour alone at 12s. per rod. Ridge tiles were generally of clay, and old drawings show that several houses retained late medieval ridge tiles into the last century. One late medieval example was found ((368); Fig. 186), and the rear wing of 17 Barn Hill (104) has crested ridge tiles perhaps of the early 17th century.

Both plain tiles and pantiles were introduced to the area by the late 17th century (Wing, 269). Plain tiles survive from the 18th century but do not appear to have been common, despite the fact that they were probably a little cheaper than stone slates and were certainly less expensive to lay. Pantiles cost even less, and were much cheaper to lay: 1s. 8d. for laying 100 sq. ft. as opposed to 3s. for plain tiles and about 3s. 8d. for stone slates (Wing, 269). Pantiles appear to have been used for humble buildings, and the earliest surviving examples are on small houses and outbuildings of the early 19th century. Welsh slates were introduced at the beginning of the 19th century, their first documented use being on the new roof at the Town Hall in 1819. They are at first associated with better-class houses, and with the lower-pitched roofs then coming into fashion.

Plaster floors

Plaster was used as a flooring material from the Middle Ages, and several plaster floors, laid directly on the earth, have been found in excavations, for example at the Castle (10). All surviving examples in standing buildings are upper floors; because of their tendency to crack when the supporting joists sag, few can be expected to be of an early date. The plaster floor in the attic of 40 St. Mary's Street (368) was laid and relaid on at least three separate occasions. The earliest reference to such floors in Stamford is in an inventory of St. Martin's Vicarage in 1582, where the chamber over the hall had a plaster floor (Ex. MS, 33/11); probate inventories of the 17th and 18th centuries sometimes refer to them incidentally, as 'plaster floor garret' (LAO, 211/280). Perhaps by this time, but certainly by the 18th century, the technique was used mainly for attic floors (e.g. Ex. MS, 89/24, referring to 15 St. Mary's Street). The latest example recorded dates from c. 1820 (274).

The plaster was run on to a layer of straw or reeds laid directly across the joists; as it set rapidly no other formwork was necessary. The plaster was generally between 1 and 2 ins. thick, and contained a little crushed brick. In 1700 a hundredweight of plaster was deemed sufficient for a square yard of flooring and this agrees tolerably well with examples noted in Stamford. At the same date 40 cwt. of plaster, at the pits, cost 4s. to 4s. 6d. (Wing, 269). In 1775, John Burton charged 1s. a square yard for materials only (Ex. MS, 89/24); this equates with Wing's figures of 4d. to 6d. a yard for workmanship, and an inclusive cost of 1s. 4d. a yard (Wing, 269).

ARCHITECTURAL STYLE

During the Middle Ages domestic buildings of stone, on surviving evidence, were built in coursed rubble. Some houses were further elaborated with buttresses and one, 17 St. George's Square (297), of very high quality, had both a string-course and an eaves cornice. The crocketed gable coping now reset at 3 Broad Street (128) must also have come from a high-quality building, but most buildings, for example 6 Barn Hill (95), were less elaborate.

Surviving timber-framed houses appear to have exploited the decorative effect of vertical stripes given by close-studding (Plate 79). The timber-framed range of 11–12 St. Mary's Street (349) had traceried heads to the panels between the studs. Occasionally gables had raking struts instead of vertical studs, a fashion which was probably confined to the late 15th and 16th centuries. The frame of 6–7 Red Lion Square (280) is unique in Stamford, and was probably intended as a bold decorative extravaganza. The external rendering of timber-frame probably began in the second half of the 17th century. Only two examples of decorative pargetting are known in Stamford, the crest of Cecil on 25 High Street St. Martins (216) and a windmill dated 1690, formerly at 51 High Street (189). Generally surfaces are pecked overall, scoring to imitate ashlar being surprisingly rare.

During the 17th century stone superseded timber-frame for all new buildings. Coursed rubble was still the common building material although ashlar slabs were used for facing an increasing number of the better houses. Windows, when mullioned, were almost always ovolo-moulded, and were protected by a weathered label or string. Doorways in the early years of this century had depressed four-centred heads with sunk spandrels; square-headed openings with mouldings which were stopped as much as 2 ft. above floor level came into use about the middle of the century.

Several houses were built with a cross wing, the gable giving interest and an asymmetrical liveliness to the street elevation. In about the third quarter of the 17th century the commonest form of external display was to build a two-storey gabled bay window. Frequently this was added to the main range of a cross-wing house, as at 12 St. Paul's Street (375), partly balancing the cross-wing gable, and giving the house a busier outline. The gables have finials and kneelers, and are often decorated with a date-slab. Bay windows were usually faced in ashlar (Plates 82, 83).

The final quarter of the 17th century saw the introduction of new ideas into Stamford's architecture. The change is heralded by 19 St. George's Square (299), built in 1674 in the most up-to-date style available to local builders (Plate 88). Mullion-and-transom windows of vertical proportions in a moulded surround mark a radical break with the past. Here and in several other buildings the surround consists of a pair of symmetrically moulded ribs dropping from a platband and terminating on a moulded sill. The last manifestation of this concept is seen at 35 High Street St. Martins (220) where the ribs have, by the second quarter of the 18th century, become plain architraves. More conventional windows of the late 17th century may be seen at 1 Ironmonger Street (240) and 32 Broad Street (142). In a few buildings, notably 14–17 High Street (178, 179), bolection ribs are extended over the whole building, forming a complete web incorporating and linking all elements of the elevation. Usually platbands have a small moulding on the lower edge. Ashlar is essential to this style, and the walls generally have a plinth with moulded top. Emphasized quoins occur for perhaps the first time, usually chamfered but in two cases with recessed centres. The eaves overhang on boldly-bracketed wooden cornices.

The late 17th-century style developed very gradually into that of the early 18th century. Plinths remained moulded, and round-nosed window sills finally gave way around 1720–5 to plain-sectioned sills with a cyma or other moulding below. Window surrounds are usually framed with a cyma moulding, a bold cavetto being less common. Unmoulded projecting window-surrounds, mostly with three keystones, only became common after about 1740, although they were in use from at least 1704. Chimney stacks on the more lavish houses were boldly rusticated, as at 33 High Street St. Martins (218). Ovolo-moulded mullioned windows continued to be used in basements of even the best houses.

By the end of the second quarter of the century these architectural details had become fused to form a mature classical style which prevailed until about 1760, the Theatre (60) being the last, belated, expression. The mouldings used were simple and confined to cavettos, ovolos and cymas; significantly the Order most commonly used was the Tuscan. An exuberant version of the style appeared between about 1730 and 1740. Bold and assertive, its chief characteristic is the exaggerated use of keystones, and this, sometimes coupled with rustication, produces a rich but somewhat old fashioned effect (Plates 101–103). This individuality might suggest the work of one designer. The style is best illustrated in a group of five houses (100, 133, 182, 220, 237). Towards the middle of the century several new elements appear, most of which are found in Stamford only at this period. These include pediments, Venetian windows, pedimented windows, and roundheaded windows on the street fronts of houses. Keystones were broad and often multiple, and at about the same time architraves eared top and bottom were introduced. The finest of these buildings are marked by a competence in design and a satisfactory balance of composition.

The second half of the 18th century in Stamford is by contrast a period of sober and relatively unambitious building. Unmoulded projecting window surrounds are found mainly between c. 1740 and 1770, and the ashlar surface of the wall is usually broken only by platbands or continuous sills. After about 1760 buildings were in an even more severe style. Only platbands or continuous sills are proud of the surface, all other dressings being flush. This is sometimes augmented by a modest dentil cornice. The interplay of texture between the neat rubble of the walls and the deliberately arranged freestone dressings provides the only other decoration (Plate 116), but some houses lack even this, being of ashlar throughout. Three buildings put up by John Hames are in this austere style (147, 239, 342), and several others were designed by W. Legg after 1778.

Several threads can be traced through the fabric of early 19th-century architecture. The century began with generally more economical and severe versions of late 18th-century classical architecture. The Stamford Hotel (352) is a metropolitan building in design, and has no place in the development of architecture in the town (Plate 152). Rutland Terrace (288) is essentially in the tradition of the great 18th-century squares of London and Bath, and its decoration is in the Grecian style of the time. In 1842–3 Bryan Browning introduced new stylistic ideas in his Institution (59) and refronting of Barn Hill House (96); more Italianate forms were at the same time appearing in Scotgate in Rock Terrace (426) and Rock House (427). Charles Richardson seems to have worked in a plainer and more severe style; he designed 5, 7, 8 Broad Street (129) and therefore perhaps 14 and 15 Barn Hill (101, 102) which are very similar (Plates 156–159).

The Gothic Revival hardly affected Stamford. Hopkin's Hospital of *c.* 1770 (51) is the earliest clumsy essay in the style. The Bath House of 1823 (110) and 21 St. Mary's Street (357), soon after 1827, are little better informed. The local architect Thomas Pierce designed Snowden's Hospital in 1822, Basevi designed two almshouses and Gandy a hospital (50, 53 and 62) in a fairly accurate Tudor style characteristic of the period before the Camden Society's influence. Gothic House (176) is the only domestic building seriously in the style, and is surprisingly early, being completed in 1849. The Jacobean style was more frequently imitated, perhaps because of the number of buildings in the town already displaying 17th-century fronts. Bryan Browning, charged with replacing a bay-windowed house of 1666, designed one on identical lines (380); nos. 4–5 Red Lion Square (279) and the buildings flanking the Bridge (333, 450) are large-scale projects in the style. Some houses, such as 54 and 55 High Street St. Martins, appear to have been largely rebuilt as faithful reproductions of their 17th-century predecessors (Plates 160–163).

Windows

Few domestic windows survive from before the 17th century. Tympana from two round-headed two-light windows of the 12th and early 13th centuries are no longer *in situ* (232, 362; Plate 62). A 13th-century traceried window from 17 St. George's Square (297) is now reset in St. Mary's church vestry (Plate 62). A wooden traceried 15th-century window, mutilated, remains at 6–7 Red Lion Square (280; Plate 76). Both the window in the rear range of 6 Barn Hill (95) and the mullioned-and-transomed window of Digby House (255) have hollow mouldings and date from the 16th century. The hood mould, seen at Digby House, continued in use until the middle of the next century. Early 17th-century windows have ovolo-moulded mullions, the central mullion sometimes being larger in section better to support the masonry above. Such windows were used as late as the beginning of the 18th century to light basements, as at 33 High Street St. Martins (218) and Brazenose House (383). Ovolo-moulded arrises are also found occasionally in the early 18th century, for instance at 28–29 High Street (185).

Architraves (Figs. 10, 11)

Raised moulded surrounds first appear in the late 17th century, associated with mullion-and-transom windows. The internal frames seem to have been mainly of wood rather than stone, as at 19 St. George's Square (299). The earliest surviving windows with architraves, at 32 Broad Street and 12 St. Paul's Street (142, 375), are approximately square, with a stone mullion, and the architrave has a cyma moulding that was to continue to be the commonest form until this type of window-surround went out of use in the late 18th century. The architraves of 20 High Street (181) are interesting examples of conservative design, though the mouldings are of an early 19th-century type (cf. Fig. 175). Windows in smaller buildings and subsidiary positions had wooden frames in unornamented openings, as at 17 Barn Hill (104).

Cavetto-moulded architraves occur in the late 17th century at King's Mill (65) on a door, and in 1725 at the George Hotel (239). Later, in the second quarter of the 18th century, all but two of the houses with rusticated doors and windows have this architrave moulding, as at 13 Barn Hill and 14 Broad Street (100, 133). The exceptions are (220) and (237). Between about 1730 and 1760, windows in many high-quality houses have eared architraves; the unusual example at 25–26 High Street (184, Plate 99) may be compared with Plate 45 of James Gibbs' *Rules for Drawing* (1732). Unmoulded architraves exist from the earliest years of the 18th century, 33 Broad Street (144) being dated 1704, but they are most common from *c.* 1740 to *c.* 1770, none being found after that date. Many of the early examples have a bead cut on the inner arris, as at 68 High Street St. Martins (238), whereas others have a chamfer, as at 18 St. George's

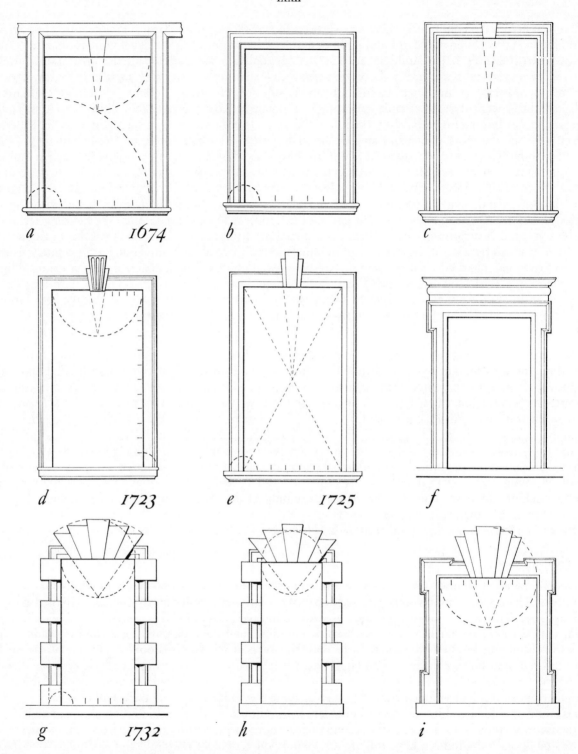

Fig. 10 WINDOW SURROUNDS arranged chronologically with building dates indicated where known.
a.(299) 19 St. George's Square; b.(72) 3 All Saints' Place; c.(218) 33 High Street St. Martins;
d.(383) Brazenose House; e.(239) George Hotel; f.(246) 9–10 Ironmonger Street;
g.(182) 21 High Street; h.(133) Former Stag and Pheasant Inn; i.(229) 47–50 High Street St. Martins.

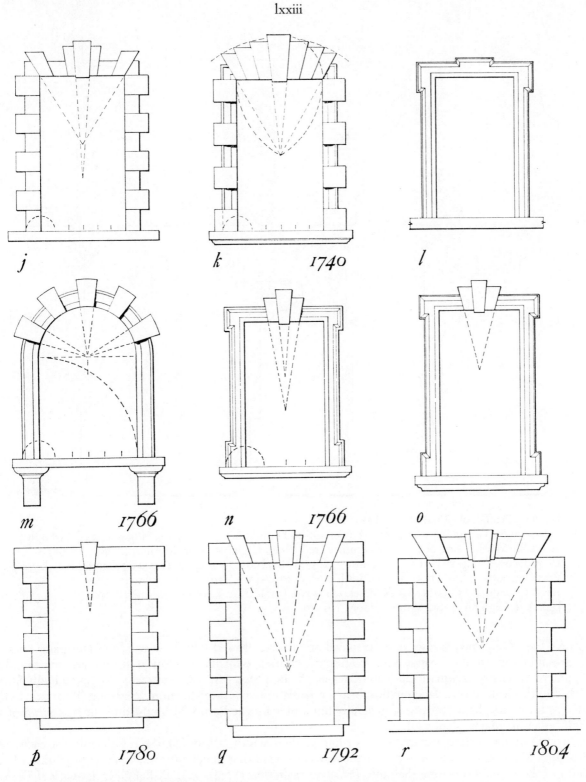

WINDOW SURROUNDS arranged chronologically with building dates indicated where known.
j.(237) 66–67 High Street St. Martins; k.(100) 13 Barn Hill; l.(184) 25–26 High Street;
m.(60) Theatre; n.(60) Theatre; o.(188) 41 High Street;
p.(337) 11–12 St. Mary's Hill; q.(361) 27 St. Mary's Street; r.(98) 10 Barn Hill.

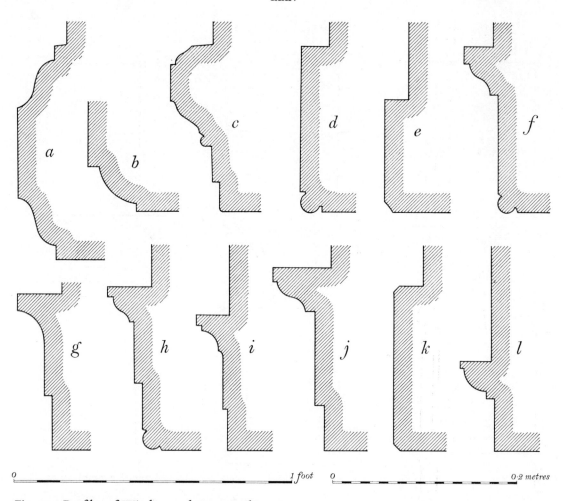

0 ⸺ 1 foot   0 ⸺ 0·2 metres

Fig. 11   Profiles of Window and Door Architraves.
a.(299) 19 St. George's Square, 1674; b.(185) 28–29 High Street, early 18th-century; c.(218) 33 High Street St. Martins, first quarter 18th century; d.(238) 69 High Street St. Martins, c. 1700; e.(298) 18 St. George's Square, early 18th-century; f.(383) Brazenose House, 1723; g.(239) George Hotel, 1725; h.(220) 35 High Street St. Martins (door), c. 1730–40; i.(136) 19 Broad Street, early 18th-century; j.(385) 31 St. Paul's Street, c. 1747; k.(301) 21 St. George's Square, c. 1768; l.(221) 36 High Street St. Martins (door), c. 1770.

Square (298). Frequently houses have moulded architraves around first-floor windows and plain ones on the ground floor. Moulded bands hung from string-courses to form a window architrave are first found in 1674 at 19 St. George's Square (299) and later at 33 High Street St. Martins (218). At 14–17 High Street (178, 179) this feature was elaborated to form a reticulation covering the entire elevation (Plate 92). In the early 18th century these bands were generally unmoulded, as at Barn Hill House and the rear wing of 35 High Street St. Martins (96, 220).

In 1700 masons priced architraves according to their width; a foot length cost a penny for each inch of width (Wing, 267). Contemporary manuals recommend that the architrave should be one-sixth of the width of the window-opening (Salmon, *Palladio Londiniensis* (1734), 128; B. Langley, *Treasury of Designs* (1745), 45). This relationship, though found in most buildings in Stamford, was not universally adhered to. In better-quality buildings, windows are generally between 3¼ and 3¾ ft. wide, and architraves often appear to have been cut to a standard width of 6 or 7 ins., thereby giving an approximately 'correct' relationship in most windows. At 14 Broad Street and 35 High Street St. Martins (133, 220) the architraves are 7 ins. wide and the windows considerably narrower than is usual in Stamford.

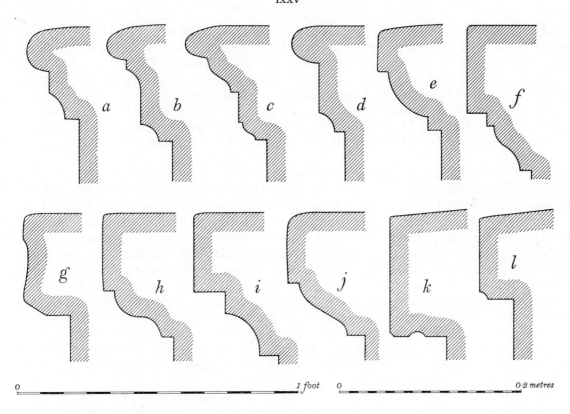

Fig. 12 Profiles of Window Sills.
a.(299) 19 St. George's Square, 1674; b.(72) 3 All Saints' Place, first quarter 18th century; c.(218)
33 High Street St. Martins, first quarter 18th century; d.(383) Brazenose House, 1723; e.(239) George
Hotel, 1725; f.(100) 13 Barn Hill, 1740; g.(341) 2 St. Mary's Place, second quarter 18th century;
h.(385) 31 St. Paul's Street, c. 1747; i.(57) Town Hall, 1776–79; j.(60) Theatre, 1766; k.(301) 21 St.
George's Square, c. 1768; l.(358) 23 St. Mary's Street, mid 18th-century.

Sills (Fig. 12)
During the early 17th century mullion-and-transom windows had weathered sills. Projecting sills first
appeared on windows with architraves in the last quarter of the century. These sills are moulded and have
a rounded nosing at the top as at 12 St. Paul's Street, 32 Broad Street and 19 St. George's Square (375,
142, 299); they continued in use into the early 18th century at 3 All Saints' Place, 33 High Street St. Martins
and Brazenose House (72, 218, 383). In the early 18th century a plainer-sectioned sill was introduced, with
a square top and a single moulding below; the earliest example is the George Hotel of 1725 (239). During
the second quarter of the century the upper, square, part became gradually heavier at the expense of the
moulding, a progression seen at 13 Barn Hill of 1740 (100), 23 St. Mary's Street of a few years later (358)
and the Theatre of 1766 (60). Plain square-sectioned sills appeared about 1730 and became universal in the
later 18th century. The earliest of these sills are continued across the elevation as platbands, and such continuous sills remained in use until the early 19th century, few being found after 1820. Sometimes plain sills
were relieved by a small moulding such as the hollow chamfer used at the Town Hall in 1776 (57). The
subtly-moulded sills of 2 St. Mary's Place (341) are exceptional.

Keystones (Fig. 10)
Although keystones are significant elements in the design of the windows of 19 St. George's Square (299)
they were not generally used until the early 18th century. Usually a single or triple keystone is used, only
occasionally decorated as at Brazenose House (383), 33 High Street St. Martins (218) and 57 High Street

(193), all of the early 18th century. Between about 1730 and 1750 large and widely-splayed keystones were fashionable, sometimes with as many as five to a window. The windows of 66–67 High Street St. Martins (237) have rusticated heads that compare with that on Plate 29 of Langley's *Treasury of Designs* (1745); the only other examples of this form date from the end of the 18th century (98, 239, 361). Several geometrical constructions were used in the design of keystones (Fig. 10). Batty Langley's precept that their base should be one-fifth or one-seventh of the width of the opening seems to have been followed by few Stamford masons or designers (Langley, *Treasury of Designs*, Plate 46) though 21 High Street and 13 Barn Hill (182, 100) conform to this rule. Their sides almost invariably radiate from a common point whose distance below the top of the window is usually related to the width of the opening. In the second and third quarters of the 18th century most keystones radiate from a point half-a-width from the top of the window, a few from one width, and several from the centre of the opening. The tops of the keystones on the more elaborate buildings are often defined by the arc of a circle sometimes sharing the same centre as the keystones, and whose radius is the width of the opening. This is seen for instance at 14 Broad Street and 21 High Street (133, 182) where the construction is similar, and 13 Barn Hill (100) where the radius of the circle is eight times the width of the architrave. At 47–50 High Street St. Martins (229) the radius of the defining circle is half the width of the opening, and is therefore centred on the top of the opening itself. This same construction can also be seen in the doorcases of 14 Broad Street (133) and 35 High Street St. Martins (220).

Very few windows have pediments. No. 13 Barn Hill and the N. gable of 41 High Street (100, 188) are the only 18th-century examples, and there is a small pediment to the stair window of Austin House (85). No. 9–10 Ironmonger Street (246) has a hood of crude design above the windows. Roundheaded windows were commonly used to light stairs from the early 18th century, Brazenose House (383) having the first dated example of 1723. They were rarely used on the fronts of buildings, exceptions being the Theatre (60), 20 High Street St. Martins (210) and the notable ground floor of 2 St. Mary's Place (341). Segmental-headed windows were rarely made in the 18th century, 1 St. George's Square (291) being the earliest; at Vale House (250) they are associated with a tall roundheaded recess. Venetian windows are also rare in Stamford; one survives at 26 St. Mary's Street (360; Plate 104) resembling Portwood's unexecuted design for 9 Barn Hill (97) (Fig. 181); there is a late one at Barn Hill chapel (37), and a third probably existed at 8 High Street (174) where there is also the only example of a lunette window (Plate 110). Oval or oeil-de-boeuf windows are almost unknown; one remains at 51 High Street St. Martins (230). Console brackets were only rarely placed below windows, the few buildings having this feature dating mainly from the middle of the 18th century (26 St. Mary's Street (360); Theatre (60)).

In the early 19th century the window sills of several houses were lowered to conform to contemporary fashion. Such elongated windows exist at 9 Broad Street (130), Vale House (250), and 8 High Street (174); more damaging to the appearance of the house are the lowered sills of 22 St. Mary's Street (357).

Doorways and doors

Doorways with depressed four-centred heads and moulded jambs gave way towards the end of the 17th century to rectangular openings with externally-applied moulded architraves. At 12 St. Paul's Street (375) the architrave has a bolection moulding. During the 18th century the moulding of the door surround commonly matched the windows of the same building, differing only in being wider; 31 St. Paul's Street (385) is a prominent example. Shaped hoods were introduced at 19 St. George's Square (299), in 1674, and that at 12 Barn Hill (99; Plate 124) is a notable example of *c*. 1700. Only one shell canopy survives (224) although a second was recently removed from the rear wing of (220). Pedimented hoods were introduced in the second quarter of the 18th century; the earliest is at the entrance to the Assembly Rooms (58; Fig. 55) and other examples include 23 St. Mary's Street (358; Fig. 179) and 20 St. George's Square (300; Fig. 155). Two pedimented hoods (72, 357) are almost identical, and a third (220) differs mainly in having more elaborate mouldings and keystones (Figs. 65, 118, 177). Later pedimented doorcases and porches, after *c*. 1760, resemble national styles. Frequently a semicircular fanlight intrudes into the pediment, as at the Theatre (60; Fig. 56) and 25 St. Mary's Street (359; Fig. 182), both of 1766, and 20 High Street St. Martins (210; Plate 124). That at 21 St. George's Square (301) is of cast iron. Porches were erected outside a few houses, notably at Barn Hill House (96), 9 Barn Hill (97; Plate 124), 30 High Street St. Martins (217) and Vale House (250).

Among surviving doors is a mid 18th-century group with decorative panels resembling those illustrated on Plate 23 of Salmon's *Palladio Londiniensis* (1734); it includes 66–67 High Street St. Martins (237; Plate 102) and 26 St. Mary's Street (360; Plate 109).

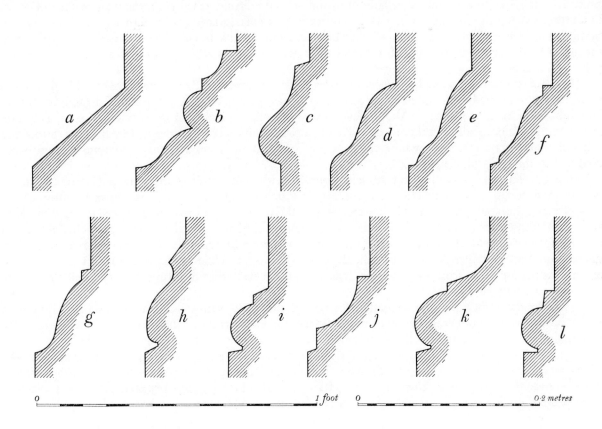

Fig. 13   Profiles of Plinths.
a.(299) 19 St. George's Square, 1674; b.(218) 33 High Street St. Martins, first quarter 18th century; c.(72) 3 All Saints' Place, first quarter 18th century; d.(383) Brazenose House, 1723; e.(298) 18 St. George's Square, early 18th-century; f.(58) Assembly Rooms, 1727; g.(134) 15 Broad Street, early 18th-century; h.(352) rear wing of Stamford Hotel, early 18th-century; i.(300) 20 St. George's Square, early 18th-century; j.(237) 66–67 High Street St. Martins, c. 1730–40; k.(358) 23 St. Mary's Street, mid 18th-century; l.(357) 21 St. Mary's Street, c. 1827.

Plinths (Fig. 13)
Early 17th-century domestic buildings of stone generally have plain chamfered plinths which continued in use into the early 18th century, as at the George Hotel (239) of 1725. In the early 18th century a wave moulding becomes more usual, though erosion often makes the profile uncertain (Brazenose House (383) of 1723, Assembly Room (58) of 1727, 17 St. George's Square (297) and 15 Broad Street (134)). Although unweathered plinths now come into use, many of the more ambitious 18th-century buildings have elaborately moulded plinths. No. 3 All Saints' Place (72) has a plinth with weathering of almost medieval profile. A heavy roll moulding is the most usual, sometimes combined with a wave as at 33 High Street St. Martins (218). The wave may be elaborate as at the former Black Bull (352); this type of moulding persisted into the early 19th century at 21 St. Mary's Street (357). Cavetto mouldings are found at 66–67 High Street St. Martins (237) and are the mark of an exceptional building.

Quoins (Plate 121)

In larger medieval buildings with rubble walls, freestone quoins were used, set flush with the wall-face. In smaller buildings (e.g. (61)) the angles were worked in rubble without formal quoins, a technique which persisted to the 19th century. A similar lack of emphasis on quoins is found in the late 18th and early 19th centuries when freestone quoins were laid flush, and are only distinguished from the wall by the difference in texture. During the first half of the 18th century in particular, many of the higher quality buildings in Stamford had rusticated quoins, although on a number of impressive houses the quoins are not emphasized, the ashlar walls usually merging with those of their neighbours, as at 21–22 and 23–24 St. Mary's Street (357, 358) and 20–21 St. George's Square (300, 301).

The basic form of rusticated quoin comprised alternate header and stretcher blocks with chamfered margins, and remained in use longer than any other, from 1674 at 19 St. George's Square (299) to 1771 at 36 High Street St. Martins (221). About eleven examples survive from before 1800 (57, 60, 96, 126, 139, 194, 227, 242, 306). In addition there is an early variation found on two buildings, 13 All Saints' Street and 1 Ironmonger Street (78, 240), where the centre of each quoin is sunken; this technique was probably confined to the late 17th century.

Two buildings have header and stretcher quoins with unchamfered margins and square channels between the stones. At 13 Barn Hill, of 1740, this is formed by cutting a rebate on top and bottom of the smaller blocks only, whereas at 33 High Street St. Martins a rebate is cut from the upper face of each block (100, 218). Only three other houses have similar unchamfered quoins, but the blocks are unchannelled and date from the middle of the 18th century (132, 167, 381). Seven buildings have alternately large and small unchamfered quoins which are set so that the larger blocks project further than the smaller ones. The earliest example is perhaps 9–10 Ironmonger Street (246), and the style persisted during the 1730s and 1740s (136, 184, 188, 220, 237, 389).

A similar date-range may be suggested for one of the most common forms of rusticated quoins in which blocks are set at intervals, proud of the wall-face; the margins are unchamfered. Twelve houses share this bold form of rustication which does not appear to have been used after the middle of the 18th century (146, 150, 173, 180, 186, 191, 197, 200, 223, 284, 298, 305). Equal-sized projecting quoins are found at 11–12 St. Mary's Street (349) of c. 1748; at 2 St. Mary's Place (341) the quoins form a rusticated pilaster. Finally mention should be made of the rustication at 10 Barn Hill (98) of c. 1804, where variations in the projection of the quoins gives a complex interplay of light and shade.

Superimposed and giant orders (Fig. 14)

Following 17th-century practice, three early or mid 18th-century buildings in Stamford have super-imposed orders. No. 33 High Street St. Martins (218) has Tuscan pilasters above Ionic (Plate 113) and is probably the earliest. The other two (223, 341) are entirely of the Tuscan order. In addition, the ground-floor pilasters of 22 St. Mary's Street (357) reflect the same theme.

There are only two 18th-century buildings in Stamford with giant orders. At 21 High Street (182) of 1732 there are Corinthian pilasters on the upper two storeys of a three-storey house (Plate 101); it is not known how the ground stage was originally treated, but masonry round the door is rusticated with horizontally-channelled joints. The rusticated equal-sized quoins of 2 St. Mary's Place (341) have bases and Tuscan capitals and are in reality a giant order on a two-storey house. The giant order was not used again in Stamford until 1810 when the London architect Bond designed the Stamford Hotel (352). Six Corinthian half columns, standing on a rusticated ground stage, reflect the ballroom inside and dominate the centre of the main elevation. Later in the century pilasters are used to form giant orders at Rutland Terrace (288) and Rock House (427), and superimposed orders at Rock Terrace (426).

Cornices (Plates 122, 123)

The late 17th and early 18th-century eaves cornices have either large dentils (modillions) or shaped brackets (called 'cantalevers' in contemporary manuals); most are made of wood but a few, e.g. at Brazenose House (383), are of stone. In 1700 a plain modillion cornice, presumably in wood, cost 1s. 2d. to 1s. 4d. a foot, whereas a stone cornice 18 to 20 inches deep cost 5s. to 6s. a foot and a carved wooden cornice cost 7s. a

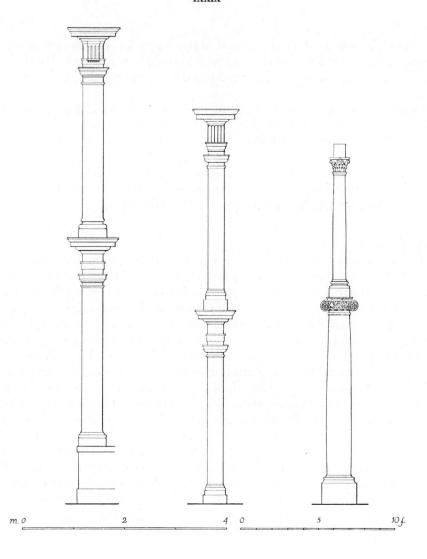

Fig. 14 Pilasters composed of superimposed Orders.
a.(341) 3 St. Mary's Place; b.(223) Lady Anne's House; c.(218) 33 High Street St. Martins.

foot (Wing, 267–8). An elaborate cornice of this more expensive type is that at 59 High Street (194). Eaves boards from 18 St. George's Square (298) have rosettes painted between the brackets (Plate 85), while at 1 St. George's Square (291) there are carved paterae in this position. Few plain coved cornices remain, but one at the rear of 8 High Street (174) is enriched with grotesque masks in plaster. The plainest form of 18th-century cornice was a moulded wooden strip below the eaves, as at 15 St. Mary's Street (351). In the early 19th century, deeply projecting eaves were given shaped brackets; Henry Tatam's cornice at 9 Barn Hill (97) is a unique application of cabinet-maker's motifs.

When parapets were introduced in the early 18th century, they were generally ornamented with block cornices at eaves level. Often, as at the George Hotel (239), they were of small projection, but during the second quarter of the century they were sometimes bold and deep as at 66–67 High Street St. Martins (237). In the second half of the 18th century tightly moulded bracketed cornices were used, particularly on the buildings associated with the 9th Earl of Exeter, but also on the Town Hall (57) and Vale House (250).

Chimney stacks

Early chimney stacks in Stamford rarely survive above eaves level, although drawings by Twopeny (290/b.3, p. 32) show that several medieval stacks with louvred tops still existed in the early 19th century. The only remaining stack, apparently of late medieval date, is the circular shaft at 11 St. George's Street (304) (Plate 61).

In the 17th century rectangular shafts built of thin ashlar blocks laid on their sides first appeared. Throughout the later part of that century and the 18th century their standard ornamentation was a moulded string and cornice. Variations are few and limited to houses of highest quality. The stacks of 19 St. George's Square (299) and 33 High Street St. Martins (218) are rusticated, and that at 2 Broad Street (127) has a blind arch on each face. At 22 St. Mary's Street (357) the shafts are linked to form arcades (Plate 120). These exceptional stacks all belong to the late 17th or early 18th centuries. In 1747 George Portwood, junior, charged 6d. a foot for building chimney stacks (Ex. MS. 55/93).

Reset architectural fragments

The amount of reset masonry in Stamford is considerable, and in many gardens are preserved early architectural fragments. Brazenose gate (383) is not a fortuitous survival but the deliberate retention of part of a building with historical associations, and the preservation of the remaining fragments of the Castle hall (10) may have a similar explanation. This same approach, partly antiquarian, partly aesthetic and partly sentimental, can be detected elsewhere. Two other medieval doorways, both plain, lead to yards (258, 434) and a third leads to a garden (109). A more ornate doorway forms a prominent feature of the garden of Vale House (250), and stands between the pleasure and the kitchen gardens. William Stukeley preserved the magnificent gate at 9 Barn Hill (97), partly for its historical associations and partly because it could easily be converted into an imposing garden alcove. Several carved medieval details probably from the Austin friary site (43) were incorporated in the near-by Hopkins' Hospital (51). During the early 18th century several townsmen formed collections of medieval sculpture, usually incorporated in garden features. Little of William Stukeley's collection survives, but at least one fragment formerly in Alderman Feast's collection from the Austin Friary, originally at 31–32 St. Peter's Street, is now reset in a garden terrace at 14 Barn Hill (101). Other architectural features appear to have been deliberately preserved, such as buttresses (188, 345), and sometimes pieces of earlier sculpture were placed prominently on a new building (256). The process continues to the present day, for three medieval doorways have been moved to new and irrelevant positions (253, 412) in recent years, and 17th-century datestones were reset from the 18th century onwards (133, 168, 225).

Interior decoration and fittings.

The only remaining evidence for 13th-century interior decoration is the survival of blind arcading in the end-walls of the halls of two houses, and similar arcading in a ground-floor room of a third house (Plates 60, 62). This last arcade, at 13 St. Mary's Hill (338), resembles a feature of comparable date at Bull Cottage, Witney Street, Burford (M. Laithwaite in *Studies in English Urban History*, ed. Everett (1973), 74–7). No wall painting survives from such an early period, though Stukeley records that there were scriptural quotations painted round the hall of 16 Barn Hill (103), presumably of the late 15th century. He also described the open halls of 16 Barn Hill (103) and 11–12 St. Mary's Street (349) as having coves at the upper ends, the latter being gilded. Nos. 11–12 St. Mary's Street and Peterborough Hall both retained medieval painted glass in their windows (Stanfordia Illustrata II, 86, 91, 115).

In the 15th and 16th centuries the studs of timber-framed houses were commonly left exposed internally; the hard white plaster did not need painting. Only two houses of this period retain painted decoration. At 51 High Street (189) a floral design was painted on the exposed studwork, but at 20 High Street St. Martins (210) the walls were given a rendering of plaster before the elaborate floral design was applied (Plate 85). In the better houses such as Digby House (255), moulded ceiling beams and joists contributed to the decorative appearance of rooms.

The amount of 17th and 18th-century internal decorative detail surviving in Stamford is neither very great nor of outstanding quality. Although much panelling was removed in the 18th and 19th centuries in

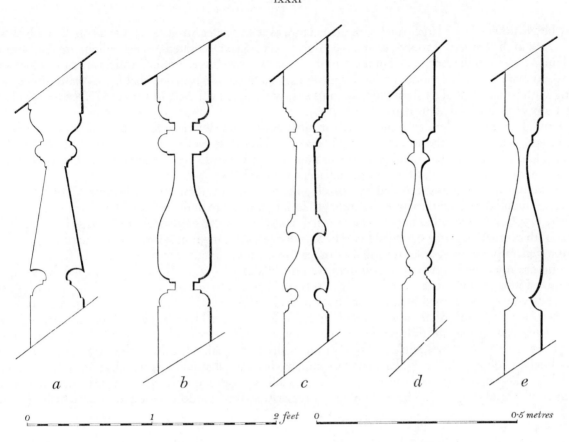

Fig. 15   Splat balusters on staircases.
a.(299) 19 St. George's Square, 1674; b.(179) 16 High Street, *c.* 1700; c.(99) 12 Barn Hill, early
18th-century; d.(133) 14 Broad Street, early 18th-century; e.(249) 13 Ironmonger Street, late
18th-century.

the pursuit of current fashions in interior decoration, it is likely that the amount which survives is a reasonable sample of that which originally existed. The degree of interior ornamentation in English town houses
of the 18th century seems to vary and Stamford is not alone in lacking many richly decorated rooms.
The explanation perhaps lies in the social structure of the town. Landed gentry appear not to have had
houses in Stamford, so that merchants and professional men formed the most affluent section of society.
In York, by way of contrast, the elaborately decorated houses in Micklegate were mainly those of the
gentry (RCHM, *York* III).

W̱all-panelling does not survive from before the 17th century, when small panels in a scratched-moulded
framework, often with a carved frieze, occur in a few houses, such as 12 St. Paul's Street (375). A plaster
frieze survives at 5 St. Mary's Hill (333). Overmantels, as at 5–6 Barn Hill (95), were usually more elaborate
sections of panelling, the panels themselves bearing carved decoration. Elaborate 17th-century plasterwork
at 3 St. Peter's Street (398) is exceptional. Towards the end of the 17th century bolection panelling was
introduced. First seen at 19 St. George's Square (299) of 1674, it remained fashionable into the following
century. Sometimes it was worked in plaster as at Brazenose House (383). Fireplaces with heavy wooden
surrounds survive more frequently than panelling, and were doubtless always more common. Beams were
then often encased, sometimes plastered over and decorated with panels.

Eighteenth-century fielded panelling, usually in two heights with chair-rail and block cornice, does
not differ from that found elsewhere. During the first half of the century the panelling around fireplaces is
generally of greater elaboration, full-height fluted pilasters sometimes flanking the fireplace, which itself

may be surmounted by a large panel with shaped top, as at 12 Water Street (442). Occasionally lobbies were contrived in the corners of rooms, as at 25–6 High Street (184). Decorated plaster ceilings are rarely found, and most date from the second half of the century, as at 7 Crown Street (168). Cornices are more commonly of wood than of plaster. Some of the larger houses have only a panelled dado, the walls above being hung with paper or, as at 13 Barn Hill (100) in 1812, with tapestry (LAO, LD 40/45A). Decorative plaster-work on walls is found at 19 Broad Street (136).

Round or elliptical-headed arches were for most of the 18th century a feature of hallways, where they pierced the spine wall of the house. They were decorated in the style of the period, as at 23 St. Mary's Street (358) (Plate 135) and 13 Barn Hill (100) (Plate 135), and in the early 19th century were sometimes echoed by shallow recesses of similar form in the adjacent walls (Fig. 147).

None of the stone vices recorded by Stukeley in 1736 survives (Stanfordia Illustrata II) and the earliest staircases found date from the late 17th century. The larger ones are built around a well, as at 19 St. George's Square (299), and have either flat or heavy turned balusters; similar staircases exist in large buildings in the early 18th century, as at the George Hotel. In Stamford development in staircase construction and baluster design generally resembles that recorded in other towns, but some of the more intricate forms of wood-carving are not found and twisted balusters are rare (Plates 132–134). The use of splat balusters (Fig. 15) continued into the third quarter of the 18th century; they are frequently confined to the upper flights of staircases which have turned balusters on the principal stages.

Fireplaces in Stamford are not outstanding and follow national trends (Plates 126–128). Sub-medieval types gave way in the late 17th century to bolection-moulded surrounds in wood or stone; the series of fireplaces at 19 St. George's Square (299) is of unusually high quality. In the 18th century a plain fireplace was much in vogue, the rectangular stone surround having a small moulding on each arris; only occasionally was there a keystone. Kitchen fireplaces were wide, usually with an elliptical arch, flanked by narrow openings with round heads (Fig. 67). The neo-Grecian fireplaces at the Stamford Hotel are noteworthy (352).

URBAN DESIGN

Stamford is a town of discrete buildings. Terraces and groups of buildings forming a unified design are notably few, and where they exist are on a small scale. Each house is an individual creation and bears but little relationship to its neighbour. Gilbert of Cestreton may have built a terrace of three tenements just W. of All Saints' Church in 1257, but they do not survive (Rot. Hund. 1, 351). Nos. 15–17 High Street (179), of c. 1700, form a terrace of three houses and no. 14 matches them very deliberately, and this group is the earliest remaining example of conscious street design (Plate 92).

Occasionally in the 18th century imposing elevations were produced by building pairs of houses. Nos. 66–67 High Street St. Martins (237) are an unusually impressive example, and the front of 8–10 High Street St. Martins (206) gives no indication of the meanness of the houses behind. Nos. 9–10 Ironmonger Street (246) are an unequal pair of houses, the two bays of no. 9 adding to the grandeur of the four bays of no. 10. Nos. 18–19 and 25–26 High Street (180, 184) are similar pairs, where the appearance of a very large house is produced.

The Earls of Exeter were the major landowners in the town, but most new work on their estate was done on building leases, so that control was usually indirect and houses were rebuilt as individual tenements rather than as parts of a large scheme. Indeed, it seems that in the early 18th century the finest buildings in Stamford were mostly put up by people other than the Earl and his tenants. The 9th Earl (1725–93) was the first to engage in a programme of systematic rebuilding to a uniform design, though the piecemeal nature of the operation resulted in a series of individual buildings. Between 1780 and 1795 seven blocks of houses were built in St. Mary's Hill and St. Mary's Street. Nos. 11–12 St. Mary's Hill (337) were built in 1780, and 14–16 St. Mary's Hill with 31–32 St. Mary's Street (339) followed in 1781. In 1784–5, 34–36 St. Mary's Street (366) were built; in 1790–1, 1–2 St. Mary's Hill (331). After the 9th Earl's death, 27 St. Mary's Street (361) was built in 1794–5, and 14 St. John's Street (313) in 1795–7. In addition, the Assembly Rooms (58) were enlarged and several other houses were improved either directly, as at 33 St. Mary's Street (365) in 1784, or by building lease, as at 19 High Street St. Martins (209) in 1797. These houses were built by his surveyor Thomas Lumby and have an overall uniformity of style and scale. The result of this work, together with the new Town Hall of 1776 in St. Mary's Hill and the associated demolition of the old gate on the bridge, was a complete change in the character of St. Mary's Hill and the approach to the town, and a considerable improvement to St. Mary's Street. About the same time the 9th Earl rebuilt much of the W. side of Ironmonger Street to the same general design.

Other individuals lacked either the resources or the compact blocks of property necessary for similar schemes. James Bellaers *c.* 1760–70 built a new office in St. Mary's Street to match his existing house next to it (358). John Hopkins, currier, had to proceed slowly in creating the uniform group at the E. end of St. Mary's Street. He lived at 26 St. Mary's Street, the front of which he raised and altered about 1766 to match no. 25, which he built in the same year (359, 360). No. 13 Maiden Lane was added to the row after he bought the site in 1773.

Rows of houses of uniform design became more common in the early 19th century. Most of them, such as the groups in St. Leonard's Street, erected by men like William Gregory, a builder, are of a humble status which is reflected in their unambitious design. Rutland Terrace was a bolder project of 1829 which bankrupted its originator, a veterinary surgeon whose aim was to create a terrace of high-class houses comparable with those in the larger fashionable towns. Between 1839 and 1845 the N.W. end of Scotgate was completely transformed by Richard Newcomb. First he built the Clock House (152) forming a termination to the street; then in 1841 he built Rock Terrace (426), followed in 1842 by Rock House (427) and in 1844 by a row of shops with warehouses and cottages behind (425).

Proposals to link the top of St. Mary's Hill with High Street were mooted in 1834 (*Stamford News*, 16 Dec.) but nothing was done until about 1849 when Richard Newcomb began the building of a street lined with shops on the site of the George and Angel Inn (*Mercury*, 21 Sept.). The scheme was abortive, but the S. end of the new road remains with its impressive shops (350). In 1840 the Blackfriars Estate was initiated by Lord Brownlow. A grid of streets was laid out, and plots of varying sizes intended for a wide range of houses were auctioned. Covenants controlled the size of the smaller houses on the N. of the estate, but the plots intended for large houses were not built upon and remained as gardens until the present century.

ORGANIZATION OF THE BUILDING TRADES

During the 18th century the different building trades remained distinct, except for the traditional conjunction of plumbers and glaziers into a single trade, and slaters and plasterers into another. Frequently craftsmen combined for the purpose of a single project, as in 1772 when William Clarke, mason, Robert Pilkington, carpenter, and John Burton, slater, presented a joint estimate of £217 for repairs to the Bull Inn (Ex. MS, 90/55). Earlier in the century Portwood and Pilkington had worked together on the task of refronting and modernizing the George Hotel (239) (Ex. MS, 51/21/23, 24).

The master craftsmen were able to call on what appears to have been a relatively fluid force of journeymen. Portwood employed ten men at the George Hotel in 1724–5, and 14 at the adjoining cockpit; Pilkington employed only about half-a-dozen journeymen. Portwood's work-force included both apprentices and freemen, some of the latter being his former apprentices (Ex. MS, 15/21/24). As architect, Legg was responsible for organizing direct labour on several of his projects, including Vale House (250) (*Mercury*, 25 Jan. 1788) and the Burghley Lodges (*Mercury*, 28 June 1799).

The practice of masons and carpenters combining for specific undertakings continued into the early 19th century. Charles Collins, carpenter, often worked with Robert Woolston, bricklayer, and Moses Peal and Robert Tinkler had a similar relationship. General builders seem to have first emerged about the beginning of the 19th century. By 1790 John Boyfield was doing painting and glazing work in addition to joinery (Exeter Day Books, Jan. 1791); in 1832 James Richardson, formerly a carpenter, was able to undertake the complete rebuilding of Truesdale's Hospital (53). Most general builders, like the Gregory family, appear to have begun as carpenters, an exception being the firm of Woolston, the founder being a bricklayer.

The master masons of the 18th century appear to have undertaken a wide range of work. Many, like Portwood and Hames, quarried their own stone, and John Pearson organized the Earl of Exeter's quarrying and lime-burning interests at Wothorpe in addition to his own building activities. George Portwood, junior, advertised in 1737 that he could provide chimney-pieces and monuments in both freestone and marble, as well as ordinary masonry work, yet in 1751 he built footings for the mundane Shambles in High Street (*Mercury*, 24 Nov. 1747; Chamberlains' Accounts). William Clarke levelled Castle Dyke, but he was also a competent builder and possibly a designer.

George Sparrow seems to have been the first specialized marble mason in Stamford although he was also a house painter. In 1793 he provided monuments, chimney-pieces and 'vases' in marble and Swithland slate (*Mercury*, 18 Apr.); by 1806 composition chimney-pieces were also available from him (*Mercury*, 17 Oct.). During the early 19th century marble masons became a separate group from general masons. The Gilbert family were specialist carvers rather than builders; John in 1807 was a marble mason, stone-cutter and house-painter, producing mainly monuments and chimney-pieces (*Mercury*, 9 Oct.), but by 1822 he had added mortars to his repertoire (*Mercury*, 16 Aug.).

Architects and Craftsmen

This biographical list is confined, with few exceptions, to those masons, carpenters, builders and architects who lived and worked in Stamford and whose work may be identified. Journeymen and men whose status is at present uncertain have been excluded. The chief sources used in compiling the list are the Hall Books, recording admissions to freedom and to scot and lot; the Chamberlains' Accounts, recording expenditure by the Town Council after 1710; and the Exeter Day Books recording the building activities of the Earls of Exeter between 1770 and 1800. Other information comes from the court rolls, churchwardens' accounts, Browne's Hospital accounts, parish registers, Exeter MSS, the *Mercury*, and the *Dictionaries* of Colvin and Gunnis.

BINGHAM, EDWARD (d. 1796). Marble mason, of Peterborough. Best known as a monumental mason; he signed tablets in 1751 and 1782 at All Saints', and 1788 and 1789 in St. Martin's. He did work for Lord Exeter at Burghley including two lions in 1775 and marble window sills in 1790. He made a chimney-piece in 1787 for 35 St. Mary's Street (366) costing £8.11.6., two more for the Assembly Rooms (58) in 1793 costing £26.9.0., and two for 27 St. Mary's Street (361) in 1795 for £20.12.0.

His son James continued the business and must be responsible for the monument of 1803 in St. Martin's.

BOOTH, JOHN. Cabinet maker and carver, freeman 1784. He was employed by Lord Exeter from 1770 to 1796, and his work included chimney-pieces at 34–36 St. Mary's Street (366) in 1785–6.

BOYFIELD, JOHN I. (1733–79). Carpenter, freeman 1764. Did small jobs for the town, made furniture, and established the family business.

BOYFIELD, JOHN II. (*c*. 1754–1825). Builder, first worked under Christopher Staveley at Melton Mowbray as carpenter; on death of cousin(?) John I, joined his widow Elizabeth to run firm (*Mercury*, 4 Feb. 1779). Lived at, and rebuilt in 1791, 1 All Saints' Place (70). Important business; employed by the Town and at Burghley. Worked in 1785 at the George Hotel (239); in 1791 at 4 St. Mary's Place (342); in 1796 at Corporation Buildings, Scotgate (422); and in 1799 at Assembly Rooms extension (58).

BOYFIELD, JOHN III. (*c*. 1796–1836). Builder, continued the family business. In 1831 his plans for remodelling St. Michael's church adopted, leading to its collapse in 1832.

BROWNING, BRYAN (1773–1856). Architect, born at Thurlby, Lincs. (parish register). Around 1819–22 had a London address; 1835 said to be at Northorpe, Lincs.; in 1826 married Ruth Snart of Stamford and moved to Stamford *c*. 1838. In 1840s he was retained by Exeter as architect for £180 p.a.; by 1847 was practising at 16 Broad Street. His Stamford work includes the workhouse of 1835 (demolished); rebuilding S.E. pillar in St. Mary's church, and layout of Blackfriars Estate in 1840; internal vestry, St. Mary's church, 1841; Stamford Institution (59), 1842; remodelling of Barn Hill House (96), 1843; Grant's iron foundry (451), 1845; 4–5 Red Lion Square and 1 High Street (279), 1848; and Byard House, St. Paul's Street (380), 1851.

BROWNING, EDWARD (1816–82). Architect, son of Bryan by first wife; began in father's firm and may have been involved in some of his later work. His Stamford work includes Town Bridge and adjacent work (64), 1847–9, the bridge with his brother Henry; cemetery chapels, 1852; Corn Exchange, Broad Street, 1858; St. Michael's National School, 1860; Butter Market, Red Lion Square, 1861; High School, St. Martin's, 1875; and St. George's vicarage, 1881. He or his father were responsible for the W. porch of St. George's in 1848, and the restoration of St. Mary's chancel in 1849.

BROWNING, HENRY B. (1822–*c*. 1908). Son of Bryan, began in family office where his mathematical abilities must have been of use; 1851 went to Cambridge, graduated and in 1855 was ordained.

CHARLESWORTH, JOHN (d. 1781). Brickmaker, with kilns in St. Martin's by 1763; after his death his widow had kilns N. of the river in 1788.

CLARKE, WILLIAM (d. 1786). Mason, admitted to scot and lot 1738. Lived at 13 St. Paul's Street (376) which he bought as sitting tenant in 1743 and probably refronted. Married Mary daughter of William Lindsey, carpenter, and his relations with that family appear to have been close. Besides small jobs for the Town he built in 1761 a house in Water Street for £60 (demolished), the Theatre (60) in 1766, and in c. 1768 he rebuilt a house 'near Burghley Lane'. In 1758 he arbitrated in a dispute over damages to a house in Broad Street (deeds, 9 Broad Street).

COLE, JOHN (d. 1797). Mason, freeman 1766. Did maintenance work at Browne's Hospital, 1783–1800, his business being continued by his widow and son. In 1791 he advertised for no less than 10 journeymen; in 1792 built 37–9 St. Mary's Street (367), and in 1794, 1–2 St. Mary's Hill (331). He also was a monumental mason, signing an oval tablet at Tinwell in 1796; his only known apprentice was William Harrison (1790–7). Subscribed to George Richardson's *New Designs in Architecture* (1792).

COLLINS, CHARLES (c. 1788–1863). Builder, began work in Stamford c. 1828; admitted to scot and lot 1834. Contractor with R. Woolston for St. Michael's church, 1835–6. In 1844 made pews in St. Martin's and St. George's churches with R. Woolston; in 1849 built 10 High Street (176).

COSIN, THOMAS (fl. 1686). Signed engraved coffin-plate to James Langton, St. Michael's church. Probably related to Richard Cosins, goldsmith, who owned 9–11 Ironmonger Street in 1696 (deeds).

DIXON, JOHN (d. 1782). Joiner, son of Joseph, carpenter; admitted to scot and lot 1748; his marriage settlement in 1750 included 2 All Saints' Place. In 1762 he bought 33 St. Peter's Street (413), and in 1778 he leased 34 St. Peter's Street (414), where he seems to have lived. He did small jobs for the Town between 1760 and 1781; maintenance at Browne's Hospital; and in 1759, with Robert Timperon, cabinet maker, wainscotted St. George's church. Having helped survey the new sheepmarket in 1777 he made the pens for it in 1781, and in the same year rebuilt a house, probably (384), in St. Paul's Street. In 1780 he made plans for wainscot and removable seating for the Court at the Town Hall.

DIXON, JOSEPH (d. 1777). Carpenter, father of John, Richard and Joseph. Freeman 1722, worked for Town and Browne's Hospital, and in 1742 demolished buildings at 9 Barn Hill.

DIXON, JOSEPH (d. 1787). Mason, son of Joseph, carpenter; admitted to scot and lot 1767 when he was said to have been born in Stamford and to be a citizen of London where he became free of the Mason's Company in 1760. In 1783 Lord Exeter paid him for drawing plans. He is probably the Joseph Dixon who built Blackfriars' Bridge, London, to Mylne's designs, 1760–9; worked for Holland 1767–70; became bankrupt in 1778; died in 1787 (PRO, PCC 171 Major); buried in St. Mary's church, Battersea, which he designed in 1775.

DIXON, RICHARD (fl. c. 1765–78). Carpenter, son of Joseph, carpenter; admitted to scot and lot 1767. In 1766–78 was surveying and working for Lord Exeter at Burghley and London. His brother John is described c. 1767–71 as being of Pimlico, so Richard may be the builder of St. Mary, Battersea, 1775–7, designed by Joseph Dixon. He was surveyor for the Westminster New Lying-in Hospital, 1765, and became bankrupt in 1778.

DIXON, SAMUEL (fl. 1789–c.1823). Carpenter, apprenticed 1772, admitted to scot and lot 1789, died before 1835. By 1794 had large building business; 1801 valued premises in Water Street; 1822–3 did carpenters' work at Snowden's Hospital (52).

EXTON, JOHN (c. 1695–1785). Glazier and plumber, apprenticed 1711, freeman 1718, retired 1773 in favour of his journeyman George Bacon. Removed glass from St. George's church, and 1758–62 worked for Lord Exeter at Burghley and St. Martin's church.

FEARN, GEORGE (fl. 1843–61). Monumental mason, born in Derbyshire, began business in High Street, Stamford c. 1843; by 1856 had moved workshop to Scotgate. Sold business in 1861 and is said to have died in Halifax in 1877. Monuments survive in All Saints', 1845, St. Michael's, 1849, St. Martin's, 1850.

GILBERT, DANIEL (d. 1862). Monumental mason, with workshops on S. side of Tinwell Road from at least 1841. Signed wall-slab and gravestone, 1847, in St. John's church.

GILBERT, HENRY (fl. 1827–45). Monumental mason, son of John; by 1827 working in his father's former premises in Broad Street, and had recently copied Roubiliac's bust of Newton at Trinity College, Cambridge. In 1845 carved lions in Ketton stone for a bridge at Burghley.

GILBERT, JOHN (c. 1773–1839). Monumental mason, born at Deeping St. James where a James and William Gilbert were working in the late 18th century. John was journeyman to George Sparrow before

1807, when he set up on his own in Broad Street. He was admitted to scot and lot in 1813 and moved to Cambridge *c.* 1825 (RCHM, *Cambridge City*; *Cambs.* I and II). By 1822 he had an agent in Spalding (*Mercury*, 16 Aug.).

GOODWIN, ROBERT. Mason, admitted to scot and lot 1792 after an apprenticeship to John Hames; in 1788 he helped to repair St. Mary's spire. He did work for the Town in 1796–1819, and signed a monument in St. John's in 1796.

His son, also Robert (1799–1871) was admitted to scot and lot in 1820. Father or son built Snowden's Hospital (52) in 1822, and signed a monument in Barnack church in 1823.

GREGORY, FRANCIS (born *c.* 1798). Carpenter, and builder; in 1832 began the alterations in St. Michael's church which ended in its collapse. Still alive in 1851.

GREGORY, WILLIAM (*c.* 1772–1852). Builder, admitted to scot and lot 1827. Member of Improvement Committee 1845. He and Francis hard to distinguish. William sold 47–52 St. Leonard's Street (325) in 1835, and one of them, with Tinkler, built Grant's iron foundry (451) in 1845.

HAMES, JOHN, junior (d. 1828). Mason. His father John had in 1743 been apprenticed to Richard Bunch (1672–1753) and died in 1782. John the son built 34–36 St. Mary's Street (366) in 1786, repaired St. Mary's spire under Christopher Staveley in 1787, built 39–40 Broad Street (147) in *c.* 1786, 11–12 St. Mary's Hill (337) in 1790, 4 St. Mary's Place (342) and the S. range of the George Hotel (239) in 1791, and a stable at 36 St. Mary's Street (366) in 1790. No. 16 All Saints' Place (74) may also be by him. In 1786 he inherited five houses, probably 70–73 Scotgate and 14–15 All Saints' Place (432), from William Clarke and in 1790 took over Clarke's old limekiln in St. Martin's. He is not known to have done any building after his bankruptcy in 1794; he valued stone in Bellaer's yard in 1801 and surveyed houses built by John Boyfield in 1815. Of signed monuments, the floor slab in All Saints' is by father or son; the son repaired Truesdale's monument in All Saints' in 1786, and made a tablet in St. John's in 1789.

HAMES, ROBERT (fl. 1784–1810). Mason, probably brother of John, junior, with whom he worked at Burghley in 1788–99. Before 1796 he had a quarry in St. Martin's at TF 036069. In 1784 he refronted 33 St. Mary's Street (365), in 1792 he rebuilt Tickencote church under direction of S. P. Cockerell, in 1794 and 1797 repaired Great Casterton church, in 1797 built 14 St. John's Street (313), and in 1810 built new walls round St. Michael's churchyard. He demolished St. George's Gate in 1805 and opened a quarry at Ketton in 1807. In 1788 he set up, for £40, the monument to Elizabeth Cecil, relict of William, 2nd Earl of Exeter, in Tinwell church after its removal from Clerkenwell.

HARRISON, WILLIAM (probably 1760–1845). Mason, apprenticed to John Cole 1790, freeman 1797. In 1808 rebuilt porch at Browne's Hospital under John Walters, architect, and carried out maintenance work from 1800 onwards. He is known mainly as a monumental mason, his first signed work being of 1798 at Uffington; other tablets of 1808 and 1810 are in St. Martin's, of 1812 in St. Mary's, and two illegible floor slabs in All Saints'.

HOLMES, JOHN (fl. 1780–97). Mason, laid flagged floors in 1780 but known mainly as monumental mason with tombstones at Great Casterton (1783, 1784) and Tickencote (1790, 1797).

KIDSON, HENRY I, II, III. Carpenters. Henry Kidson I bought 54 St. Leonard's Street in 1702 and his son Henry Kidson II (1695–1760) became freeman in 1718, doing work for the Town between then and 1743. His son Henry worked at Truesdale's Hospital between 1768–73.

LAMFORD, JOHN (fl. *c.* 1805–25). Carpenter, apprenticed 1797 to Bartholomew Richardson. In 1821 he adapted a building to serve as the Congregational schoolroom (56).

LEGG, WILLIAM DANIEL (d. 1806). Architect. Legg set up in business in Stamford *c.* 1778. By 1788 he had completed Vale House (250), in 1797 was concerned with an unexecuted municipal project for housing the poor of Stamford, and in 1799 began the new Lodges to Burghley Park. In 1804 he designed the new Shambles (61). He employed masons and provided stone. In 1790, 1793 and 1799 he was paid as architect by the Earls of Exeter; the extent of his responsibility for the 9th and 10th Earls' buildings in Stamford is uncertain. He cannot be proved to be the carpenter of Coleman Street, London, in 1774, and designer of stables at Panton Hall, Lincs., in 1777, but he certainly made alterations at Casewick Hall, Lincs., in 1785.

LINDSEY, WILLIAM (d. 1763). Carpenter, son of Thomas, carpenter; apprenticed to Benjamin Tipping, cabinet maker, 1725; admitted to scot and lot 1733. William lived at 1 St. George Square (291), which he must have fitted up. In 1748 he sold a house, possibly 22 St. Mary's Street (357), to Leonard Stevenson; in 1759 with his son John (admitted to scot and lot in 1750) and Robert Pilkington he built a gallery in St. George's church. His daughter Mary married William Clarke, mason (q.v.).

LUMBY, THOMAS. Surveyor, presumably of Lincoln. He surveyed and valued for Lord Exeter between 1780 and 1794, staying at the Crown when he visited Stamford. He specifically worked in St. Mary's Hill in 1780–1 and St. Mary's Street in 1784; his visits in 1780–1, 1784, 1789–94, correspond with the building activities in Stamford of the 9th Earl of Exeter, and he may have been employed primarily as a surveyor. In 1780 he was working at Burghley.

MANTON, THOMAS (d. 1789). Mason, freeman 1769. He did much work for Lord Exeter at Burghley, 1775–84, and in Stamford. He built new houses in 1777 and 1778; 14–16 St. Mary's Hill (339) in 1780, and stables at 34–36 St. Mary's Street (366) in 1785. Between 1784 and 1789 he was working at the George Hotel (239) on the stables and other work, including the N. range, in 1787. He carved a tombstone at Great Casterton, 1782.

NEWARK, JOHN. Brickmaker and confectioner, began brickmaking in St. Martin's in 1754.

NORRIS, TOBY (d. 1626). Bellfounder, freeman 1607. He cast a bell for St. John's church in 1605 (now gone), two for St. Mary's church in 1625 and a third in 1626. He lived at 12 St. Paul's Street (375), which he bought as sitting tenant in 1617. His bell-metal monument is in St. George's church.

He had two sons Toby II, freeman 1628; and Thomas, freeman 1625, to whom the house and business passed, who may have cast a bell for St. Mary's in 1638, and who resigned from the Town Council in 1678. Thomas' son Toby III (1634–99) also lived and worked at 12 St. Paul's Street until 1689.

PEAL, MOSES (c. 1786–1855). Builder, born at Northborough; admitted to scot and lot 1813 as a carpenter. In 1838 repaired nave roof of St. Mary's church; 1841 constructed an internal vestry and made several pews at St. Mary's and built the Stamford Institution (59); 1842 with R. Tinkler made alterations to the gaol (demolished); 1847 built a fever-ward at the workhouse, and in 1848 built 1 High Street and 4–5 Red Lion Square (279). His small houses include 1–8 Adelaide Street (114), c. 1840–1, eight houses in Ryhall Road (289, 290), before 1838, and 4 St. Leonard's Street (317), 1845.

PEARSON, JOHN (d. 1808?). Mason, son of Thomas. Quarried at Wothorpe for Lord Exeter from 1777 onwards. He built houses in 1777 and 1782 and 11–12 St. Mary's Hill (337) in 1791. He rebuilt part of 15 St. Mary's Street (351) in 1775, and following enclosure of St. Martin's was in charge of building the new wall round Burghley Park in 1798.

A second John was born c. 1776 and died 1817.

PEARSON, WILLIAM (1737–1806). Mason, freeman 1762; to be distinguished from a second William (c. 1758–1835). He did small jobs for the Town between 1765 and 1788; in 1767 dismantled part of Scotgate Gate. In 1795 he built 27 St. Mary's Street (361) and worked on 23a High Street St. Martins (213) in 1794.

PEPPER, JOHN (fl. 1784–1810). Surveyed masons' and carpenters' work for Lord Exeter in 1787–93; apparently lived in Stamford.

PIERCE, THOMAS. Architect. In 1819 he redesigned the roof and probably the entrance hall of the Town Hall (57). He designed a new gaol behind the Town Hall in 1821 and Snowden's Hospital in 1822, and in 1825 he and James Richardson gave an estimate of £260 for repairs to the school (54).

PILKINGTON, GEORGE (d. 1785). Carpenter, son of Thomas. Admitted to scot and lot 1764. He worked at Burghley for Lord Exeter, in 1778 he built a house in St. Martin's, and in 1775 demolished and rebuilt part of 15 St. Mary's Hill (339). After his death the family business was continued by his widow Alice until at least 1795, she doing work at Burghley, the George Hotel (239) in 1788 and 37–39 St. Mary's Street (367) in 1793.

PILKINGTON, ROBERT, senior (fl. 1714–36). Carpenter. His father, also Robert, worked for the Town 1709–22 and did maintenance work at Browne's Hospital; he died in 1723. The younger Robert became freeman in 1714 and worked for the Town between 1727 and 1736. In 1725–6 he worked at the George Hotel (239) making the S. stair in 1726.

PILKINGTON, ROBERT, junior (fl. 1752–91). Carpenter, son of Thomas, admitted to scot and lot 1752. He worked for Lord Exeter and also the Town 1757–91. In 1759 he made a gallery at St. George's with John and William Lindsey; in 1772 he estimated with William Clarke and John Burton, slater, for work at the

Bull Inn (352); he was working at 14–16 St. Mary's Hill (339) in 1780 and the George Hotel (239) in 1786. In 1771 he leased a yard in Scotgate.

PILKINGTON, THOMAS. The first Thomas, carpenter, was apprenticed to his father Robert in 1718, became free in 1724; he worked for Lord Exeter 1758–61, and in 1751 helped rebuild the Shambles in High Street. A second Thomas, carpenter (c. 1732–1809), did work at the extension to the Assembly Rooms (58), at 27 St. Mary's Street (361), and 14 St. John's Street (313) in 1795. The third Thomas, carpenter, freeman 1797, was calling himself architect and builder in 1822, retired in 1829 and died 1830. He built 1–4 Blackfriars Street (124) and 10–12 St. George's Square (295), both designed by him or his son.

PILKINGTON, THOMAS. Architect, son of Thomas Pilkington III, carpenter. He 'received instruction under an eminent carpenter and builder in London' and entered partnership with his father in 1822, being admitted to scot and lot in 1830. In 1832 he demolished the tower of St. Michael's church and submitted an unsuccessful design for the new building, and in 1836 he built the Union Workhouse with Richardson. He moved to Bourne before going to Edinburgh in 1854, returning to Bourne in 1874.

PORTWOOD, GEORGE, senior (d. 1742). Mason, probably took Robert Skynnar as apprentice in 1707. In 1710 he was working in St. Michael's church, in 1713 was repairing Browne's Hospital, in 1723 dismantled steeple of Pickworth church, Rutland, in 1724 refronted the George Hotel (239) and in 1726 built a cockpit there. In 1725–6 he did the surveying work for Lord Exeter, in 1730 was involved in the choice of site for a new gaol, for which he built a 'necessary' in 1733, and in 1737 designed the steeple of Witham-on-the-Hill church, Lincs. (built by another mason). The unexecuted design for 9 Barn Hill (Fig. 181) was drawn in 1741; in 1742 he was engaged in a large project at Browne's Hospital, which was taken over at his death by Benjamin Stanmore.

PORTWOOD, GEORGE, junior (d. 1761). Mason, son of George, senior. In 1720s working as journeyman for father; in 1737 became freeman and set up independent business. He did lesser work for Lord Exeter, and for Truesdale's and Browne's Hospitals. He died in 1761 (All Saints' parish register). His brother Samuel worked for their father and died in Browne's Hospital.

RICHARDSON, CHARLES (1813–63). Architect and builder, son of James; freeman 1835. His known works in Stamford are 5–8 Broad Street (129) of 1846 and the shopfront at 31 Broad Street (141) of 1848.

RICHARDSON, JAMES (c. 1782–1860). Builder and carpenter, admitted to scot and lot 1808. Became Borough Surveyor 1825; lived at 16 Barn Hill (103) as had his father Bartholomew. In 1845 took sons Charles and Samuel into the business. He worked on the Town Hall improvements of 1819; repaired the School (54) in 1825 with Thomas Pierce, and made further alterations to the Town Hall in 1839. In 1832–3 he built Truesdale's Hospital (53), followed by an extension in 1844. In 1843–4 with R. Tinkler he altered Barn Hill House (96), and in 1847 repaired Bourn Court (73). Small houses built by him include 11–12 Bath Row (108) of 1834 and 16–19 Adelaide Street (116) of c. 1840–1. In 1820 he took an auctioneer's licence, and this branch of the business remained in Barn Hill until 1971.

SHARPE, EDWARD (d. 1764). Mason, freeman 1714. Marble monument, 1736, in North Witham church, Lincs. His son Edward became freeman 1749.

SMITH, THOMAS (fl. 1828–42). Mason, admitted to scot and lot 1832, and lived at 19 St. George's Square until he sold his stock and left Stamford in 1842. In 1828–32 he built a house in St. Martin's and worked at Burghley under Gandy; in 1836 he was clerk of works at the Union Workhouse; in 1841 he repaired St. Mary's Church and tendered for the Stamford Institution. He submitted an unsuccessful design for St. Michael's church in 1834. As a monumental mason his work was prolific, in the plain Grecian style of the day: 13 wall-monuments survive in Stamford, and a gravestone of 1833 at Tickencote.

SPARROW, GEORGE (fl. 1788–1805). Mason, freeman 1792 as a housepainter but by 1793 was working as a marble mason; in 1806 he moved to W. D. Legg's former house in Broad Street. He was a member of the Sparrow family of monumental masons and may have come from Grantham.

STAVELEY, CHRISTOPHER (c. 1727–1801). Architect, of Melton Mowbray. In 1787 he repaired the tower and spire of St. Mary's church, and in 1794 drew plans of sluices for an improvement in the Welland navigation. John Boyfield II was his foreman before 1779.

SUTTON, JOHN. Mason, freeman 1662. In 1672 he contracted with Sir Abel Barker to build part of Lyndon Hall, Rutland.

TATAM, HENRY (fl. c. 1772–1804). Cabinet maker, worked with Cobb in London before starting business in Stamford; freeman 1772. Made furniture for Burghley House. Acting as representative of the Wansford Road Trustees he 'explained' the plan of the proposed Town Hall to the Council in 1775, signed the building proposals, and in 1780 designed an embattled folly to replace Scotgate gate. In 1777 he planned and estimated for new sheep pens with John Dixon, and in 1804 unsuccessfully submitted a plan for the new shambles. He was almost certainly responsible for the design of 9 Barn Hill (97), *c.* 1796–1801.

TINKLER, ROBERT (1797–1868). Mason and builder, born at Woolsthorpe, Lincs. Among his works are repairs to St. Mary's spire in 1842, alterations to Barn Hill House (96), 1843–4, various stations for the Midland Railway, *c.* 1847, and the W. porch of St. George's church in 1848.

WILLFORD, JOSEPH (d. 1780). Brazier. He made a chandelier for St. Martin's church in 1732, a bell for the Town Crier in 1740, and did unspecified work for Lord Exeter, 1770–80.

WING, JOHN (fl. *c.* 1674–1714). Surveyor, of Pickworth, Rutland. In 1714 a Mr. Wing was paid 10s. for 'measuring joiners work' at Browne's Hospital. This was probably the campaign of work costing over £150, George Portwood being paid £50. In 1700 he published a revised version of his uncle Vincent Wing's work *Geodaetes Practicus Redivivus*, in which he advertised himself as a land and quantity surveyor and architect.

WOOLSTON, ROBERT (d. 1856). Builder, admitted to scot and lot 1825 as bricklayer. In 1847 began building Town Bridge (64), became bankrupt 1848 but continued in business, tendering for the Infirmary Lodge (45) in 1849. He was a brickmaker, and a monument signed by him in 1829 is in All Saints' church. Contractor with Charles Collins for St. Michael's church, 1835–6. In 1844 he made pews in St. George's church with Collins, and in 1847–8 was building lodges for the Midland Railway.

SOURCES FOR STAMFORD HISTORY

The earliest historical account of Stamford was written by Richard Butcher, a town clerk, and published in 1646 as *A Survey and Antiquity of the Town of Stamford*. Frances Howgrave, printer of the *Stamford Mercury*, published *An Essay on the Ancient and Present State of Stamford* in 1726, allegedly to annoy Peck; it derived much from Butcher. Francis Peck (1692–1743) was a serious historian and in 1727 he published the first volume of a projected history of the town called *Academia Tertia Anglicana*. Arranged as a series of Annals up to 1461, it includes much useful material such as the lost medieval conveyances formerly at Browne's Hospital and has as appendices Butcher's *Survey* of 1646 and two letters from the Reverend W. Forster, vicar of St. Michael's, to Mr. Tanner and John Stevens, concerning antiquarian topics. Peck's two volumes of miscellanea, *Desiderata Curiosa*, published in 1732 and 1735, contain little of relevance to Stamford. His friend and contemporary William Stukeley (1687–1765), vicar of All Saints' from 1730 to 1747, did not publish any of his work on Stamford. 'Designs of Stanford Antiquitys' is a collection of plates from Peck and drawings by Stukeley compiled in 1735; this is complemented by 'Stanfordia Illustrata', an attempted history of the town written in 1735–6. In his 'Designs' Stukeley drew reconstructions of several medieval buildings which he believed had been academic halls. He based these reconstructions partly on memory but mainly on visible evidence, observing that 'a discerning eye, that is a little conversant with our Stamford manner of building, will not find it very difficult' (Stanfordia Illustrata II, 73). Further notes on these houses are included in Stanfordia Illustrata where, on the fifth day of their conversation, Palaephatus (Stukeley) takes his friend Panagius on a tour of the town. Much of the value of the descriptions lies in their reference to features which have not survived. Among the buildings described, the following are of particular importance:

(1) Black Hall (Plate 70; Designs, 78; Stanfordia Illustrata II, 88). This building lay on the site of 1 Barn Hill, but faced S. towards All Saints' Place.

(2) Peterborough Hall (Plate 70; Designs, 73; Stanfordia Illustrata II, 86) was immediately W. of monument (281) at the E. end of All Saints' Street, on the site of the present G.P.O. William White, who died c. 1720, had altered the front which Stukeley restored partly from memory. The window at the upper end of the 'large and elegant hall' had painted glass including quarries depicting cocks; the cross wing on the W. had a parlour and a lodging room over. Behind was a small courtyard with ancient but altered buildings.

(3) Sempringham Hall (Plate 70; Designs, 75; Stanfordia Illustrata II, 73) was a farmhouse in 1736 and remains as 31–32 St. Peter's Street (412). Stukeley's drawing is a reconstruction based on visible evidence. His notes are incomplete but mention four stone staircases.

(4) Thurney Hall (Plate 70; Designs, 20; Stanfordia Illustrata II, 115). Part of this house remains in St. Mary's Street (349). The hall was 'handsomely coved at the upper end', and the kitchen, originally the parlour, had painted glass, golden portcullisses recurring frequently. There was a stone staircase, and 'a necessary closet in every room'.

(5) All Saints' Vicarage (Plate 71; Designs, 28; Stanfordia Illustrata II, 91) survives as 16 Barn Hill (103). 'The front of the house was originally of this form. A hall with a cove at the upper end . . . many old latin verses still visible painted on the timber. By a stone staircase we go up to his lodging room, handsomely coved, the wainscot ledge along the cornish for tapestry hangings'.

Later historians relied heavily on Butcher and Peck, adding later material from their own experience. William Harrod published *The Antiquities of Stamford and St. Martins* in 1785, and John Drakard, printer of the shortlived *Stamford News*, published a *History of Stamford* in 1822; both books consist largely of borrowed material. In 1813 Thomas Blore, a lawyer, published *An Account of the Public Schools, Hospitals and other Charitable Foundations of the Borough of Stamford* as part of an attack on the corrupt way the Town Council ran its charities; it provides much valuable information. George Burton's *Chronology of Stamford*, arranged alphabetically by topics, was published in 1846 and contains much useful material relating to the 19th century. Later histories, such as M. E. C. Walcott's *Memorials of Stamford* (1867), are generally short and derivative. One of the most important printed sources for the 18th and 19th centuries in Stamford is the *Stamford Mercury* which began in 1695 and became the *Lincoln, Rutland and Stamford Mercury* after 1783. Copies before c. 1720 are rare.

The first attempt at a modern history of Stamford is the series of short essays edited by A. Rogers in *The Making of Stamford* (1965). The chapter on the 19th century must be qualified by the work of S. Elliott, for instance in *Lincolnshire History and Archaeology* 1, No. 4 (1969). Recently, the Stamford Survey Group has produced two reports, on medieval buildings and religious institutions respectively. Since 1966 excavations have been carried out on many sites in the town by the Stamford Archaeological Research Committee; interim reports have been published in *Medieval Archaeology*.

The diocesan records of Lincoln are in the Lincoln Archives Office and cover Stamford N. of the Welland; St. Martin's is in the diocese of Peterborough and the archives are in the Northamptonshire Record Office. In Stamford Town Hall are the municipal records including court rolls, and the Chamberlains' Accounts which record briefly corporate expenditure between 1697 and 1835. The Hall Books contain the minutes of the council and record decisions and admissions to freedom from 1465 until they were superseded by council and committee minute books in 1835. The Marquess of Exeter's manuscripts at Burghley House include maps, conveyances and court rolls. The Day Books of the estate, recording expenditure between 1770 and 1800, are in the Burghley Estate Office.

There are very few maps of Stamford. Speed's map was drawn *c.* 1600 and was reprinted several times with slight amendments. James Knipe made a survey of the whole town in 1833, which was published early the following year (Plate 56). In Burghley House are maps of St. Martins made in 1773 by W. Murray (Plate 3), and in 1799 by J. Baxter.

Of the topographical artists who visited Stamford in the early 19th century, W. Twopeny is the most important. He was particularly interested in medieval buildings and recorded many features which have not survived. J. C. Nattes made some drawings in 1804 and J. C. Buckler and E. Blore drew a few outstanding buildings during the first half of the 19th century.

AN INVENTORY OF
THE ANCIENT AND HISTORICAL MONUMENTS
IN THE TOWN OF STAMFORD

EARTHWORKS AND ALLIED STRUCTURES

ROMAN

At least two Roman coins have been found within the town, one of the 4th century, at TF 03260735 in 1874, the other unlocated (OS Record Cards).

(1) ROMAN BUILDINGS (?) (possibly about TF 031069). In or just before 1839 a large piece of Roman tessellated pavement was found in digging a cellar, near the bridge. It was broken up and moved. (*Gent's Mag.*, (1839) pt.2, 527; *Arch. J.*, XC (1935), 182; fragment in Spalding Museum).

(2) ROMAN (?) FINDS (about TF 027072). The following were found in the garden of 9 Barnhill (97), at that time the home of William Stukeley: in June 1743, a possible Roman urn in a stone cist, 7 ft. below the surface, and a few days later a Roman coin in the same area; early in 1744, another 'whiteish' urn, also said to be Roman (*Surtees Soc.*, LXXVI (1883), 330).

(3) ROMAN (?) CREMATORIUM (about TF 030071), found in 1744 in the High Street, included an empty urn covered with a slate, possibly Roman, a barrel-shaped urn which William Stukeley thought was pre-Roman, and other urns. These urns were said to be associated with two 'perpendicular hewn arches made without mortar against the side of the rock'. The arches were filled with 'black mould' and adjoining ground was paved with stone and blackened by burning (*Surtees Soc.*, LXXVI (1883), 326).

(4) ROMAN POTTERY (TF 03230754) all of 4th-century Nene Valley types, and a worn coin, possibly of Severus Alexander, were found in a drainage trench on the W. edge of Stamford School playing fields in 1957–8. No definite building is recorded, though a few large stones were seen in the trench (OS Records; Stamford Museum).

(5) SETTLEMENT (TF 020063) in the S.W. corner of the borough, on land sloping S.E. towards the R. Welland on limestone at 100 ft. above OD. Air photographs (in NMR) show crop-marks of a small settlement covering some 2 hectares, and comprising a markedly rectangular ditched enclosure. There are traces of an internal ditch, dividing it into two unequal parts, and further ditches in the surrounding area.

(6) ROMAN ROAD, Ermine Street (Margary 2c; TF 027064–002086) ran diagonally across the W. part of the borough from S.E.–N.W. No trace of it exists on its presumed alignment on the S. side of the Welland, although in the 18th century William Stukeley recorded it just outside the borough as being 20 ft. wide with a 3 ft. high agger made up of stony soil on a foundation of 2 ins. of pebbles and black material (W. Stukeley, *Itinerarium Curiosum* (1776), 84). The Roman road crossed the river (at TF 027063) where it flows in a wide alluvial flood-plain. Immediately W. of the modern footpath is a much mutilated low bank, 10 m. wide and 0·5 m. high on the presumed alignment, traceable for about 35 m. This lies outside the 'walled garden' which Margary assumed to be on the line of the road (Margary, 225).

Beyond and to the N.W. the line of the road is taken by a rough track known as Water Furlong and, after crossing the Tinwell Road, by a modern street called Roman Bank. This street is still slightly raised above the surrounding land. N.W. of the Empingham Road (TF 018672) the remains of Ermine Street have been completely destroyed by modern housing estates for a distance of 1 km. Before this destruction (Plate 2) a well-preserved agger existed up to 1·5 m. high and 12 m. wide, and traces of side ditches were visible on air photographs (Margary, pl. VII). A section across the road was excavated in 1956 before destruction (at TF 015075) and the S.W. side ditch was discovered but that

I

on the N.E. had already been destroyed. The road itself consisted of a 7 m. wide and 0·25 m. thick layer of limestone, overlaid by a compact mass of lime-cement, up to nearly 1 m. thick. Above this was the road surface 4 m. wide, composed of small limestone pebbles or chippings (*Antiquaries Journal*, 39 (1959), 77).

On the N.W. side of the borough Ermine Street meets and runs parallel with the Great North Road (TF 010079–002087). Along this section, where it is undamaged, the agger is a massive bank up to 18 m. across and 1 m. high with a flat top 6 m. wide. However, owing to the proximity of the Great North Road it has been dug into for road material in many places and the result is that the agger is either 'filleted' with a trench along its summit, or completely dug away by a number of pits and quarries. At the extreme N.W. corner of the borough the Ermine Street turns slightly N. on to the line of the present road, to cross the R. Gwash and enter the town of Casterton (Margary, 225–7).

MEDIEVAL

(7) SAXON CEMETERY (TF 04096768), found in 1854 when the Essendine–Stamford Railway was cut. It lay just N. of the Uffington Road bridge between the Rivers Welland and Gwash. A complete urn and fragments of at least three other vessels, an iron spearhead, a human skull and some animal bones were discovered. Further human remains later came to light in the adjacent limeworks. The present location of the pottery from the site is in doubt. There is a mid 6th-century urn, with stamped ornament and incised lines at Burghley House, which may be the one discovered in 1854. There is also a small plain urn from 'Stamford' in Cambridge University Museum of Archaeology and Ethnology and an early 6th-century Anglo-Frankish urn with vertical and horizontal linear decoration, said to have been found in 1848 in Stamford, in Lincoln Museum. There may in fact be more than one cemetery site from which this pottery has come. (A. Meaney, *Gazetteer of Early Anglo-Saxon Burial Sites* (1964), 163–4)

(8) DANISH BURH (Fig. 4) occupied much of the area covered by the central part of the later medieval town. It was established in 877 by the Danish army which built a fortified stronghold at Stamford. Nothing now remains on the ground of the defences of this burh, though topographical evidence suggests the approximate area (see also Plate 1).

The W. boundary may have been on the E. crest of the shallow valley, now occupied by Red Lion Square and Castle Dyke. The actual defences perhaps lay along the E. side of the Square and St. John's Street. The N. boundary is probably marked by the curving line of Broad Street, which may have been developed immedi-

ately outside the Danish defences. At the E. end of Broad Street the right-angled corner into Star Lane is perhaps the N.E. corner of the defences which ran S., then E. of St. George's Street, to a point at or near St. George's church. The boundary then probably turned W. and ran along the main crest of the Welland valley, approximately where St. Mary's Street now lies. These defences enclosed an area of approximately 15 acres (6·2 hectares) and have a total length of about 940 yards (860 m.); although not fully proven, their existence on this assumed line would account for some of the otherwise unexplained changes of alignment in the existing street plan, such as the Broad Street–Star Lane corner and St. George's Street–High Street–St Paul's Street junction. On this hypothesis High Street would then have been the original axial road through the burgh.

Excavations E. of St. George's Street on the presumed line of these defences (TF 032072) revealed a large Saxo-Norman quarry which had obscured any earlier ditch. The quarry had cut through an iron smelting hearth which had in turn cut through earlier, presumably Saxon or Danish, structures. These consisted of a linear arrangement of slots and post-holes along the line of the supposed defences, and were associated with a series of dark laminated layers, perhaps turf and brushwood, and interpreted as a possible rampart (*Med. Arch.*, XV (1971), 127).

(9) SAXON BURH (Fig. 4) occupies the greater part of Stamford S. of the R. Welland, now St. Martin's parish. The burh was erected by King Edward in 918 when the town was again brought under English rule (see p. xxxviii).

Nothing of any major significance now remains on the ground but the bounds of the burh are perhaps reflected in the rectangular layout of the existing streets in the area. The boundary on the E. may therefore have been along the line of Park Lane with a N. extension towards Lumby's Terrace. There is a low bank on the E. side of the disused St. Martin's graveyard but this may be a later feature. The S. boundary may be reflected by the present borough boundary which turns S.W. at the S. end of Park Lane and runs to High Street St. Martins. This line is continued W. of the High Street by Pinfold Lane which then turns N.W. parallel to High Street. At this point, a broad low bank, much damaged by modern development, lies along the W. side of the lane. It is now 8 m. across and nowhere above 0·5 m. high. To the N. of Kettering Road there are no significant alignments; the defences may have extended in that direction but there is no clear N. boundary. The burh could have extended as far as the river, but a more likely line would have been immediately N. of St. Martin's church, where there is a marked break in the slope down to the Welland flood-plain. Such an explanation would also account for the alignment of High Street St.

Martins. S. of the church the road is almost straight and as such could have originated as the main axial road of the burh; on the N. it deflects slightly to cross the river by the town bridge. The marked double bend of the Old North Road, S. of High Street St. Martins, can also be explained as the result of diverting into the burh the older route which ran northwards along Wothorpe Road to the river.

Excavations to find the E. side of these presumed defences were carried out in the yard at the rear of Stamford High School (TF 032067). A Saxo-Norman quarry was found which had been cut through an earlier N.–S. ditch some 4 ft. deep (*Med. Arch.*, XV (1971), 127).

(10) CASTLE (Fig. 16) occupied a large area to the S. of Sheepmarket, on the crest and slope of the Welland valley. It was built soon after the Norman Conquest for Domesday Book records that five houses were destroyed to make way for it. It was twice besieged and finally captured during the civil wars of the mid 12th century. It was in use throughout the 13th century, but by 1340 had clearly outlasted its usefulness, a survey of that year describing it as 'old, and the walls decayed; within are an old tower, a great hall, a chamber with a solar, a chapel, a turret, and a house for a prison, all of no value beyond outgoings; the site of the castle contains two acres and is called the manor' (*Cal. Inq. Misc.* 2, no. 1703). The buildings continued to deteriorate and none remained by 1600 (Speed's map). A small room used for the Court Leet (Designs, 15) had been formed at the E. end of the former hall, and is still marked as such in 1833 (Knipe's map). By that time the site was used mainly as gardens; part was levelled for an omnibus station in 1936. A length of the ditch on the N. side was filled and levelled for a sheepmarket in 1781.

Before 1936 the castle consisted of two parts, usually described as the motte and the bailey. On the crest of the valley-side was a large circular bank with an overall diameter of about 50 m. This was drawn by Stukeley in 1735 (Plate 2, Designs, 4). When the bank was levelled in 1936, a circular structure of rubble about 60 ft. in diameter and standing 7 ft. high was revealed (PRO, Works 14/515); photographs show it to have had a slightly battered profile. This may be interpreted as a circular keep, the 'old tower' of 1340, standing within a ringwork. A short distance away stood a length of 12th-century ashlar wall; this is presumably related to the massive ashlar wall running N.–S. found in the 19th century on the W. side of the ringwork (*Mercury*, 30 May 1879). Limited excavations on the site in 1933 by H. F. Traylen produced little information (*Antiquary* 16 (1936) 410–11) and a well of 12th to 13th-century date was excavated in 1962. The ditch to the S. of the ringwork was located in 1972; it had been filled in and paved over by the 13th century.

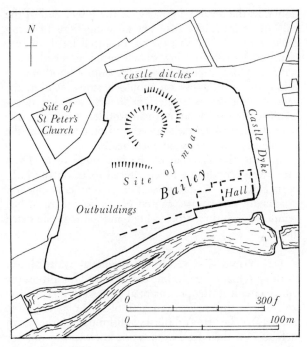

Fig. 16   (10) Site of Castle.

The S. part of the castle site is a broad area sloping to the S., and has been terraced for gardens. Stukeley shows it bounded by stone walls (Plate 2) but these have been largely replaced, especially on the E., where he shows a gateway. The present W. wall does not appear to be ancient. Of the four buttresses shown by Stukeley at the E. end of the S. wall, one may survive, of 'Barnack' stone, now set in 19th-century masonry. A reset doorway (109) is of no significance.

Excavations in 1972–5 showed that the W. part of the area had been extensively quarried for stone in the Saxo-Norman period; these quarries were filled in and by the 13th century the area had been covered by a number of buildings partly terraced into the slope, including grain-drying kilns and a complex garderobe. The principal domestic buildings were discovered built against the E. end of the S. boundary wall. This wall was very thick and was clearly the original curtain wall. Against its N. face was built a long range with a hall at its E. end and a solar to the W.; this range conformed in width to the row of three doorways surviving at the S.E. corner of the site, but the floor level was considerably lower. Later, the hall was widened to the N. and remodelled with a nave and two four-bay aisles with timber posts. This hall was later remodelled to have a single N. aisle of three bays, the nave again conforming to the width and floor level of the surviving doorways.

The only part of this building standing above ground is the E. wall of the hall, formerly the E. wall of the small Court Leet building and now incorporated in a modern shed (Plate 64). There are three door openings, doubtless the service doorways at the lower end of the hall, of 13th-century date but showing signs of being reset. These doorways have two-centred heads of two chamfered orders resting on clustered attached shafts with moulded capitals and bases, and a hood mould resting uncomfortably on moulded stops. Within the central doorway is a later, medieval, wooden door-frame with ogee head and nail-studded door; the side openings are blocked. The restored rear arches on the E. face have pointed segmental heads.

In 1936 the W. wall of the rear wing of 62 High Street was rebuilt in a much-altered form on the N.E. corner of the Castle site as a public convenience. Originally there was a canted N. and a square S. bay window, each three storeys high and gabled, one dated 1664.

(11) TOWN WALLS. Of the medieval walls almost nothing remains but the line can be traced for almost the entire circuit in the present road pattern (Fig. 17; Plate 56). The walls enclosed an area of about 75 acres (30 hectares). The date of the establishment of the town defences on their final lines is not known, but murage grants dating between 1261 and 1352 presumably refer to the walls now traceable (H. Turner, *Town Defences in England and Wales* (1971), 238). The line is broadly preserved by West Street, North Street, Elm Street, part of Brazenose Lane, and Wharf Road. Several gates are recorded but all have been demolished: Bridge Gate, St. Peter's Gate, Scot Gate, New Gate, St. Paul's Gate, St. George's Gate and Water Gate. Butcher ((1646), p. 2) refers to a postern near Bridge Gate, but this is probably the doorway of the 12th-century house in St. Mary's Hill (336). He also lists five towers (Beesfort, Holme, Carpe and White towers, and North Bulwarke), but only one tower which stands near the former St. Peter's Gate now remains. Butcher further states that most tenements adjoining the town wall had a postern by his time, a fact borne out by the Hall Books, which record that in 1574 and 1614 general walling-up ordinances were passed (Hall Books, I,206, 309). Licences for posterns were given, for example, in 1472 to William Hykeham (Hikham) and as late as 1694 to Mr. Fryerye. The only surviving postern gate is probably that to 9 Barn Hill (97; Plate 90).

The principal features of the walls are located on Fig. 17.

(a) Site of BRIDGE GATE. The gate stood at the N. end of the bridge, housing the Town Hall in its upper room, and was demolished in c. 1778 in order to improve access to the town (64).

(b) Site of ST. PETER's GATE. The gate was demolished in c. 1770 in connection with the building of Hopkins' Hospital which stands on the S. side of the road. The gable of the hospital is reflected by a similar gothic gable on the other side of the street (51).

(c) BASTION (Plate 57), of two stages with weathered external set-backs, and parapet which is pierced by a single loop of uncertain antiquity. The coursed rubble walls are heavily repaired including internal thickening and partial filling with concrete. The tower was originally open at the back. Flanking walls are post-medieval and modern but follow the old line.

(d) GARDEN WALL, 38 St. Peter's Street, built in about 1840 on the line of the town wall, incorporates a terrace with a 17th-century doorway, perhaps as a postern (417).

(e) Site of SCOT GATE, also known as Clement's Gate. The gate was partly demolished in 1767 when the lower arch was removed, and finally in 1780 when the Turnpike Trustees bought it for road materials at a cost of £20. They replaced it by an embattled and turreted structure on either side of the road to the design of Henry Tatam (Hall Books), but this is now only represented by a modern buttress with a reset panel inscribed '1780', and a length of classical dentilled cornice.

(f) WALL, in school playground, West Street. The wall is 19th-century and follows the line of the town wall.

(g) GATEWAY, in garden of Stukeley House, 9 Barn Hill, large early 17th-century postern, built into the town walls and altered by William Stukeley in 1744 (97).

(h) WALL, 14 Barn Hill, is early 19th-century and forms a terrace and loggia (101).

(i) WALL, in former garden of 3 Broad Street, is of well-dressed and coursed stonework and of early date. Against its inner face is a garden terrace, and on its outer side are five raking buttresses. Above three stone spouts which drain the terraces is a string course of simple profile. The coping is inscribed 'GD 1721', possibly for George Denshire.

(j) Site of NEW GATE. The gate was in existence in the late 16th century (NRO, Fitzwilliam Misc. 433).

(k) WALLING, behind 15–16 Broad Street and giving onto Elm Street, several lengths, mostly of post-medieval date, perhaps 17th-century. The line of the wall continues E. behind Nos. 18–19 (136), and behind 15 St. Paul's Street (378) where, for a short distance, the wall is thicker and possibly medieval.

(l) Between 24 and 25 St. Paul's Street (381, 382), the garden wall is tall and thick, and may be medieval.

(m) Site of ST. PAUL's GATE; demolished c. 1780.

(n) SCARP, now the S.E. boundary of mon. (383), is 12 ft. high and has a rubble retaining wall of post-medieval date. On the S.E. side of wall a strip of land approximately 8–10 yds. wide, and now occupied by cottages and garden, probably indicates the ditch.

(o) Site of ST. GEORGE's GATE; the gate, also known as Cornstall Gate until c. 1727, was demolished c. 1805 (Chamberlains' Accounts. Illustrated in c. 1789 in Torrington Diaries by Hon. J. Byng (1954), 153).

(p) Site of WATER GATE; a postern at S. end of Gas Lane, mentioned between 1570 and 1689 (Ex. MS, 201/27; Hall Books; Blore (1813), 285–9).

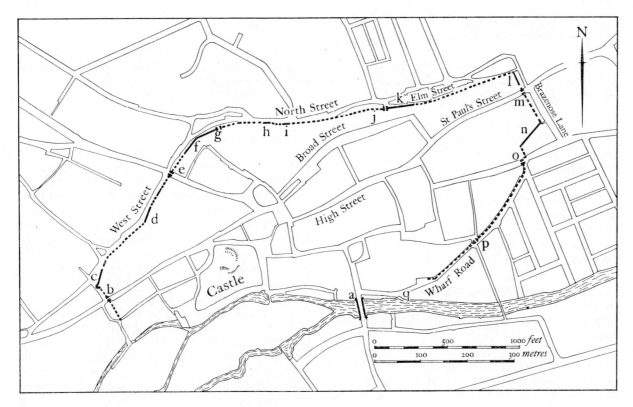

Fig. 17 (11) Map showing medieval town walls.

(q) Reputed site of TOWER; marked on OS map of 1886 but not now traceable; probably outside the line of the medieval walls.

(12) MEDIEVAL OCCUPATION SITE (?) (TF 027073) found in the gardens of shops between North Street and Scotgate. Quantities of Saxo-Norman pottery, mostly Stamford Ware, were discovered (*Med. Arch.*, IX (1965), 195).

(13) MEDIEVAL OCCUPATION SITE (TF 032068) found E. of High Street St. Martins. Excavations have led to the discovery of pits and occupation levels, containing Saxo-Norman and later pottery (*Med. Arch.*, IX (1965), 195).

(14) MEDIEVAL OCCUPATION SITE (TF 032073) discovered during the excavations at Nos. 46–47 High Street. Late Saxon occupation, represented by traces of slight timber buildings or fences, was recorded. Subsequent occupation in the 11th century included industrial workings shown by iron slag and hearths. A 12th-century timber building followed on this site, and was in turn superseded by a substantial stone building. Near by a stone-built malt-drying kiln, probably of 14th-century date, was found overlying earlier material including iron slag. An underground stone

barrel-vaulted chamber of unknown date was also discovered (*Med. Arch.*, XI (1967), 267, 293).

(15) MEDIEVAL OCCUPATION SITE (?) (TF 030070) found during the renovation of 5 St. Mary's Street (345). A well, a drain and large stone foundations were recovered (*Med. Arch.*, XI (1967), 283). The suggestion by the excavators that the remains belong to an early phase of the adjoining St. John's church is unlikely.

(16) MEDIEVAL OCCUPATION SITE (TF 031069) was excavated in Water Street. Traces of late Saxon timber buildings were recovered as well as quarry and rubbish-pits. These remains had been disturbed by a line of four 13th and 14th-century tenements. Two were substantial stone buildings with deep garderobe pits (Fig. 8). One contained a cellar (*Med. Arch.*, XIII (1969), 234, 265).

(17) POTTERY KILN (TF 033074) was excavated in Elm Street in 1963. It was oval, of up-draught type, producing mostly 'developed' Stamford Ware of the late 12th or 13th centuries (*Med. Arch.*, VIII (1964), 294–6; *E. Midland Arch. Bulletin*, (1962), 18–19).

(18) POTTERY KILN (TF 033071) in Wharf Road. A single flue up-draught kiln producing Stamford Ware was excavated (*Med. Arch.*, XIII (1969), 234 and Fig. 70).

(19) POTTERY KILN (TF 032073), found 1874. No significant details (*Mercury*, 2 October 1874).

(20) POTTERY KILN (?) (unlocated) found in 'the car-park'. Pottery, including wasters, all apparently Stamford Ware, is recorded (OS Record Cards).

(21) QUARRY PIT (TF 035074) found in St. Leonard's Street was partly excavated. Large quantities of glazed Stamford Ware, including many wasters, were recovered (*Med. Arch.*, XIII (1969), 234).

(22) IRON-SMELTING WORKINGS (TF 031072) found N. of High Street. A slag heap associated with a clay-built shaft furnace and two hearths were discovered. Pottery was almost all Stamford Ware, some of late 11th or early 12th-century date (*Med. Arch.*, VIII (1964), 294).

(23) IRON-SMELTING WORKINGS (?) (TF 034073) found during road works on the site of St. Paul's Gate. A slag heap, similar to (22), was noted (*Med. Arch.*, VIII (1964), 294).

(24) IRON-SMELTING WORKINGS (?) (TF 033073) found during building works. An area of iron slag and late Saxon to 13th-century pottery were discovered (*Med. Arch.*, IX (1965), 195).

(25) IRON-SMELTING WORKS AND QUARRY (TF 032072) found during excavations on the line of the presumed Danish burh defences (8). A large Saxo-Norman quarry had been cut through an iron-smelting hearth (*Med. Arch.*, XV (1971), 127).

Discoveries referred to in (20)–(25) were made in the 1960s.

(26) CULTIVATION REMAINS. The medieval open fields of Stamford were not finally enclosed until 1875, following an Act of Parliament of 1870. Before that time there had been four large open fields, covering some 1,300 acres and occupying most of the borough area. These were Ketton Dale, Pingle, New Close and Low Fields, though a three-field system was operated (S. Elliot, 'The Enclosure of Stamford Open Fields', unpublished M.A. thesis, University of Nottingham, 1965; *Agrarian History Review*, 20 (1972), 155–69).

Ridge-and-furrow of these fields can be traced over wide areas, especially to the N. and W. of the town (TF 025084 and TF 016070). It is arranged in rectangular or C-shaped furlongs. In the far W. of the borough (around TF 015080) air photographs also show further traces of ridge-and-furrow, here associated with broad low ridges which still exist, up to 300 m. long. These latter are headlands between the former furlongs.

POST MEDIEVAL

(27) CANAL (TF 041073–048076; Plate 87) runs roughly parallel to the R. Welland, from near Hudd's Mill to the borough boundary on the R. Gwash.

The proposal to construct a canal from Stamford to Market Deeping, and so improve the navigation of the Welland, was first made shortly before 1570. In that year an act for making a navigable canal was obtained by the Corporation of Stamford, though nothing was done apart from some construction work at the W. end. In 1620 further authorization was obtained and work resumed. Owing to severe financial difficulties construction ceased in 1621 and in spite of numerous attempts to complete it no progress was made. In 1664 Royal approval was obtained and a contractor appointed. By 1673 it was completed and carried considerable traffic. It was abandoned in 1863 (A. Rogers, 90–2; N. Birch, Stamford, *An Industrial History* (1972)).

The finished canal ran for some 9½ miles (15·5 km.) from Stamford to a point just W. of Market Deeping. There were twelve locks, each of 17 ft. beam. It started just above the weir at Hudd's Mill (TF 041073) where there are still traces of the original entrance below the old railway bridge. For the next 170 m. the remains have been obliterated by sewage works, and the following stretch has been filled with quarry spoil. Further E. (from TF 043074–046074) it survives as a shallow depression 12–15 m. wide with a well-marked S. bank 1 m. high, running due E. The canal then turned N.E. and ran for 300 m. in an almost exactly straight line until it met the R. Gwash and passed outside the borough. Along this section the canal survives as a dry ditch 10–12 m. wide and 1–1·5 m. deep with a flat bottom, 5 m. across. On both sides are low banks 3–4 m. wide and 0·5–1 m. high. Beyond the borough boundary the remains are much more massive, with a large retaining bank up to 3 m. high in places along the S. side. The stone abutments of a number of bridges also remain outside the borough.

ECCLESIASTICAL BUILDINGS

CHURCHES

(28) PARISH CHURCH OF ALL SAINTS (Fig. 18; Frontispiece and Plate 13) stands in a small churchyard on the N. side of Red Lion Square. It consists of a *Chancel* with *S. Chapel*, *Nave* with *N.* and *S. Aisles*, *N.W. Tower*, *N.* and *S. Porches* and a *Vestry*. The walls are of coursed limestone, either squared or rubble, and the roofs are covered with lead. The plan, an irregular parallelogram, may have been

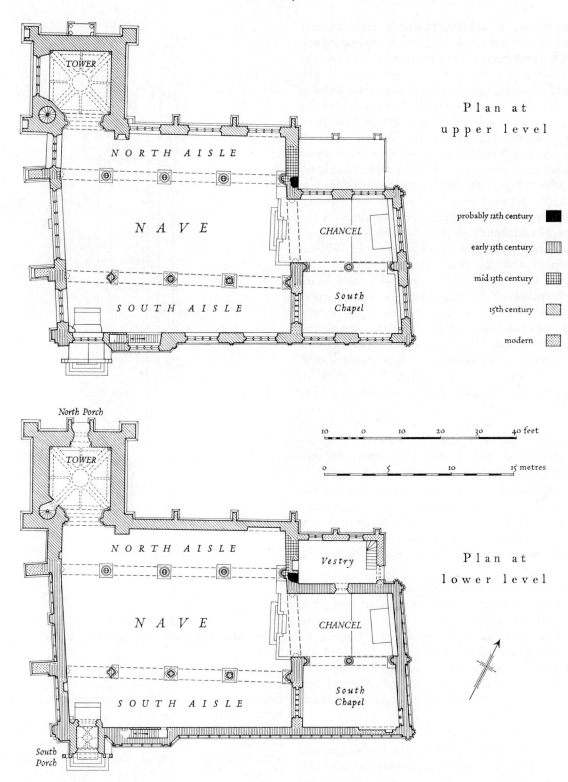

Plan at upper level

TOWER

NORTH AISLE

NAVE

CHANCEL

SOUTH AISLE

South Chapel

probably 12th century
early 13th century
mid 13th century
15th century
modern

North Porch

TOWER

NORTH AISLE

Vestry

NAVE

CHANCEL

SOUTH AISLE

South Chapel

South Porch

10 0 10 20 30 40 feet

0 5 10 15 metres

Plan at lower level

Fig. 18 (28) Church of All Saints.

influenced by an earlier, probably 12th-century, church of which the N.E. angle of the nave survives. With the exception of the tower and the vestry, the main fabric is entirely of the 13th century. The chancel, S. chapel, nave and S. aisle date from *c.* 1230, but the N. aisle is slightly later. Access to the church in the 13th century appears to have been through an internal porch in the W. bay of the S. aisle. The porch had an upper floor and rose above the aisle roof as a turret. Considerable rebuilding was undertaken in the late 15th century at the expense of the wool-merchant family of Browne, as attested by the merchant's mark carved on the tower. No document survives to show which member was responsible but John (d. 1475) and William Browne (d. 1489) are usually credited with the work (see (48) Browne's Hospital for family tree). With the exception of the pilaster buttresses at the corners of the building the walls above the 13th-century blind arcading were rebuilt, and the tower and spire constructed. This 15th-century work included new windows throughout, a larger chancel arch, a nave clearstorey, a vestry and the introduction of an arch at the W. end of the S. arcade. This last alteration involved the removal of an upper room in the W. bay of the aisle. Access to this room had in the 13th century been gained by a stair in the thickness of the aisle wall; in the 15th century the stair was lengthened to reach the aisle roof.

In 1857, a subterranean compartment, 9 ft. 6 ins. wide and 12 ft. high, with a quadripartite vault, and passages on S. and W., 6 ft. wide and 7 ft. high, was found within the churchyard on the N. side of the church, but the precise location is not known (Burton, 10).

Galleries, since removed, were inserted in the 18th century. There were restorations in 1856 when the vestry was rebuilt and new oak pews were made to the design of E. Browning, in 1871 when T. G. Jackson rebuilt the W. wall of the S. chapel and added two buttresses to the W. wall of the nave, and in 1878 when the present reredos and low chancel screen were designed by T. Treadway Hanson (*Associated Architectural Societies' Reports* iv, 1856–7; LRO. Faculty Books 14/5, 71/521, 8/41).

The church is noteworthy for the extent and elaboration of the early 13th-century architecture and for the sophistication of the 15th-century alterations and additions.

Architectural Description (arranged chronologically) — Several quoins existing at a high level at the N.E.

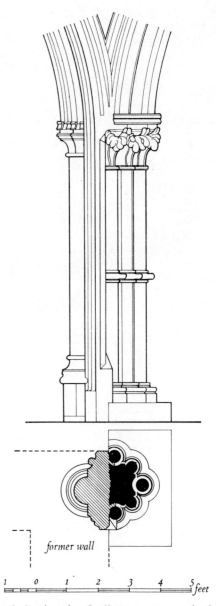

Fig. 19   (28) Church of All Saints. S. arcade showing 15th-century adaptation of 13th-century W. respond.

corner of the nave survive of an early, possibly 12th-century, nave. Externally the walls of the 13th-century fabric are marked by blind arcading consisting of detached shafts with moulded arches and continuous moulded labels; the capitals are alternately bell-shaped or carved with stiff-leaf foliage (Plate 11). This arcading survives unaltered on the S. and E. sides, but on the W. the heads of the arches were rebuilt in the 15th century with four-centred cinquefoiled heads. The walls are strengthened by pilaster buttresses: those on the E., at the W. end of the N. arcade and under the W. window have chamfered angles, but those at the W.

end of the S. aisle are distinguished by angle shafts, capitals and bases, in two stages.

Internally the principal 13th-century features are the arcades, the northern of which is plainer and later than that on the S. The S. arcade, originally of three bays only, consists of piers composed of clustered shafts with water-holding bases, annulets, stiff-leaf capitals and deeply moulded arches (Plates 8, 13). The responds and the first pier have keel-moulded shafts on the diagonals, but on the second they are set axially; the E. arch has nail-head ornament on the soffit. In the narrower W. bay a 15th-century arch (Fig. 19) with battlemented capitals was set into the wall which was presumably pierced only by a doorway in the 13th century. On the S. side of the third pier are indications of a former wall enclosing the W. bay of the aisle. A shaft in the S.W. angle of the aisle with 13th-century detail comparable to the N. arcade probably implies a vault over the ground floor of this area. The N. arcade consists of round columns with water-holding bases, coved capitals and arches of two chamfered orders. The arcade of two bays separating chancel from S. chapel is transitional in character between the two nave arcades, the outer order of the arches being moulded while the inner is chamfered. Four human heads, much restored, are incorporated in the stiff-leaf foliage with which the capital of the round column is decorated.

The 15th-century additions and alterations are characterised by considerable architectural elaboration and by some degree of fantasy. Battlements are freely used as decoration on capitals, on wall surfaces of the tower, and as cresting to the arcading on the west front, as well as more conventionally on all the external parapets. The windows have graduated lights of predominantly vertical tracery in four-centred, two-centred or triangular heads. The porch on the N. side of the tower is conceived as a miniature fortified gateway complete with cruciform arrow slits (Plate 17); one of its two pinnacles is set diagonally while the other is square. The S. porch (Plate 17), replacing the earlier internal porch the entrance to which is traceable over the porch roof, has an archway with panelled jambs within a tall ogee framework, flanked by linked pairs of crocketed and panelled buttresses, the outer set diagonally; inside, the porch had a barrel-vault with decorative cusped panels. Panelling on jambs is also a distinctive feature of the vestry doorway. The arrangement for down-pipes on the exterior of the N. and S. aisles is unusual; vertical channels for pipes, cut in the face of the N. buttresses, lead to gargoyles on the swept-up weathering (Plate 17), or to corbels above the earlier arcading on the S. (Plate 11).

The tower (Frontispiece and Plate 19) is of four external stages; the third is enriched with cusped panelling, band of quatrefoils and battlemented cornice, the remainder are in plainer ashlar. The clasping buttresses are subordinated to the decorative treatment but terminate in prominent turrets, diagonally placed and projecting back to the spire. On the second stage, facing E., is a two-light window having a moulded surround integral with the adjacent string courses, deep casement-moulded jambs and a large circular stone clock face interrupting the mullion; on the rim of the dial are twelve embossed discs and in the centre are radiations; all late 15th-century (Plate 19). On the N. a lozenge-shaped panel contains a shield suspended by a hand and flanked by birds, charged with the merchant's mark of the Browne family: a sub-divided heart with letter B in base, surmounted by a cross, all within a border; the lozenge had a moulded surround with elaboration at the corners, now all cut back. The octagonal spire with broaches has crockets on each arris and three tiers of lucarnes with finialled gables. Inside, the ground stage has a stone vault with broad panelled ribs and a large aperture for bell-raising; some of the shaft capitals are carved with grotesque male figures in contorted attitudes, apparently blocking their ears (Plate 18).

The vestry, entered by a 15th-century doorway with panelled reveals (Plate 19), was rebuilt in 1856. It stands on medieval basement walls below ground; an area window on the N. has splayed jambs and a blocked opening in the S. has a pointed head. The stone steps are perhaps medieval.

The following *Roofs* are low-pitched and 15th-century. Those over the chancel, nave, and S.E. chapel have cambered tie beams, intermediate principals, purlins, wall posts supported on carved stone corbels, and gilded bosses; the chancel and chapel roofs have three-quarter winged angels at the ends of the principals, and the chapel roof is further enriched by a boarded soffit with diagonal mouldings, bosses and radiating foliage (Plate 23). Decoration on bosses in chancel include an unidentified crest (*lion's head collared between two spears erect*), two with storks and '+ me spede' on label, swans or pelicans and mitred heads. The S. aisle roof of single pitch but ridged internally has moulded rafters and purlins.

Fittings — *Bells*: six, of which four are inscribed in Roman capitals, three being signed by R. Taylor of St. Neots and dated 1808; the previous ring was recast in 1808 by Taylor and a new bell added, at a cost of £230 (Burton, 8).

Brasses and Indents. Brasses: in S. chapel — (1), (Plate 32), in Purbeck slab, male civilian in cloak, feet on two woolsacks, female figure with horned headdress, small dog at foot, canopy partly recessed for inlay, spandrel-roundel with stork on nest, separate labels inscribed '+ me spede' and 'oer lady help at nede', four indents for shields, and rectangular plate with two Latin verses in black-letter, between which are engraved two storks on woolsacks; the brasses have been ascribed to William and Margaret Browne (both died 1489) (M–S. II); (2), to

Fig. 20 (28) Church of All Saints.
Monument (2) to George Denshire, 1743.

Margaret, daughter of John Elmes, 1471, in slab possibly of Alwalton marble, small figure with horned headdress, plate with Latin black-letter inscription (M–S. III); (3), (Plate 53), in same slab as (2), to John Saunders, 1693, rectangular plate with inscription in capitals and with shields of arms and crest of Saunders of Sapperton (M–S. VIII). On S. wall — (4), priest in cope, head missing, c. 1500 (M–S. VII); (5), to Henry Wykys, vicar, 1508, plate with black-letter inscription, probably belonging to (4) (M–S. VII); (6), to Alice Bredmeydew (Browne), February 1491, plate with Latin black-letter inscription (M–S. V). In N. aisle — (7), male civilian and female figure with horned headdress, late 15th-century (M–S. VI); (8), (Plate 30), male civilian in cloak over tunic, with belt recessed for inlay, and purse, feet on twin woolsacks, and female figure with horned headdress, dog at feet, mid 15th-century, in reused slab with indent for shield; figures possibly belonging to (10) (M–S. I); (9), (Plate 31), male civilian in

cloak, 1475/6, the lining recessed for inlay, and female figure with veil headdress, tall pleated collar, and plate with Latin verse in black-letter, with indent for shield below; inscription (. . est m(ih)i nome(n) idem q(ue) p(at)ri, labor un(us) ut(r)iq(ue) . .) suggests that this brass commemorates John Browne the younger, and Agnes his wife (M–S. IV). On N. wall (10), to John Browne (the elder), woolmerchant of Calais, 1442, and Margery his wife, 1460, rectangular plate inscribed in raised black-letter against a hatched background with flanking merchant's marks of Browne, on reused Purbeck slab in moulded stone frame cut down at top, possibly 17th-century; perhaps belonging to (8) (M–S. I); (11), to Catherine Wilson, 1836, plate with black inlay. *Indent*: in S. chapel, for small figure and inscription plate, 15th or early 16th-century.

Chest: oak, with shaped bracket feet, 18th-century. *Clock face*: see Tower. *Coffin*: in churchyard, tapered stone coffin, perhaps 13th-century. *Font*: Purbeck marble, octagonal, buttressed stem with cinquefoil-headed panels, buttresses on the arrises, moulded plinth, bowl with blank shields in shallow cusps and sub-cusps, 15th-century (Plate 40). *Glass*: in S. chapel, E. window, in tracery, yellow-stain, 15th-century. *Hour-glass stand*: on S.E. nave respond, wrought-iron with scrolled ends to holder, and bracket of twisted bars, 17th-century (Plate 55). *Ironwork*: four gates in churchyard wall, with delicate uprights and scrollwork, c. 1800. *Masons' marks*: in tower, 15th-century (Fig. 6).

Monuments and Floor slabs. Monuments: in S. chapel — (1), of Elizabeth Truesdale, January 1683, black tablet with limestone frame and broken pediment; (2), of George Denshire, January 1743, and Mary his wife, 1741, coloured marble, central urn in broken curved pediment, shaped apron with shield of arms with escutcheon and crest, signed 'E. Bingham Peterbro' Fe' (Fig. 20); (3), of George Denshire, 1782, Sarah his wife, 1779, Langton their son, captain in the 34 Regiment who died at the siege of Havannah, 1762, and Sarah their daughter, 1782, marble, shaped apron, pilasters with urns, shield of arms as (2), and central urn and swag against obelisk background; (4), of Cornwall Tathwell, February 1773, coloured marble enriched with cherubs' heads, books and shield of arms; (5), of Francis Butler, February 1726, white marble classical design with broken pediment and shield of arms of Butler; (6), of Thomas Truesdale, 1700, cartouche with elaborate surround of swags incorporating two shields of arms of Truesdale, one impaled and one quartered. In nave — on W. wall (7), of Jane Warren, 1827; (8), of Edward Brown, 1838, by T. Denman, 83 Quadrant, Regent's Street; (9), of Margaret Scott, 1835, by Smith; (10), of William Scott, 1826, by Gilbert; (11), of Mary Holmes, 1834, by Smith; (12), of Emma Thompson, 1845, by Fearn. In N. aisle (13), of Emma Rode, 1826. In S. aisle — (14), of John Wyche, 1820, and Sarah Clarke his daughter, 1836; (15), of Frances Gilchrist, 1806, neo-Greek design with scrollwork top; (16), of Ann Barker, 1829, lozengewise tablet with cusped decoration, by Woolston; (17), of Thomas Haynes, 1834, and Elizabeth his wife, 1837, by Smith; (18), of David Watson, 1818, and Mary his wife, 1843; (19), of George White, 1790, Phoebe his wife, 1799, and Woods their son, 1832. Monuments listed above without full description are of white marble with black backgrounds, and of simple design. Tablets attached externally — on N. aisle wall, (20), of Ann Edgson, 1806, and Frances Edgson, 1807, by Gilbert; (21), of Charlotte Edgson, 1815; (22), of David Edgson, 1817; (23), of Ann Edgson, 1788; on S. aisle wall, (24), of Bridget Webb, Jan. 1715, oval cartouche with scroll surround and cherubs' heads; (25), of William Baker, 1796, and wife, open book beneath obelisk. In churchyard — 18th-century tomb chest with baluster-shaped terminals; approximately 20 embellished headstones of the 18th century. *Floor slabs*: in S. chapel — two slabs with bitumen inlay, one coffin-shaped, the other possibly dated 1764. In tower — eleven slabs include (1) of Eliza Lafargue, 1780, signed 'J. Hames', two others, mostly illegible, with bitumen-filled lettering and scroll flourishes, signed 'Harrison', and another with bitumen-filled scrollwork surround.

Niches: in N. and S. aisles, W. wall, two small recesses with miniature vaulting in the head, 15th-century. *Painting* (Fig. 21): in tower, high on N. wall, with pilasters, curved pediment, and verse: 'If you that do pretend to ring; you under take a dangerous thing; if that a bell you over throw; two pence must pay before you go. 1694'. The ringing gallery at the level of this painting was removed in 1856 (LAO, Faculty Book, 14/5). *Piscinae*: in S. chapel — (1), in E. wall, double recess with central shaft and engaged side-shafts, water-holding bases, bell-shaped capitals carrying roundheaded arches, and two fluted drain sinkings, 13th-century (Plate 9); (2), in S. wall, recess with cinquefoil head, mutilated shelf on rear wall, 15th-century. *Plate*: cup (ht. 8 ins.), tapered stem with knop, inscribed 'gift of Richard Cumberland vicar . . .', and cover paten, by Anthony Nelme 1691; flagon (ht. 10 ins.), flat domed lid, inscribed as gift of Edward Curtis on 25 December 1709, by John Wisdom 1709; funnel with detachable strainer by Samuel Godbehere 1811; plate or paten (diam. 8¼ ins.), inscribed beneath as gift of Anna Lawson in 1707, London 1706; stand paten, inscribed as bequest of John Palmer in 1706, by William Looker 1706. *Recess*: in W. wall of vestry, plain jambs and pointed head, with brick repairs, medieval. *Sundial*: on parapet of S. aisle, pedimented stone panel, early 18th-century. *Table*: oak, with turned baluster legs and shaped rails, repaired, 17th-century. *Miscellaneous*: over chancel arch, stone shield with merchant's mark of Browne, possibly brass, date unknown.

Fig. 21   (28) Church of All Saints.
Wall painting in tower, 1694.

(29) PARISH CHURCH OF ST. GEORGE (Fig. 22; Plate 27) stands at the E. end of St. George's Square within a small churchyard. The walls are of limestone, some being 'Barnack' with diagonal tooling, and the roofs are lead-covered. The church consists of a *Chancel*, *Nave* with *Aisles*, *Transepts* and *W. Tower*. The church received a gift of timber from Henry III in 1229 (10 copulas . . . ad operationem ecclesie Sancti Georgii', *Cal. Close*, 1227–31, 273). A later gift, in 1244, was specifically for an aisle ('iiij quercus ad maeremium ad constructionem unius ale, que de novo construitur in predicta ecclesia', *ibid.*, 1242–7, 208). The surviving nave pier bases are in accord with this latter date. Also of the mid 13th century is the E. part of the tower and the reset tower arch.

Early in the 14th century the nave arcades were remodelled and heightened, reusing the pier bases and ashlar from the earlier shafts. Later in the 14th century the chancel arch was rebuilt, and the wall between it and the N.E. respond pierced with an archway. During the mid 15th century the chancel was rebuilt, the completion of the work being made possible by the bequest of Sir William Bruges, first Garter King-of-Arms, who died in March 1450 (Lambeth Palace, Register of Archbishop Stafford, ff. 186v–187v); at the same time an archway was inserted in the long E. respond of the S. arcade, perhaps in connection with one of the

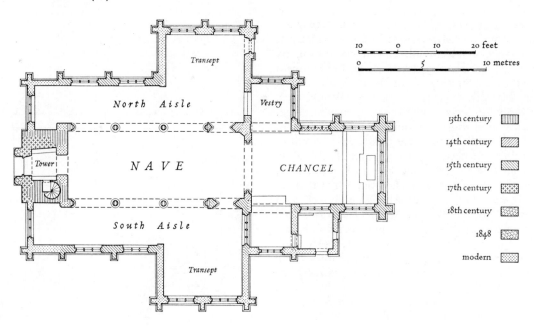

13th century
14th century
15th century
17th century
18th century
1848
modern

Fig. 22　(29) Church of St. George.

chapels referred to in Bruges' will. In the second half of the 15th century the nave was reroofed and the aisles were rebuilt. The markedly oblong plan of the W. tower appears to be the result of the rebuilding of the western half and the upper two stages, possibly in the 17th century. The addition of the clearstorey, perhaps also in the 17th century, necessitated the resetting of the 15th-century roof at a higher level. A number of alterations were made in the late 19th century: a 'new vestry' referred to in 1862 may relate to the present N. vestry (church documents); an organ chamber and porch, S. of the chancel, were added at a cost of £164 by E. Browning in 1878; the N. and S. transepts were built, the aisles lengthened to the W., and the organ chamber and vestry altered at a total cost of £800 by J. C. Traylen in 1887 (LAO, Faculty Books 8/97, 9/423). The church is notable for the documented date of the chancel, and its association with the order of St. George.

Architectural Description — The *Chancel* has a battlemented parapet with large beast-head gargoyles. The E. window has a four-centred head with vertical tracery and transom over the central light. The side walls have windows of four graduated lights in four-centred heads; the third on the N. has been reset in the E. wall of the vestry, and the third on the S. in the E. wall of the S. transept. The 15th-century S. doorway, replaced by a modern one, has been reset in the E. wall of the organ chamber (engraving of 1727 in Peck, XIV,

opp. p. 23). The late 14th-century chancel arch with two-centred head has two orders, the outer continuous, the inner rising from semi-octagonal shafts with plain bases and moulded capitals. The *Nave* (Plate 14) has uniform N. and S. arcades with long E. responds. The central bay is wider than those on the E. and W. The 13th-century water-holding bases to piers and responds are circular, and the piers are in three sections: the central is circular, and the octagonal form of the lower and upper sections is continued in the coved capitals. The circular elements are 13th-century, the octagonal 14th-century. The arches are double-chamfered, the first and the third bays being two-centred and the wider central bays depressed. In the long E. respond on the N. is an inserted late 14th-century opening with continuous moulded jambs and head of three orders, symmetrical on the N. and S., the two outer wave-moulded and the inner hollow-chamfered, all stopped on a plain chamfered plinth. On the S. the corresponding 15th-century opening has a four-centred head, moulded jambs and head of three orders, the outer two being continuous and hollow-chamfered, the inner having wave-moulded head with moulded caps and bases; the mouldings stop on a high chamfered plinth, much renewed. High up at the E. end of the N. wall is a blocked two-centred doorway to the former rood loft; across the N.E. angle is a 19th-century blocking, until 1887 pierced with an opening to the pulpit. The embattled clearstorey, perhaps of the early 17th century, has windows of two lights with two-centred heads within rectangular openings. The N. and S. *Aisles* are uniform and were rebuilt, apparently totally, in the mid 15th century. The embattled parapets have beast-head gargoyles. Windows which survived the 19th-century alterations have triangular heads and three cinquefoiled lights; others have been reset in the N. wall of the vestry, the S. wall of the organ chamber, the transepts and the aisle-extensions. The rear arch of the E. window of the N. aisle remains, but the jambs have been cut straight. Four rounded corbels in the aisle related to an earlier aisle roof.

The *N.* and *S. Transepts* incorporate some reused medieval masonry in the lower courses of the wall. A gargoyle with fabulous beast's head has been reset in the N. transept wall.

The *W. Tower* is of four stages without buttresses (Plate 27). The plan is oblong as a result of the W. part being rebuilt, and a straight joint in the S. wall indicates the limit of this rebuilding in the 17th century. The entirely rebuilt upper two stages have battered sides and the parapet is battlemented. The 13th-century tower arch has been reset at a higher level; it has two quadrant-shaped shafts on the E., a double-chamfered arch and bell capitals with abaci enriched with nail-head. The 14th-century W. window with flowing tracery forming a pattern of intersecting ogee curves has been reset (cf. similar window at Canford church, Northamptonshire); other windows at belfry level, with pointed heads, transoms and wooden rear lintels are 17th-century. On the E. an area of masonry with a small two-centred opening, at nave roof level, is a survival of the 13th-century tower. On the N. and S. are rough projections being the remains of the former W. walls of the aisles. The shallow projecting W. porch, built in 1848 to a design by E. Browning (vestry book), has a trefoil-headed doorway of 13th-century character and a 17th-century rear arch.

The mid 15th-century *Roof* over the chancel is low-pitched, in three bays with cambered tie beams, moulded purlins, ridge piece with square foliated bosses at the intersections, battlemented cornice, and intermediate principal rafters at the feet of which are winged demi-angels holding shields carved with (a) cross of St. George, (b) hands and feet, (c) a heart, all painted in modern times. The E. and W. end trusses have moulded arch braces and battlemented wall posts. The central bay and the two unmoulded tie beams are renewals. The reset nave roof follows the design of that in the chancel, but is in four bays; the tie beams are arch-braced, and mortices in the intermediate principal rafters indicate former demi-angels which were removed when the roof was reset, to avoid the clearstorey windows. One boss is carved with a swan, the remainder are foliated. The N. and S. aisle roofs, originally of four bays, are single-pitch versions of the foregoing but much renewed; some square foliated bosses and the mortices for demi-angels survive. The N. roof is at a higher level than the S.

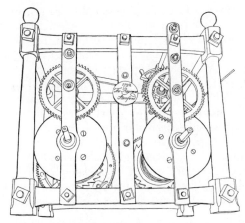

Fig. 23   (29) Church of St. George. Clock, 1792.

Fittings — *Bells*: 1st by Thomas Eayre, 1761; 2nd, 1777; 3rd by Arnold, 1797; 4th, attributed to Toby Norris III, 1697. *Bell frame*: possibly medieval but reset and altered with addition of upper tier to take bell of 1697. *Clock* (Fig. 23): iron frame with round standards, ball finials, and circular plate inscribed '1792 Thos. Rayment, Stamford'; it cost £24 (Churchwardens' Accounts). *Clock dial*: on W. face of tower, wood, octagonal, 18th-century. *Font*: limestone, lead-lined, octagonal bowl cut with vertical and tapering sides, moulded stem and base, probably medieval. *Glass*: in chancel (1) in first window on N., 130 complete quarries and 60 half-quarries, many being copies, depicting the Garter with black-letter motto (Fig. 25), yellow-stain, reset remnants from backgrounds of portraits of the Knights of St. George, second half 15th century (W. A. Rees-Jones, *The Order of St. George*; H. Stanford London, 'The Life of William Bruges...', *Harleian Soc.* CXI, CXII (1970); copies by Dugdale, 1641, Earl of Winchelsea collection); (2) in S. window (Plate 38), crowned figure of St. Catherine with emblems of martyrdom, under architectural canopy, against modern background, fragments of black-letter inscription (recorded fully by Peck (1727) XIV, 24); roundel with head of mitred prelate (Plate 39); figure of St. Anne, heavily restored, teaching the Virgin to read, under architectural canopy, and with modern background; roundel with head of man, probably a Garter portrait; all 15th-century. In N. aisle (3) in W. window, assembly of fragments including Garter quarry, lion's head, angel, architectural decoration and black-letter inscriptions, all 15th-century. In S. aisle (4) three Garter quarries, head of the 14th century, architectural decoration, 15th-century, made up with head of man, *c.* 1500. Much of the medieval glass remained until the 18th century; Stukeley records that 'walking by Exton the glaziers door I saw a cart load of painted glass just taken from St. George's Church' (*Surtees Society* 76 (1883), 328).

Monuments: in chancel — on N. wall (1), of John Wyldbore, 1674, on sill of first window, dark stone inscription tablet set in limestone surround with jewelled pilasters and scrolled cresting enclosing painted shield for Wyldbore (Fig. 24); (2), of Rev. Richard Atlay, 1832, white marble tablet with scrolled cresting, signed 'Smith'; (3), of Savile Cockayne Cust, 1772, marble, circular inscription panel between fluted pilasters supporting cornice and urn of coloured scagliola, within a draped niche, surmounted by oval shield of arms of Cust, Cockayne and Savile, signed 'W. Tyler' (Plate 52); (4), of Ursulah Cust, daughter of Edward Woodcocke, 'Jan. 1683/4', marble cartouche with floral and drapery swags at top and sides, crest and shield of

Fig. 24 (29) Church of St. George.
Wall monument (1) to John Wyldbore, 1674.

arms of Cust impaling Woodcocke, six oval plaques, applied later to swags, to Sir Pury Cust, 'Feb. 1798/9', Sir Richard Cust, 1700, Samuel Cust, 1662, Mary Woodcocke, 'Feb. 1682/3', Sir Richard Cust, 1734, and Mary Thompson, 1718, together with Ursulah Newton, 1757 (Plate 52); (5), of Sir Richard Cust, 1734, and Anne (Brownlow) his wife, 1779, white marble statuary with veined marble obelisk background, set against rusticated ashlar blocking of second window, with plinth bearing inscription flanked by low relief panels depicting a lion with staff, and hand mirror with snakes, and supporting statuary consisting of female figure and

pillar carved with arms of Cust quarterly impaling Brownlow, and carrying a male portrait-bust, signed on plinth 'J. Bacon R.A. Sculptor London 1797' (Plate 51); on S. wall (6), of Rev. Thomas Darke, 1839, repeating design of (2), signed 'Smith'; (7), of Dr. James Oldershaw, 1796, white marble inscription panel with enriched classical surround including emblems of Aesculapius, surmounted by veined marble obelisk, urn, and shield of arms of Oldershaw with escutcheon for Roe, signed 'Sparrow'; below, added triangular apron to Anne (Roe) his wife, 1801; on W. wall (8), of Rev. R. L. Carr, 1811, plain marble tablet with obelisk, signed 'Spencer'; (9), of Francis Butt, 1840, and daughters Mary, 1838, Leonora, 1839, and Selina (Welby), shaped white marble tablet signed 'Smith'; (10), of Henry Smith, 1833, white marble tablet signed 'Smith'. In nave — on N. wall (11), of Margaret Thompson (Northon), 1805, white marble tablet surmounted by urn, signed 'Sparrow'; (12), of Rev. John Northon, 1781, Elizabeth his wife, 1796, and two sons, white marble tablet with fluted pilasters, moulded cornice, terminal urns and stunted obelisk; (13), of Martha Merveilleux, 1824, and daughter Caroline Aird, 1825, by Gilbert; on S. wall (14), of Caroline May, 1837, and brother, Henry, 1837; (15), of Sarah Clay, 1830, Samuel and Arthur, 1842, and five infants, with later apron; (16), of John Butt, 1831. Monuments listed above without full description are of white marble and simple design. In N. aisle (17), of Tobie Norris, inscribed bell-metal panel composed of bell-founders' dies, 'Here lieth the body of Tobie Norris Belfoun: who decea: the 2 of No 1626' (Plate 53); indent for panel is in limestone slab in the N. aisle. Attached externally — on N. transept (18), of John Cole, 1797, mason, tablet with floral frame surmounted by obelisk carved with cherub's head, possibly executed by Cole family; on S. side, five oval or shaped tablets, dated between 1789 and 1823. In churchyard — approximately 25 headstones, the earliest dated 1699, the remainder 18th-century, many enriched with scrollwork and emblems of mortality; also four in slate, the earliest dated 1777, and a large number of later headstones.

Plate: Stand paten (diam. 8 ins.), inscribed '1707 given to St. George's in Stamford for the service of ye Communion by E.G.', by Henry Greene, 1706; cup (ht. 7 ins.), beaker-shaped bowl with wide stem, inscribed 'given by the will of Dame Alice Cust to St. George's Church in Stamford 1715', by Michael Boult, 1715; flagons, a pair (ht. 11 ins.), tapered sides, domed lids, inscribed as on cup, by Boult, 1715. *Rainwater heads*: on chancel and transepts, half-round, lead, embossed with cherubs' heads, 18th-century. *Screen*: lower part reset in N. transept, in four bays with blind cusped tracery, foliage in spandrels, 15th-century. *Sundial*: on S. face of tower, limestone panel, 18th-century. *Table*: oak, with bulbous legs, early 17th-century, remodelled.

Fig. 25 (29) Church of St. George.
Glass (1) depicting Garter.

(30) PARISH CHURCH OF ST. JOHN BAPTIST (Fig. 26; Plate 26), has a churchyard on the S. and houses built close to it on the E. and N. It comprises a *Chancel, N.* and *S. Chapels, Nave* with *Aisles, N.W. Tower* and *S. Porch.* The walls are mostly of limestone ashlar and the roofs are lead-covered. The earliest survivals are some late 12th-century voussoirs said to have been found built into the chancel arch (see *Miscellaneous*); rough masonry N. of the chancel arch may be the remains of the E. aisle wall of the same date, subsequently cut back. Sloping weathercourses on the S. and E. sides of the tower relate to a continuous roof over a former nave and N. aisle; the low pitch of the weathercourse over the aisle, implying a late medieval date for its former roof, suggests that an earlier structure had been, or was intended to be, reroofed. In either

event these features show that the construction of the tower preceded the rebuilding of the nave and aisle. The present church is in appearance entirely of the 15th century. Peck in 1727 (Peck, XIV, 36–7) records that two windows, in the N. chapel and N. aisle, had glass inscribed 1451, a date which is also reasonable for the structure. Restorations in 1897 under J. C. Traylen, architect, included a new vestry, removal of the font from nave to S. aisle, and restoration of screens to their original positions (LAO, Faculty Book 11/9).

The church is noteworthy for its unified design resulting from its construction within a short span in the 15th century. It has been little altered. Notable fittings include 15th-century glass and screens, and an 18th-century English altar frontal and pulpit cloth.

Architectural Description — The *Chancel* has lateral buttresses of two stages with cusped gabled tops, and battlemented parapets. The E. window, of five cinquefoil lights and no tracery, has a low internal sill; the N. and S. windows repeat this design. The low sill of the N. window has a projecting chamfered slab. The S. doorway, now serving the vestry, has a four-centred inner and square outer head and foliated spandrels. The N. and S. arches are of two wave-moulded orders, the outer continuous with label and grotesque headstops, the inner carried on half-rounded responds with semi-octagonal bases and crenellated caps; the chancel arch is similar but has semi-octagonal responds. The *N.* and *S. Chapels* and the *Aisles* have windows of cinquefoil lights and vertical tracery. Arches between chapels and aisles die into the side walls. The rood loft stair, entered from the S. aisle, is part octagonal below the parapet

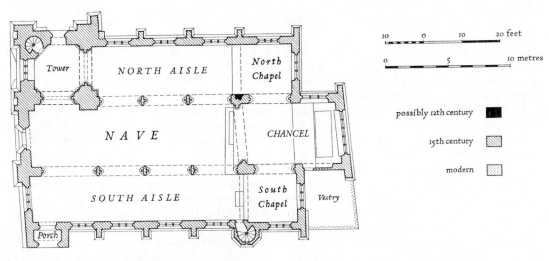

Fig. 26 (30) Church of St. John Baptist.

and octagonal above, with a band of blind quatrefoils, false battlementing and stone octagonal top.

The *Nave* (Plate 21) has arcades with piers and responds having half-rounded shafts, semi-octagonal bases and caps, and arches of two moulded orders, the outer continuous but terminating on a lower base. The W. window, of five cinquefoiled ogee lights, has intersecting tracery over the centre and outer lights and vertical tracery over the remainder. The W. doorway, blocked internally, has continuous moulded jambs and four-centred head, and human head stops. The battlemented clearstorey has two-light cinquefoiled windows with triangular heads.

The *N.W. Tower* of five external stages has clasping and pilaster buttresses, battlemented parapets enriched with band of quatrefoils, crocketed pinnacles and diagonally-placed gargoyles carved as grotesques. The lowest stage, above a high weathered plinth, has a N. doorway with two-centred head and continuous wave-and-hollow moulded jambs; the W. window of three cinquefoiled lights with simple tracery rises into the second stage. On N. and W. of the third stage are quatrefoil openings in a square surround. All four faces of the fifth stage have belfry windows each of four lights with a mullion rising to the apex. Inside, the tower arches repeat the design of the nave arcades but are lower, narrower and with mouldings of bolder profile. Engaged angle shafts rise to the ringing chamber and terminate with the moulded springing for intended vaulting. Weathercourses on the E. and S. faces relating to former nave and aisle roofs are referred to in the introduction; blocked recesses for rafters of the earlier nave roof are traceable below the weathercourse on the S.

The very shallow *S. Porch* has an archway with numerous engaged shafts with caps and bases supporting a multi-moulded two-centred arch with ogee crocketed label and demi-angel stops; the battlemented parapet has central and terminal pinnacles and side gargoyles carved as animals.

The *Roofs* are mid 15th-century; that over the chancel (Plate 21), of three bays, has cambered tie beams, short king posts, queen struts, pierced arcade infilling, braces to wall posts each with three-quarter angels holding shields, a book and other emblems; the central bosses are floriated. The angels are crudely carved and the wings are missing; in 1623 John Bassett was paid 18d. for cutting angels' wings (Vestry Book). The nave roof (Plate 22), of eight bays, rests directly on cambered tie beams and the wall posts are supported on stone demi-figures carved as human grotesques; the intermediate principals terminate as three-quarter angels either in prayer or holding emblems which include a crown, sceptre, musical instrument and a flask (?) (Plate 23). At the intersections of the main members are foliated bosses. The roofs over N. chapel and N. aisle are lean-to

with moulded purlins and principals alternately arch-braced to wall posts or terminating as three-quarter angels; the S. aisle roof repeats the design but the wall posts are longer and terminate as small demi-angels. At the junctions of the purlins and principals are foliated bosses.

Fittings — *Bells*: four; 1st, with floriated cross, shield and inscription in Lombardic capitals, 'Richard Snamdon Parson Anno 1561'; 2nd, recast in 1814 by Taylor of St. Neots and formerly dated 1516; 3rd, uninscribed, with three foundry marks, *c.* 1550–1650; 4th, as 1st, inscribed 'Robert Medoens Gent Tobe Lovadaie 1561' with some letters reversed. The number 6 on bells 1 and 4 is probably a reversed 9; Snowden was incumbent from 1572 to 1604. *Bell frame*: probably 1814. *Brasses and Indents. Brasses*: in S. chapel (1), on E. wall, of Phillip Johnson, January 1683, rectangular plate (Fig. 27; M–S. IV); (2), of Henry Sargeaunt, rector, died 1497, priest in vestments, indent below for inscription plate and in each corner quatrefoil indents (M–S. III); the slab (6 ft. 9 in. long) was reused in the 18th century and inscribed to Thomas Bright, 1774, and below brass is inscribed 'H.S. MCCCCLXXX . . .'. (Peck, XIV, 66–7, for inscription and evangelists' symbols). In Nave (3), of Nicholas Byldysdon and Kateryn his wife, 1489, male civilian in fur-lined gown, and female figure, plate with black-letter inscription in English, evangelists' symbols, two of which are modern, and two small plates for four male and five female children (M–S. II) (Plate 44); the brass was formerly in S. chapel and the present slab is only partly ancient (Peck, *ibid*). In N. aisle (4), of William Gregory and Agnes his wife, rectangular plate, black-letter inscription in Latin, 15th-century (M–S. I). In S. aisle (5), of Robert Ridlington, 1766, shaped plate. *Indents*: in S. chapel (1) and S. aisle (2), both rectangular. *Chest*: oak, 18th-century. *Dial*: scratched on first buttress of S. aisle, 15th-century. *Font*: limestone, octagonal with waisted stem, flared foot, roll-moulded arrises, and panels containing quatrefoils; 15th-century (Plate 40). *Font-cover*: oak, octagonal with scroll panelling, conical spire with debased crockets and leaf finial; 17th-century, repaired (Plate 54).

Glass: probably all installed in 1451 (see introduction). The glass was cleaned and partly rearranged in 1974 and some panels were reset in other windows. In chancel — (1), N. window, fragments in border. In N. aisle — (2), 1st window (reading from left to right): (a) and (b) saints; (c) 'Scs Augustin'; (d) 'Scs Ambro'; (e) and (f) mitred saints; demi-angels in tracery are *in situ*, remaining figures are new arrangements of old glass; canopy-work in heads of main lights. (3), 2nd window, six figures in tracery *in situ* (Plate 34); (a), (b), (e) and (f) show tonsured saints in blue habits with black-letter inscriptions below: (a) holding crozier and book, with hind at foot, inscribed 'S. Egidius' (Giles); (b) holding crozier and book, inscribed 'Scs Botulpus'; (c) mitred saint holding woolcomb, inscribed '. . Blasius' (Blaise); (d) mitred saint; (e) holding fetters, crozier and book, inscribed 'Scs Leonardus'; (f) holding tall cross and book, with knife in chest, inscribed 'S. Petrus de Mille' (St. Peter Martyr). (4), 3rd window, mostly *in situ*, six figures under canopies with feathered angels in tracery; (a), (b), (e) and (f) represent Cardinal Virtues, each holding swords, and are inscribed 'Sca Spes', 'Sca Fides', 'Sca Caritas' and 'Sca Sapiencia'; (c) Virgin of the Mantle sheltering miniature figures; (d) God the Father holding souls in folds of garment (Plate 34); also canopy-work. In S. chapel — (5), E. window, in tracery, figures *in situ* including 'S. Elizabet'; in main lights, assemblage of fragments, formerly in S. window of chancel and elsewhere, including a large demi-figure of a mitred saint holding crozier and in act of blessing, with inscription 'S. Oswaldus'; also fragments of prophets, heads of donors, a phoenix with halo, angels and lions. In S. aisle — (6), 1st window, in tracery partly *in situ*, six figures: (a) female figure; (b) 'Scs Marcus'; (c) St. Christopher and Christ child; (d) St. George and dragon; (e) 'Scs Matheus'; (f) 'Scs Johes'; also canopy-work. (7), 4th window, six figures of female saints including (a) 'Sca Petronilla', (b) St. Mary Magdalene, (c) 'Sca Etheldreda', (d) St. Catherine, (e) and (f) saints. *Masons' Marks*: throughout building, 15th-century (Fig. 6).

Monuments and Floor slabs. Monuments: in Nave — on N. wall (1), of Susanna Allen, 1825; (2), of Chamberlin White, 1847, by Daniel Gilbert; (3), of James White, 1820, and Phillis his wife, 1834, by Gilbert. In N. aisle — (4), of Rev. Charles Stokes, 1776, limestone cartouche; (5), of Cassandra Whitley, 1769, and Elizabeth Carrighan her daughter, 1813, and children, marble tablet with scrollwork sides and overthrow enclosing shield of arms and crest of Whitley; (6), of Samuel Allen, 1796, and Mary his wife, 1812, twin limestone tablets, obelisk and urn; (7), of William Gardner, 1792; (8), of Mary Mills, 1822; (9), of John Mills, 1832, and Jane his wife, 1840. In S. aisle — (10), of Ann Howgrave, 1764, and sons, shaped limestone tablet; (11), of Thomas Smith, 1760, and Sarah his wife, 1782, and Thomas, 1798, and Elizabeth his wife, 1792, marble tablet with reeded surround, shaped apron surmounted by urn and shaped background, by Sparrow; (12), of Mary Digby, 1737, limestone cartouche; (13), of William Ashby, 1820, and Ann, 1842, by Gilbert; (14), of John Booth, 1810, and Mary his wife, 1813, by Gilbert; (15) of John Booth, 1799, Coade stone relief of female figure mourning over urn, obelisk top, with inscription altered by infilling and painting, signed 'Coade London 1800' (Plate 52); (16), of John Bushby, 1788, and Martha his mother, 1789, limestone cartouche, by J. Hames; (17), of Solomon Woodroffe, 1769. Monuments listed above without full description are in

white marble and of simple design; (2), (3) and (13) are of some elaboration. Attached externally — (18) of Joseph Goodwin, 1825, Jane his wife, 1834, sarcophagus-shaped tablet; three undeciphered tablets. In churchyard — approximately nine enriched headstones of the 18th century and about 50 of later date; slate headstones include (1) of Elizabeth Irving, 1833, signed 'Danl. Gilbert'. *Floor slabs*: in chancel (1), of Robert Ste . ., 18th-century. In S. chapel — (2), of George Searson, 1772; (3), of Ann Smith (Woodroffe), 1837, black marble, lozenge-shaped; (4), of Thomas Bright, 1774, reinscribed slab of brass (2). In N. aisle — (5), date only, 1793; (6), of Richard and Mary Jennings, 1766; (7), of Elizabeth Ridlington, 18th-century, reinscribed slab of brass (4). In S. aisle — (8), of M.M., 1822, and C.M., 1845; (9), of Robert Ridlington, 1766, inscribed slab with brass (5).

Piscinae: in chancel (1) in S. wall, square recess with miniature vaulting; in S. aisle (2) in S. wall, recess with cinquefoiled head; both 15th-century. *Plate*: paten (diam. 9 ins.) with foot, inscribed as gift of Eli Mergerum in 1733, engraved with emblem of St. John Baptist, London 1691. *Screens* (Plate 41): at E. ends of N. and S. aisles, oak, each with dado of cusped arcading, double doors beneath segmental lintel entwined with foliage; above, are cusped ogee heads within two-centred arches containing window forms; carved on rear face and with indications of a former coved cornice; the S. screen returns without doors on S. of chancel; 15th-century. *Textiles*: Altar frontal, dark blue serge with yellow embossed embroidery depicting sacred monogram, emblems of Passion within a sunburst, and on lower edge 'With desire I have desired to eat this passover with you before I suffer. For I say unto you I will not any more eat thereof until it be fulfilled in the Kingdom of God. 1718' (Plate 53). Pulpit cloth, of dark blue material with white embossed lettering, 'St. John 1701' within a garland (Plate 53). *Miscellaneous*: in S. aisle, roll-moulded voussoirs of late 12th century, extracted during repairs to chancel arch.

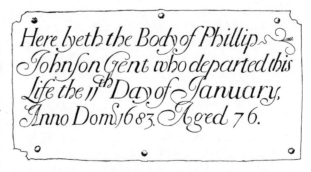

Fig. 27 (30) Church of St. John Baptist. Brass (1) to Phillip Johnson, 1683.

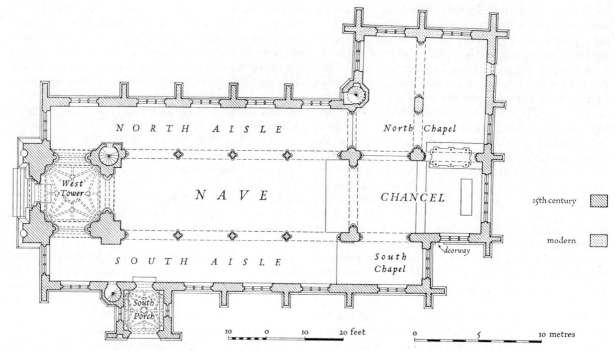

Fig. 28 (31) Church of St. Martin.

(31) PARISH CHURCH OF ST. MARTIN (Fig. 28; Plate 26) stands at the W. end of a rectangular churchyard part of which was removed in 1803 when the road was widened (NRO, C.C. Papers 19). It consists of a *Chancel* with *N.* and *S. Chapels*, *Nave* with *Aisles*, *W. Tower* and *S. Porch*. The walls are of limestone ashlar and the roofs are covered in cement tiles or lead. The church is entirely of the second half of the 15th century, but the steeply-pitched weathercourse associated with an earlier nave roof survives on the E. face of the tower; this weathercourse returns on the N. and S. of the tower indicating that the former nave and tower-aisles were left standing while the present tower was under construction. No early medieval feature survives but small-sized masonry in the lower part of the tower may be reused material. The chancel was reported as ruinous in 1473 but rebuilding appears not to have started before 1482 (Stamford Report 2, 31; LAO, Visit Vj. 4, f. 80d). Heraldry displayed on corbels in the nave implies that the rebuilding of the main body of the church was not completed before *c.* 1485: the arms are those of Chedworth, Bishop of Lincoln 1452–71; Russell, Bishop of Lincoln 1480–94; Rotherham (Scott), Archbishop of York 1480–1500; and probably Shirwood, Bishop of Durham 1485–94. The corbels were apparently inserted after

the arcade had been finished, perhaps to commemorate patronage on the completion of the rebuilding of the whole church; the inclusion of Chedworth's arms may indicate that the tower was built during his episcopacy. Although the arms here attributed to Shirwood are those normally given to Sherard, it is known that the names were interchangeable at least in the 17th century (J. Foster, *Alumni Oxoniensis*, 1500–1714); the appearance of the Bishop of Durham's arms is reasonable in view of the known association between that See and Stamford. The arms of Russell, Rotherham and Chedworth are repeated in the 15th-century glass where also the arms of Richard Fleming, Bishop of Lincoln 1421–31, are depicted.

The church has been little altered since the 15th century with the exception of the N. Chapel which was increased to double its area by additions on the N. in 1865. Fittings designed by E. Browning in 1845 included the Marquess of Exeter's pew, an altar screen, a pulpit and reading desk (Burghley Estate, Account books). The church is a notable example of late 15th-century architecture; the 15th-century glass and the Cecil monuments are the principal fittings.

Architectural Description — The *Chancel* has four-stage weathered buttresses and battlemented parapets.

The five-light E. window has vertical tracery in a four-centred head. Arches on N. and S. have half-round respond shafts, semi-octagonal moulded bases and caps with arches of two wave-moulded orders, the outer continuous with labels; this design is repeated through the church. In the S. wall the three-light window has a battlemented transom and simple tracery; the aisle windows also follow this pattern. A doorway on the S., with wave-moulded jambs and four-centred head, is blocked internally. The *N. Chapel*, doubled in size to the N. in 1865, has an acutely pointed arch which divides the original chapel E. and W. The arch between aisle and chapel is 19th-century; the aisle roof formerly continued as far as the dividing arch in the chapel (Plate 46). The 19th-century arch partly masks the blocked doorway to a semi-octagonal stair turret with conical roof, serving the rood loft. The *S. Chapel* has no arch between it and the aisle. The E. window has a higher sill below which the face is recessed for a reredos.

The *Nave* has lofty arcades with labels which terminate on eight widely projecting corbels carved as demi-angels holding shields (Plate 20); on the E. the labels pass below the rood-loft openings in the respond. The four E. shields are carved, on the N. with arms of Russell (*two chevronells between three roses*) and Shirwood or Sherard (*a chevron between three roundels*), and on the S. with arms of Archbishopric of York impaling Rotherham (Scott) (*crozier in pale surmounted by pall charged with four crosses paty fitchy impaling three bucks trippant*) and Chedworth (*chevron between three foxes' heads erased*). The four W. shields are blank. These corbels, evidently inserted soon after the completion of the arcade, may have served as bases for figures. The *N.* and *S. Aisles* continue the architectural treatment of the chancel. The S. doorway has wave-and-bracket moulded jambs and four-centred head.

The *W. Tower*, of four external stages with clasping buttresses, rises to ornate cusped and battlemented parapets with crocketed pinnacles (Plate 26). The W. doorway has continuous wave-and-casement mouldings; the W. window has three lights with vertical tracery and labels returning as string-courses. The belfry windows of four cinquefoiled lights each have a pronounced central mullion rising to the apex of the almost semicircular head. Above the E. tower arch is a hollow-moulded weathercourse, following the roof line of the former nave, which returns on N. and S. indicating a nave without clearstoreys, and aisle roofs of slightly lower pitch than that of the nave (Plate 20). Impinging upon the sloping weathercourse is a deeply weathered offset of external character which continues on N., S. and W.; above, on the E., is a blocked opening with cambered head. The N. and S. tower arches are lower than the E. arch but are continued within higher, plainly chamfered, arches on the tower sides. Engaged shafts with moulded caps and bases carry the springing of wall, diagonal and

intermediate ribs of a vault completed in modern times. Squinches for an intended spire survive.

The *S. Porch* of two storeys has a pitched roof with battlemented parapets. Above the archway of many orders is a three-light window in a four-centred head. The upper floor is carried on a quadripartite vault of minimal pitch with intermediate ribs springing from four demi-angels holding shields carved with unidentified devices; the ribs meet at a central boss carved as a demi-angel holding a shield with arms of See of Lincoln (*two lions passant facing sinister, on a chief the Virgin and Child throned*) (Plate 18). The upper compartment is reached by an externally projecting stair turret with conical stone roof.

Fittings — *Altar*: stone slab with five crosses, on main altar, probably medieval but totally recut (*Gent's Mag.*, Sept. 1861, 278). *Bells*: six by Meares dated 1850. *Bell frame*: 1850. *Benefactors' table*: large wooden panel with eared surround, open pediment, recording charities from 1592 by Cecil and other families; 18th-century. *Bracket*: in S. aisle, E. wall, battlemented, 15th-century. *Brass*: in nave, panel inscribed 'ID 1815, EKD 1828, EH 1839'. *Chandelier*: brass, inscribed 'Robt Phillpott Chris^t Burtoff Church-wardens 1732', doubtless by Joseph Willford, brass founder, who was paid £20 (churchwardens' accounts, 1732–3); now in Victoria and Albert Museum. *Chests*: four, three of oak, one of softwood with fielded panelled front; all 18th-century. *Doors*: to tower vice (1), oak, of two planks with strap hinges; to porch vice (2), oak, with strap hinges and original lock; to chamber over porch (3), oak, keel-section planks, some original furniture including escutcheon and ring, and bolt; all 15th-century. *Font*: octagonal limestone bowl, tapering sides decorated with window forms in shallow relief, early 14th-century (Plate 40).

Glass: Five windows contain an assemblage of glass of various dates and provenances; some has always been in St. Martin's although in 1737 it is recorded that all the painted glass was taken away (Surtees Soc. 76 (1883), 325). Much of the existing glass was removed from Tattershall church (see below) in February 1757 having been given by Lord Fortescue to the Earl of Exeter (*Lincolnshire Notes and Queries* (1889), 1–3). Other glass from Tattershall is in Burghley House. Two windows were assembled with ancient glass by Peckitt of York in 1759, and four in 1760, but only five windows are now traceable (York City Art Gallery, Peckitt MSS Box D3; VCH, *Northamptonshire II*, 528; Burton, 267; *Gent's Mag.* (1862), 336–41; A. E. Dixon, 'Shields in Ancient Glass . . .', Northants. and Oakham Arch. Soc. XXXVII (II) (1925), 316). The glass listed below is of the second half of the 15th century unless otherwise stated. In chancel — E. window (1) (Fig. 29), in tracery, shields (a) perhaps of Latimer (*gules a cross flory within a border azure with eleven crosses potent argent*), (b) St. Gilbert of Sempringham perhaps of the Gilbertine hall in Stamford (*argent three bars gules overall a long cross in bend azure*), (c) Archbishopric of York impaling Rotherham (Scott) (*azure a crozier in pale surmounted by a pall argent charged with five crosses paty fitchy impaling vert three stags trippant argent*), (d) Abbey of Peterborough (*gules two keys in saltire between four crosses fitchy or*), (e) Fleming, for Richard, Bishop of Lincoln 1421–31, (*argent two bars azure on a chief three lozenges gules*), (f) monastery of St. Cuthbert, Durham, or the abbey of Bardney, Lincs. (*azure a cross flory or between four lions rampant argent*), and late 16th-century shields of (g) Walcot, (h) Gylby, (i) unidentified (*three birds or*), (j) Ogell, (k) Ayscough and (l) Panell; in the two central lights (A) is an Annunciation scene (Plate 35) with scrolls inscribed ' . . . . gra plena' and 'ancilla dñi'; in main lights, shields of (m) Chedworth, for John, Bishop of Lincoln 1452–71 (*azure a chevron between three wolves'/foxes' heads or*); (n) Russell (twice), for John, Bishop of Lincoln 1480–94 (*azure two chevronells or between three roses argent*); (o) St. George in Garter, crowned; (p) 16th-century shields with Royal Arms in Garter, (q) Sheffield (quarters: 1 Sheffield, 2 Gonston, 3 Beltoft, 4 Delves, 5 Rochford, 6 Ferriby, 7 Staunton); (r) Borough (quarterly: 1 and 4 Borough, 2 Cobham, 3 Percy quartering Athole), and late 16th-century shields of (s1) Holland, (s2) Bertie, (s3) Irby, (s4) Meeres, (t1) Bilsby, 1565, (t2) Copledyke, (t3) Baude, with date 1565, and (t4) Bushy; (u) shield of Cecil, possibly that supplied by Peckitt in 1759 for £1 11s. 6d. (York City Art Gallery, Peckitt MSS, 6); in upper parts of main lights, (B) four demi-angels (Plate 35); in centre part, (C) four mitred saints, one an Archbishop, three with croziers, and (D) figure of God enthroned; the window was completed by Peckitt with panels of chequer work and other patterns composed of ancient glass fragments, and a variety of miniature heads of the 15th and 16th centuries (Plate 39). The demi-angels (B) and the saints (C) are certainly from Tattershall church; the shields (a) to (f) and (m) and (n) have always been at St. Martin's. S. window of chancel (2), in tracery, angels playing dulcimers; in part above transom, two demi-angels, angel holding raiment; in heads of main lights, canopy work; in centre, male heads, late 15th and 16th-century; below transom, three figures, one with halo, crown, sceptre and book, the second an amalgamation of two figures, the third with book; completed in brightly coloured glass by Peckitt. In S. chapel — E. window (3) in tracery, crowned saint's head and angel's head; above transom, two demi-angels and 16th-century shield of Clinton quartering Say within Garter; in centre, shield of Lord Cromwell of Tattershall (*argent a chief gules overall a bend azure, a label ermine*); below transom, three hieratic saints, two with mitres, the centre holding cross staff (the head extraneous), apostle's head; completed with patterns of

Fig. 29 (31) Church of St. Martin. Diagram showing arrangement of glass in E. window.

brightly coloured glass by Peckitt and incorporating four heads probably of the 16th century. S. window (4), in tracery, two heads; above transom, two demi-angels and two figures from a Trinity (?), early 16th-century, and below, two 19th-century shields; below transom, two saints one with crozier and book (the heads modern or from elsewhere); and in centre fragmentary figure with extraneous crowned head; made up with miniature heads in cinquefoils, medieval from various sources, and patterns of garish glass by Peckitt. In S. aisle — first window (5), in tracery, heads; above transom, three Old Testament scenes, Moses striking the rock, Samson carrying gates of Gaza, and David slaying Goliath; below transom, three New Testament scenes, the Crucifixion, the three Maries at the Tomb (one head extraneous) and the Resurrection; the scenes include appropriate inscriptions in black-letter on scrolls; included are 15th-century shields of Goldsborough (*azure a cross flory argent*), possibly of Marmyon (*vair a fess gules*), of Grey of Rotherfield (*argent three bars azure a bend azure*), family of Russell (*argent a chevron between three crosses crosslet fitchy sable*), the See of Lincoln (*gules three lions passant or, on a chief azure, the Virgin and Child enthroned*) and Bishop Russell, all flanked by angels. The six scenic panels (Plate 35), based on illustrations in the *Biblia Pauperum* and representing type and antitype episodes, come from a large series originally in the chancel of Tattershall church. Stamford glaziers were paid for providing glass in the nave of Tattershall church in 1480–2 (H.M.C., 77, Lord De L'Isle and Dudley, I, 198–9), but the glass in the chancel was probably slightly earlier. The shields of Cromwell, Goldsborough, Marmyon and Grey also come from Tattershall (Holles' Church Notes, BM, Harl MS. 6829).

The shield of Borough, and other 16th-century shields, probably came from Snape; Lord Borough married Katherine Parr later wife of Lord Latimer of Danby and Snape. The arms of sees, monastic houses and bishops, now mostly in the E. window, are likely to have been made for St. Martin's; vanished shields of Gray, Alnwick and Lumley, recorded by Peck in 1727, complete a sequence of arms of Lincoln bishops from Fleming (1420–31) to Russell (1480–94) (Peck, XIV, 68, Plate 68(I)). Besides the four demi-angels and the four mitred saints in window (1), the two demi-angels and three major figures in each of windows (2), (3) and (4) also came from Tattershall where fragments in the same style remain.

Hatchments: in Burghley chapel, one of 1st Marquess of Exeter, 1804 and three of late 19th century. *Masons' Marks*: in tower, 15th-century (Fig. 6).

Monuments, and *Floorslabs*. *Monuments*: in chancel — beneath N. arch (1) (Plates 47, 48), of William Cecil, first Lord Burghley d. (1598), elaborate free standing composition of various coloured marbles, some painted, consisting of tomb chest on podium supporting Corinthian columns, canopy of twin arches with coffered soffits, and cresting comprising obelisks, strapwork and pilastered centre-piece with scroll finials and shaped pediment; the chest has inscribed panels and carries alabaster effigy on rolled mat, in Greenwich armour, mantle with Garter badge, wand of office in right hand and lion at feet; shields in cresting are of Cecil, Cecil impaling Cheek, and Cecil impaling Cooke, with crests of Cecil as central finials. (2), of Elizabeth Plumptre, 1806, by W. Harrison; (3) of Cyril Jackson, 1797, and Judith his wife, 1785, by Westmacott. In N. chapel — (4) (Plate 46), of Richard Cecil, 1552, and Jane his wife, 1587, ornate composition of various marbles comprising plinth with cypher-and-square decoration, podium with miniature kneeling children, Corinthian columns flanking arch within which are male and female kneeling figures, he in Greenwich armour, central inscription tablet with pediment as prayer desk; above, cresting consists of obelisks, strapwork and centre-piece incorporating arms of Cecil quartering Winston, Heckinton, Walcot, Caerleon. (5) (Plates 49, 50, 51), of John Cecil, fifth Earl of Exeter, 1700, and Anne (Cavendish) his wife, 1703, classical statuary group comprising male and female figures reclining in Roman attire on inscribed sarcophagus, flanked by figures of Victory and the Arts (Plate 51), against a grey marble background composed of urns and a pyramid topped by a putto holding snake, and enriched by scroll-cartouche with arms of Cecil impaling Cavendish; the plinths to the figures are crudely inscribed 'Petrus Stephanus Monnot Bisuntinus fecit Romae MDCCIV'. The monument was commissioned by Cecil but was not completed until the year after his widow's death. It was installed by William Palmer

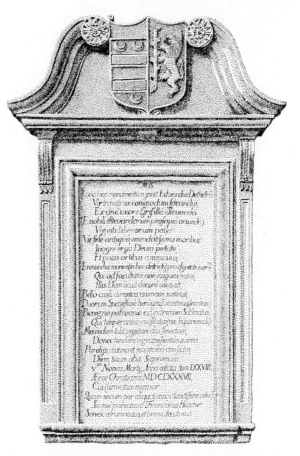

Fig. 30   (31) Church of St. Martin. Monument (11) of Edward Dethe, 1687.

(Gunnis, 261–2, 287–8, on the evidence of Le Neve, *Monumenta Anglicana*) who may have also carved the architectural setting; the flanking figures, unfinished at the back, are not integrated into the design of the monument and the central group is placed directly, without a moulding, on the sarcophagus. Payment in 1706 of £208.5.4. for 'Mr. Balle's bill freight and charges on a monument' and in the following year of £8.2.6. for 'charges of a monument lying in London' (Child's Bank ledgers) may refer to this monument. Monuments (4) and (5) were originally sited against the N. wall of the former N. chapel (engraving publ. by S. Sharp and Ackermann) (Plate 46). In S. chapel — (6), of John Truman, January 1788, and his wives Mary, February 1747, and Lettice, 1762, and the latter's sister Margaret Mawby, 1773, white and polychrome marble, circular tablet with cusped pilasters, urn and apron with arms of Truman, signed 'Bingham, Peterbro' '; and incorporated above, (7), of Thomas Truman, 1810, by Harrison; (8), of Martha Etough (Sanderson), 1833, and others, with arms, by Smith of Stamford; (9), of James Davie, 1785, Ann, 1797, and Catherine Bellaers, 1788, shaped tablet with apron incorporating circular plaque,

Fig. 31   (31) Church of St. Martin. Monument (19) of William Wissing, the painter, 1687.

swags and urn on cornice, signed 'Bingham, Peterbro''. In N. aisle — (10), of Mary and Henrietta Mottram, 1814 and 1817, with heavy floral swag beneath lozenge of arms of Mottram, flanked by reversed torches; (11), of Edward Dethe, 1687, limestone, with impaled shield of arms in scroll pediment (Fig. 30); (12), of George Neunburg, 1822; (13), of William Mackenzie, 1770, Colonel in the Russian service, ' . . . his private virtues are impressed on the souls of all connected with him in characters more legible and permanent than any of which marble is susceptible . . .', white and grey veined marble with shaped apron, crest of Mackenzie, and obelisk background (Plate 52); also of Mary Humberstone, 1813; (14), of John Lawson, 1828, and Frances his wife, 1834, by Gilbert; (15), of William Harper, 1803, and Catherine his sister, wife of Healy Chapman, 1797, in white, yellow and grey marbles, signed 'Bingham, Peterbro' ' (i.e. James Bingham); (16), of Bridget, daughter of Sir Arthur Hesilrige, 1813, and Hannah her sister, 1822, tablet, apron enriched with lozenge of arms

of Heselrigg, and background obelisk and urn; (17), of Joseph Phillips, 1833, and Judith his wife, 1837, and others, by Gilbert; (18), of James Holman, 1831, and Mary his wife, 1838, by Smith; (19) of William Wissing, the artist, 1687, limestone, scroll pediment and emblems of mortality (Fig. 31). In S. aisle — (20), of Henry Fryer, 1789, and Ann his wife, 1793, with apron and obelisk background; (21), of Henry Fryer, 1823, and Martha his sister, 1801, Gothic design with arms of Fryer; (22), of Joseph Michael, 1838, and Amelia his wife, 1833, as (8); (23), of Kirby Freer, 1830; (24), of Samuel Judd, 1826, and children, with arms of Judd impaling; (25), of John Davies, 1815, and Elizabeth Hodson, his grandaughter, 1839, and Elizabeth Hodson his daughter, 1848, with arms of Davies; (26), of Henry Allin, 1850, and others, by Fearn; (27), of Samuel Judd, 1801, and Susanna his wife, 1818, and five children, with shaped apron, obelisk and side brackets; (28), of Elizabeth Judd (Strachan), 1802, and Louisa Judd (Woodlett), 1814, and children; (29), of George Betts, 1814; (30), of John Neale, 1797, oval; (31), of Noah Neale, 1769, and John Neale and Elizabeth his wife, 1782 and 1780, limestone tablet with apron and obelisk, and black marble rectangular and circular plaques; (32), of Rev. John Serocold, 1835, and Mary his wife, 1830, with arms of Serocold, by Smith; (33), of Richard Millington, 1811; (34), of Sophia Baker (Tathwell), 1803; (35), of George Betts, 1806, and Alice his wife, 1822; (36), of William Symonds, 1796, and others; (37), of Sarah Stafford (Newbold), 1811; (38), of William Bury, 1823, by Gilbert. Monuments listed without full description are of simple design; (3), (8), (34), are of some pretension or have high-quality lettering. Attached externally — on tower buttress (39) of . . . . . Pollard, 1760, shaped tablet with cherubs' heads; five 19th-century tablets. In churchyard — approximately 30 enriched headstones of the 18th century; also (1) of Harriet Stokes, 1840, by Goodwin. *Floor slabs*: in tower — (1), to Mary Boyden, 1807, with bitumen inlay; (2), Sarah Osborn, 178(6?), circle with bitumen inlay; (3), Nathaniel Popple, 18th-century; (4), Samuel Judd, 1826, with bitumen inlay. In porch — (5), to Capt. William Bury, 1823; (6), to Kirby Freer, 1830. *Painting*: on responds of chancel arch, red damask patterns, 15th-century. *Panelling*: in N. aisle, fielded panelling in two heights, 18th-century. *Piscinae*: in chancel (1) and S. chapel (2), both in S. walls with depressed heads and continuous moulded jambs, projecting slabs with drain sinkings, 15th-century. *Plate*: cup (ht. 6 ins.), foot with egg-and-dart decoration, modern inscription between original bands, with flat fish mark of Thomas Buttell, *c.* 1570; cup (ht. 10 ins.), stem with knop, inscribed as gift of Margaret Lamb, '1722' roughly inscribed beneath, by James Smith 1722; flagons (ht. 11 ins.), a pair, domed lids, straight sides, inscribed, and engraved with lozenges of arms, by

Thomas Folkingham 1722; plates, a pair, inscribed beneath 'the gift of Margaret Lamb' with initials MW for Margaret Walburge (Lamb), London 1682; stand paten, the foot and attachment probably modern, inscribed on rim '1688', modern donation inscription, no marks, late 17th-century. *Recess*: W. of piscina (1), with four-centred head, renewed moulded jambs, perhaps an adaptation of former sedilia. *Royal Arms*: over chancel arch, canvas in moulded frame, repainted arms of 1801–16, date 1808 over painting 1758. *Seating*: oak pews of Gothic design, installed by Browning in 1844 (Burton, 274). *Stoup*: W. of porch archway, four-centred head, front of bowl mutilated, 15th-century. *Table*: oak, turned legs, stretchers, 18th-century. *Tiles*: in chancel with Gothic and architectural decoration, perhaps Minton, mid 19th-century.

(32) *Burial Ground*, belonging to St. Martin's church, contains tombstones dating from the year of opening in 1796. Signed headstones include (1), of Daniel Lambert, 1809, by 'Pollard and Shenton, engravers, Lester'; (2), of Tho. Dobney, 1841, by J. Perkins; (3) of William Hornsby, 1844, by Daniel Gilbert. Historically the most noteworthy is that to Daniel Lambert who weighed 52 stone 11 lbs. at his death in 1809.

(33) PARISH CHURCH OF ST. MARY (Fig. 32; Plates 10, 12, 14, 15), consisting of a *Chancel*, *N.* and *S. Chapels*, *Nave* with *N.* and *S. Aisles*, *W. Tower* with spire, and *S. Porch*, has a small churchyard on the S. The walls are of rubble and limestone ashlar, the nave and aisles are lead-covered, and the chancel and N. chapel stone-slated. External plinths and string-courses on the E. buttresses of the tower and now visible in the aisles, and the weathercourse of a nave roof, indicate that an older nave was standing when the W. tower was built in *c.* 1220. At the same time a chancel, narrower but almost as long as the nave, was added to the E.; shortly after, the W. respond of a S. arcade was built against the angle of the tower, the face of which was cut back to receive the stones, but the work does not then seem to have proceeded further. In the late 13th century a N. aisle, extending the full length of nave and chancel, and a S. aisle, one bay shorter than that on the N., were added; arches were cut through the chancel walls to the new chapels. The responds of the N. arcade, the E. respond of the S. arcade, the base of the E. wall of the N. chapel, and the S.E. buttress of the S. chapel, survive of this building phase in the 13th century. At the same time the roof of the nave was raised; its weathercourse, of slightly steeper pitch than its predecessor, is visible on the E. face of the tower. In the early 14th century the N.

chapel was widened on the N. and another arch cut through the chancel wall; also, a stone spire was added to the tower. During the second half of the 15th century the character of the church was transformed: the nave and aisles were rebuilt with a nave clearstorey and S. porch, an elaborate stone vault introduced into the tower, new windows added to the chancel and chapels, the chancel arch rebuilt and heightened, and a decorative ceiling installed in the N. chapel. In the nave, all four 13th-century arcade responds were allowed to remain. The following restorations have taken place: in 1788, strengthening of tower and spire with iron bands, to designs by C. Staveley (drawing in vestry) with John Hames as builder, for £300 (Burton, 279); in 1842 repair of tower by Robert Tinkler for £68 (Vestry Book); in 1852–3, repewing and other alterations to designs by Rev. T. James for £703.16.5; in 1859–60, repair of chancel roof, rebuilding of upper part of chancel wall and introduction of new E. window by Edward Browning (*Associated Architectural Societies' Reports*, V., pt. 1 (1859)); in 1890, under direction of J. D. Sedding, rebuilding of vestry, installation of screens, new altar with gilded metal panels by Sterling Lee, and painting of chancel ceiling by Farrell and Wilson, and E. Sedding (LAO, Faculty Book 10/130); in 1953, cleaning of N. chapel ceiling by E. Clive Rouse.

Guilds associated with the church were those of St. Mary, perhaps founded in 1310, and of Corpus Christi which is recorded in 1350 (PRO, CH/174, 172); the latter perhaps used the N. chapel.

The tower, impressively enriched with tiers of blind arcading, has long been recognised as an important example of 13th-century architecture; the N. chapel, with 14th-century tomb recess and a carved and painted ceiling of *c.* 1480, is particularly noteworthy. The chief fittings comprise a large 14th-century stone figure and the Phillips tomb of the early 16th century.

Architectural Description—The *Chancel* has at corners and centre of the E. wall early 13th-century pilaster buttresses with chamfered angles, pronounced weathering at base, and weathered tops. The lower part of the wall is early 13th-century and is capped by a moulded string course, perhaps medieval; the upper part was entirely rebuilt in 1860, the E. window replacing a late medieval one without tracery (drawing by Buckler; BM. Add MS. 36. 369, f. 134). The N. wall has two intruded arches; the eastern, of the 14th century, is the narrower and has a semi-octagonal E. respond, coved capital, and double-chamfered arch; the W. respond has been largely removed to accommodate the Phillips tomb and adjacent doorway (monument 1). The W. arch, of the late 13th century, has half-round responds, water-holding bases, deeply-coved capitals and double chamfered arch. Between the arches, on the chancel side, is a moulded string-course, perhaps an early 13th-century survival. The S. wall is of two periods: the E. half is early 13th-century and has a late 19th-century window in the position of an earlier one (Buckler's drawing) and a doorway, probably medieval, with chamfered jambs and modern square head. The W. half, of the late 13th century, has a slightly thinner wall, the transition being made by chamfered quoins which are capped by a moulded string-course. The W. bay is occupied by an arch corresponding with that on the N. of the chancel; above it is a projecting course aligning the wall with the thicker E. half. The chancel arch with late 13th-century details was rebuilt and heightened in the 15th century; it has triple half-round responds, modern bases, coved capitals, and an arch which is not set centrally on the capitals and has two chamfers on the W. and one on the E.

The *N. Chapel* was formed in the 14th century by widening the late 13th-century aisle; it was refenestrated in the 15th century. It has a steeply-pitched roof with parapeted gables. Between the buttresses are high protective plinths added in 1818 by the mason Gilbert at a cost of £90 (Vestry Book). The E. wall, built slightly E. of the chancel wall, consists partly of squared ashlar and partly of rubble, the former being a survival of the 13th-century aisle extension. The late 15th-century E. window has vertical tracery and mouchettes. Inside (Plate 15), the N. wall has three tomb recesses of the 14th century; the first (Plate 16) has a trefoil head at high level with crocketed and finialled ogee surround with paterae in the hollow moulding, slender side shafts carried on corbels, and now contains a tomb and effigy of *c.* 1380 (monument 2). In the rear wall is a four-centred window with three cinquefoil lights and cusped openings in the head. The other recesses form a pair and are plainer; each has an unornamented ogee head with cinquefoil cusping, the spandrels either pierced or blind, and renewed head stops. In the W. wall is the N. jamb and springing of a tall window opening, presumably 14th-century, which was blocked in the 15th century by the external stair turret within which the opening's external jamb is visible. Between aisle and chapel is a 14th-century arch with double chamfers which die into plain responds.

The *S. Chapel* has a low weathered buttress on the E. unbonded with the wall but perhaps a 13th-century survival. In the thin E. wall, probably rebuilt in the 15th century, is a blocked medieval window with later central mullion rising to apex. The tracery of the S. window varies slightly from that of the aisle windows. Inside, a

water-holding base on a high plinth in the N.E. corner, and a similar plinth in the S.E. corner, are perhaps survivals of an unfulfilled intention to vault the chapel in the 13th century.

The *Nave* has N. and S. arcades of three bays (Plate 14). The N. arcade has E. and W. late 13th-century responds with half-round shafts, water-holding bases and coved capitals, the W. respond being set against the cut-back surface of the tower; the late 15th-century piers each have octagonal bases, four engaged shafts with fillets, and moulded capitals with battlemented tops. The S. arcade has an E. respond uniform in design with that on the N.; it was rebuilt in the 19th century. The S.W. respond is of the early 13th century, and has clustered shafts, alternately engaged and free-standing, all with water-holding bases, two tiers of annulets and stiff leaf capitals. The 15th-century arches on both arcades are uniform and of two chamfered orders. The late 15th-century clearstorey has battlemented parapet and triangular-headed windows, each of two cusped lights.

The *N. aisle*, entirely of the 15th century, has at the E. end a rood loft stair turret with steeply-weathered stone roof; inside, the stair is served by upper and lower doorways with four-centred heads. Between the aisle buttresses are weathered infillings at the base, continuing the treatment to the E. The side and W. windows have vertical tracery. Below the third window is a segmental-headed recess with chamfered jambs and head. The N. doorway has continuous hollow and wave-moulded jambs and head with paterae in the hollow. The *S. Aisle* has side buttresses the top stages of which have gabled tops and niches with nodding ogee heads and crocketed finials. The windows are uniform with those in the N. aisle but the third is cut short below the springing to allow for the S. porch. The S. doorway has four-centred continuous hollow and wave-moulded jambs and head; to the E. is a segmental pointed recess.

The *W. Tower* (Plate 10), of five main stages and three storeys, has wide, shallow, clasping buttresses against which are narrow chamfered pilasters rising to the top of the third stage. The 13th-century W. doorway has an inner plain roundheaded opening of the 18th century below a blocked rear arch; the original doorway has stiff-leaf imposts (Plate 9), semicircular roll-moulded arch, and an outer surround comprising engaged nook shafts, stiff-leaf capitals, two-centred arch of three moulded orders, two with nail-head decoration, and a crescent-shaped typanum with central lozenge and roundels, one surviving with quatrefoil cusping. The lower three stages are enriched with blind arcading of varying forms, the lower two having plain capitals and the third stiff-leaf decoration; the latter also returns on the W. All four faces of the fourth stage have blind arcading with trefoil arches with cinquefoil spandrels, the wall being pierced with trefoil-headed lancets and roundels. Tall belfry windows in the fifth stage have clustered shafts, annulets, nail-head decoration, stiff-leaf caps and an arch of three moulded orders, the inner slightly trefoiled. Above, a corbel course has trefoil arches and mask stops. The 14th-century spire has broaches which terminate against crocketed tabernacles for statues, on the face of the spire; two statues are of nimbed figures blowing trumpets, a third probably of St. William of Norwich holding a tall cross and

on the N.E. and S.E. pilaster buttresses, now appearing in the N. and S. aisles, do not return on the E. side, implying that the tower was built against the W. end of the pre-existing nave. Across the internal angles of the tower are 18th-century infillings which mask the springing of the 15th-century stone vault above the second stage; the diagonal vault ribs are cusped-panelled and meet at an aperture for bell-raising.

The single-storey *S. Porch* has a low-pitched roof. It is

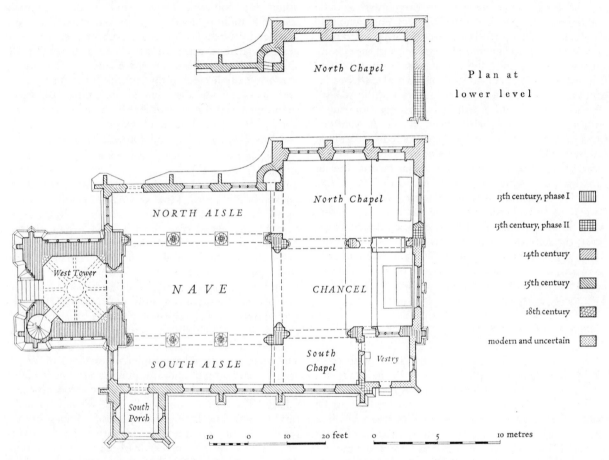

Fig. 32   (33) Church of St. Mary.

a hammer and nails, and the fourth is mutilated (Plate 16). The spire has three alternating tiers of gabled and crocketed lucarnes (Plate 12). Inside, the tower arch has triple half-round responds, stiff-leaf capitals, water-holding bases, and an arch of two chamfered orders separated by a keel moulding with label and mask stops. Above the arch are two blocked 13th-century windows with trefoil heads and above again two redundant weathercourses of slightly different pitch, the lower probably relating to the pre-13th-century nave roof, the upper to the 13th-century roof (Plate 14). Formerly external plinths, string-courses and weathering

contemporary with the S. aisle and incorporates the penultimate buttress in its E. wall. The archway and the side windows have four-centred heads. The *Vestry* has an E. window reset from No. 17 St. George's Square (297) (*Mercury*, 29 April 1881); it has two lights and trefoil in the head, 13th-century but considerably renewed (Plate 62).

The late 15th-century nave *Roof* is low-pitched with cambered tie beams, arch-braced to wall posts carried on stone corbels carved as grotesque heads, short king posts, purlins, foliar bosses and intermediate principals with nimbed demi-angels at the ends of each. The lean-to

N. aisle roof is ridged internally with 'false' rafters; 15th-century. The roof-space of the N. chapel is sealed but the steep pitch points to a 14th-century date. The 15th-century ceiling of waggon type, of five sides, is of plaster with a diapering of applied moulded oak ribs running diagonally with bosses of radiating leaves at the intersections (Plate 24). The plate-like bosses include carvings of a crowned Host, a stag, grotesque heads, crowned and mitred heads, Tudor rose, angel holding crown, and foliar and arboreal designs (Plate 25). The central boss and radiating leaves are carved with a falcon and fetterlock, the badge of the Dukes of York who held the manor of Stamford. The plaster panels, painted blue, have central stars containing letters W., and the ribs are mostly red and gilt; this decoration is in the main original. On the S. cornice is depicted a black-letter inscription in gilt: 'Orate specialiter pro a(n)i(m)ab(u)s Wille(l)m(i) Hikham et Alicie uxoris ejus q(uo)ru(m) a(n)i(m)ab(u)s p(ro)picietur deus amen'. A vanished brass showed that the ceiling was ordered by William Hikham, alderman, and his wife:'. . . testudinem fieri fecerunt', presumably implying a benefaction during their lifetime (Gervase Holles, B. M. Harley MS. 6829, compiled 1634–42, LRS, *Lincolnshire Church Notes*, I (1911), 201). The ceiling may be dated shortly before 1484, the year of Alice Hikham's death, as attested by the brass; the surviving painted inscription was added after 1486, the last year in which William Hikham was recorded as a member of the Guild of St. Katherine, Stamford (Gonville and Caius College, Cambridge, MS. 266/670, 18v. and 20v.).

Fittings — *Bells*: eight; 1st, 2nd, 6th by T. Mears 1802; 3rd inscribed in capitals 'Sum Rosa Pulsata Munda Maria Vocata Tobie Norris Cast Me 1625' with coins set in rim (Plate 55); 4th by Henry Penn, 1727; 5th inscribed in capitals 'Omnia Fiant Ad Gloriam Dei Tobie Norris Cast Me 1625'; 7th inscribed in Lombardic capitals 'iesus spede us stamfordiensibus inserviens ipsa conteror tobie norris cast me 1626' with arms of King Charles I (Plate 55); 8th inscribed in Lombardic capitals 'feare god honour the king IB TT gardeani 1638', probably by Thomas Norris; the Corporation's gift of £5 in 1624 towards the casting of the old 5th bell may refer to one of those by Tobie Norris (Burton, 280). *Bell frame*: probably 17th-century. *Brass*: in S. aisle, to Richard Warwick, alderman and mayor, 1684, rectangular plate with italic script. *Font*: limestone, octagonal bowl and stem, the former enriched with cusped panels, on modern base and foot pace, 15th-century. *Glass*: in N. chapel, fragments in border; in N. aisle, fragments of yellow-stain including crowned M and a wheel-pattern roundel, all 15th-century. *Inscription*: on W. face of spire, incised, 'R. Goodwin helped to repair 1788 T.T.' (recorded *Mercury*, 4 Sept. 1885).

Library: now in tower, was initially formed by Richard Banister (*c.* 1570–1626), the eye surgeon; he bequeathed £10 for books for the library (LAO, Lincoln Consistory Court 1626, 496). Further books were added to the collection, some in 1636 from William Dugard, schoolmaster of the Grammar School, who had received them from Banister (notes on flyleaves), and others as a result of a committee formed in the 18th century to administer the library and to collect subscriptions. The books dating from the 16th century onwards are mostly theological and number about 162 volumes. They include some with early stamped bindings, notably one by Garrett Godfrey and another by Nicholas Spierinck both of the early 16th century (stamps classified as 503 and 502 by J. B. Oldham, *English Blind-stamped Bindings*). The library was originally housed in the 'South Quire'; in 1704 the area it occupied was granted to Joshua Blackwell (monument 28) for burials. At Blackwell's expense the library was 'repaired and made exceeding neat' (Churchwardens' Book 1831–94 and notes on flyleaves).

Monuments: in chancel, occupying first bay of N. arcade (1) (Plate 45), limestone and clunch tomb chest with canopy, effigies, and doorway on W., probably of Sir David Phillips (d. 1506) and Anne his wife; his will records a wish to be buried in St. Mary's (PRO, Prob. 11/15), but Anne was buried in Chenies church, Buckinghamshire (RCHM, *Bucks*. I, 89). The long sides of the chest are both enriched with crocketed ogee niches containing attached figures of the Apostles and a wider central bay with demi-angel holding blank shield. The canopy has four-centred arch with cusped and subcusped trefoils below, foliated spandrels, and jambs with carved paterae including a crest (head of animal erased and collared) and vertical feathers rising from a crown. The main spandrels have undercut carvings of Welsh dragons and greyhounds supporting crowned Tudor roses or lily issuing from crown, motto scroll, rose and foliage. The cornice on N., S. and W. has undercut carving including Evangelists' symbols, grapes, branch forms, central crown and shield with I.H.S. in blackletter; on the W. the underside of the cornice is slotted, demonstrating the method of securing the panels below it. The reveals of the canopy have on the E. three enriched ogee cusped niches against an overall background of shields in cusped quatrefoils. The soffit of the canopy is missing. The figures comprise a military effigy in plate armour over mail shirt, head on crested and mantled helm, feet on lion, and hands in prayer; the female figure has hands in prayer, head on cushion supported by angels, and feet on crouched animal. Both figures wear reversed SS collars. The doorway on the W. is integral with the monument. It has four-centred head, enriched and moulded plinth, double row of cusped quatrefoils on jambs, and spandrels decorated with fleurs-de-lis, Tudor roses, feathers issuing from crowns and portcullis.

In N. chapel — N. wall (2), within recess, tomb chest with cusped panelling on long side, partly with transoms, central blank shield in cusped surround, and military effigy of alabaster in mail and plate armour with basinet, aventail and jupon, head on diagonally placed cushion supported by angels now mutilated, and on jupon in low relief *three lions' gambs erect and erased,* perhaps for Brown or Usher; *c.* 1380. (3), of Ann Wright, 1829; (4), of John Blackwell, 1770, Mary his wife, 1772, daughter of Williams Winder of Dufton, cartouche with scroll surround, painted arms in head of Blackwell impaling Winder; (5), of Ann Wright, 1798, as (3) by Gilbert; (6), of Mary Blackwell, 1699, tablet with side scrolls, console brackets, swags and central cherub's head, surmounted by broken curved pediment enclosing cartouche of arms of Blackwell impaling Rogers. In N. aisle — (7), of Mary McGuffog, 1840, by Gilbert; (8), of Thomas Althorp, 1834, by Smith; (9), of Mary Althorp and child, 1838, by Smith; (10), of Lady Georgina Ramsay, daughter of Earl of Dalhousie, 1794; (11), of James McGuffog, 1829, as (7); (12), of Caroline Rocher, 1840; (13), of James Althorp, 1828, and Elizabeth his wife, 1812, and child; (14), of James Yorke, 1824, signed 'Hampd. Road, London'; (15), of John Lumby, 1842, and Catherine his wife, 1842; (16), of Mary Broughton, 1802; (17), of William Whitby, 1837; (18), of William Allen, 1844; (19), of Rebecca Baker, 1848. In S. aisle — (20), of Mary Davis, 1842, '. . from an attack of apoplexy directly after bathing . .', and Thomas her brother, 1843; (21), of William Davis, 1810, and Mary his wife, 1838; (22), of Thomasin Davison, 1805; (23), of Richard Askren, 1800, and Mary his wife, 1798; (24), of Elizabeth Bowker, 1843; (25), of Frederick Piercy, 1827, died at Burrhampoor, by Gilbert; (26), of Joseph Piercy, 1823, Jane his wife, 1835, and infant; (27), of Mary Roberts, 1824, as (22); (28), of Joshua Blackwell, 1727, and Lettice his wife and co-heiress of William Williams, 1770, white marble epitaph tablet, fluted pilasters, entablature with triglyphs surmounted by painted cartouche of arms for Blackwell, and below, a shaped and carved apron, console brackets and rococo leaf corbel; (29) of William Allen, 1829, by Gilbert. Monuments listed above without full descriptions are generally of white marble with black backgrounds, and of simple design; (7), (8), (17) and (26) are sarcophagus-shaped and of some elaboration. In porch — (30), of Margaret Stevenson, 1813, tablet with emblems of mortality, by Harrison; (31), of Sarah Stevenson, 1796. In churchyard — (1), coped slab with inscription on sides, of Ann Barry, 1660; approximately 12 embellished headstones of the 18th century, and a number of later date. Slate headstones include (2), of Mary Charlesworth, 1767, signed 'T. Smith, Grantham'; (3), of Edward Atter, 1841; (4), of David Atter, 1847; (5), of Henry Atter, 1848, all three by John Hibbitt of Colsterworth; (6), of William Parker, 1836, by Smith;

(7), of Jas. Boyfield, 1848, by H. Gilbert.

Piscinae: (1), in N. chapel, E. wall, with ogee head, chamfered jambs, modern corbelled drain, 15th-century; (2), in S. chapel, S. wall, with chamfered jambs, head invisible, medieval. *Plate*: cup (ht. 9 ins.), flagon (ht. 16 ins.), paten and pair of plates, all with foliage decoration and other scrollwork, engraved with sacred monogram, inscribed as gift of Mrs. Mary Yorke in 1825, by Emes and Barnard, 1825. *Rainwater head*: on S. aisle, lead, 1718. *Statue*: in N. chapel, three-quarter life size, probably of the Virgin, robed, veiled, right forearm raised with restored hand, mid 14th-century (Plate 33). *Stoup*: external, W. of N. doorway, blocked recess with four-centred head, 15th-century. *Tables*: three of oak including one with round tapered legs and spreading feet, 18th-century. *Tomb recesses*: see N. chapel.

(34) PARISH CHURCH OF ST. MICHAEL (Fig. 33; Plates 27, 28) stands at the E. end of High Street on the site of the medieval church which partly collapsed during alterations in 1832. It consists of a *Chancel, Nave* with galleries, and *West Tower*. The walls are of ashlar and the roof is covered in Welsh slates. In April 1832 the former church was closed to allow for the introduction of new pews at a cost of £600. In June of that year attempts were made to improve the church under the supervision of John Boyfield (the third) by the removal of alternate pillars, with consequent loss of support to the tower; heavy rain caused the collapse of the roof, and the tower developed cracks and inclination (Vestry Book; *Mercury*, 13 April, 8 June 1832). Total replacement of the church was decided on, and in 1834 John Brown's design and estimated cost of £2,800 were accepted, the design to be 'in exact imitation of the architecture of Salisbury Cathedral' (*Stamford News*, 7 Oct. 1834). The foundation stone was laid on 12 May 1835, the contractors being Woolston and Collins, and the church was opened on 19 October 1836; the final cost was £4000 (*Mercury*, 13 Feb., 8 May, 21 Oct. 1836; *Burton*, 287). In a restoration in 1866 the pulpit and reading desk were removed from the centre of the nave (*Mercury*, 30 Nov. 1866).

The building has a pronounced 13th-century character, the details of that period being faithfully reproduced. The E. elevation is the most elaborate having two tiers of lancets beneath the central gable and single lancets with trefoils beneath the side gables; the side compartments are entered through twin porches with gables. Four tall buttresses terminate with gables at parapet level, the centre pair continuing as octagonal pinnacles. The side walls of the nave have pairs of lancets, only those facing the road being enriched with labels and shafts. Decoration to the tower (Plate 27) is concentrated at belfry stage, each face of which is pierced by three tall graduated lancets; the parapet is arcaded and the corner pinnacles are octagonal with attached shafts. The chancel has a plaster vaulted ceiling with wooden ribs. A stone gallery staircase in the N. compartment rises in three straight flights; the corresponding S. compartment is a vestry with register room above. The nave (Plate 28) has N., S. and W. galleries supported on quatrefoil cast-iron columns with capitals and bases. The ceiling, divided into rectangles, has painted cross-ribs terminating on carved corbels; the N. and S. sections of the ceiling are slightly pitched.

reset and recut; a similar respond-capital in the former church was drawn by William Twopeny in October 1834 (Twopeny, 290/d. 13, p. 59). The stone floor of the tower and the lower treads of the stone staircase are supported on brick barrel vaults introduced in 1876 by J. Woolston, builder, who signed the brickwork and one stiff-leafed capital. The crypt appears to have been designed as a catacomb for burials from the previous church (see wall monument (14)); it was then filled in with earth, but in 1876 was partly excavated in order that the brick vaults could be built beneath the tower.

Fittings—*Bells*: six (not accessible); all dated 1762 and bearing inscriptions mostly of a laudatory nature; 2nd and 4th signed by J. Eayre of St. Neots (North, *Church*

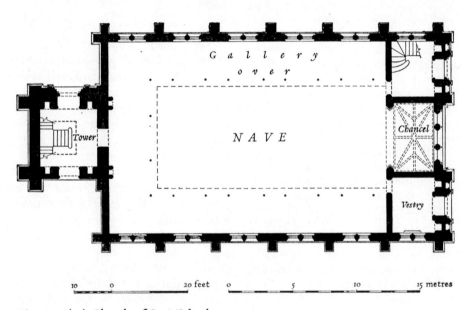

Fig. 33   (34) Church of St. Michael.

The eastern of three circular and enriched ventilator grilles is inscribed 'John Brown architect, Norwich, 1836'. In the tower, a stone stair with cast-iron balusters and swept handrail has a central lower flight which divides on the N. and S. to reach the organ and gallery. Beneath the E. end of the church a narrow crypt running N. and S., and reached by the N.E. stair, has eight segmental vaults on the E. and three on the W., each constructed of stone and brick; the central opening on the W. has a modern blocking and may have led to a passage axial with the church. The vaults contain tombs, mostly from the former church (see *Monuments*). A crypt under the tower, contemporary with the church, has stone walls. On the E. a roundheaded archway with circular responds and stiff-leaf capitals is blocked by a later brick apse. The capitals are possibly 13th-century,

Bells of Lincolnshire (1882), 681–2). *Benefactor's Table*: recording the rebuilding and enlarging of the church in 1836. *Books*: Bibles, one of 1825, another of 1842 and a third mid 19th-century; Common Prayer, two of 1730, two of 1743, one of 1809, one of 1825 and one of 1846; and others, early 19th-century. *Brasses*, coffin plates: in nave (1), to Catherine Austin, 1758; (2), to Elizabeth Wigmore, 1662 (M–S. I); (3), to children James and Joan Langton, 1686, Latin epitaph ending '... Tho Cosin sculp' (Fig. 34) (M–S. II); (4), to Richard Nevison, 1759; (5), to Mary Potter, 1759. *Chest*: oak, rectangular, carved with date '1662'. *Font*: octagonal, buttressed shaft, bowl enriched with pointed quatrefoils arranged lozengewise, 15th-century (Plate 40). Recently moved to St. Nicholas' church, Leicester. *Monuments*: in N.E. stair hall — on E. wall (1), of

Henry West, 1835, Mary his wife, and others; (2), of Rebecca Gouger, 1824, sarcophagus-tablet inscribed 'Near this spot is deposited until the archangel's trump shall summon from its resting place, the perishable part of Rebecca . . .'; (3), of Henry Ward, 1781, Sarah his first wife, 1776, and Hannah his second wife, 1780, Mary Harper, 1799, and others, tablet surmounted by urn; on S. wall (4), of Robert Hunt, 1846, sarcophagus-tablet, by Hibbins of Ketton; (5), of Sophia Wilson (Drakard), 1824, and child, by Gilbert; (6), of Elizabeth Robinson (Wells), 1773, Prudence Robinson (Ansell), 1780, Mary Robinson, 1815, tablet surmounted by draped urn, with addition to base by Gilbert inscribed to Joseph Robinson, 1823; (7), of William Johnson, 1819, by Gilbert; on W. wall (8), of Thomas Robinson, 1798, and Anne his wife, 1836, and child, tablet with shaped sides surmounted by urn against grey marble oval background; (9), of Elizabeth Hunt (Coddington), 1836, and daughter; (10), of Margaret Hunt, 1826, sarcophagus-tablet,; (11), of William Chamberlin, 1792, and Rebecca, his wife, 1797, tablet surmounted by draped urn; (12), of William Harper, 1814, and daughter, tablet surmounted by draped urn, by Gilbert; (13), of Sophia Hunt (Broughton), 1830, and William her husband, 1834; (14), of Alfred Harper, 1831, Charles his brother, April 1831, Anna his sister, 1836, 'in the fifth Catacomb beneath the chancel of this church'; (15), of Rev. Thomas Hurst, vicar of All Saints', 1802, and Margaret his wife, 1814, tablet with scroll cresting; (16), of Elizabeth Snow, 1808, and Thomas her husband, 1813; (17), of James Hurst, 1787, Phillipa his wife, 1793, and daughters, twin tablets with reeded pilasters and frieze, obelisk background with central and flanking urns, and apron with inscription added by Gilbert to Rev. Thomas Hurst, 1838; (18), of Clement Rubbing, 1838, by Gilbert. In nave (19), of Mary Betton, 1849, by Fearn. In tower — on N. wall (20), of William Baker, 1791, semicircular tablet against carved background with shaped apron, cresting and flanking urns; (21), of Jeremiah Belgrave, twice Mayor, 1818, and Jane his wife, 1796, and infants, tablet with brown marble classical surround surmounted by shield and crest of Belgrave, against shaped grey marble background, by Gilbert. A number of burials in the E. crypt, having inscribed tablets, are also commemorated on wall tablets listed above (nos. (1), (3), (4), (9), (12) and (14)); a tablet of 1822 on the second vault is signed 'Harrison'. In W. crypt, (22), of James Bowker, 1828. All monuments are in white marble unless otherwise stated, and those without descriptions are of plain design. Attached externally — (23), of Sam. Wilson 1838, circular cartouche with enriched top. In churchyard — tomb chest with mortality emblems, late 17th-century; approximately 30 headstones of the 18th century, some with rococo decoration; slate headstone (1), of Joseph and Elizabeth Coddington, 1791, signed 'Sparrow, Stamford'.

Plate: flagons (ht. 11 ins.), a pair, cylindrical, spreading bases, cap-shaped covers, inscribed, engraved with contemporary lozenges of arms of Scott (?) impaling Collins (?), plume-like mantlings, London 1693; plates (diam. 11 ins.), a pair, inscribed, engraved with lozenges of arms of Collins (?), 1725 by Thomas Tearle; plates (diam. 7 ins.), a pair, as larger pair; pewter dish for baptisms, inscribed '. . . 1820'. *Pulpit*: wooden, rectangular, in two stages, the lower pierced by arches, the upper enriched with arcading and floral decoration in 13th-century manner, resited, 1836. *Reredos*: plaster, cusped blind arcading beneath three crocketed gables, 1836. *Seating*: box pews in nave and galleries, 1836, those in nave cut down in 1866.

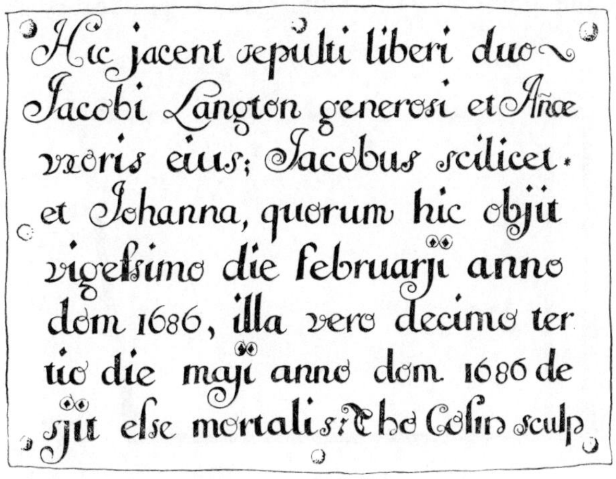

Fig. 34 (34) Church of St. Michael.
Brass coffin plate (3) to James and Joan Langton, 1686.

For the former CHURCH OF ST. PAUL, see (54) STAMFORD SCHOOL.

(35) THE CHURCH OF OUR LADY AND ST. AUGUSTINE (Plate 163), Roman Catholic, in Broad Street, was designed by George Goldie in 1862 and opened two years later. The *Stamford Mercury* of 26 December 1862 anticipated that it would be 'the prettiest modern Gothic building in town'. It consists of an apsidal-ended sanctuary, nave, side chapel, short N. aisle, and N. porch. The bell turret, enriched with Gothic arcading and having a steeply-pitched roof, is the external focus of the building.

(36) CONGREGATIONAL CHURCH, Star Lane (Fig. 35; Plate 29), stands on land purchased in 1719 following the destruction by a mob in 1714 of an earlier chapel in St. Paul's Street. In 1739 considerable alterations were made to the building owing to its excessive roof span, but it remained until 1819 when it was demolished (*Mercury*, 5 Feb. 1819). The present building was started in March 1819 and opened in September. It cost £1800 and seated 800. In 1862 a new vestry was built and a section of the old corn market arcade, below Browne's Hospital, was transferred and adapted as an entrance (see Broad Street, street introduction). Further alterations in 1876 included new windows in the W. wall (church minutes, Jan. 1862; manuscript 'History' in church).

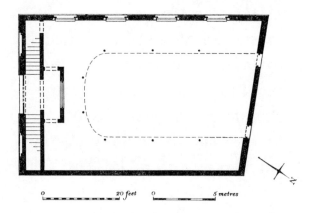

Fig. 35   (36) Congregational Church, Star Lane.

The church has red brick walls, ashlar plinth and hipped slated roof, and is entered on the narrower S. side from a small yard. The wide entrance has segmental head and double doors with reeded joinery; above is a stone panel inscribed 'MDCCCXIX'. The building was originally lit only at gallery level by roundheaded sash windows, with marginal panes, but on the W. blind roundheaded recesses at ground-floor level were opened as windows in 1876. On the E. there are blind lunettes below the main sash windows. Set in N. wall is a stone slab inscribed '1720', from the previous building. Doors have Gothic glazing bars. Around three sides of the interior is a gallery with curved corners and panelled front, supported on eight Doric cast-iron columns. The ceiling has a plaster cornice with bead-and-reel ornament. Most of the early 19th-century box pews, and some benches with shaped ends in the gallery, remain. In entrance, small table with turned legs and moulded rails, early 18th-century.

(37) Former TRINITY METHODIST CHAPEL, Barn Hill, with ashlar walls and slated roof was built at the expense of Miss Frances Treen on land purchased in 1803; licence for worship was granted in December of that year (LAO, Faculty Book 3, f. 169). A gallery was added in 1838. The chapel was extended to the S. in 1863 (*Mercury*, 26 June) and the present S. front is a reconstruction from the original building probably without alteration except for the introduction of a doorway with Tuscan surround (Plate 29). It comprises roundheaded windows and a central Venetian window with Gothic glazing bars, and arbitrarily placed oval panels carved in relief with emblematic representations of Faith, Hope and Charity (Plate 119). The interior now has an inserted upper floor.

(38) Former BAPTIST CHAPEL, now a pair of dwellings, No. 13 Bath Row, coursed rubble walls, hipped roof, was opened in October 1835 (*Mercury*, 9 Oct.). It was no longer in use by 1846 (*Mercury*, 18 Sept.), but the present conversion is probably late 19th-century. Originally with two tiers of windows, the openings have since been modified and augmented. A gallery probably existed at the S. end. The plaster ceiling has a cove, moulded frieze and roses for pendant lights.

(39) CHAPEL, Strict Baptist, North Street, was originally built by Dr. J. G. de Merveilleux in 1834 at his own cost (*Mercury*, 12 Aug. 1864). The chapel was enlarged in 1838 and a gallery added, but in 1901 it was dismantled except for the N. and W. walls which were incorporated in a new structure. The old walls, of coursed rubble, have tall roundheaded windows, one blocked, and at a higher level are trefoiled openings (Chambers R. F., *The Strict Baptist Chapels of England*, IV, 116–17).

SITES OF CHURCHES

(40) CHURCH OF ST. MARY BYNNEWERK, site of, probably located where All Saints' Tithe Yard stood; land to the N., known as Bonney's Paddock in the 18th century, was possibly named after the adjacent churchyard (LAO, Glebe terrier, 1800). In 1854 a coffin 'dated 1464' was dug up in the tithe yard (*Mercury*, 14 Sept.) and in 1895 a vault measuring 10 ft. by 8 ft. was discovered (*Mercury*, 21 June).

(41) CHURCH OF ST. PETER, site of. The churchyard stands on ground W. of the castle, several feet
higher than the road. In 1828 about 10 ft. was taken
from the N. side of the yard for road widening
(*Mercury*, 8 Aug.); later a gun captured from the
Russians during the Crimean war was placed here
(General Purposes Committee, Aug. 1859). The
church remained standing in 1543 (LAO, LCC
Wills, 1541–3) and in 1736 Stukeley recorded that
fragments, believed to be from it, were built into
several houses (Corpus Christi College, Cambridge,
MS. 619 f. 149). In 1858 the N. wall and part of the
floor of the church were uncovered, and various
fragments including a pier base, stained glass and a
foliated capital were discovered (*Mercury*, 3 and 17
Sept., 8 Oct. 1858).

(42) CHURCH OF ST. MICHAEL THE LESS, site of,
also known as the church of St. Michael, Cornstall,
is recorded in the 12th century but in 1308 was
amalgamated with St. George's church because of
its poverty (LAO, Reg. 2, 24). The boundaries of
the site which became known as St. George's Tithe-
yard can still be traced, but no structure survives
above ground.

CHURCH OF ST. STEPHEN AND HOLY TRINITY, site
of, marked on the OS map on the N. side of St.
Paul's Street (map in end pocket). This small extramural parish was united with that of St. Michael's in
1556, after which the church is not mentioned; there
are no visible remains.

MONASTIC BUILDINGS AND SITES

(43) SITE OF AUSTIN FRIARY (TF 025068; Fig. 36)
lies on the W. of the town, opposite Rutland Terrace, on land sloping S. to the R. Welland. The site
was first occupied by a house of the Friars of the
Sack, though little is known of its history. It was
a small community and only four friars were living
there in 1300 (VCH *Lincs.*, II, 230). This house was
probably suppressed with the rest of the Order in
1317, and in 1341 the land was granted to the
Austin Friars. In 1342 Robert de Wodehous had a
licence to build and found a house for 12 friars, and
at least part of the church there had been built by
1345 (VCH *op. cit.*, 225–6). By 1538, when the
friary was dissolved, there were only six friars, and
the buildings were soon destroyed.

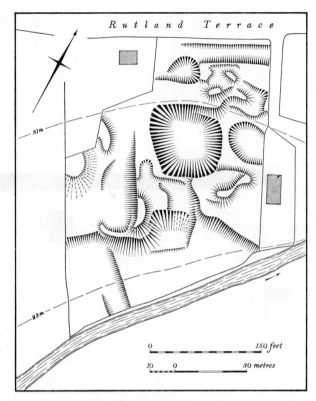

Fig. 36　(43) Site of Austin Friary.

The site was excavated in 1712 and a record of the
plan then recovered was made (Peck, Forster's Letters,
10–11). The buildings appear to have been arranged
around a central courtyard but no satisfactory reconstruction is possible. Forster recorded that during the
excavations human bones and glazed tiles were discovered and that 'the stone pillars and windows, which
have been dug up in the ruins, render the structure very
magnificent'. A central vault-boss found on this site in
1712 is now in the garden of 14 Barn Hill (101) (Plate 44).

The area is at present grass land and those earthworks
that remain are largely uninterpretable. The most
prominent feature is a large rectangular depression up to
2 m. deep which appears to be a pond of relatively late
date. Otherwise, only low uneven mounds, probably
spoil heaps from the excavation, exist.

(44) SITE OF BENEDICTINE NUNNERY OF ST.
MICHAEL (TF 028064) lies on the S. side of the
Welland and W. of the town. The nunnery was
founded in 1155 as a cell of Peterborough Abbey,
originally for both nuns and monks. The latter
ceased to exist as a significant group in 1323. The
house was always a small one, and was dissolved in
1536 (W. A. Sturman, 'The History of the Nunnery
of St. Mary and St. Michael', unpublished M.A.

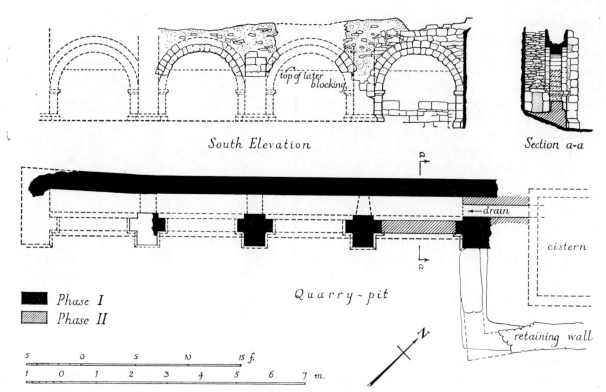

South Elevation   Section a-a

top of later blocking

←*drain*

cistern

■ *Phase I*
▨ *Phase II*

Quarry-pit

retaining wall

Fig. 37   (44) Nunnery of St. Michael. Plan, elevation and section of reredorter.

Thesis, University of London, (1944)). By 1727 all the buildings on the site seem to have been destroyed. Stukeley (*Designs*, 46) records a female tomb effigy from the site. During the construction of the Stamford–Leicester railway in 1846 many finds were made including 'ancient foundations . . . broken mullions of windows and other carved stones, five stone coffins, a quantity of human bones, coloured glass' etc. One coffin lid with a long Latin inscription was discovered, as well as a small crucifix of jet (*Gent's. Mag.* (1846), 305).

Late in 1973 excavations for a new school building revealed part of a reredorter on the S. side of the nunnery site (Fig. 37; Plate 5). It was built on the N. edge of a large hole, presumably a quarry. The surviving 12th-century remains consisted of an arcade of four bays, entirely below ground level, with a parallel retaining wall about 2 ft. to the N., subsequently partly rebuilt. The arcade carried the S. wall of the reredorter, and the retaining wall supported the fronts of the seats. The arches are of two unchamfered orders springing from square piers against which are pilaster buttresses with chamfered plinths. Short lengths of wall bridge the space between the retaining wall and piers; a fragment of tomb slab supports the bridging wall at the E. end. Originally, drainage must have been towards the S.,

through the arches into the quarry, but later the level was raised and stone slabs were laid in the space behind the arcade; low walls were also added between the piers to form a water-channel running in a W. direction. In addition, the E. wall was reconstructed to incorporate a stone-lined conduit at channel level; the conduit continues E. for at least 6 ft. and may be associated with a retaining wall of coursed rubble which was added at right angles against the E. pier. The upper part of this retaining wall was in turn partly rebuilt at an unknown date. It contained a clay-lined reservoir at ground level, presumably for flushing the reredorter. In the later Middle Ages, the arches were almost completely blocked with small masonry thereby enclosing the water-channel. The three W. arches were destroyed during recent building operations but the E. arch has been preserved.

(45) SITE OF CARMELITE FRIARY (TF 035073; Fig. 38) is located immediately E. of the town walls on land sloping gently to the R. Welland. The situation of this friary has been frequently confused with that of the Grey Friars (see (46)). The house was founded sometime before 1268, at which date the church was apparently built. Records show that between 1285 and 1350 the friars were acquiring

existing buildings and gardens to enlarge the site (Cal. Pat. (1281–92), 172; (1317–21), 54, 65; (1334–8), 325; (1348–50), 512). The priory was dissolved in 1538 when seven brothers were in residence, and the site passed to the Cecils. By about 1600 all the friary buildings had been pulled down, and apart from one or two later buildings the site was probably left empty until the early 20th century when three houses were erected on the N. side.

The earthwork remains, now divided between three gardens, are in a fragmentary state and interpretation is difficult. Excavations ('a' on Fig. 38) in 1971 revealed a number of stone footings and a stone-lined drain or culvert. The surrounding stone wall is said to have once contained pieces of sculpture (Designs, 69) but these no longer exist; into the coping are built reused fragments of window dressings and chamfered stones of post-medieval date. On the S. side is part of a gateway which survived complete in 1735 when drawn by Stukeley

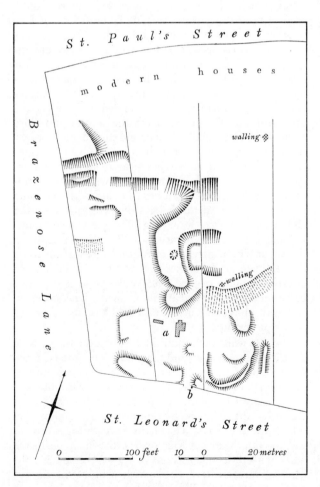

Fig. 38 (45) Site of Carmelite Friary.

(Designs, 67). He showed an opening with pointed head, flanked by two-stage buttresses. The E. jamb ('b' on Fig. 38), splayed and rebated internally, double-chamfered externally, remains together with some limestone blocks to the W., possibly representing the corresponding jamb.

(46) SITE OF FRANCISCAN FRIARY (TF 036075). The Friars Minor or Grey Friars were established in Stamford by 1230 when it is recorded that Henry III gave them fuel (Cal. Close (1227–31), 283). They were engaged in building by 1235 in which year the king gave them timber for making stalls (Cal. Close (1234–7), 138). By 1239 there were sufficient buildings to hold a provincial chapter (VCH Lincs. II, 228). After the suppression the site was given in 1541 to the Duke of Suffolk, by which time many of the buildings were demolished (Letters and Papers, Henry VIII, vol. XIII part ii 220, 236, 275, XVI 326) but enough remained standing for Sir William Cecil, who later bought the site, to entertain Queen Elizabeth there in 1566 (Harrod, 40). The site remained in the hands of the Cecils until 1826 when it was sold to provide a site for the infirmary (62).

Early historians confused this site with that of Whitefriars, and this error has persisted to the present day. In 1595 Greyfriars was described as being in St. Paul's parish (NRO, Fitzwilliam Misc. 433) and in 1714 and 1735 it was referred to as Far Friars whereas the adjacent area to the S.W. was called Little Friars (Ex. MS 33/27, 201/30). There can be little doubt therefore that the Grey Friars occupied the present site, further from the town, and hitherto called Whitefriars (see 45).

In 1881 excavations for a new building revealed a stone coffin 4½ ft. long, and plain glazed floor tiles said to be medieval (Mercury, 15 Apr.). In 1884 excavations for new buildings to the W. of the infirmary revealed two skeletons, and on the E. a deep pit was discovered, apparently a stone quarry (Mercury, 30 May).

At the W. extremity of the site the medieval Gateway of the friary survives (Plate 57). It belongs to the second quarter of the 14th century and is built of 'Barnack' limestone with repairs in similar stone. The approach elevation, on the W., consists of an archway of two chamfered orders with depressed head and label, flanked by two-stage buttresses, each upper stage bearing a niche with nodding trefoil head; pinnacles rising behind the niches vary in design. Over the arch is a niche uniform with the others, and flanking it are blank shields in square panels. The wall is weathered back to a parapet with crocketed pinnacles and a central merlon containing a blank shield.

Built against the back of the gateway is a *Porter's Lodge*. In 1848 Mrs. Hodson of St. Martins bequeathed £200 to Stamford Infirmary for the lodge to be built in the style of the 'ancient gate'; the contract was given to Thompson of Peterborough for £367 (*Mercury*, 28 Jan. 1848; 19 Feb. 1849). The designs were by one Cotton (Hospital Records). The lodge is generally similar in style to the friary gate. The entry has a two-centred vault and over the archway are two single-light trefoiled windows flanking a diapered panel with a shield of arms of Fryer.

(47) PRIORY OF ST. LEONARD (TF 038073), remains of, stand on the E. side of the town and S. of Priory Road (Fig. 39; Plate 7). A 15th-century document states that the priory was built on the site of a monastery which was founded by St. Wilfrid in 658 and destroyed in the Danish invasion, but the association between St. Wilfrid's foundation and St. Leonard's priory is open to doubt (VCH *Lincs.* II, 127). A further statement in the document refers to the Stamford house being jointly refounded by the Conqueror and William Carileph, Bishop of Durham, in *c.* 1082, and becoming a cell of Durham. In the later Middle Ages the number of monks was much depleted and in 1440 was reduced to the prior and one monk. It remained a cell of Durham until its dissolution in 1538.

Excavations carried out under the supervision of Miss C. M. Mahany between 1967 and 1972 show that the Benedictine church comprised a long sanctuary with apse, a N. transept with apse, a nave of six bays which survives, and a N. aisle; excavated conventual buildings on the S. included a rectangular cloister with ranges on the S. and W. (*Med. Arch.*, XII (1968), 167, 8). A reredorter at the S.W. corner perhaps implies that the dorter was in the W. range, an abnormal arrangement but also to be found at Durham, where the dorter was moved from the E. to the W. side of the cloister. The frater may have stood on an undercroft in the S. range. Of the standing remains, all but the W. three bays of the nave are of the early to mid 12th century, and presumably the destroyed parts of the church to the E. were also of this date. Very late in the 12th century, the nave was completed by the addition of three bays and a W. wall; the earliest identifiable features of the claustral buildings belong to this period. Excavations N.E. of the sanctuary revealed an L-shaped foundation probably implying a rebuilding of the sanctuary, on a wider, square-ended plan, perhaps in the 13th century.

The date of destruction of the priory is not recorded; five and a half bays of the nave, and the W. front, were allowed to remain but the E. and S. walls are Tudor, suggesting that dismantling followed soon after the dissolution. In 1747 stone coffins were found in the region of the choir (*Surtees Soc.* 76 (1883), 293), and in *c.* 1772 six coffins were found when one Ridlington, tenant of Priory House (276), 'levelled a hill before the N. front of the house' (*Mercury*, 24 May 1833). The *Mercury* of 24 May 1833 records that 'the West front fell down a few months ago and is now being rebuilt'. In *c.* 1844 William Fenton pulled down the walls filling the arches on the N. side, and glazed the W. windows (Burton, 265); it may be assumed that the long axial wall, with door and window openings in the Romanesque style, was built at this time.

The *Nave* has a 16th-century E. wall of coursed rubble and reused 'Barnack', built almost one bay W. of the crossing; at its N. end is a small doorway with triangular head. Also 16th-century are tall E. buttresses of two weathered stages in continuation of the side walls. The N. arcade is composed of five complete bays and the springing of an incomplete bay at the E. end. The round piers are substantial; the first three have chamfered bases, scalloped capitals and square abaci with re-entrant angles (Plate 8). The incomplete arch has zig-zag ornament on N. and S. sides; the second and third arches have roll-moulded inner and square outer orders. 'Barnack' stone fills the spandrels, and above is a string-course, chamfered above and below; above again are two roundheaded clearstorey windows, the W. complete, but the E. blocked externally and with one inner splay only. The W. three bays of the arcade are taller and wider than the foregoing. The piers have water-holding bases, capitals carved with stylized foliage on the S. but with plain coves or rudimentary leaf-forms on the N. (Plate 8); the arches have roll-moulded inner and chamfered outer orders. The W. respond has a small half-round pier flanked by nook shafts. The spandrels and wall above are in coursed rubble without string-course or openings.

The W. wall was rebuilt in 1833 except for parts of the clasping buttresses, and the plinth. The wall is in two stages; a blind vesica with roll-moulded and chamfered surround is in the gable. The lower stage has a blocked central doorway, blind side bays, all with round heads and nook shafts linked by annulets which continue as sills in the side bays. The shafts have stiff-leaf capitals and the doorhead has four orders, the inner plain, the outer with different versions of zig-zag ornament; the flanking recesses have heads with nebuly and zig-zag ornament (Plate 9). The second stage has an arcade of seven bays, alternately blind and open, with shafts having

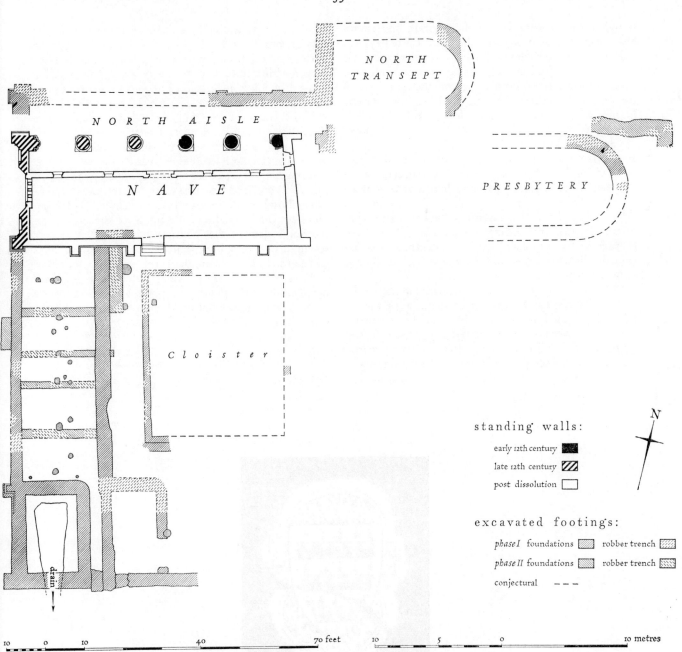

NORTH TRANSEPT

NORTH AISLE

PRESBYTERY

NAVE

Cloister

drain

standing walls:

early 12th century
late 12th century
post dissolution

excavated footings:

phase I foundations   robber trench

phase II foundations   robber trench

conjectural   – – –

N

10   0   10   40   70 feet   10   5   0   10 metres

Fig. 39   (47) Priory of St. Leonard. Plan showing standing building and excavated remains.

simple foliage decoration on the capitals, and round heads enriched with zig-zag; the three open bays are slightly taller and have straight-splayed inner jambs and wooden lintels. Roll-moulded string-courses divide each stage, the lower string returning round the clasping buttresses. The N. buttress has some disturbed stones on the N. indicating the W. wall of the former aisle; Buckler's drawing of 1811–12 (BM Add. MS. 36369, f. 62) shows the stub wall more pronounced. Similarly, a drawing by Blore (BM Add. MS. 42000, f. 38) indicates a tall pilaster on the S. of the S. buttress, presumably a survival of the W. wall of the claustral buildings; there is now no trace of this feature.

The S. wall has four tall buttresses and excavation has shown that it is not exactly on the line of the 12th-century wall; it is probably early 19th-century. Stukeley records in 1747 'narrow upper windows' which do not now exist (*Surtees Soc.* 80 (1887)).

Excavations in 1967–72 have revealed: (a) part of the apse of the sanctuary; (b) part of the apse of the N. transept; (c) an L-shaped wall N.E. of the sanctuary, perhaps 13th-century (see above); (d) cloister (garth, 34 ft. by 40 ft.); (e) W. range of cloister with central line of post holes, apparently replaced by stone piers, subsidiary post holes indicating cross partitions, and late medieval cross walls; (f) a masonry projection in the cloister, possibly related to a stair from the conjectured dorter in the W. range; (g) reredorter at S. end of W. range, with reinforcing arch in N. wall, roundheaded splayed opening in S. wall, sloping footings on E., N. and W., but without indication of its upper floor (Plate 5); (h) S. range with a round pier-base to undercroft, perhaps late 12th-century, and later cross walls, two with chamfered door jambs; (i) some lengths of N. aisle of church, having buttresses of pilaster form.

Immediately W. of the standing buildings in a pasture field are traces of very low indeterminate *Earthworks*, nowhere more than 1 m. in height. These may represent other buildings. To the S. of the priory, on the flood-plain of the Welland (TF 039072) is a large rectangular pond lying parallel to the river, 60 m. long and 20 m. wide and 1 m. deep. It is connected at either end to a series of shallow drainage ditches which extend northwards of the pond. This pond does not appear to be of great antiquity but the drainage ditches may have originated as the fishpond of the priory.

For site of DOMINICAN FRIARY see introduction to Blackfriars Estate (114–23).

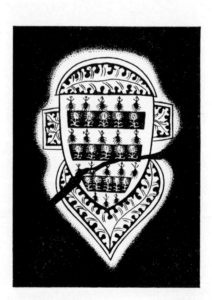

Fig. 40 (48) Browne's Hospital. Shield of Elmes in Audit Room, window (4).

SECULAR BUILDINGS

PUBLIC BUILDINGS AND INSTITUTIONS

(48) BROWNE'S HOSPITAL (Figs. 41, 42; Plates 66–69) stands on the N. side of Broad Street and consists of a courtyard with the main range with Chapel on the S., a cloister on the W., almshouse accommodation on the N. and the warden's house on the E. The hospital was founded by William Browne, merchant (see *Brass* below), and was completed in 1475/6 (Bodl. MS Rawlinson B., 352 ff. 1–2; quoted in full by P. A. Newton in *Antiquaries Journal* XLVI (1966), II, 283). It was endowed in 1485 (Cal. Pat., 1476–85, 505), and after Browne's death in 1489 new letters patent were obtained by his brother-in-law, Thomas Stokke, Canon of York, in 1493.

The hospital provided accommodation for ten poor men and two women under the supervision of a warden and confrater. The Chapel was 'beautified' sometime between 1769 and 1785 (Harrod, 11, 370). The porch was rebuilt in 1808 when payment was made to John Walters, architect, and Harrison, mason (Hospital account book). A mid 19th-century proposal to rebuild the S. wall with alterations to the elevation, but retaining the gatehouse in its original position, was not adopted (drawings in Hospital archives). The buildings were recorded before the late 19th-century restoration by Buckler in 1811, by Blore at about the same time (BM Add. MSS. 36369, 42036), by Dollman (*Antient Domestick Architecture* (1858), II pls. 1–4) and in early photographs (Plates 66, 67, 69). The S. range contained the Chapel, a long dormitory with side cubicles, and a gatehouse opening into an unroofed external passage which led, indirectly, into the cloister; on the first floor, and reached by an external stair block on the court side, was a hall (Audit Room) and subsidiary rooms (Plate 67). The original cloisters had an arcade of three arches, the N. of which was wider for an entry; the upper floor was jettied. Accommodation for the warden was in the E. range and on the N. were service rooms. Beyond were gardens on to which later outbuildings had encroached (Fig. 41).

Members of the Browne family to whom references are made in this inventory are tabulated as follows:

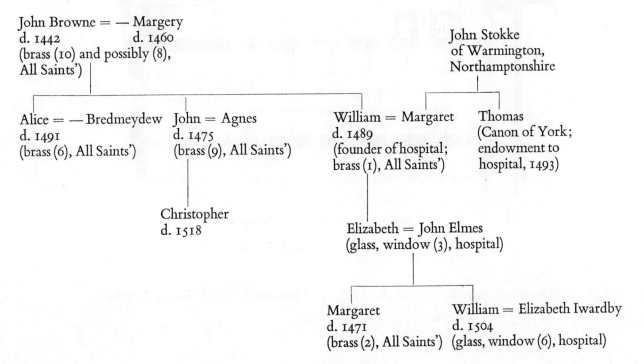

John Browne = — Margery
d. 1442　　　　d. 1460
(brass (10) and possibly (8),
All Saints')

John Stokke
of Warmington,
Northamptonshire

Alice = — Bredmeydew　John = Agnes
d. 1491　　　　　　　d. 1475
(brass (6), All Saints')　(brass (9), All Saints')

William = Margaret　Thomas
d. 1489　　　　　(Canon of York;
(founder of hospital;　endowment to
brass (1), All Saints')　hospital, 1493)

Christopher
d. 1518

Elizabeth = John Elmes
(glass, window (3), hospital)

Margaret　　　　William = Elizabeth Iwardby
d. 1471　　　　　d. 1504
(brass (2), All Saints')　(glass, window (6), hospital)

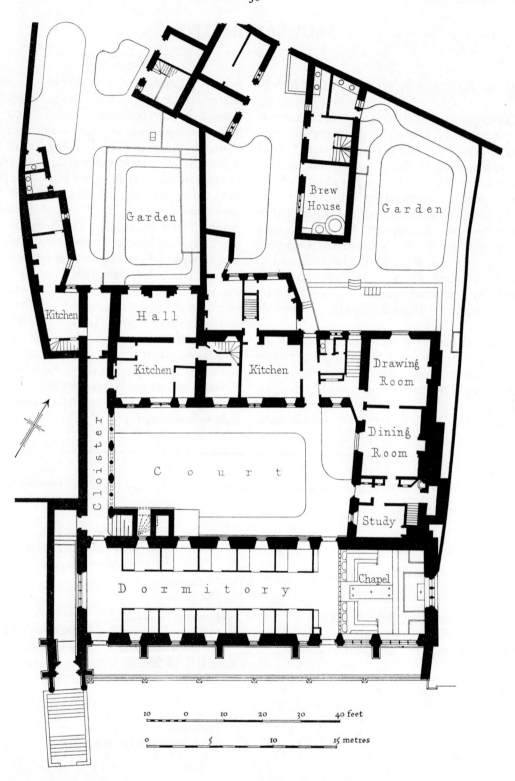

Fig. 41 (48) Browne's Hospital. Copy of plan by F. T. Dollman made in 1858 before alterations.

In 1870 James Fowler, architect, of Louth, began a complete restoration of the main range facing Broad Street. He replaced the other ranges by ones in Gothic style further to the N. and E., and extended the cloisters to the N. The general arrangement and appearance of the main range were preserved with the exception of the gatehouse which was rebuilt as a porch against the W. bay, in line with the cloister. An octagonal stair turret was added at the S.W. corner of the main range. The dormitory ceased to be used as such and the cubicles, shown by Dollman, were removed. The Hospital, built on an impressive scale, retains contemporary glass of special importance in the Chapel and Audit Room.

The main range on the S. has coursed rubble walls with ashlar dressings, buttresses and parapets; a terrace on the S. has an ashlar retaining wall, a feature which existed in one form or another at least as early as the 18th century (Peck, Forster's Letters, opp. p. 11). On the S. elevation are four intermediate two-stage gabled buttresses, but on the N. the end of the W. wall of the former E. range is reflected as a 'flying' buttress. The E. wall of the *Chapel* and probably some lengths of the side walls appear to have been rebuilt by Fowler; the former three-light E. window cannot be traced in the present blank wall. The W. wall of the S. range was probably rebuilt from the ground by Fowler but the original windows were retained; the lower has four graduated lights in a four-centred head, and above is a pair of single-light windows with trefoil heads and

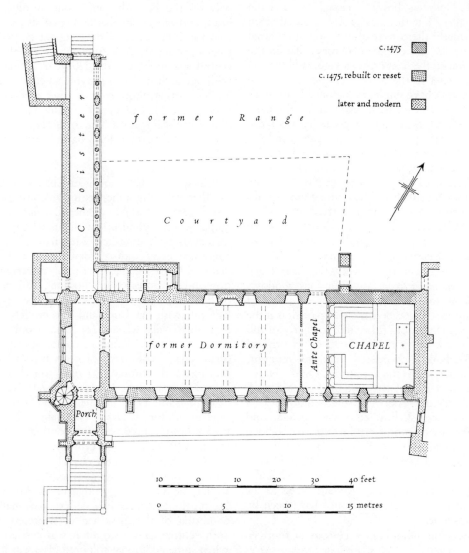

Fig. 42 (48) Browne's Hospital. Plan as existing.

square labels. The S. windows of the chapel, of four and three lights, have battlemented transoms, cinquefoiled lights and mullions rising into the almost round heads. At the W. end of the chapel are opposing doorways on the N. and S. each with continuous moulded jambs and head; above, on the N., is a single light with cinquefoil cusping in a scarcely pointed head, and on the S. a tall window with a cinquefoiled light above and below a transom.

The screen wall between chapel and *Dormitory* is close-studded with intermediate rails and a moulded bressummer which is coved and embattled on the E. and carries the jettied upper wall; in the centre is a wide opening with four-centred head, hollow-and-roll-moulded jambs, caps and bases, but on the first floor no original openings to the gallery are traceable in the stud work. The hard plaster infilling is decorated with compass work. Dollman showed a closed screen at the front of the gallery but this was probably an addition (Plate 67). Formerly there were also opposing external doorways at the W. end of the dormitory; that on the N. remains *in situ* (in the later cross passage), and that on the S. has been reset in the E. wall of the porch. The dormitory windows have single cinquefoiled lights with almost round heads and square labels; beneath the stairs on the N. is a reset 15th-century doorway with depressed head, in the position of a former window. Small external blockings with relieving arches in the N. wall at upper floor level coincide with the ends of the beams. The W. wall of the present room is of 1870; the reset central door is probably 15th-century but heavily repaired. The ceiling has old rafters carried on modern braced cross beams. Reset in the N. wall is a limestone fireplace with depressed head and moulded jambs; partly renewed but perhaps 16th-century.

Rooms over the dormitory, known as the *Audit Room*, *Anteroom* and *Confrater's Room*, are lit by four windows on the S. and one on the N., each of two cinquefoiled lights with transoms. The wooden screen partition at the W. end of the Audit Room (Plate 68), formerly of full height, was rebuilt in 1870 slightly E. of its original position; it has hollow-chamfered stiles and muntins, with coved cornice, and is much restored. On the N. is a fireplace with moulded and depressed four-centred head, probably 17th-century. Between the windows is a wooden cornice with shallow cove with paterae and pierced cresting, each length terminating on moulded uprights; a modified version of the cornice returns on the E. wall. The Confrater's Room at the W. end has an inserted doorway to the upper part of the porch and a reset or modern fireplace in the N. wall; access to the upper room of the original porch must have been by ladder and trap-door.

The roof over the whole range consists of fourteen bays with cambered tie beams, moulded ridge pieces and purlins, and solid arch braces.

The stair block (Plate 68) was probably totally rebuilt in 1870 when the ground-floor was extended to the E., and a medieval window, presumably from the dormitory, reset in the new wall. At the foot of the stairs is a roundheaded moulded arch with an attached shaft on the N. and corbel on the S. and battlemented capitals. Towards the head of the stairs is a moulded arch springing from the wall face. The original handrail consists of a roll-moulding in a hollow recess.

The present porch incorporates some original masonry, including carved and moulded stonework. The S. archway has bracket-moulded jambs and head, with half-round battlemented responds; the doorway has continuous moulded jambs and head, and between archway and doorway is cusped panelling. The outer buttresses are octagonal with moulded and battlemented tops, the inner are simple and gabled. A doorway on the E. with continuous moulded jambs and head, and label with battlemented stops, is reset. The two surviving bays of the original cloister each have twin openings with battlemented capitals and pierced central spandrels; the third bay, of similar design but with one arch wider to provide an entry, has been reset in the northernmost bay. A reset 15th-century doorway at the N. end of the cloister has moulded head dying into plain jambs. The formerly jettied upper floor was replaced in 1870 by a battlemented parapet (Plate 69).

Principal fittings, mostly in Chapel or Audit Room — *Altar slab*: limestone, with five consecration crosses, upper part reworked; medieval. *Alms box* (Plate 55): maple wood, cylindrical with funnel top, iron-bound, medieval. *Bell*: inscribed with names of warden and confrater; early 19th-century. *Brass*: at foot of stairs, plate with black-letter inscription referring to foundation and purposes of the hospital, and bearing shield of Browne; 15th-century. *Chair* (Plate 54): oak, plain, half tub with flat front and one crudely-worked rear leg; medieval. *Chests*: (1) oak, front carved with arcade pattern enclosing lozenges, inscribed 'TE 1629' (Plate 54); (2) oak, front carved with roundels and chip carving, 17th-century; (3) oak, rounded top, heavily bound in iron, three hasps, medieval (Plate 54). *Clock*: of chair-frame type, installed 1840 (*Mercury*, 20 Mar.), reset in W. turret. *Desks*: two pairs of bench ends, the poppy heads carved with confronting eagles, beasts and foliation (Plate 43); 15th century.

Glass: Windows in the chapel contain glass (Plate 36) which is probably contemporary with the building and so may be dated *c.* 1475; that in the Audit Room may be, on the evidence of heraldry, marginally later. The condition of the glass had deteriorated by the early 19th century and restoration was carried out in 1869 when some additional coloured glass was introduced; it was cleaned, and to some degree rearranged, by D. King in 1967. It has been suggested that it is the work of John Glazier of Stamford on the analogy of glass installed by him at Tattershall church (J. P. Hoskins, *The Hospital of William Browne* with supplement on the medieval glass by P. A. Newton and D. King where inscriptions on the glass are given in full). Windows in the chapel depict large figures beneath canopies, against coloured backgrounds; the method of representing jewelled decoration, by coloured glass individually leaded in settings of clear and yellow stain glass, is a technical peculiarity. In the chapel — S. wall (1), above transom: St. James the Great in pilgrim's dress with hat slung on shoulder and holding staff; St. John Baptist, in camel-skin cloak, holding Lamb on book, background diapered with scrolls inscribed 'Ecce agn(us) dei', and at base modern device of a stork rising from nest (perhaps a rebus of Stokke), and inscription '+ me spede'; the Trinity represented by God the Father, Christ on the Cross and the Dove, with orb and scroll inscribed 'S(an)c(tu)s (Trini)tas', and modern diapered background; a Royal Saint, crowned and nimbed, holding sceptre, possibly St. Edmund or St. Edward the Confessor, but the crown and head have been amalgamated. Below transom: head

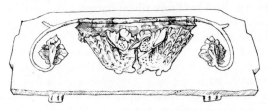

Fig. 43   (48) Browne's Hospital. Misericord in chapel.

and shoulders of female saint, possibly the Virgin, with demi-angel above; female saint, lower part missing, with head-garland of roses and leaves, holding lilies and roses, possibly the Virgin with symbols of Conception; head of the Virgin with Dove descending; the Virgin, lower part missing, crowned and holding model of three-light windows symbolic of the Conception; male head, bearded, perhaps a prophet; head and shoulders of crowned saint, probably the Virgin, with demi-angel above; in tracery are fragments including a spiked wheel presumably from a St. Katharine scene, and a closed door perhaps once associated with a figure of the Virgin. The figures mostly have architectural borders with niches containing lions and eagles alternately, and canopies incorporating miniature heads; along the base of the lights are fragments of an invocatory inscription referring to William and Margaret Browne. Window (2), head of centre light: St. Michael spearing Devil (Plate 39), with background diapered with roundels each depicting a sun; other fragments include the stork device, and sacred monogram 'MR'. In entrance passage to hospital, W. window (3): shield of

Browne (*sable three mallets argent*); shield with Browne's merchant's mark (heart with letter B, surmounted by cross); shield of Browne impaling Elmes (*ermine on three bars couped sable fifteen elm leaves or*) for Elizabeth, daughter of William and Margaret Browne, and husband John Elmes (Plate 39); roundel with stork device. In Audit Room — N. wall (4), shield of Elmes (Fig. 40). S. wall (5): King David, with scroll bearing name, holding second scroll with text from *Psalm CXII*. (Plate 37); St. Paul, head extraneous, with name on scroll, holding sword and scroll inscribed with text from *Colossians III*. 1–2; in tracery, shield of Browne. Window (6): King David, modern head, with namescroll, holding scroll inscribed with contraction of *Psalm CVI*.43; St. Paul, name-scroll, holding scroll inscribed with text from *Corinthians III*. 19 (Plate 37); in tracery, shield of Elmes, impaling possibly Iwardby (*ermine a cross sable*) for William Elmes (1465–1504), son of John and Elizabeth Elmes (see window 3), and wife Elizabeth Iwardby. Window (7): King Solomon, name-scroll bearing text from *Proverbs XV*. 18 (Plate 37); figure composed of unrelated fragments including a male saint wearing a doctor's black cap (Plate 37), and a scroll with composite lettering which contains the name 'Seneca', the classical philosopher. Windows (5)–(7) have backgrounds of yellow-stain quarries with floral designs, and borders with flowers, strapwork, and merchants' marks and stork devices of Browne family (Plate 39), some modern, in the heads.

Paintings: (1), on canvas, copy and translation of inscription on brass (q.v.), in Audit Room formerly in Chapel, dated 1662; (2) (Plate 53), flanking (1), two panels with texts in black-letter in English from *Acts X*.1–5; perhaps 16th-century. *Piscina:* recess, partly under window jamb, with cinquefoil head, sinking in projecting shelf on attached pedestal; 15th-century. *Plate:* cup (ht. 6 ins.), tapering stem with knop, inscribed as gift of Dr. Thomas Cawdry in 1635; inventory of 1677 shows that Dr. Cawdry's gift included a cover to the cup (Account Book); salver (diam. 6 ins.) with three scroll feet, inscribed as gift of James Hurst in 1782, engraved with corn sheaf on rim, by Robert Jones 1781; flagon, (ht. 11¼ ins.), Sheffield plate, by Thomas Law & Co., 19th-century. *Screen* (Plate 41): at W. end of chapel, in ten bays, the centre pair being doors, each divided into two sub bays with elaborate crocketed finials against a traceried background, and coves on each side enriched with miniature vaulting; late 15th-century. *Squint:* in N. wall of chapel, at high level and originally serving warden's lodging, rectangular, blocked; 15th-century. *Stalls* (Plate 42): six, at W. end of chapel, with curved backs, hand rests in form of angels, beasts or birds, and misericords (Plate 43) carved as (a) mermaids, (b) dragons (Fig. 43), (c) eagles, (d) beasts, (e) eagle, (f) grotesque head, perhaps modern; 15th-century. *Tables:* (1) oak, turned legs, inscribed

'1583 PR', for Peter Routh, warden; 17th-century, apparently reusing some earlier pieces. (2) in former dormitory, leaves inlaid with diamond and square pattern; 17th-century, legs and base modern.

(49) LORD BURGHLEY'S HOSPITAL, High Street St. Martins (Fig. 44; Plate 80). The Hospital of St. John the Baptist and St. Thomas the Martyr was founded in c. 1170–80 for the relief of travellers and the local poor. In 1548–9 it was described as 'on the bridge' (Cal. Pat. 1548–9, 358–60). By the end of the Middle Ages its function as a hospital appears to have fallen into abeyance; only the chapel con-. tinued in proper use (Chantry Cert. XXXV; Val. Eccl. (Record Commission) IV, 143) and by the 16th century it was called a free chapel. The hospital was bought by William Cecil in 1549 (Cal. Pat. (1548–9), 358) and part was maintained as an alms-house by 1595 (NRO, Fitzwilliam Misc., 433), but the present hospital was not formally reconstituted until 1597 in which year Lord Burghley endowed it (Ex. MS, 75/44). There were to be thirteen old men one of whom was to serve as warden.

The building at the E. end of the site dates from the late 16th or early 17th century and incorporates part of the substructure of the 12th-century hospital. Also in the 17th century a new range was added on the W. to accommodate ten of the thirteen men stipulated in the Founder's ordinance. The date stone on the central gable is eroded but probably reads 1616. Various alterations were made subsequently and in 1964–5 the rooms were completely rearranged.

The 12th-century work, in 'Barnack' stone, consists of a barrel-vaulted tunnel running diagonally beneath the N.E. corner of the building, between two semicircular arches, each of two unchamfered orders, on the N. and E. faces of the 12th-century hospital (Plate 4). There is a clasping buttress on the corner of the 12th-century building, now partly obscured and visible externally as a pilaster. Above the arches and continuing across the buttress is a chamfered string-course; a second, higher, string-course survives only on the buttress. Reset on top of the buttress is a band of 12th-century tooth-ornament. On the S., a smaller half-arch spans the 6 ft. gap between the 12th-century hospital and the earlier bridge-pier (see mon. 64). The 12th-century hospital was built partly in the river and the tunnel prevented total obstruction of the S. arch of the bridge.

The present hospital comprises an L-shaped block next to the bridge, presumably of the late 16th or early 17th century, and a long W. range which was added in 1616. The former, of coursed rubble and two storeys,

has its E. wall built above the parapet of the 12th-century bridge, and its N. wall follows that of the original hospital. The S. wing, parallel with the street, has a blocked central doorway with moulded jambs and head, leading to a cross passage which was the original entrance to the hospital. The N.E. corner of the building as far as the 12th-century buttress is of pindle and was rebuilt by Browning in 1849 when the present bridge was erected. The windows have ovolo-moulded mullions, but a number of openings have been blocked. The N. wing has been considerably patched and the S. elevation much altered with the insertion of new windows; three wooden four-light windows with diamond mullions survive on the S. and another on the N. Inside, there are chamfered cross beams, some with run-out stops, others stop-moulded. A large window in the W. gable has been blocked by the later W. range.

The W. range, straight-jointed against the foregoing, has a chamfered plinth on the N. of reused 12th-century masonry, and the walls contain a number of blocks of this date laid in alternating courses with rubble; some have roll-mouldings. Other reused blocks have masons' marks. On the N. (Plate 80) six tall chimney stacks rising from the wall are 18th-century, replacing earlier stacks. Between them are flush gabled dormers, formerly with finials. The windows have ovolo-moulded mullions with labels, but one has been enlarged. The S. elevation, considerably altered in 1964, is dominated by three large flush gabled dormers. In the apex of the central gable is a slab carved with figures '1 . . 6', probably for date 1616, although the third digit might be a 4. The windows have moulded mullions but many are modern. Before the recent changes there were eight doorways but five were not original; an old plan reproduced by Peck shows only a central and end doors (Peck, Desiderata Curiosa, I (1732), pl. opp. p. 14 of lib. 5). These additional doorways were probably inserted when the interior arrangement was altered from one with a long corridor and rooms leading off, to one with larger rooms each with separate outside doors (Fig. 9). Formerly, alternate partitions terminated against the central mullions of windows in the rear wall, and each stack served fireplaces in adjacent rooms. A stair at the E. end led to a long semi-attic lit from both sides. It was probably originally without divisions. On a jamb of a ground-floor window is a metal plaque inscribed 'Easter Flood in the year 1640 the water came up to this mark'.

(50) FRYER'S HOSPITAL, Kettering Road (Fig. 45; Plate 160), one storey, coursed rubble walls with freestone dressings, was built in 1832 to designs by George Basevi following bequests in the will of Henry Fryer. The accommodation originally comprised six single rooms entered from three shared lobbies but recent alterations have closed these

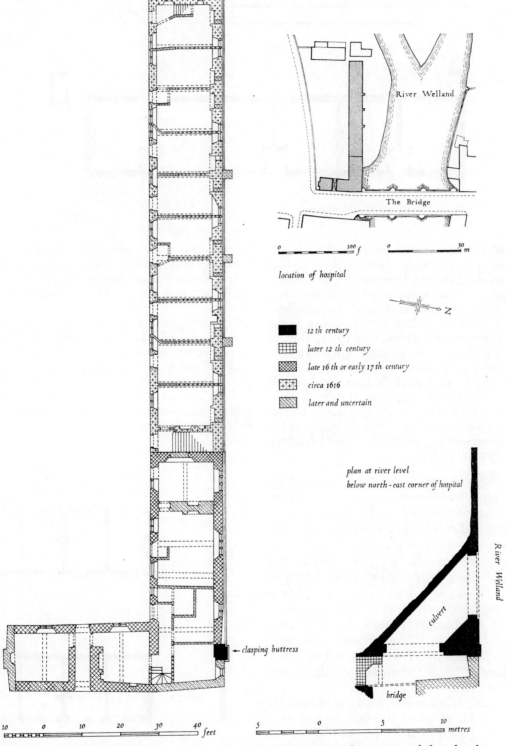

River Welland

The Bridge

0   100 f   0   30 m

location of hospital

Z

■ 12 th century

⊞ later 12 th century

▨ late 16 th or early 17 th century

⊞ circa 1616

▧ later and uncertain

plan at river level
below north - east corner of hospital

River Welland

culvert

bridge

← clasping buttress

10   0   10   20   30   40 feet

5   0   5   10 metres

Fig. 44   (49) Lord Burghley's Hospital, before recent alterations. Plan at ground-floor level and of N.E. corner at river level.

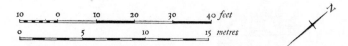

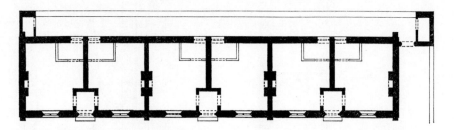

Fig. 45   (50) Fryer's Hospital.

entrances and access is now from the back.

The main elevation in the Tudor style is divided into three identical units by buttresses. Each unit has a central doorway with four-centred head beneath a parapeted gable with Gothic pinnacle, and windows from which the transoms have been removed. In the three gables are carved mullioned panels: 1, arms of Truesdale, inscribed in raised Gothic letters 'Thomae Truesdale insig:'; 2, arms of Fryer and crest of Hurst, inscribed 'Hen. Fryer Fundatoris insig:' and 'Iacobi Hurst. Benefactoris insig:'; 3, arms of Burghley, inscribed 'Gul: Dni: de Burghley. insig:'. Above the W. buttress is an inscription 'Geo. Basevi: Archt. 1832'. Low gate piers with cusped panelled sides have been reset from a central position.

(51) HOPKINS' HOSPITAL, St. Peter's Street (Fig. 46; Plate 160), was founded on the initiative of John Hopkins who opened a subscription in 1770 when he was Alderman. The Corporation gave the site which was on the Town Walls, and the Earl of Exeter the gardens on the W. The proceeds of a special performance by Mr. Whitley's Company at the Theatre (Blore, 221–2) were donated, and subscriptions were received in 1770 from the Town Council and Alderman Hopkins, and in 1772 from the Earl of Exeter (Chamberlains' Accounts; Exeter Day Books). By 1773 the hospital had been built (bequest of James Hurst). In 1962 the rooms were replanned and several doors blocked.

The almshouse, of two storeys, has ashlar walls and is built in the Gothic style with two-light pointed windows, embattled parapets and depressed four-centred doorways. Two upper windows are blind to preserve a regular design, and between the central windows is a scrolled cartouche with the arms of Stamford above which is a reused and recut gargoyle of a crowned head against a background of a traceried windowhead

(Plate 119). On the parapet are openwork pinnacles. Each floor had four rooms which were entered separately from the outside, those on the ground floor from the W. and those on the first floor from a raised platform on the E.

Opposite, on the N. side of St. Peter's Street, is a projection with a false gable which reflects the N. gable of the almshouse; it was built *c.* 1770 and replaces the medieval gate in the Town Wall. The Council's gift of £70 in 1770 was for repairing the gate as well as for building the almshouse (Chamberlains' Accounts). The gable feature was reset early in the present century when the road was widened.

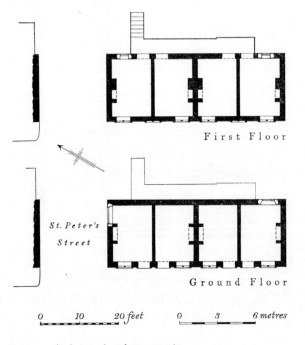

Fig. 46   (51) Hopkins' Hospital.

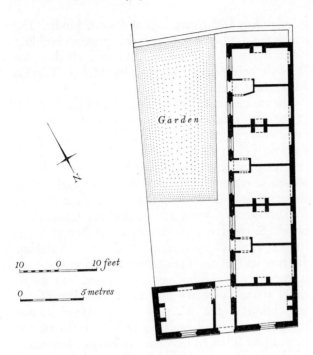

Fig. 47 (52) Snowden's Hospital.

(52) SNOWDEN'S HOSPITAL, Scotgate (Fig. 47). The almshouse was founded under the will of Richard Snowden who died in 1604. He left all his land for the benefit of seven poor widows who were at first housed in a building he owned on the site of the present almshouse. In 1822 the hospital received the interest on £1,000 by the will of Henry Fryer, which probably led the way towards rebuilding (PRO, PCC, 17 June 1823). The new almshouse, entirely replacing the old and providing for eight widows, was built at a cost said to be £450 (Burton, Appendix 11–13; contracts advertised in *Mercury*, 18 Apr. 1823). The architect was Thomas Pierce (Chamberlain's Accounts, 1822). Recently accommodation was reorganized to house three widows.

The hospital, of one storey, slate roofs, with red brick stacks of 1877 (Municipal Charities Treasurer's Book), is built in the Tudor style. The ashlar street front has a central doorway with depressed four-centred head between two-light side windows. Across the front, below the eaves, is inscribed 'Snowden's Hospital rebuilt 1823 H.P. West Esq. Mayor'. The dwellings have rubble walls; doors and windows have Tudor heads.

(53) TRUESDALE'S HOSPITAL, Scotgate (Fig. 48; Plate 160). Thomas Truesdale, attorney, died in 1700 leaving land in Morton and Boston, Lincolnshire, and a house in Scotgate, for the benefit of six

poor men. By 1831 accommodation for eight men had been provided but in that year George Basevi reported that the building needed replacement and proposed a hospital to house twelve men. Building began in 1832 to designs by Basevi, and was completed the following year at a total cost said to be £3,300. In addition to the twelve almshouses a

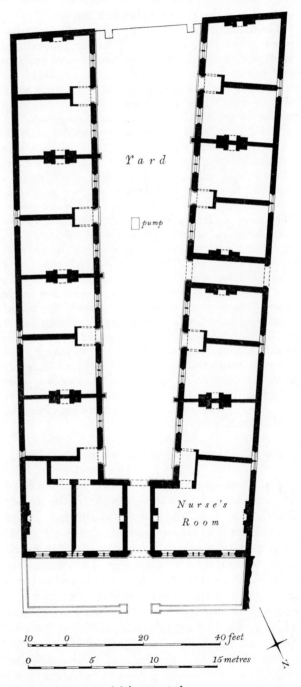

Fig. 48 (53) Truesdale's Hospital.

committee room and two rooms for a nurse were provided (Burton, Appendix 45, 47, 48). Richardson was contractor, stone carving was by W. G. Nicholl and iron railings were by W. and S. Summers at a cost of £47.10.0. The rooms at the S. end of the E. range were added in 1844 by Richardson, continuing Basevi's design, for £447, and coalhouses were rebuilt (account book at Kelham's, 9 Broad Street; Knipe's map).

The building is in the Tudor Gothic style with parapeted gables over archways all having four-centred heads with square labels; the windows have mullions and square heads. The single-storey dwellings are arranged in two confronting rows behind a street block with a central through-archway. The forecourt is flanked by gable walls against adjoining properties. The ashlared street block has angel-stops to the entrance archway, probably supplied by W. G. Nicholl, and in the spandrels are the letters 'Th' and 'T' for the founder. In the central gable is a cusped quatrefoil containing a quartered shield for Truesdale; in the side gables are quatrefoils enclosing blank shields. The string-course is inscribed 'G. Basevi Archt. 1832'. Chimney shafts are either octagonal or rectangular set diagonally, in groups or in pairs, the pair above the entrance linked with cusped arches. The entrance passage is vaulted and flanking it are lead rainwater heads inscribed '1832'. The almshouses, in coursed rubble, consisted of single rooms entered from shared open lobbies, but recent alterations have amalgamated the rooms into larger units. Over the entrances are square panels with blank shields. On the W. an almost central cross passage leads from the yard to ground behind Snowden's Hospital; in the gable over the archway is an inscribed panel recording the hospital's rebuilding and enlargement. A tall retaining wall with two-stage buttresses closes the yard on the S.

For WILLIAMSON'S ALMSHOUSES see mon. (398).

(54) STAMFORD SCHOOL stands on the N. side of St. Paul's Street and incorporates part of the former church of St. Paul. The school was founded in 1532 and perhaps in c. 1548 moved into the church of St. Paul, the parish of which had recently been amalgamated with that of St. George. The church was probably shortened at this time, the E. end remaining in use as a schoolroom until 1930 when it was restored as a chapel. A second schoolroom was added on the N. in 1833. (Deed, *History of Stamford School*, 14, 42–6.)

The Chapel (Fig. 49; Plate 6) is a rectangular building with a combined *Nave* and sanctuary, and a *N. aisle*. The walls are of 'Barnack' stone, coursed

rubble with ashlar dressings and some pindle. The roofs are lead-covered. Of the present building (65 ft. by 29 ft.) only the E. half is of early date, the W. half being added in 1930 by Messrs. Traylen and Lenton, architects.

The two E. bays of the S. wall are of the first half of the 12th century, but the plan of the church of this date is not known; it may have been rectangular without a chancel. In c. 1200 a N. aisle was added, and the present arcade of four bays seems to be an authentic restoration of the aisle's original length although only the two E. bays are ancient. The E. wall also dates from c. 1200 and either replaced an earlier E. wall or, alternatively, a chancel arch. Larger windows were added to the S. wall during the first half of the 14th century. Late in the 15th century new windows were introduced into the E. walls of the sanctuary and aisle. The date of the demolition of the W. part of the church is not known, but a wall built across it just W. of the second pier (Plate 6) may date from the conversion of the building into a schoolroom in the 16th century. Excavations in 1902 (Deed, *op. cit.*, 66) revealed the 'original floor level'. In 1929–30 excavations were carried out ahead of the restoration of the building as a chapel. Two pier bases, fragments of medieval carving and window tracery were found (*Stamfordian*, no. 8, 4, 5).

Architectural Description — The *Nave* and sanctuary has an E. wall, probably of c. 1200, with a low central pilaster buttress flanked by areas of 19th-century pindle facing; not exactly in line with the arcade is a taller pilaster buttress. Above the facing are lengths of string-course, chamfered above and below, some enriched with saw-tooth decoration; these decorated pieces are probably 12th-century, reset, the remainder contemporary with the wall. The wall was thickened internally in the 15th century and the E. window inserted; the window has four graduated cinquefoiled lights in a triangular head with external label and grotesque head-stops. The two E. bays of the S. wall have a corbel-table with miniature arches and rounded corbels, supporting a later battlemented parapet. The lower part of the wall has a refacing of pindle. In the E. bay the corbel-table is lower by about 18 ins. than in the adjacent bay, and in a different plane, indicating the rebuilding of the E. bay in the 14th century when a window of that date was inserted. Only one pilaster buttress is 12th-century, that at the S.E. angle being replaced by a long projecting buttress perhaps in the 14th century; a former pilaster between the two bays is shown by Peck but is now obscured by a wide projecting area of ashlar of unknown origin. In the E. bay a short length of chamfered string-

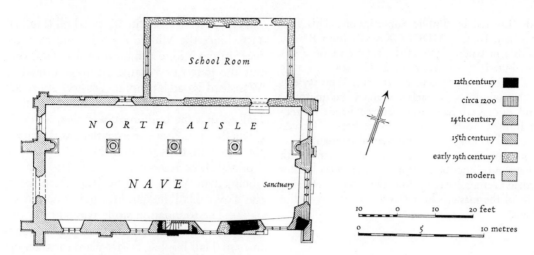

Fig. 49 (54) Former Church of St. Paul.

course with saw-tooth and billet ornament survives and continues in the W. bay. Early 14th-century windows with rectangular heads and demi-reticulated tracery are in each bay, one with a grotesque headstop, the other with one light blocked internally; the windows interrupt the string-course which is reset below the sills. Reset between the bays is a 15th-century doorway with continuous moulded jambs and head; it was formerly internal and is now solely decorative. In the S. wall is a doorway to a former rood loft stair; it has a chamfered ogee head without rebates and is 14th-century. One jamb of the upper opening to the loft is original.

The N. aisle has a N.E. buttress of slight projection, presumably of c. 1200; against it is a later buttress with a reset chamfered string-course. The E. window of three trefoiled lights is 15th-century. The N. arcade, comprising two original and two modern bays, has an E. respond capital with leaf and volute-type decoration; the capital incorporates a further lobe on the S., supported on a long conical corbel, but it was apparently not designed to carry an arch (Plate 9). This respond is partly hidden by the 15th-century thickening of the E. wall. The two round piers with chamfered, square sub-bases, water-holding bases and stiff-leaf capitals (Plate 8) carry double-chamfered arches; the E. part of the third arch is original. The third pier and W. respond have original square sub-bases, presumably in situ. The aisle wall is early 19th-century and modern.

The Roof, over the E. part of nave, is flat-pitched and comprises tie beams, short king posts, and purlins, probably of the 17th century. The second tie beam is supported on a later projection with moulded corbelling.

Fittings — Coffin lids: (1) (Plate 33), under first recess on S., limestone slab with black-letter inscription arranged crosswise. 'Henri Elyngton jadiz Parson de sa glyse gyt iscy; dieu de sa alme eyt mercy amen; Katerine & Margarete preie: p li; a vost chapel il fut pour: amy'; Elyngton was rector of St. Paul's between 1384 and 1400; at end of inscription is incised floral decoration. (2), under second recess, miniature lid (2 ft. 1 in. long), tapering sides with central ridge and fish-tail motifs indicating crosses, probably 13th-century. Images: (1, 2) found in 1930, probably a facing pair; lower half of draped figure, and another similar but less damaged, both medieval. (3), over W. door, male head, perhaps 17th-century. Monument recesses: (1), in S. wall, with chamfered imposts, double chamfered arch, medieval, much renewed; (2), adjacent to (1), with moulded imposts, continuous roll-and-hollow moulded jambs and head, and a second chamfered arch at back of recess, 14th-century; (3), reset over W. doorway, formerly on N. side of church, segmental-arched string-course, chamfered below, with Lombardic inscription in two lines, the letters misleadingly accentuated in paint, '+HIC IACET ... IUSTACIUS MALERBE .... N... IS STAM(orN)FORDIE CUIUS ANIME PROPICIETUR DEUS AMEN'. The eroded words after the name have been read as '.. quondam burgensis ..'; Malerbe was Parliamentary representative for Stamford in 1322 (Parl. Writs, II, 1134) (Plate 33). Piscina: in S. wall, three recesses, the central with trefoil drain, modern projecting shelf, 13th-century; the side recesses, probably credences, with chamfered ogee heads, 14th-century. Miscellanea: (1), reset in N. wall, window head found in 1930, 14th-century but much restored; (2), over first recess, a keystone with rectangular decorative panel containing an oval or heart within looped branches, perhaps 13th-century (Fig. 50).

The Schoolroom, built in 1833, necessitated the rebuild of most of the north wall of the church. The walls are of pindle with freestone quoins. The foundation stone is inscribed, 'Erected by Public Subscription. This first Stone was laid IX Oct MDCCCXXXIII John Roden Esq Mayor'; in truth £373 of the total cost of £522 was contributed by the Rev. F. E. Gretton, recently appointed headmaster (Deed, *op. cit.*, 45). The style is Tudor; the windows at each end have cinquefoiled lights and doorways have four-centred heads in rectangular frames. The open roof has tie beams, curved braces secured to king posts, and shaped pendants.

Reset in room N. of schoolroom is a stone panel with scroll surround, inscribed 'Donum M: Tho Bellot Stamfordiae Gymnasi Archis Ano Dni 1609', referring to the gift of the master's house to the school by Bellot and others.

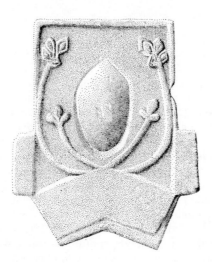

Fig. 50   (54) Former Church of St. Paul. Carved keystone.

(55) Former SCHOOL AND SCHOOLHOUSE, Wharf Road, built in the early 19th century as a Girls' National School. The schoolroom of six bays has walls of coursed rubble and the openings have flat arches in brick. The detached schoolhouse with coursed rubble walls, class 10 plan, has wooden ovolo-moulded mullioned windows with iron casements, of two and three lights; it was built in plain Jacobean style in 1851 (*Mercury*, 2 May).

(56) Former CONGREGATIONAL SCHOOL, behind No. 7 St. Paul's Street, opened in 1821 (Burton, 200). The walls of coursed rubble have roundheaded windows in red brick surrounds; above are small dormers. The school consisted of a single room. The church accounts for 1821 record only repairs by Lamford, a carpenter, suggesting that the school may have been formed out of a previous structure.

(57) TOWN HALL, St. Mary's Hill (Fig. 51; Plate 117). Since the Middle Ages a room over the gateway on the bridge had been used as the Town Hall, but the gateway became an impediment and the Wansford Road Turnpike Trustees approached the Council in 1774 over the resiting of the Town Hall so that the building could then be demolished (Hall Book 4, f. 26). Agreement was reached with the town in 1775 (Hall Book 4, ff. 30–1) and the Council chose a site on St. Mary's Hill. The Trustees obtained an Act in 1776 enabling them to demolish the Town Hall and build a new one (16 Geo. III, c. 74). The foundation stone was laid the same year (*Mercury*, 16 May) and the building was completed in 1779 (Hall Book 4, f. 81); plans for seats and other woodwork were made in 1780 by John Dixon, carpenter. Payments for improvements and maintenance are recorded in 1807 and 1819 (Hall Book 5). In 1819 Thomas Pierce, surveyor, reported on the state of the roof, suggesting its replacement for £158 (Hall Book 5, f. 152). A sum of £250 was said to be necessary for work on the Hall. However, bills amounting to £330 were presented including £159 from Jas. Richardson, carpenter (Chamberlains' Accounts). Following the Municipal Reform Act of 1835 improvements were made to the Hall and to the Gaol behind it. In 1838 the kitchen was partitioned to form a Town Clerk's office which contained a safe; Richardson received £75 for both plans and workmanship. Sometime in the early 19th century, possibly in 1819, the entrance hall was remodelled and the present stair installed. Later, perhaps in *c.* 1836, a wing was built in the angle at the rear, originally of two storeys but later heightened. Further buildings were added at the rear in 1891.

Although no designer is known it is recorded that Henry Tatam, cabinet maker, 'explained' the proposed plans to the Council in 1775 on behalf of the Turnpike Trustees (Hall Book 4, f. 40). It may be suggested that the small-scale architectural details evident on the main elevations may be due to Tatam's involvement with the proposals for the new building (see also mon. (97)).

The building has almost identical N. and W. elevations of ashlar; the remainder is of coursed rubble. It has three tiers of windows but the front range is two storeys high over a basement and part at the rear has three storeys. The symmetrical W. elevation of seven bays rises above a terrace with two modern flights of steps and railings, the central three bays breaking forward slightly. The ground stage below a platband is rusticated; all the lower openings have round heads but the window-

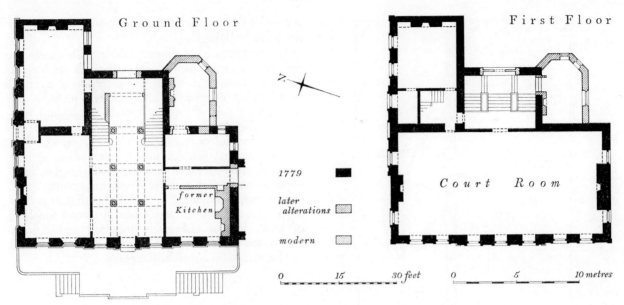

Ground Floor

First Floor

Court Room

former Kitchen

1779

later alterations

modern

0   15   30 feet   0   5   10 metres

Fig. 51   (57) Town Hall.

tympana are solid. The central doorway is emphasized by projecting rustication and a keystone. The two upper tiers of windows, in plain ashlar walls with rusticated quoins, have keystones and surrounds enriched with alternate paterae and fluting (Plate 121). Between the top tier of windows is a cartouche (Plate 119) with scroll surround in bold relief, bearing the arms of Stamford (*gules three lions pass. in pale or impaling chequy or and az.*). The moulded cornice has slight projection. The N. elevation repeats that on the W. but, owing to the sloping ground, the terrace is omitted. The second bay from the W. conceals a chimney stack and all openings in the bay are blind.

Internally, the entrance hall has six large wooden Doric columns and a double-flight staircase with turned newels, all of the early 19th century. The N.W. room was divided in the early 19th century and a second doorway inserted from the entrance hall; the partition has since been removed. The S.W. room, originally a kitchen and divided in 1838 (see above), was provided with a safe above which are the painted arms of Stamford and date 1849. The N.E. room has a plaster cornice of *c.* 1830. In the S.E. angle a small room with canted sides was built in 1836 and formerly had access from the S. On the first floor the Hall or Session Room occupies the W. range. It has two tiers of windows on all but the E. side, where there is an elliptical-headed opening forming a small gallery. Two benches with fielded-panelled backs and shaped tops are part of the Court fittings made by John Dixon for £25 in 1781 (Hall Book); a third bench and a central seat with higher back, recorded in an old photograph, no longer survive. Other fittings include: a portrait on panel of William Cecil, Lord Burghley (1520–98), 16th or 17th-century;

a board inscribed in black-letter with list of mayors to 1700; two boards listing mayors from 1700 to 1749 and from 1750 to 1800, and Royal Arms of 1780 on canvas, all in shaped and eared surrounds of 1780.

(58) ASSEMBLY ROOMS, St. George's Square (Figs. 52, 53; Plate 91). In 1727 the site was let to Askew Kirk on condition that an Assembly Room be built (Ex. MS, 88/42). Assemblies had been held monthly

5   0   10 feet   0   5 metres

Fig. 52   (58) Assembly Rooms. Front elevation.

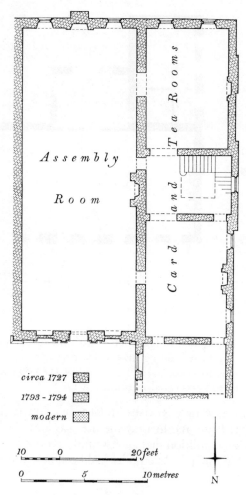

Fig. 53   (58) Assembly Rooms.

corner of the square and contrasts with the adjacent domestic buildings.

The buildings have coursed rubble walls except for the N. elevation which is ashlared; roofs are hipped. The street front of the main Room consists of a central roundheaded doorway with rusticated pilasters and pediment, a pair of flanking roundheaded blind windows, and angle pilasters supporting an architrave, frieze and cornice, below a parapet (Figs. 13, 54, 55). Few original internal features survive; exceptions include some bolection-moulded panelling in two heights, and a stone fireplace with a carved wooden surround and overmantel, surmounted by a broken pediment enclosing a cartouche draped with husks. A second fireplace, of 1868, has an elaborately moulded 18th-century overmantel with scroll side-brackets, eared surround and broken pediment as the foregoing.

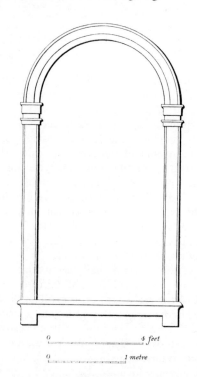

Fig. 54   (58) Assembly Rooms. Blind window.

The later rooms occupy a two-storey range parallel to the earlier Rooms; it has coursed rubble walls with flush dressings. The E. front, facing the square, has stepped window lintels and continuous sills uniform with the neighbouring house, No. 27 St. Mary's Street (361). The range has a central stair hall, now with later stair, between the former card and tea rooms. In the N. room is a late 18th-century wooden fireplace surround enriched with agricultural emblems (Plate 130).

at a house in Barn Hill since before 1720, and monthly assemblies were maintained at the present building after Kirk's death in 1738 (*Mercury*, 14 Apr. 1720, 15 Aug. 1745). It is recorded that in 1721 Kirk had given up the governorship of his boarding school to his wife, hitherto a mantua maker, so that he could devote his time to teaching dancing at the school (*Mercury*, 9 Mar. 1721). The building of *c*. 1727 consists of a large room end-on to the street. In 1793 and 1795 payments were made for various works on the new rooms adjoining the Assembly Rooms; Thomas Pilkington undertook the joinery work in 1795. In 1797 Robert Hames carried out sundry masonry repairs for £16.10.0. These new rooms are presumably the late 18th-century 'card and tea rooms' on the W. of the main Room (Burton, 13). In 1868 the Rooms were restored unsympathetically by William Langley. The classically-designed entrance front brings emphasis to the

have eared surrounds and cornices and originally had truncated pediments; the attic stage comprises an architrave, plain frieze, cornice with lion's-head waterspouts and balustrade having central wreath and ribbon motif with openwork side bays. The interior has been much altered. The lecture room on the first floor remains undivided; part of the gallery, now a room, survives on the S. and is supported on two fluted cast-iron columns and contains part of a heavy dentilled plaster cornice. The stair to the former observatory remains in the S.E. corner.

(60) Former THEATRE, St. Mary's Street (Figs. 57, 58, 59; Plate 91). In 1766 William Clark, a Stamford mason, and James Whitley 'comedian', leased the site from the Earl of Exeter (Court Roll, Easter 1766) and immediately began construction of the theatre. It was completed in 1768 (*Mercury*, 17 Mar.) at a cost of £806 (Harrod, 368). Whitley had a company of actors and was involved in the management of at least six Midland theatres (Baker, *Biographica Dramatica*, 746–7). He was closely connected with Stamford and his wife was buried in St. John's church. As built, the theatre had a large stage, a gallery, pit and two tiers of boxes (hand bills in Stamford library). A cellar belonging to an earlier

Fig. 55 (58) Assembly Rooms. Doorway.

(59) Former STAMFORD INSTITUTION, St. Peter's Hill (Plate 156), was built in 1842 to a design by Bryan Browning (Stamford Institution *Report* (1842), 17) at a cost of £1,724; the contractor was Moses Peal (*Mercury*, 27 Aug., 24 Sept., 1841). It contained a concert and lecture room with a gallery to be used as a museum, a library and reading room, newspaper and committee rooms, laboratory, and apartments for a resident. An octagonal observatory and camera obscura, formerly rising from the roof as a cupola but now demolished, were not part of the first plan (*Mercury*, 3 Sept. 1841).

It is of two storeys and cellar with Ketton ashlar front wall and coursed rubble rear walls. The Greek-style street elevation in three bays has rusticated ground stage, central pedimented doorway with battered, moulded and eared architrave and carved axial brackets supporting a pediment (Plate 157), and flanking roundheaded windows in square recesses. The tall first-floor sash windows

Fig. 56 (60) Theatre. Central doorway.

house on the site was incorporated in the structure. In 1849–53 extensive alterations were made by the Marquess of Exeter and his tenant, Mr. Cople, when the floors of the pit and the stage were apparently levelled (*Mercury*, 15 Dec. 1848, 23 Sept. 1853). The theatre finally closed in June 1871 and the building was put to other uses (*Mercury*, 26 May).

below the modern floor is lit by side windows and has a number of stone partitions of *c*. 1768; the S. half below the stage must have been dressing rooms from which the stage was reached by a stair on the E. A narrow rectangular area in the centre may be the orchestra pit. A wall defining a passage on the E. side, and two further

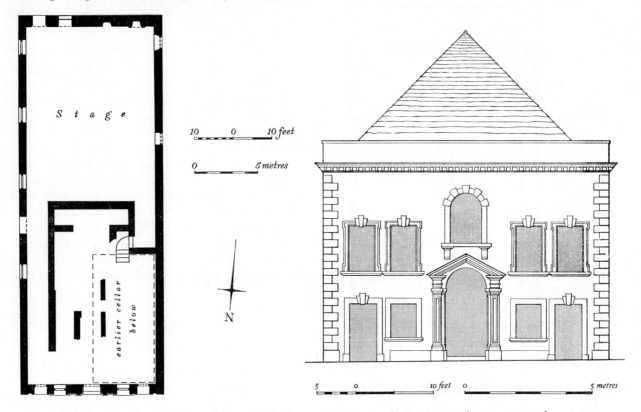

Fig. 57   (60) Former Theatre. Plan at basement level.

Fig. 58   (60) Former Theatre. Front elevation.

The walls are of coursed rubble except for the ashlar front wall. The classically designed main front on the N. has openings of domestic proportions but arranged in an unorthodox manner in order to comply with the internal floor levels required by the theatre. It has rusticated quoins, cornice with shaped brackets, and a parapet. A central roundheaded doorway with panelled pilasters and open pediment is flanked by side doorways and windows each with wide but plain architraves (Figs. 10, 12, 56). The side doors may have given access to the upper levels of seats. The four upper windows, in two pairs, have moulded eared architraves, triple keystones and moulded sills; a slightly higher central window has a round head with moulded architrave and bold, spaced rustication, and a sill supported on shaped brackets. Doorways and windows in the side walls have flush dressings. Internally, the main floor is now reached by a short flight of stairs from the street level. The space

short walls to the W., probably formed part of the support for the boxes. The early 18th-century cellar in the N.W. corner has an ashlar barrel vault. At main-floor level are further windows in the side walls including a pair at the N. end, which are at different levels to conform with a former sloping gallery; scars of a stair to this gallery survive in the E. side wall.

The hipped roof is in eight bays with tie beams, kingpost trusses, and square-set staggered purlins, three pairs to a bay. At the N. end, poles set at a slope between the tie beam and the end wall held a former plaster ceiling over the gallery; some plaster painted bright blue survives. The auditorium is now divided by a cross wall presumably introduced in 1871; in the centre is a large reset doorcase with double doors, fluted Ionic side pilasters, pulvinated frieze, dentil cornice, and broken pediment. This doorway may have come from the entrance hall.

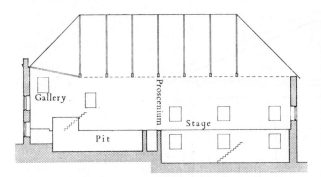

Fig. 59 (60) Theatre.
Diagrammatic section showing former arrangement.

(61) LIBRARY, High Street (Figs. 60, 61; Plate 151), formerly the 'Portico' to the market and shambles which stood beyond. This market replaced the butchers' shambles which were in the High Street, opposite St. Michael's church; they had last been rebuilt in 1751 and in 1801 the town decided to buy the White Lion Inn in the High Street as a new site for them (Hall Book III, 193; IV, 325, 321, 337). Schemes by Henry Tatam, costing £2,200, and W. D. Legg, costing £1,500, were considered and Legg's design chosen (Hall Book IV, 364–7, 169–71). Work started in 1804. The completed building was vested in the council in September 1808, but by 1868 the market had become dilapidated and one row of shambles was demolished (General Purposes Committee, Sept. 1868; Jan. 1881). Its adaptation as a library was completed in 1906 (Stamford Council minutes book G, May and July 1903; date-panel).

The ashlar portico originally consisted of an open propyleum with lower side wings, one being a watch-house (police station) the other a house for the Beadle; there was also provision for a fire engine. The butter market was within the portico, the fish market stood to the N., and beyond were 53 stalls of shambles in four rows (Burton, 77). The front elevation comprises four Tuscan columns, no frieze, and wide pediment producing deep overhangs at front and sides; immediately behind the columns is a modern wall. The W. side wing has a new, lower roof and a window has replaced the former doorway; the E. wing, now the library entrance, has a roof which partly obscures the windows which lit the portico on this side.

(62) STAMFORD AND RUTLAND INFIRMARY, Deeping Road (Fig. 62; Plate 161). Henry Fryer in his will of 1823 bequeathed a large sum of money for an infirmary to be built within five years of his death. A competition was held in 1825; Basevi refused to

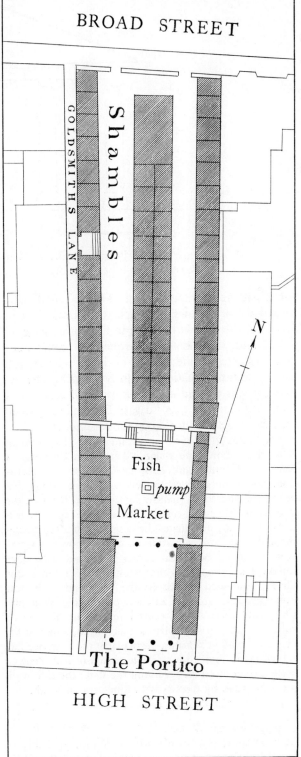

Fig. 60 (61) The Library. Plan of Shambles showing original arrangement (1:500).

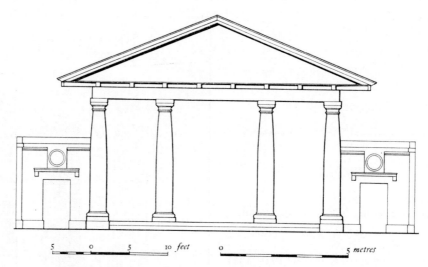

5   0   5   10 *feet*

0   5 *metres*

Fig. 61   (61) Portico to former Shambles, now the Library.
Reconstruction of elevation.

participate in a competition and H. E. Kendall submitted a Norman design which was passed over in
favour of the present building in the gothic style by
J. P. Gandy. In 1826 the Marquess of Exeter conveyed 2½ acres of land, the site of the Greyfriars (46),
for £250, and building began forthwith. The infirmary was opened on 5 August 1828 and cost a
total of £8,700. In 1841 Edward Brown left £5,000
for a fever ward and £6,000 for its support.

The building, of two storeys and cellars, has walls of
Wittering pindle with ashlar and freestone dressings of
Ketton and some Stamford stone. The front, S., elevation, consisting of a centrepiece and cross wings, has
been little altered. A shallow light-well in front of the
side wings serves the cellars. The centrepiece, which is
faced in ashlar, punctuates the design with a tall battlemented oriel above a continuous band of cusped diaper-
work, and tall octagonal corner buttresses with ogee
finials. The wings, in a more restrained Tudor gothic
idiom, contained wards. At the back and sides new
buildings have masked and altered the old structure.
Originally there was a central rear wing of coursed
rubble. Inside, in spite of much alteration, some of the
original building remains, particularly the entrance hall
which is sub-divided by a triple arcade of four-centred
arches, the central arch framing the stair; the side walls
are articulated by recesses with four-centred heads.

For Porter's Lodge, see mon. (46).

(63) Former WORKHOUSE of St. Martin's Parish,
Water Street, consists of three buildings, probably of
late 18th-century date. A separate block to the S., of
two storeys with rubble walls, contains seven dwellings arranged as reflecting pairs with one room on each
floor; they may be the 'new cottage houses' built by the

Earl of Exeter, payments being recorded for slating in
1796 and masonry in 1798 (Day Books). A second range
on the west side, with coursed rubble walls, one storey
and attics, consists of three rooms. A workshop, on
the street side, with rubble wall, slate roof, three storeys,
has three large segmental headed windows on the first
floor, small ones above, and none on N. side; probably
built in 1825 (*Mercury*, 29 July).

(64) TOWN BRIDGE (Plate 157). A bridge at Stamford is mentioned in Domesday Book and a stone
bridge of five arches was built over the Welland on
the present site in the 12th century. By the end of the
Middle Ages this bridge had a gateway at its N. end,
the upper part of which was occupied as the town
hall. The gate was demolished in *c.* 1778 when the
Wansford Road Turnpike Trustees improved the
road and provided a new town hall on St. Mary's
Hill. In the 1840s, after much discussion, it was
agreed between the Marquess of Exeter and the
Midland Railway Company to replace the old
bridge. The contract for building the present bridge,
to a design in the Norman style by Edward and
Henry Browning, was given to Robert Woolston,
who was to use Bramley Falls stone from near
Leeds, and to complete the work by summer 1848
(*Mercury*, 14 May, 11 June 1847). An alternative
crossing was provided by diverting traffic along
Wothorpe Road across George Bridge, The
Meadows, and Lammas Bridge to Sheepmarket.
Demolition of the old bridge then began, but by the
beginning of November work had been brought to
a halt by the flooding of a coffer dam (*Mercury*,

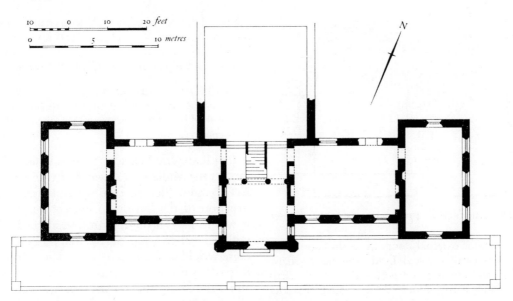

10   0   10   20 *feet*
0   5   10 *metres*

N

Fig. 62   (62) Stamford and Rutland Infirmary. Plan before alteration.

5 Nov. 1847). It was not until early in the following year that the dam was pumped dry and workmen could resume the task of removing the foundations of the old bridge (*Mercury*, 28 Jan. 1848). The dam soon filled again and Woolston, who had made a loss of £2,000 by March, obtained a second contract with completion scheduled for January 1849. The problems remained unsolved, however, and he relinquished his contract the next month and declared himself bankrupt (*Mercury*, 17 Mar., 21 Apr. 1848).

Edward Browning, the architect, then assumed direct control of the building operation, and, favoured by better weather, had one pier above water level by August (*Mercury*, 18 Aug. 1848). The bridge was completed by March 1849 although it remained closed because of the scaffolding on the new facades he was building to the Toll House (450) on the E. and a house (333) owned by the Marquess on the W. (*Mercury*, 30 Mar. and 13 Apr.). The N.E. corner of Burghley Hospital was rebuilt at the same time. The bridge was opened on 1 May 1849, having cost about £8,000, of which £5,000 was contributed by the Midland Railway Company (*Mercury*, 4 May) under terms of a deed of covenant dated 30 May 1845 (Ex. MS, 48).

The bridge, of ashlar except for pindle in the spandrels, is of three low arches with cutwaters and solid parapets. The medieval bridge had five arches, of which the S. was obscured by early encroachments and survives beneath the S. approach of the present bridge (Fig. 44). Built of 'Barnack' stone and now blocked, this 12th-century arch has a span of about 21 ft., a plain soffit and two unchamfered orders (Plate 4). The four free arches of the medieval bridge were recorded before demolition by J. H. Buckler in 1804 and W. Twopeny in 1826 (BM Twopeny 290/b.11, p. 90; Plate 4). The two N. arches were similar to the one surviving, with two unchamfered orders and plain soffits and were presumably of the same date; the two S. arches were of three chamfered orders and of later date. The hospital of St. John and St. Thomas was built in front of the S. arch of the bridge in the 12th century, and part of its substructure remains (49).

(65) KING'S MILL, No. 1 Bath Row (Plate 86), was formerly known as North Mill and is so called in a list of King John's possessions (BM, Harley, Roll Y.21). In 1629 a conveyance of nearby land refers to a new millstream being dug for King's Mills or North Mills. This new dyke was presumably completed in *c.* 1640 when the present mill was constructed; in that year the Earl of Exeter covenanted with an adjoining landowner to repair the banks of the 'new dyke' and to prevent flooding (deeds at Messrs. Evans, Pope and Dalton). Also in 1640 the Corporation determined to petition the Dowager Countess of Exeter concerning damages suffered 'by cutting the water course to the new mill now building' (Hall Book).

The 17th-century building has two storeys, coursed rubble walls, ashlar plinth, and an L-shaped plan, the E. arm of which may be slightly later. The mansard roof is early 19th-century. A number of ovolo-moulded mullioned windows survive at varying levels and on the

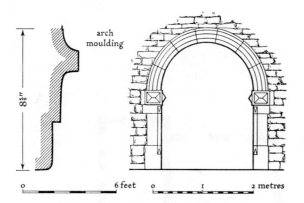

arch moulding

8½″

0   6 feet   0   1   2 metres

Fig. 63   (65) King's Mill. 17th-century doorway, reset.

W. is a first-floor external doorway with Tudor head and label, now partly blocked. Inside, two heavy chamfered beams are supported on posts, and a third, partly chamfered and partly moulded, is reused. External water-wheels on the N. and S. are of iron and the machinery is of wood with iron cogs; each wheel drives two pairs of stones on the first floor.

In *c.* 1793 a long granary was added on the N. It was built by Joseph Robinson, the tenant miller, under a building lease of January 1793 in which he was obliged to spend £400 within two years on the work (Ex. MS, 88/50). It is of two storeys, with slated mansard roof, coursed rubble walls, but has been opened up on the E. to form garages. Other additions, abutting the original block, include two-storey granaries on the E. and S., both early 19th-century, a single-storey compartment also on the S. but slightly later than the foregoing, and a two-storey building on the N.E. of *c.* 1800 but much altered. In the E. elevation of the E. granary, and reset from the N. wall of the original structure, is a wide doorway of the 17th century, with chamfered jambs, pyramid stops, jewelled capitals and moulded semi-circular head (Fig. 63); scratchings include 'John Sellers 1699', 'IF 1704' and 'IK and IS'.

(66) HUDD'S MILL, off Priory Road (Plate 86), two storeys, of large squared masonry, stands across the mill stream. It dates from the first half of the 17th century. The S. end of the building was probably the miller's house and has remained domestic. A modern N. gable indicates a slight shortening; the E. elevation has been much altered and partly rebuilt. On the W. are a number of one, two and three-light windows with ovolo mullions and moulded cornices. In the S. gable is a deeply-incised inscription, 'IRELAND 164..'. Some jambs and sills of original windows remain on the E., where, on the first floor, there is a reset doorway with four-centred head of the early 17th century; adjacent is a wide chamfered opening with four-centred head, either a fireplace or an aperture connected with a sack hoist.

Several stones are incised with names and 18th-century dates. In 1770 the mill was leased to Thomas Boughton on condition that he spent £200 on building a house and repairing the mill (Hall Books).

(67) HODGES' MILL, off Empingham Road, circular, on a low mound, coursed rubble; all but lowest stage demolished in 1869 (*Mercury*, 3 Dec.); late 18th or early 19th-century.

(68) RAILWAY STATION, Station Road (Plate 161). In 1845 the Midland Railway Company obtained an Act (8 and 9 Victoria cap. 56) authorizing the construction of the Syston to Peterborough Railway. It was to pass through Stamford along Bath Row, with a level-crossing on St. Mary's Hill on which there would be a 4 m.p.h. limit. The Company was to pay a sum not exceeding £5,000 for widening and rebuilding the Town Bridge, ostensibly to alleviate the inconvenience caused by a level-crossing at the foot of a narrow medieval bridge. Although the route was amended in 1846 to pass S. of the river, the Company was called on to honour the covenant signed with the Marquess of Exeter to pay the £5,000 towards the bridge (Ex. MS, 48; 9 and 10 Victoria cap. 51). Work on the railway began in March 1846, and in July the section through the site of St. Michael's Nunnery was cut (*Mercury*, 20 Mar., 12 June, 13 July); the deep cutting through High Street St. Martin's was finally completed in March 1847 (*Mercury*, 19 Mar.). The station was designed by Sancton Wood (Midland Railway Company minute book Min. I/319) and the work supervised by Cleverley (*Lincs. Chronicle*, 16 June 1848); the tender submitted in July 1847 for £8,700 by Groocock and Yates of Leicester was accepted (Company minutes) and building was completed in June 1848 (*Mercury*, 7 May, 23 July 1847; 16 June 1848).

The station buildings have coursed and squared rubble walls, freestone dressings, parapeted gables, and consist of a single-storey range with a station master's house of two storeys and attics on the W. They are designed in a plain Tudor style or, as the *Mercury* described it in 1847, 'in an Elizabethan style similar to Burghley House'. The main approach is through a loggia of three bays with a large entrance hall behind and waiting rooms to one side; a booking office appears to have existed on the ground floor of the station master's house, there being a window opening into the entrance hall for the purpose. The various waiting rooms have pointed windows and are provided with parapeted gables, an octagonal turret (Plate 163) and tall chimney stacks adding to the romantic appearance of the whole building. The modern platform canopy is supported on original cast-iron columns.

(69) Former RAILWAY STATION, Stamford East, Water Street (Plate 161). The Station for the Stamford and Essendine Railway was begun in 1855 on the site of the temporary station built for the Peterborough and Syston Railway. The architect was William Hurst (*Mercury*, 1 Sept. 1854, 13 July 1855). It is mostly of two storeys with ashlar walls and is designed in the Tudor style. Except for a three-storey square block on the S.E., the plan is symmetrical; a central entrance hall is flanked with waiting rooms in gabled cross wings between which is a screen wall pierced by a round-headed entrance and an unglazed upper window.

For BATH HOUSE see mon. (110).
  ,,   CONDUIT see mon. (387).

HOUSES

ADELAIDE STREET
Laid out in 1840 on the Blackfriars Estate (see mons. 114–116).

ALL SAINTS' PLACE (Fig. 70)
This open space to the N. of All Saints' church formed part of a large medieval market place.

(70) HOUSE, No. 1 (Fig. 64), two storeys and attics, has ashlar and stone rubble walls. It was rebuilt in 1791 after damage by fire. In 1791 the lease was renewed by Browne's Hospital, the owners, to John Boyfield, carpenter, with a covenant to rebuild according to a plan and elevation prepared by the Warden. The front range of three bays has sash windows rising from plat-bands. The plan now approximates to class 12, the side passage giving access to an entrance hall as well as to workshops at the rear. The kitchen has a late 18th-century fireplace with keystone.

(71) HOUSE, No. 2 (Plate 148), two storeys and attics, with ashlar walls, incorporates an earlier, perhaps 17th-century, timber-framed building which was encased in ashlar in the first half of the 18th century; a two-storey kitchen wing was also added at the rear. The three upper windows of the main front, above a platband, are symmetrical and have keystones and moulded architraves. A wooden cornice with brackets carries the gutter (Plate 122). The unevenly spaced ground-floor openings of varying widths are later alterations; each has keystones and channelled lintels imitating voussoirs. Inside, the main room has fielded panelling in two heights; early

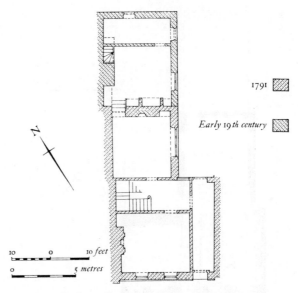

1791

Early 19th century

Fig. 64   (70) 1 All Saints' Place.

in the 19th century, the interior was refurbished and the lower flights of the stairs were reset probably from the N.E. corner where the upper flights survive in a hipped turret. The stairs have turned balusters. Against the side wall an arcade of three elliptical arches was built in the early 19th century. In 1750 John Dixon, carpenter, acquired the property through his wife, Alice Newcomb, and the present building may date in part between then and his death in 1782 (Ex. MS, 90/27).

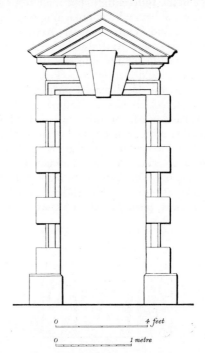

Fig. 65   (72) 3 All Saints' Place. Doorway.

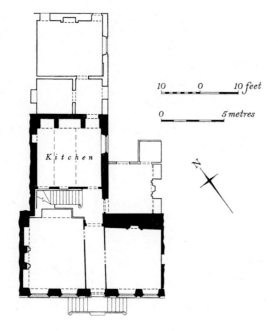

10   0   10 feet

0   5 metres

Kitchen

N

Fig. 66   (72) 3 All Saints' Place.

(72) HOUSE, No. 3 (Figs. 65, 66; Plate 96), two storeys and attics, with ashlar front wall, rubble gable, is early 18th-century. The plan is L-shaped and in the entrant angle a small timber-framed block was added in the late 18th century to give a class 11b plan; the rear arm was lengthened in the 19th century. The main front on the S. is in five unequal bays with approaching steps, moulded platband and a later central doorway having a moulded architrave with spaced rustication, double keystone in relief, and a pediment; the uniform upper and lower windows have moulded architraves (Figs. 10, 12, 13, 65). Above is a central shield-shaped plaque. The wooden cornice has square brackets (Plate 122). Inside, the entrance hall and two front rooms have fielded panelling in two heights with chair-rail and cornice of the 18th century. The kitchen in the rear wing has a wide elliptical-headed fireplace and flanking roundheaded openings (Fig. 67). Doorcases with angle-roundels, and the staircase, are early 19th-century. The roof has staggered purlins; principal rafters have curved feet.

Fig. 67   (72) 3 All Saints' Place. End wall of kitchen.

(73) BOURN COURT, Nos. 4, 5, two storeys, attics and cellar, hipped mansard roof, rubble walls, comprises two separate dwellings which were built in c. 1800 by the Bourn Charity. By 1813 there were four houses, two barns and two stables on the site (Blore, 235–50). The two surviving houses each had a front of three bays with central doorway but both have been recently altered. Wooden-framed windows have fixed glazing with small metal casements. No. 4 incorporates a large stack from an earlier building.

Nos. 14–15, see mon. (432).

(74) HOUSE, No. 16 (Plate 146), three storeys, cellars and attics, ashlar walls, wooden cornice, mansard roof with three dormers, class 10, is probably the house described in 1793 as newly built, James Hames being tenant (*Mercury*, 15 July). The cellars comprise three parallel vaults. The front elevation is dominated by three-storey twin bow windows in timber-framing and of slight projection; the central doorway has a fanlight with gothic tracery in a round head. Contemporary interior features include fluted pilasters and a plaster acanthus frieze. Carved fragments reset in the yard behind are probably from the workshop of John Hames.

ALL SAINTS' STREET (Fig. 70)

This street, a continuation of St. Peter's Street, crosses at its E. end a possible market-place, partly infilled, although any such infilling was complete by the 13th century (Peck, IX.34). At its W. end is St. Peter's Callis, an almshouse which is of ancient origin, and which possibly dates from before 1466 (Hall Book I, 7). Two inns, Millstone and Salutation (75, 80), doubtless arose because of proximity to Red Lion Square. In 1826 the first Roman Catholic church in the town was built on the site now occupied by No. 19.

(75) THE MILLSTONE INN, No. 1, of two storeys, has coursed rubble walls. The street front, of the 17th century, has a wide rectangular two-storey bay window with hollow-chamfered mullions; the proportions of the building, which approximates to class 1 or 2, suggest an earlier origin. A carriage entry on the W. has been blocked to form additional accommodation. A wide projecting chimney stack is built in the back wall. A rear wing on the S. may have been timber-framed, perhaps 17th-century, but the walls are now of stone.

(76) HOUSE, No. 3, three storeys, coursed rubble with flush dressings, class 10, now has a shop on the ground floor. It was described as newly built in a lease of 1812 and was presumably constructed after a previous lease of 1805 (Browne's Hospital, leases).

(77) TERRACE, Nos. 4–8, two storeys and attics, red brick front wall, remainder coursed rubble, with mansard roof, class 14a, was built between 1792–8 (Browne's Hospital, leases). Openings in the rear wall have brick dressings. Modern shops occupy most of the ground floor.

(78) Former WHEATSHEAF INN, No. 13 (Plate 73), now class 12, two storeys, consists of an early 17th-century timber-framed rear wing of one-room plan, having a jetty on one side and a slightly later wooden mullion-and-transom window, and a late 17th-century front range. The latter has ashlar walls, moulded string-course, and a two-storey bay window with flat roof and ovolo-moulded mullions; the quoins have raised margins. Between the front room and the rear wing is a staircase which replaces a former winding stair, the scar of which remains.

(79) HOUSE, Nos. 14–15, two storeys and attics, slate roof, is 17th-century but was substantially renovated in the 19th century; the original walling is in squared ashlar, the remainder coursed rubble. The original street front comprised two bay windows with canted sides, ovolo-moulded mullions and parapeted gables, but the E. bay has been removed, the gable being reset over the main wall (drawing by Twopeny, 1827; OS map). The front range, of class 6, originally consisted of two rooms. The central entrance has depressed four-centred head and ovolo-moulded jambs, and internally there is a similar doorway but with sunk spandrels. At the rear is an 18th-century wing with a diamond-patterned panel in the gable. To the E. is a reset arch from the former Corn Market (see Introduction to Broad Street).

(80) HOUSES, Nos. 16–17, two storeys, attics in mansard roof, rubble walls, continuous sills, large flush quoins and dressings, were rebuilt in the late 18th-century by Alderman Robert Hunt as the Salutation Inn (Blore, 253). No. 17, marginally earlier than No. 16, of class 9, has been gutted for a shop but the symmetrical front of No. 16 remains.

(81) ALBION TAVERN, No. 20, three storeys, ashlar walls and Welsh slate roof, class 14b, is early 19th-century. The sash windows and round-headed doorway have flush dressings. The deeply overhanging eaves have plain widely-spaced brackets.

(82) HOUSE, No. 21 (Fig. 68), now with two storeys and attics and stone walls, originated as a class 1a timber-framed medieval building of three bays, the two W. bays comprising the hall; both the hall and the single bay, on the E., were originally open to the roof, and the upper section of the partition between them survives in the roof. In the E. wall is a fireplace with chamfered

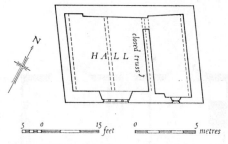

Fig. 68   (82) 21 All Saints' Street.
Plan at upper level omitting later additions.

jambs, and brackets supporting a vestigial hood; it is in a stone wall and is presumably secondary. The roof has tie beams, collars, clasped purlins, curved windbraces and principals diminishing above the collars. These members and the faces of the W. wall and the partition are smoke-blackened. The house now has a central stack of unknown but possibly early 19th-century date. Several mullion windows are modern reproductions.

(83) HOUSE, No. 22, two storeys, attics, coursed rubble walls with 18th-century wooden eaves course, is 16th or 17th-century. All that remain of this date are some outside walls, a central stack, a heavy axial beam with substantial joists, and a roof with clasped purlins but no ridge-piece. On the street front is a three-storey timber-framed bow window, probably of the early 19th century. Internal partitions are modern. To the side is an early 19th-century two-storey wing of rubble.

AUSTIN FRIARS LANE (Fig. 201)
This lane runs along the line of the ditch outside the town walls on the W. side of the town.

(84) HOUSE, No. 3, two storeys, coursed rubble walls, consists of the gabled cross wing of a 17th-century or earlier building of class 3, the main range having been demolished recently. An extension at the rear of the wing has an early 19th-century appearance but probably retains the plan at least of an earlier structure. Between the former main range and the cross wing is a massive stone chimney stack, partly cased in brick. Inside, an axial chamfered beam extends into the rear extension. Fittings include a mid 17th-century scratch-panelled cupboard door.

AUSTIN STREET (Fig. 201)
Forming a back lane to St. Peter's Street, this narrow street runs along the top of the scarp above the Welland Valley.

(85) AUSTIN HOUSE, No. 4 (Fig. 69; Plates 146, 149), three storeys, attics, ashlar S. wall, otherwise coursed rubble with plain quoins, mansard roof, was built in

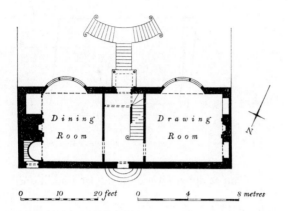

Fig. 69   (85) Austin House.

c. 1800. The house is an elegant example of Regency architecture. In plan it conforms to class 10, the entrance at street level being a storey higher than the garden level. On the street front a central door, and above it a shallow bow window of two stages rising to the attics, are the only openings. The main rooms are lit by tall bow windows on the garden side. The stair-hall was originally lit from the bow on the street side, but marginally later partitions enclosing closets now block this source of lighting. The shallow bow windows on the S. rise the full height of the house, the upper two stages having Venetian-type sash windows with Gothic glazing, but the ground stage, containing service rooms, has casement windows. Between these bays, a central roundheaded door, with porch having fluted pilasters and columns, leads to a single flight of steps which divides into two side flights, all with iron railings. Above the door is a roundheaded window with heavy architrave set in an incised surround with a pedimented hood; this incongruous feature is an insertion which may have been introduced to light the stair-hall. The interior fittings are refined. The stair has slender hollow-moulded balusters set diagonally and shaped brackets to the treads. Other fittings include moulded plaster cornices, roundheaded cupboards and recesses, and moulded panelled doors.

(86) HOUSE, No. 11, two storeys, stone walls, consists of two parallel gabled ranges on a sloping site, the main room on the garden side being therefore above ground level. This room has an original verandah. In 1801 the owner of the site, Browne's Hospital, granted a lease to Joseph Robinson conditional on his demolishing three tenements and rebuilding a 'good and more substantial messuage' (Browne's Hospital leases). However Robinson only carried out repairs at a cost of £90, which proved ineffective and the structure began to collapse (deeds). The present house was built in 1808 and was described as 'newly erected' in October of that year. The house remained unoccupied and in October

1809 Robinson exchanged five acres of land for the freehold. He immediately enlarged the house by adding the two-storey S. range above a basement. (Inside not seen.)

(87) HOUSE, No. 12, three storeys, coursed rubble walls with freestone dressings and quoins, class 10 plan with kitchen wing at side, stands on sloping ground and so has a street-entrance at a higher level than the main ground-floor rooms. It was built in the very early years of the 19th century. The garden front has sash windows with continuous sills, on both floors. The staircase has shaped tread-brackets and turned newels.

(88) Former HOUSES, No. 14, two storey, attics, coursed rubble walls, mansard roof, hipped on the W., were built as a pair of class 15 dwellings in the early 19th century.

(89) HOUSE, No. 15, two storeys, coursed rubble walls, class 15, early 19th-century.

(90) TERRACE, Nos. 16, 16A, 16B, two storeys, coursed rubble walls, ashlar dressings, projecting keystones to doors and windows, comprises a class 10 house of *c.* 1840 and a pair of slightly later class 15 houses. In the centre is a communal passage.

(91) HOUSE, No. 26, two storeys and attics, coursed rubble walls, approximating to class 10 plan, bears a panel inscribed 'I^DM 1706'. The windows have wooden lintels. On the S. elevation are two small blocked lights, probably for closets beside the stack in the gable wall. Originally there were two main rooms each entered from a central lobby, but the cross wall has since been removed.

(92) HOUSES, Nos. 27–28, a pair, two storeys and attics, coursed rubble walls, mansard roof, probably late 18th-century. Each has a class 15 plan but the W. house has a side passage to a yard. Inside, the upper floor is of plaster.

BARN HILL (Fig. 70)

The top of Barn Hill was the site of the sheep market before its removal to Sheep Market in about 1781. Nevertheless the street appears to have had relatively distinguished occupants since the later Middle Ages. No. 6 retains parts of a very large house of the 16th century, Barn Hill House incorporates reused material from another large house of similar date, and No. 9 was occupied in the 17th century by Richard Wolph, a wealthy grocer who is said to have befriended Charles I; it later passed to William Stukeley, the antiquary. The high social status of Barn Hill, which was long-standing, is revealed by the quality of the houses, especially

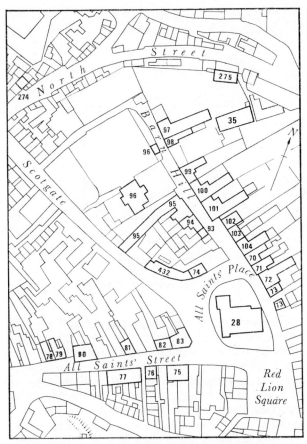

Fig. 70   Map showing monuments in All Saints' Place, All Saints' Street, Barn Hill and North Street.

Barn Hill House (96), No. 13 (100), and finally, from the middle of the 19th century, No. 14 (101).

(93) HOUSE, No. 3 (Fig. 71; Plate 146), two storeys, cellar, basement and attics, class 14b, ashlar front wall, remainder brick, with mansard roof, is early 19th-century. The narrow front elevation comprises a doorway, with a contemporary wooden porch in 'chinese' latticework and lead roof; to the side is a two-storey timber-framed and plastered bow window with curved sashes. A bracketed cornice continues round the bay. Inside and on each floor is a single room with a small room and staircase behind. The cellar is stone-vaulted.

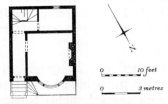

Fig. 71   (93) 3 Barn Hill.

(94) HOUSE, No. 4, now approximates to class 11b but is in two sections; that on the W., of two storeys, has a rear wing and a timber-framed stair turret in the entrant angle, and may be 17th-century; that on the E., of three storeys, is early 19th-century. The earlier range was refronted in ashlar in the late 18th century; the windows have plain projecting architraves and the doorway is pedimented. The roof over the rear wing has clasped purlins and is probably 17th-century. The later section has a street front of ashlar and a slate roof; on the ground floor two roundheaded sash windows are set in a three-bay shallow arcade. In the rear wall, of coursed rubble, is a blocked elliptically headed arch which was still open in 1886.

At the rear is a detached three-storey building in coursed rubble, described in 1843 as a six-horse stable with granaries above.

(95) HOUSE and RANGE, Nos. 5–6 (Figs. 72, 73). The house, one storey and attics, partially heightened to two storeys, stone rubble walls, has a front range and rear wing of the 17th century; the wing is continuous with a range of the early 16th century (see below). On the street front a two-storey bay window with canted sides was one of the improvements carried out by John Wyche between 1774 and 1781 (Ex. MS, 90/26); Wyche, town clerk, was fined in 1783 for the encroachment of the bay onto the street. In 1824 the house was divided and a separate tenement formed in the E. part where a hallway was partitioned; a stair and kitchen were added. Another room was built in c. 1843 when the Marquess of Exeter bought the property. The main room on the W. has fielded panelling of 1774–81; the ceiling, raised in the 18th century, is enriched with geometric pattern later elaborated with floral panels. A stair of c. 1700 in the rear wing has closed string, square newels, and turned balusters. A ground-floor room in the wing has early 17th-century scratch-moulded panelling, probably once with a frieze; the corner fireplace has elaborately carved mid 18th-century surround and 17th-century overmantel comprising three bolection-moulded lozenges, frieze panels carved with arabesques, dentil cornice, cut-work brackets, and pendants. On the first floor is an 18th-century fireplace surround with garlanded rams' heads.

The early 16th-century *Range*, extending from the rear wing of the house to Scotgate, has rubble external walls. It originally consisted of a hall open to the roof and a two-storey range continuous with it on the S. but on a slightly different alignment. At this change in alignment there was probably an internal stone cross wall. The hall is a long one and the building was doubtless part of a large and important domestic establishment. Drastic alterations included the insertion of a floor in the hall, the addition of an 18th-century chimney stack and many large openings in the walls.

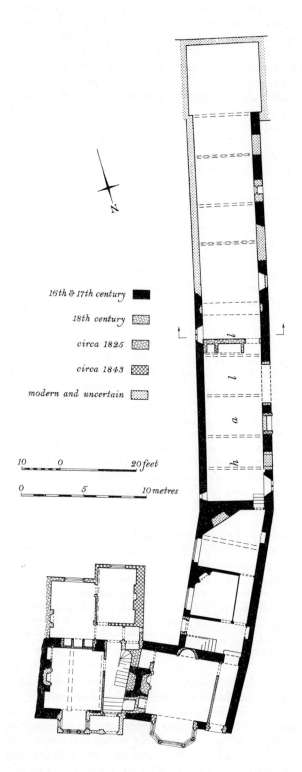

16th & 17th century
18th century
circa 1825
circa 1843
modern and uncertain

10   0   20 feet

0   5   10 metres

Fig. 72   (95) 5–6 Barn Hill.

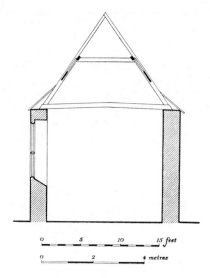

0   5   10   15 feet

0   2   4 metres

Fig. 73   (95) Range behind 6 Barn Hill. Section.

The surviving original features of the hall are two large windows and the roof. The windows, of two lights, have transoms and hollow-moulded jambs with upper lights having four-centred heads and sunk spandrels. One is at the N. end of the W. wall, the other at the S. end of the E. wall; the head of the latter has been destroyed. A small ground-floor window with splayed jambs, at the N. end of the E. wall, and another on the first floor in the S. range, may also be 16th-century. Some of the later openings, now blocked, are probably in the positions of original ones but no early details survive. The roof, of modest design, has collars clasping purlins, principal rafters with reduced thickness above the purlin, cambered tie beams and broad windbraces (Plate 77). The hall roof is in five bays of which the two on the N. are narrower; the roof over the S. section of the range, of four unequal bays with two closed trusses implying at least three rooms, originally extended further to the S. The division between the hall and the S. section is marked by two later trusses. The two N. bays of the hall have chamfered beams and wide joists, laid flat, indicating a date of *c.* 1600 for the insertion of the floor into the hall. The compartment in these bays is 'the low room now divided by a partition into two small rooms and used as a larder . . .' which Charles Snow bought from William Noel in 1720 and incorporated into his house, No. 6 Barn Hill (deeds; Ex. MS, 90/26). In the W. wall are two roundheaded early 19th-century doorways with stone surrounds and capitals.

(96) BARN HILL HOUSE, No. 7 (Fig. 74; Plates 96, 156), two storeys, attics and basement, is mainly of ashlar but with coursed rubble basement which, because of the sloping ground, is entered at ground

level on the S.; the plan, conforming to class 9, originally had fireplaces in all four corners, but one has been removed. A quoin inscribed '1698' presumably denotes the building-date. The carcase and most of the internal walls of the original house survive, but the window surrounds, which are repeated on all elevations, have a mid 18th-century character suggesting a total refacing, except for the basement, at that date. In 1843–4 Bryan Browning made considerable alterations for the Marquess of Exeter (Burghley Estate Account Books, ledger 8) including the complete transformation of the N. front.

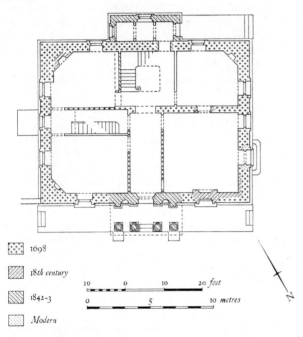

1698

18th century

1842-3

Modern

10   0   10   20 feet

0   5   10 metres

N

Fig. 74   (96) Barn Hill House.

The building has a wave-moulded plinth belonging to the house of 1698. The N. front has windows with simple projecting surrounds and triple keystones. Under Browning's instructions the central doorway was given a round head, sculptured keystone and spaced voussoir-blocks (Plate 157); it is flanked by small niches. He also added a large four-column porch in the Roman Doric style, which obliterated earlier ground-floor windows. Other alterations included the addition of an attic parapet carved with swags and rams' heads, the removal of a platband linking the heads of the upper windows, and the construction of a low rusticated terrace along the front. The S. elevation of three bays with rubble basement, moulded plinth, platband, gabled roof, has windows with simple surrounds with roll-moulded arrises and small keystones, those on the first

floor being linked by a narrow band, presumably all of the 18th century; the basement windows have either three or four mullioned lights with triangular heads, probably 16th-century, reset. A basement quoin is inscribed 'GP 1698'. A forebuilding reaching to the platband, added by Browning in 1843, has windows of the 16th and 18th centuries reused from the main wall. Both the E. and W. elevations have twin gables with a chimney stack on each apex. The windows are uniform with those on the S., and are similarly linked. The flush, roll-moulded quoins on the S. elevation remain, but those on the N. have been replaced by the later rusticated quoins. The masonry of the E. wall is of smaller size than that on the W.; in the basement is a reset three-light window of the 16th century. An early 19th-century wooden porch on the E. has Tuscan columns; the sides are now filled in.

Internally, the basement has heavy unchamfered beams, and a fireplace with depressed four-centred head, presumably 16th-century, reset; a doorway with four-centred head, and a small circular window above, are possibly c. 1698. The central room has reset early 17th-century moulded panelling. The arrangement of the ground-floor rooms in double depth with a central entrance hall is broadly original but the present principal stair is a replacement by Browning in the position of an earlier one. The stair is cantilevered and has cast-iron balusters with floral motifs. In the entrance hall are three pilasters with Ionic-type capitals, a rounded arch with keyblock, and a plaster cornice, all c. 1698. Browning was responsible for the panelling. In the N.E. room is early 17th-century reset panelling composed of larger and smaller rectangles with moulded surrounds; of c. 1740 is a fireplace with carved eared surround. The N.W. room contains early 18th-century bolection-moulded panelling in two heights with wooden cornice. The corner chimney was moved to the N. wall necessitating the blocking of two windows, the W. of which remains externally; the 18th-century eared surround of the fireplace has Rococo-style central panel and carved pulvinated frieze (Plate 127). The S.E. room is lined with reset 17th-century panelling, as in the N.E. room. The S.W. room has early 18th-century bolection panelling in two heights. The rooms on the first floor have block cornices, and a central lobby has roundheaded arches with keyblocks, all of the 18th century, but one length of plaster cornice may be of 1698, as well as a bolection-moulded fireplace surround in the S.E. room. Some early 18th-century splat balusters exist at the head of the service stair.

The garden consists of a parterre levelled from the sloping ground, with a terrace on the N. and W. On the terrace, and approached by steps at the side, is a mid 18th-century *Summer House* (Plate 104) of ashlar, having central roundheaded doorway with rustication, side sash windows, and a pediment; the window sills have been lowered. Ancillary features include 18th-century walls enclosing the forecourt, with two ashlar gate piers surmounted by classical urns; a rustic arch of undressed stone in the N.W. corner of the sunken area of the garden, originally leading to a tunnel beneath Barn Hill Lane to a garden beyond, is now blocked but was in use in 1842 (Ex. MS, 63/66).

(97) STUKELEY HOUSE, No. 9 (Fig. 75; Plate 148), two storeys, cellar and attics, class IIa, has front and rear walls of ashlar and gable walls of coursed rubble; the stone-slated mansard roof has at the rear subsidiary mansard roofs at right angles. The property, once owned by the Rev. William Stukeley, was bought by Henry Tatam, alderman and cabinet maker, in 1796 (All Saints' vestry, deposition, 1854). The house was built and presumably designed by Tatam between that date and 1801, and was described as newly built in 1802 (LRO, Barn Hill Methodist Church records, conveyance, 1802). In about 1840 the rear wing was rebuilt, perhaps by James Atter who purchased the house in that year (All Saints' vestry, allegations, 1854); it is of two storeys, in coursed rubble with freestone dressings.

The design of the main elevation derives from Tatam's calling as a cabinet maker. The central sections of the heads of the four larger windows are raised to a

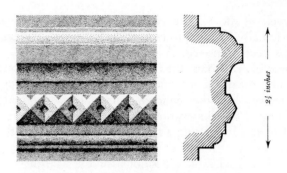

Fig. 76   (97) 9 Barn Hill. Detail of chair rail.

flat segment; the lower windows have rusticated surrounds and the upper, of slender and individual character, have shafted jambs and shallow moulded heads (Plate 120). The cornice concealing the gutter is carried on small shaped brackets reminiscent of cabinet work. Dormers have segmental heads. The Greek Doric porch was added in the early 19th century (Plate 124). Inside, many fittings of 1796–1801 remain, and include a stair with inlaid handrail, a chair-rail with nail-head ornament (Fig. 76; cf. 234), reeded door architraves, and plaster cornices. Over a back door is a reset panel 'Johanni Rogers Ob Hydram Podagrae Domitam Gratitudinis Ergo Wilhemus Stukeley MDCCXXXIII'; the panel was set up by Stukeley in his garden on 27 June 1743 (Surtees Soc. 76 (1883), 331).

Of William Stukeley's garden little remains; it was described in 1785 as having temples and an obelisk (Mercury, 9 Sept.), and a prospect mound. Set in the N. wall which follows the line of the medieval town wall are fragments, presumably from Stukeley's collection, which include a capital and a corbel of the 13th century and medieval responds. Against the wall is a rectangular summerhouse, timber-framed, with half-hipped roof, and weathervane perforated with date 1849; over the four-centred doorway is an 18th-century stone tablet inscribed with a Latin eulogy on flowers.

Adjacent is a Gateway (Plate 90) built into the town wall and altered by Stukeley in 1744 (Surtees Soc. 80 (1885), 457). It probably dates from the first half of the 17th century and may have been constructed by Alderman Richard Wolph, a wealthy grocer, who lived here. It consists of a massive roundheaded arch with rusticated voussoirs radiating to a rectangle, and heavy bracketed cornice above a plain frieze panel inscribed, 'Beatae Tranquillitati P Wilh Stukeley MDCCXXXVII'. Above is a battlemented parapet with panel carved with a shield in a quatrefoil and inscribed 'Anno Victoriae Cullodonianae 1746', and behind the arch is a half-domed recess with a doorway, and a stairway within the thickness of the wall, all of which were additions by Stukeley in the 18th century when he converted the gateway to a garden alcove.

Fig. 75   (97) 9 Barn Hill. Front elevation.

(98) HOUSE, No. 10 (Plate 149), is in three sections: that in the centre, of two storeys and cellar, is perhaps late 17th-century; that on the S., of three storeys with mansard roof and attics, was built in 1804 for Miss Frances Treen (Burton, 227) and that on the N. has a date-stone inscribed 1866. The earliest section consists of one room with two large chamfered cross beams, but has no other early features. The block of 1804, entered from the side, comprises a large parlour, stair and entrance hall; the quality of the ashlar is noteworthy. The elevations are of idiosyncratic design with voussoirs and quoins in alternating planes giving a lively effect (Fig. 10; Plate 121); the sills continue as platbands. Above the roundheaded entrance doorway with fanlight and enriched pilasters is a stair window with alternating jamb blocks, round head and gothic glazing bars. A thin projecting stone cornice conceals a gutter. Interior fittings of c. 1804 include a moulded chair-rail and plaster cornices; a moulded stone fireplace surround with enriched frieze is in the first-floor room, perhaps originally the drawing room.

(99) HOUSE, No. 12, two storeys, five gabled dormers, attics and cellar, has walls of coursed rubble. The front range on the S. is probably c. 1700 but the rear wing, originally timber-framed, is earlier. This wing was cased or replaced in stone in the 17th century and now has blocked ovolo-moulded two-light mullioned win-

dows. The front range has an abnormal plan of five principal bays with the entrance in the end bay; it has been shortened at its W. gable end. The window openings have lintels channelled to simulate voussoirs, and no sills; the proportions are squat and the present sash windows may have replaced ones with wooden mullions and transoms. The main doorway has a moulded surround with projecting hood and curved pediment carried on elaborately carved console brackets (Plate 124), c. 1700. At the rear of the main range is a large ground-floor Venetian window. In front of the house is a low wall with 18th-century wrought-iron railings with scrolled finials at intervals (Plate 125). Inside, the house has many fittings of the first half of the 18th century, the principal being the staircase, with a lower enclosed flight, first-floor balustrade with turned balusters having square knops, and the upper flight with splat balusters (Fig. 15); other fittings include bolection-moulded and fielded panelling in two heights, wooden cornices and a moulded doorcase with pulvinated frieze and entablature.

(100) HOUSE, No. 13 (Figs. 77, 78; Plate 103), two storeys, cellars and attics, class 11b, was built in 1740, the date on the two lead rainwater heads; it has been little altered. In the side wall of the rear wing, at a low level, is a blocked three-light ovolo-moulded window with hood mould indicating a

Fig. 77   (100) 13 Barn Hill. Front elevation shown with window glazing restored.

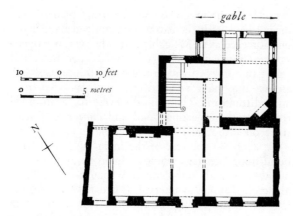

Fig. 78　(100) 13 Barn Hill.

17th-century origin for this part of the building.

The front wall is of ashlar with rusticated quoins (Plate 121), the remainder, including the elliptically-vaulted cellars, are of coursed rubble. The main elevation is in five almost symmetrical but unequal bays; the ground-floor windows have voussoirs and rusticated jambs; those on the first floor have eared surrounds, continuous sills and pediments (Figs. 10, 12, 79). The central entrance with pilasters and pediment is plainer, and a side entrance to a passage is unemphasized. Contemporary wrought-iron railings with scrolled finials survive in front (Plate 125). Internally two main rooms and the entrance hall are lined with panelling of two heights with a cornice; the long axis is accentuated by decorative doorcases in the end walls. The doorways have eared architraves, and a fireplace has shell-and-dart surround. The generous stair hall (Plate 135), reached through an elliptical archway with scrolled brackets, is

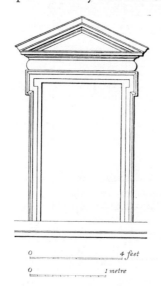

Fig. 79　(100) 13 Barn Hill. Upper window.

lit by a tall roundheaded window with panelled reveals. A rear room, now the kitchen but formerly a sitting room, has fielded panelling; the earlier kitchen was in a wing now demolished. The stair (Plate 134) rises in three flights with turned balusters, cut string with scroll brackets (Plate 130), panelled dado and ramped handrail; the walls have plastered panels above a scroll frieze and the decorative plaster ceiling has an enriched cornice (Plate 136). The large drawing room on the first floor has an elaborately carved wooden fireplace surround (Plate 127). The roof of five bays has principals with curved feet, two sets of purlins, one set square the other canted.

(101) HOUSE, No. 14 (Plate 159), class IIb, three storeys, cellars, two-storey rear wing, main walls of ashlar, remainder of coursed rubble, hipped slated roof, was probably built between 1840 and 1850. The main elevation is severe without emphasis to the window openings; above the lower windows is a string-course of corona profile on which a pediment is set un-classically over a roundheaded doorway. Beneath the parapet is a deep cornice. The side elevation, in contrast with the front, is meant to impress. On each floor are

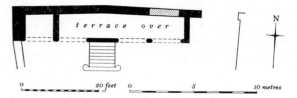

Fig. 80　(101) 14 Barn Hill.
Loggia on line of town walls.

triple windows in a vertical shallow recess; that on the first floor is accentuated by a pedimented cornice on brackets. The interior is relatively severe with simple plaster cornices providing the main ornamentation. The cantilevered stair has cast-iron balusters decorated with Greek motifs, and a continuous handrail (Plate 133). Several original fireplace surrounds of simple design remain. The drawing room was on the first floor.

At the N. end of the garden, on the line of the town walls, is an early 19th-century *Loggia* (Fig. 80) comprising a central flight of steps to an upper terrace, flanked by pairs of segmental-headed arches now blocked. In the rear parapet wall are reset three carvings (Plate 44): crocketed niche with figure of St. Lawrence with grid-iron, 15th-century; corbel head, medieval; grotesque head in octofoil probably a vault-boss, medieval, recorded in 1736 by Stukeley as coming from the site of the Austin Friary (Stukeley, Designs, 74).

(102) OFFICE, No. 15 (Fig. 81; Plate 159), two storeys, ashlar front and rear walls, coursed rubble side walls, hipped slated roof, was built as an office probably for the

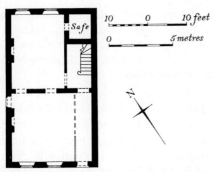

Fig. 81   (102) 15 Barn Hill. Plan of office.

firm of Richardson in the mid 19th century. The three-bay S. front has sash windows, roundheaded doorway with fanlight, platband and moulded cornice below a parapet; the N. elevation is in similar but plainer style. Inside, the strong-room, an original feature, has a brick barrel vault.

(103) HOUSE, No. 16 (Fig. 82; Plate 71), formerly All Saints' Vicarage, was built towards the end of the 15th century. It is now of two storeys throughout but originally had an open hall, class 1a. The walls are of coursed rubble. The rear wing and most internal fittings date from the late 19th century but the medieval priest's house survives substantially.

The front elevation has two-light mullioned windows of 17th-century style but mostly of early 19th-century date; their disposition may be compared with that shown by Stukeley in 1735 (Plate 71; Designs, p. 28). The hall in the E. half was previously lit by two tall two-light windows with pointed heads, transoms and labels. These have been replaced by square windows with terracotta labels, on two floors. The doorway, with depressed four-centred head, moulded jambs. square hood mould and sunk spandrels, remains as shown by Stukeley; a jamb stone is inscribed 'IH 1695', The doorway is probably late medieval; it preserves the position of the original entrance but appears to be later than the hall windows shown by Stukeley. Upper windows in the two W. bays are apparently as shown by Stukeley, but the lower window replaces one with a single light. The rear wall is now featureless, but a plan of 1841 (deeds) shows at the W. end, where the present wall is thin and rebuilt, a rectangular projection which may have been an early stair turret (Surtees Soc., 76 (1883), 324). Internally, the former open hall now has an inserted upper floor of the 17th century. In the N. wall is a partially-blocked fireplace with tall relieving arch and a flue rising within the thickness of the wall; it is probably medieval. At the W. end of the hall most of

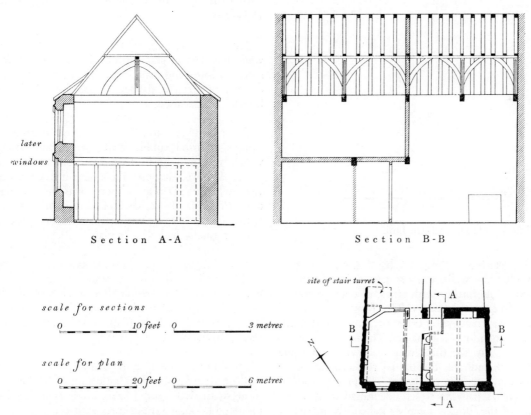

Fig. 82   (103) 16 Barn Hill. Plan as existing; sections with later floors and partitions removed.

the timber-framed screens partition survives although hidden on the hall side by a mid 19th-century elliptical headed recess flanked by cupboards. The partition consists of top rail and chamfered studs with an interval for a central entrance to the hall. The screens passage is marked on the W. by a heavy ceiling beam but the partition below it is possibly not original. At the N. end of the passage is an original but mutilated doorway, the rebate of one jamb only remaining. Over the service rooms is a chamber which overhangs 2 ft. beyond the screens passage into the hall. The roof, of four bays, has crown posts braced downward to the tie beam and upwards to the collar purlin; the central truss is closed.

Stukeley records that the open hall had 'many scripture sentences around it' (*Surtees Soc.*, 76 (1883), 324). Later fittings include an 18th-century moulded stone fireplace with eared surround.

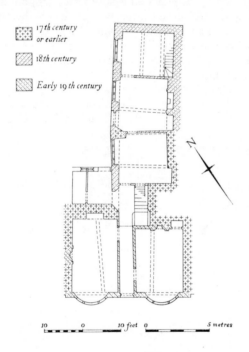

17th century or earlier

18th century

Early 19th century

10   0   10 feet 0   5 metres

Fig. 83   (104) 17 Barn Hill.

(104) HOUSE, No. 17 (Fig. 83), has a S. range of two storeys with ashlar walls, and a rear two-storey wing in two sections, the further with attics, of coursed rubble walls and freestone dressings. The front range has a central doorway flanked by timber-framed, full-height, shallow bow windows with sashes. The front wall dates from *c.* 1800, but the thick rear wall with a massive chimney stack indicates the partial replacement of an earlier structure perhaps of class 2. The present roof of unequal pitches had the street side raised in *c.* 1800; one rafter of the former, steeply-pitched, front part of the roof remains in a partition. The rear wing is 17th or

early 18th-century; the S. room is probably a rebuilding of an earlier wing. The wooden windows have mullions on the ground floor, and mullions and transoms on the first floor; internal partitions are timber-framed and of poor quality.

BARNACK ROAD (Fig. 111)
Originally the road to Barnack was a continuation of Burghley Lane and ran across open fields. The present road was made in 1796 after Enclosure and the extension of Burghley Park over the former open fields of St. Martins.

(105) Former MALTINGS, three storeys and attics, coursed rubble walls, is early 19th-century (on Knipe's map, 1833). It has two parallel, slated, mansard roofs, returned at the S. end.

BATH ROW (Fig. 138)
Running between the castle and the tail-race of King's Mill, this road takes its name from public baths which were first built here in 1722 (Burton, 19). There were a few cottages in the 18th century, but it only became a residential street in the early 19th century. The Baptists built a chapel here in 1835 (38).

(106) HOUSE, No. 7, two storeys, coursed rubble walls, has class 10 plan with roof continued at rear over service rooms and stair. Between the upper sash windows is a circular date-panel inscribed 'W.P. 1826'. Interior modernised.

(107) HOUSES, Nos. 8–10, now two dwellings, two storeys, coursed rubble walls, were built on a site which was bought in 1817 by Robert Nicholls and James Althorp, drapers; the house had been built by 1824 when their joint property was divided between them (Deeds). No. 8 has a class 10 plan of three bays with a contemporary wooden latticework porch; Nos. 9–10 originally had class 15 plans.

(108) HOUSES, Nos. 11–12, two storeys, coursed rubble walls with dressed window surrounds, were built by James Richardson after purchase of the land in 1833 (Deeds); they were completed before 1839 (Dewhirst and Nichols' map). The reflecting pair, each class 14b, has adjacent entrances.

(109) DOORWAY, E. of former Baptist chapel, reset in wall of a garden on the Castle site, of 'Barnack' limestone, with two-centred head, single chamfered jambs, moulded hood, is 13th or early 14th-century. The doorway is shown on Knipe's map of 1833.

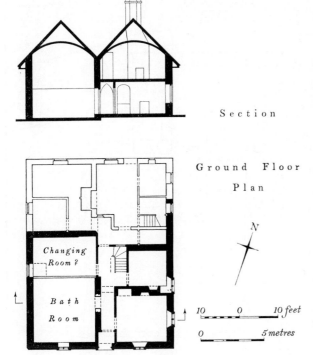

Fig. 84   (110) Bath House, Bath Row.

(110) BATH HOUSE, No. 16 (Fig. 84; Plate 151), two storeys, has walls of pindle with ashlar quoins and finely dressed surrounds to openings. It was built in 1823, the date inscribed internally on the S. wall. The openings are in the First Pointed Gothic style. It was extended at the rear in the late 19th century probably over a former yard. On the front elevation a parapet with obelisk finials and openwork cresting masks the valley between two parallel roofs, producing a truncated outline. Inside, the bathroom has a high barrel-vaulted plaster ceiling and possibly had a plunge bath, now filled in; to the N. was a ground-floor room perhaps used for changing. E. of the central passage was accommodation for the attendant; the first-floor rooms have barrel-vaulted plaster ceilings.

(111) HOUSE, No. 24, two storeys and attics, coursed rubble walls, mansard roof, is an early 19th-century single-room dwelling (class 15). It is of some topographical interest as being a survivor of the many small houses that formerly cluttered the riverside along Bath Row.

BELTON STREET

Laid out in 1840 on the Blackfriars Estate (117–18), and named after Belton House, the home of Earl Brownlow who owned the land.

BENTLEY STREET
(TL 030075)

(112) EMLYN'S COTTAGES, Nos. 15–18, two storeys, coursed rubble walls with freestone quoins, pantiles and slate roofs, comprise two reflecting pairs of dwellings of class 13a plan, under twin gables facing the street. The doorways have round heads. They were built c. 1840. A tablet is inscribed 'Emlyn's Cottages'.

(113) EMLYN'S COURT, Nos. 19 and 20, two storeys, brick walls, comprise two dwellings having plans of class 10 and 15; probably c. 1840.

BLACKFRIARS ESTATE

The Estate (Fig. 85) of about ten acres is bounded by Wharf Road, St. Leonard's Street, Cherryholt Road, the R. Welland, and partly by Gas Street. It occupies the site of the house of Black Friars which was founded in Stamford before 1241 (Knowles and Hadcock, *Medieval Religious Houses*, 187). The friary buildings stood above the flood plain on the N. side of the site but no structure or earthwork associated with them survive. Masonry and mullions were found S. of Adelaide Street in 1845 (Burton, 40); skeletons were discovered N. of the street in 1840 (Burton, 40) and in 1887 (*Mercury*, 14 Oct.). A stone coffin was unearthed in 1840 (*Mercury*, 18 Dec.), and another in 1909. Building operations in 1974 revealed traces, probably of a cloister, S. of Adelaide Street and immediately E. of Brownlow Street. The church would therefore have lain under the W. end of Adelaide Street (C. Mahany, *Med. Arch.* vol. XIX (1976)). After the Dissolution in 1538 the land passed eventually to Sir Edward Heron who built a house on the site of the friary between 1574 and 1611. In 1654 it was bought by Richard Cust (E. Cust, *Records of the Cust family*, 268). The house was demolished in 1775 (*Mercury*, 2 Mar.) and the ground laid out as separate gardens. In 1840 the 1st Earl Brownlow divided the land into streets and building plots which were sold at three auctions (*Mercury*, 12 June and 6 Nov. 1840, 6 Dec. 1844). The plots were laid out by Browning and varied in size, the larger on the S. being for freestanding houses. Covenants required the houses to be at least of two storeys, and noisome or dangerous trades were forbidden (Belton Estate Office, box 21, bundle 273). A wharf was planned between the S. ends of Brownlow and Wellington Streets. In the first auction small plots N. of Adelaide Street were bought mainly by speculators, and in the second the

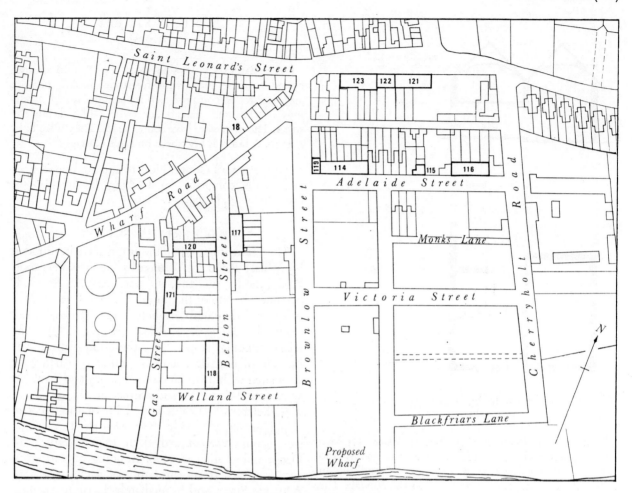

Fig. 85   Map showing monuments in Blackfriars Estate and Gas Street.

area around Belton Street was sold. The remainder, sold in 1844, was occupied almost entirely by separate gardens which had become increasingly sought after by townsfolk whose own gardens had been lost to commercial and domestic building. A number of these gardens survive as open spaces.

The principal buildings are listed below.

ADELAIDE STREET

(114) TERRACE, Nos. 1–8, two storeys, coursed rubble walls with ashlar dressings, and slated roofs, comprise dwellings of class 13b plan. The doors have lattice fanlights. The land was sold in 1840 to Moses Peal for £245 (*Mercury*, 8 Feb. 1867; Belton MSS.) Nos. 4–8 were built first and Nos. 1–3 soon after.

(115) HOUSE, No. 14, two storeys, red brick with stone quoins, class 10 plan, has panel inscribed 'J.B. 1843' for John Burton (*Mercury*, 7 Feb. 1868).

(116) TERRACE, Nos. 16–19, two storeys and cellars, coursed rubble walls with freestone dressings, has class 14b plans. The doorways are roundheaded. The plots were bought in 1840 by James Richardson, builder and house agent, who advertised a house for letting, probably in this terrace, in 1841 (Belton MSS.; *Mercury*, 10 April).

BELTON STREET

(117) TERRACE, Nos. 4–9, two storeys, coursed rubble with freestone dressings, the door and window lintels being continuous, consists of two blocks at different levels, with dwellings each of class 14a plan. It was built between 1844–6 by James Richardson (*Mercury*, 19 July 1844, 3 July 1846). Plan of No. 8, Fig. 7.

(118) TERRACE, Nos. 12–15, two storeys, coursed rubble, ashlar front wall with platband, sash windows, slate roof, was built soon after the sale of land in 1840 (*Mercury*, 6 Nov.). Before recent amalgamations, the

terrace comprised eight dwellings each with class 14a plan.

BROWNLOW STREET

(119) EVERARD HOUSE, No. 1, two storeys and cellar, coursed rubble walls with freestone dressings, class 10 plan, stands on a corner site with a large triple-sash window in the end wall facing Adelaide Street. It was built soon after 1840 by Moses Peal (Belton MSS; *Mercury*, 8 Feb. 1867).

MILNER'S ROW

(120) TERRACE of seven dwellings, two storeys and attics at front becoming three storeys at rear, ashlar front wall, rest in squared rubble, class 14 plans, was built on plots sold in 1840 (*Mercury*, 6 Nov.). In 1846 tenants of Thomas Milner who owned 13 houses in the area threatened to quit because of the smell from M. Laségue's guano factory (*Mercury*, 9 Oct.).

ST. LEONARD'S STREET

(121) TERRACE, Nos. 29–31, two storeys and cellars, have coursed rubble walls with freestone dressings. No. 29, of class 10 plan, was built after the others which have class 14b plans. The houses are on land bought in 1840 by Charles Lowe and John Horden, tradesmen (Belton MSS).

(122) HOUSES, Nos. 32–33, a pair, three storeys and cellars, coursed rubble with ashlar front wall, class 14b plans, were built in *c.* 1840.

(123) HOUSES, Nos. 34–38, two storeys and cellars at front, three storeys at rear, street elevation of coursed rubble with freestone dressings, gable and some rear walls of brick, class 14b plans, were built in three groups in *c.* 1840.

BLACKFRIARS STREET (Fig. 143)

(124) TERRACE, Nos. 1–4, two storeys, red brick front and stone rear walls, dressed quoins, was built shortly before 1829 by Thomas Pilkington who bought the site in 1813 (Ex. MS, 84/7). Upper and lower windows have continuous sills, and stone surrounds. The doorways, above which are blank walls, formerly had wooden architraves. Each dwelling, of class 15, consists of a front room, side passage and outshut containing the stair.

(125) Former BALLOON INN, No. 6, three storeys and cellar, with coursed rubble walls and brick gable walls, was described as newly built in 1827 (*Mercury*, 28 Dec.). It has an L-shaped plan (class 11) and a street front composed of sash windows and two roundheaded doorways, one leading to a central hallway the other to a side passage. In 1827 there was a parlour, bar and kitchen, with a dining room on the first floor.

BROAD STREET (Fig. 86)

As its name implies Broad Street is a wide street; it lies N. of the Danish burh (Plate 98). The W. end is now almost closed by encroachments, and at the E. end it terminates in Star Lane, which was formerly very narrow. Markets have been held in this early extramural development from an early date. The Beastmarket is mentioned in 1595 (NRO, Fitzwilliam Misc. 433) and this is the name usually applied to the W. end of the Street (e.g. Town Hall parcel 208) although a new beastmarket is recorded at the E. end in 1668 (Hall Book 2 fo. 44v). The cattle market was held in Broad Street until 1887 when it was moved to the present site near the railway station (Town Hall, minute book F).

The E. end of the street was known as the Haymarket from at least the 18th century. In 1595 the slope S. of Browne's Hospital was called the Fridaymarket and this was presumably the same market which by the 18th century was called the Cornmarket. In 1839 the sloping land was levelled and a new market, designed in the Tudor style by the Rev. Henry de Foe Baker of Greetham, was built against a retaining wall (*Mercury*, 17 Jan. 1862); it consisted of an open arcade of six bays (Plate 66). In 1859 it was replaced by a new building designed by Edward Browning on the opposite side of the street. The roof of the old building was removed on Browning's advice in the same year. It was dismantled in 1862 and parts were rebuilt elsewhere in the town. One bay of the arcade of Baker's building was re-erected by R. Tinkler in 1862 (*Mercury*, 14 Mar.) as the gate of the Bluecoat School, All Saints' Street; another bay stood between Nos. 28 and 29 St. Paul's Street but is now in pieces in the grounds of Brazenose House (383); a third serves as a gateway to the Congregational Church (36) and a fourth is at No. 41 High Street St. Martins (224) (Burton's *Guide to Stamford* (1896), 79).

Although the site of Browne's Hospital is said to have been undesirable before 1475 (*Antiquaries Journal* XLVI (1966), II, 284) the reset masonry at No. 3 Broad Street (128) indicates that not all houses were of low social status. In the 18th and 19th centuries the street retained a high level of respectability, and the markets doubtless encouraged the presence of professional men such as bankers (130 and 148) and newspaper proprietors (139).

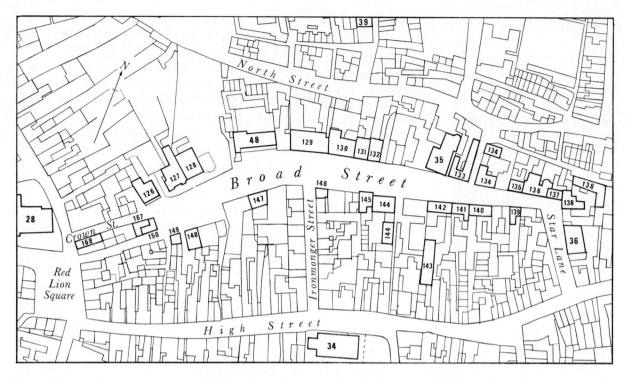

Fig. 86 Map showing monuments in Broad Street and Crown Street.

(126) HOUSE, No. 1 (Plate 118), three storeys and cellar, has ashlar front wall, rusticated quoins, and rubble side walls. It was built in the early 18th century to a class II plan. Early in the 19th century the main front was refaced and heightened, the original roof-line being visible on the gables. The new front has two-storey canted timber-framed bay windows with Gothic glazing bars; slightly later, a central porch with Tuscan columns was added. At attic level in the E. gable is a single-light ovolo-moulded window. A shallow fore-court, with semicircular steps and stone corner piers surmounted by urns, is enclosed by early 18th-century wrought-iron railings with central gates and scrollwork standards (Plate 125). Inside, a bolection-moulded door architrave and a wooden ceiling cornice of *c.* 1725 survive; otherwise the fittings are early 19th-century.

(127) WILLOUGHBY HOUSE, No. 2 (Fig. 87), two storeys, attics and cellars, stone walls, class IIb, is mostly early 18th-century, but a chimney stack in the E. wall is apparently 17th-century. It was advertised for sale in 1739 as 'new built and fashionable' and was then occupied by J. Wyche (*Mercury*, 9 Aug.), but was probably built *c.* 1717 (see *stone* below).

The main part of the 18th-century house comprises a central entrance, large flanking rooms, and a side stair-case, with lesser rooms, considerably altered, at the back; these last and the staircase are roofed at right angles to the front range. A rear wing of one storey and attics has a 17th-century origin, but the walls were refaced with ashlar in the late 18th century, and alterations made to the interior. Shortly before 1870 (*Mercury*, 27 Oct. 1871) the street front was refaced, the design being dominated by heavy quoins and large bay windows. Originally the front was in five bays (painting in Town Hall). Internally, most features date from a general redecoration scheme of *c.* 1790. The two front rooms both have wooden fireplace surrounds in the Adam style, and moulded and enriched plaster cornices. The staircase (Plate 132) with turned balusters, heavy rail and newels, and carved scroll brackets to the treads (Plate 130), is early 18th-century. In the timber-framed N. wall of the stair hall is a roundheaded window with Gothic glazing bars. Some upper rooms have plaster dentil cornices of *c.* 1790. Inside the 17th-century rear wing is a wide stone fireplace with chamfered jambs.

Set between returns in the front garden-wall are 18th-century wrought-iron gates, a pair in the centre and a single gate at the side, decorated with scroll and chinoiserie lattice work (Plate 125).

On an outbuilding is a stone inscribed 'Under this pavement is a well 1717'; this may be contemporaneous with the building of the house.

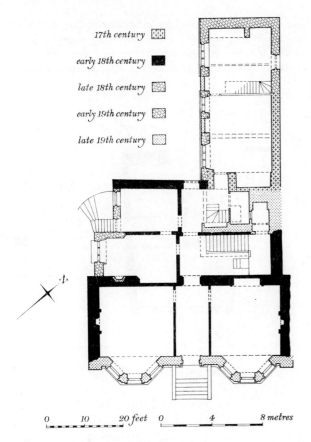

0　　10　　20 feet　　0　　　4　　　8 metres

Fig. 87　(127) 2 Broad Street.

(128) HOUSE, No. 3, two storeys and attics, coursed rubble walls, freestone dressings, is late 18th-century. The plan, now resembling class 9b, is unusual in that originally one of the main rooms on the front was entered directly from the street; the position of the doorway is now occupied by a window. Between this room and a stair at the rear is the main entrance hall, suggesting that the smaller front room had a commercial use while the rest of the house, entered from the side, remained private. On the street front the sills are now continuous and there is a wide platband. Internally, original decoration is mostly limited to plaster cornices, one of which is enriched with flowers and clover leaves. The kitchen fireplace has a roundheaded opening with moulded stone surround and keystone. On the first floor are two reeded fireplaces, late 18th-century.

On the N. gable of the modern wing on the E. is a reset crocketed coping with kneelers and a gable finial with cusped panels, crockets and carved heads, apparently 15th-century. These pieces probably came from a former building on this site, shown in a painting of a bull-running (Town Hall).

(129) HOUSES including THE LINCOLNSHIRE

POACHER (Plate 158), Nos. 5, 7, 8, three storeys, brick barrel-vaulted cellars, coursed rubble walls faced on S. in ashlar, have slated roofs. They were built for Charles Lowe, wine merchant, in 1846 to designs by Charles Richardson who applied in that year to the Improvement Commissioners for permission to set forward the W. end of the house (*Mercury*, 17 Apr.).

The long range formerly comprised three houses of which the central and western were of three bays with central entrances, and the eastern of two; the central house is set slightly forward. The range terminates with narrow, recessed, bays, that on the W. being curved. The doorways have round heads and fanlights, and the elevation is variously fenestrated, triple sashes predominating on the ground and first floor, and single sashes or blind recesses on the top floors. An upper projecting bay window with rounded sides is original. A broad platband has been partly mutilated to receive trade boards, since removed; below a shallow parapet is a moulded cornice. Inside, some plaster cornices of 1846 remain, particularly one in the Grecian taste in the W. house (Plate 153). Late in the 19th century, much of the interior was converted into a brewery.

(130) HOUSE (Fig. 88), No. 9, of two storeys with attics and cellars, ashlar walls, originally comprised two

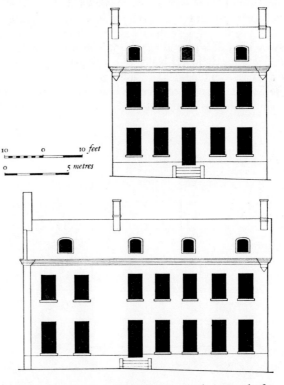

10　　　0　　　10 feet

0　　　5 metres

Fig. 88　(130) 9 Broad Street. Front elevation before and after amalgamation with adjoining property.

houses; roof construction suggests that the E. section has a late 17th or early 18th-century class 10 origin. The E. house was rebuilt or refaced in the early 19th century; soon afterwards the smaller W. house was amalgamated and its front elevation rebuilt as a unity with the E. part. Slightly later in the 19th century, the central entrance to the E. house was moved to its present position, and the sills of the ground-floor windows were lowered. These alterations may be associated with the use of the building, or part of it, as a bank after its conveyance in July 1810 (Messrs. Kelham, solicitors); it remained a bank until the late 19th century. All openings are plain and their grouping reflects the two houses incorporated in the present building. Inside, the arrangement of rooms has been much altered, but fittings include a veined marble fireplace with fluted sides of *c.* 1800, and a decorative plaster cornice of *c.* 1830.

(131) HOUSE, No. 10, two storey and attics, stone walls, has an 18th-century origin but was largely rebuilt in 1888, the date inscribed over the main doorway. Three asymmetrically spaced windows on the first floor of the street front have raised surrounds, keystones and continuous sills; these openings and much of the ashlar wall they are in are probably 19th-century reproductions of 18th-century work. The ground floor has been gutted.

(132) HOUSE (Plate 108), No. 11, two storeys and attics, is mid 18th-century, but the original class 10 plan has been disguised by later bay windows and the change in the position of the entrance; it was formerly of four bays with a doorway in the third. The front has rusticated quoins, bold platband, two original upper windows with moulded sills and architraves, and keystones. The wooden eaves cornice is bracketed. Inside, the ground floor has been gutted but traces of the central

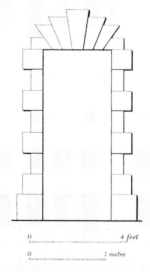

Fig. 89   (133) Former Stag and Pheasant Inn. Doorway.

passage with a roundheaded doorway in the back wall remain. Fittings include fielded panelling in two heights in the former W. room. At the rear are mid 19th-century additions, of two storeys, mainly commercial.

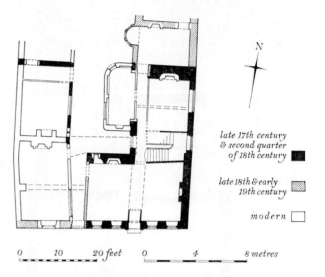

Fig. 90   (133) Former Stag and Pheasant Inn.

(133) Former STAG AND PHEASANT INN, No. 14 (Fig. 90; Plate 113), mostly of two storeys, some attics and cellars, has an ashlar front wall, remainder coursed rubble; the main block, of class 11a, dates from the second quarter of the 18th century and may incorporate parts of a 17th-century structure in a rear wing. In 1799 the building became the New Salutation Inn (*Mercury*, 10 Sept.). The W. section, partly 17th-century at the rear, was much altered *c.* 1800 when it was made into a wine shop; stables on the E. side of the plot were described as new in 1819 (*Mercury*, 24 Dec.).

The main range has an 18th-century roof with staggered purlins; the rear wing has a roof with clasped purlins perhaps of the 17th century. The symmetrical street front of five bays has a platband, openings with continuous sills and pronounced keystones; the central doorway and upper windows have rusticated architraves (Figs. 10, 89). Above, is a deeply projecting moulded cornice and a parapet. The small range on the W. has a roundheaded upper window and moulded stone eaves course; the ground-floor window is inserted in a former roundheaded opening. In each rear wing is a wooden mullion-and-transom window, probably late 17th-century. Reset in W. gable is a stone slab inscribed 'IB 1663'. Inside, the 18th-century stair has turned balusters, scroll tread-brackets and fielded panelled dado; the upper flight has splat balusters (Fig. 15). In the main ground-floor room, originally two

Fig. 91 (134) 15 Broad Street. Reconstruction of front elevation showing former central entrance.

rooms with central passage, are sections of double-height fielded panelling with wooden cornice; the fireplaces have fielded-panelled overmantels. The rooms above are now also united and similarly panelled. Other rooms contain reset sections of panelling of various dates.

(134) HOUSE, No. 15 (Fig. 91; Plate 113), two storeys and attics, ashlar front, coursed rubble side and rear walls, was probably built in the second quarter of the 18th century. It originally had a class 11 plan, but many alterations have been made to the plan, particularly the moving of the entrance from the centre to the second bay and the unifying of the former hall with the E. room. The five-bay street front has rusticated quoins, wooden eaves cornice with brackets (Plate 122), and openings with moulded surrounds and triple keystones. Inside, there is an egg-and-dart plaster cornice of the late 18th century; the late 19th-century stair incorporates turned balusters with square knops of the 18th century.

An outbuilding, originally timber-framed, of two storeys, has a roof with clasped purlins; perhaps 17th-century.

(135) Former RISING SUN INN, No. 17 (Fig. 92), one and two storeys and attics, rubble walls, has a class 10 plan and an early 19th-century external appearance. However, the W. room and the central entrance passage may originally have formed a medieval open hall, and the E. part a two-storey service end (class 1a). The

W. section and central entrance passage have a high ceiling and the W. room has a heavy cross beam; a cross partition is composed of 18th-century fielded panelling in two heights. Although there is no detail which is certainly medieval, this section probably formed the service end originally. The medieval arrangement is reflected in the disposition of the windows on the street front.

Fig. 92 (135) 17 Broad Street. Front elevation.

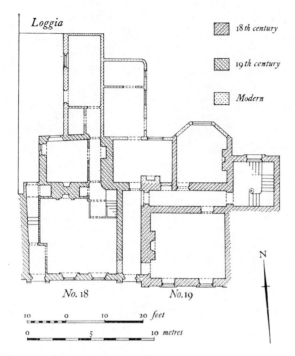

Loggia

☐ 18*th century*

☐ 19*th century*

☐ *Modern*

N

No. 18   *No. 19*

10 0 10 20 *feet*

0 5 10 *metres*

Fig. 93 (136) 18–19 Broad Street.

(136) HOUSES, Nos. 18–19 (Fig. 93), appear to have developed as one property but are now separate. The earlier, No. 19 on the E., dates from the mid 18th century. No. 18 (Plate 142) was added on the W. in *c.* 1830, possibly replacing a former structure belonging to No. 19; the E. bay of No. 18 was designed to provide the main access to the whole property.

No. 19 (Plate 115), two storeys and attics, ashlar front, coursed rubble rear walls, mansard roof, was built in the mid 18th century possibly against an older and lower building which stood to the E.; this latter has since been rebuilt (137). The street front of two bays has a broad platband and windows with moulded architraves (Fig. 11), keystones, and continuous sills to the upper pair, and a boldly projecting cornice and parapet. The upper part of the S.E. angle of the building overlaps the lower building (137) to the E.; the rusticated quoins were used only on the S.W. angle below the platband. The single ground-floor room has an elaborate decorated plaster ceiling of the second half of the 18th century with bracketed cornice, central fluted rose with radial fluting within and a band entwined with vines (Plate 137). The fireplace of white and grey marble has central panel carved with an urn spilling grapes, and vine foliage; a door has an entablature carved with fluting and central acanthus motif (Plate 131). Behind is a passage with contemporary roundheaded archways and a cupboard with shaped shelves. The passage leads to a stair hall on the E. and a further room on the N., both probably additions of the late 18th century. The N. room, with

prominent semi-octagonal bay, has a late 18th-century plaster cornice and stone fireplace. The stair hall has a plaster ceiling comprising acanthus-derived central motif and elegantly enriched cornice. The present stair is early 19th-century with bracketed treads and handrail terminating as a scroll. In an upper room is a white and orange-veined marble fireplace of chaste design, 18th-century.

No. 18 (Plate 142), two storeys and attics, coursed rubble walls, freestone dressings, platband, cornice and parapet, has rear wall and chimney stack in red brick. Stylistically it appears to date from *c.* 1830. The symmetrical street front has two side projections each with roundheaded doorways, one, on the W., leading to a through-passage with a side entrance to the house, the other now providing the main entrance to No. 19, but at one time access also to No. 18. Between the projections are sash windows and all openings have keystones. Inside, the two back-to-back rooms have no datable features.

At the N. end of the gardens is an 8 ft. high terrace on the line of the town wall. The W. end is still in the form of a loggia with two roundheaded arches, but the E. section is now largely destroyed; 18th-century.

(137) HOUSES, Nos. 20–21 (Plate 115), two storeys and attics, ashlar front wall, were built as a single house on the site of part of No. 19 in the late 18th century. Scratched on the plinth of the S. wall are initials 'IR' and a date 1770 or 1790. The street front of three unequal bays has a first-floor moulded string course; the tall sash windows have no architraves. The E. of the two doorways is an insertion, but both are without surrounds. The interior, originally conforming to class 10 plan, has been recently remodelled.

On a wall in the yard are several carvings and inscriptions including cherubs and date '1824', presumably a mason's trial pieces.

(138) HOUSE, No. 22, has a two-storey front range and a rear wing of one storey and attics. The walls are rubble. It has a 17th-century origin but the front range was considerably altered in the early 19th century when small rooms were also added in the entrant angle. The street front is rendered and has early 19th-century sash windows. Inside, one cross beam, perhaps 16th-century but certainly reused, is partly chamfered and partly wave-and-hollow moulded. The rear wing is a two-room house of class 6 with axial chamfered beam of the 17th century.

In the yard beyond is a row of mid 19th-century industrial buildings of two storeys with coursed rubble walls. They are lit by tall windows with small panes. It was built for a foundry.

(139) HOUSE and SHOP, No. 25 (Figs. 94, 95; Plate 140), two storeys, cellar and attic, class 12, of coursed

Fig. 94　(139) 25 Broad Street. Reconstruction of front elevation.

rubble, the front wall of ashlar and E. wall of S. wing timber-framed, was built in the mid 18th century; the N. room was apparently intended as a shop. The street elevation has a moulded stone plinth, alternate rusticated quoins, moulded wooden eaves cornice, and openings with moulded surrounds and keystones. The first floor is of three bays but the ground floor of four, originally with alternating windows and doors; the W. door apparently always opened into a passage leading to the back wing, and the other door with its flanking windows to the shop in the front range.

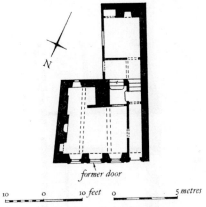

former door

Fig. 95　(139) 25 Broad Street.

(140) CONGREGATIONAL HALL, Nos. 28–30, was formed recently out of two houses, first by demolishing all but the upper storey of the stone façades and then by rearranging the window surrounds and quoins; the result is a pastiche. The former houses were a pair, of two storeys each of three bays, and had basements with 17th-century mullioned windows and timber-framed rear walls. On the first floor the moulded window surrounds of No. 29, the E. house, have been rearranged as the central three windows of the new seven-bay façade while the four plain surrounds from No. 30 form the two outer bays. All have keystones. The W. quoins are reset from No. 29. The ground floor is entirely modern. A timber-framed stair turret of three storeys formerly stood at the rear.

(141) HOUSE, No. 31, two storeys, attics and cellar, now class 10, probably originated as a timber-framed building of class 6 with a jetty to the street, which was faced in ashlar in the late 18th or early 19th century. It comprises a two-room house with a side-passage. A red brick wing with lean-to roof was added at the rear in the early 19th century. A shop front was installed by Charles Richardson, architect, in 1848 (*Mercury*, 14 April); the shop window has curved side-panes and stone side pilasters with egg-and-dart moulded capitals, also repeated as door-pilasters. The central upper window is blocked and the eaves have a plaster cornice. Interior fittings include a stone fireplace surround, and fielded panelling in two heights in a first-floor room, both perhaps *c.* 1800. Behind the house is a two-storey bake-house, with stone walls and a projection for sack-hoist, of *c.* 1848.

(142) HOUSE, No. 32 (Fig. 96; Plate 81), two storeys, cellar and attics, ashlar front and rubble rear walls, has a 17th-century main range of class 10 plan which extends over a carriage-entry to one side; a rear wing was added in the 19th century. The street elevation comprises a central doorway with an early 19th-century pedimented surround, flanked by two-storey gabled bay windows with mullions and canted sides. Over the carriage-entry is a timber-framed and gabled bay window with ovolo-moulded mullions, carried on wooden moulded brackets. The rear wing incorporates two stone mullioned windows reset from the back wall of the main range. Interior fittings include 18th-century fielded panelling of two heights, and early 19th-century door surrounds with angle-roundel decoration. The roof has collars which clasp the purlins.

(143) BUILDING, behind No. 32, a long rectangular structure with red brick walls, stone-dressed openings, and hipped roof, may probably be identified as the silk throwsting factory recorded in 1816 (Hall Book 5, f. 126). The upper of the present two storeys may be late 19th-century; windows and doorways in the semi-basement have segmental heads, stone jambs and key-stones. Inside, a row of iron columns supports the first floor which is of plaster. On the upper floor a kiln has been added.

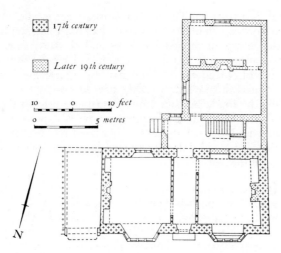

17th century

Later 19th century

10   0   10 feet
0   5 metres

N

Fig. 96   (142) 32 Broad Street.

(144) Former ROE BUCK INN, No. 33 (Plate 114), class 8a, originated as a timber-framed structure, perhaps of the 17th century. It was cased in stone early in the 18th century; at about the same time a single room with ground-floor walls of stone, the upper of timber-frame, was added at the rear. A second rear wing was built late in the 18th century and another of two storeys in red brick added in the re-entrant angle in the early 19th century. Timber-framing survives in the rear wall of the main range. The front elevation in seven ground-floor bays of coursed masonry has an almost central straight joint which aligns with a change in ridge height. The plain window surrounds with triple keystones are uniform throughout implying little difference in date between the two sections. The central doorway has no window above, and the end bays are occupied by openings to a passage on the E. and a yard on the W. On the front is a date panel with shaped top, inscribed 'EW 1704', possibly for one Walker (Plate 129); in 1717 the Roe Buck was owned by widow Walker and had stables, a large yard and a garden (*Mercury*, 25 Apr.). Inside, 18th-century fittings include stone fireplaces and some reused turned stair balusters. The W. room has fireplace and adjacent elliptical-headed arches with key-blocks and capitals, and panelled cupboards, indicating its use as a kitchen. A number of early 19th-century fireplaces have panelled surrounds and angle roundels.

Barn, of two storeys and attics, stone walls, is perhaps 18th-century; it was raised in height in *c*. 1800 to provide stables with lofts over.

(145) HOUSE, No. 34 (Plate 140), two storeys and basement, attic in mansard roof, rendered stone walls, is late 18th-century. It comprises a main range with staircase and a rear wing, resembling class 11b; the three-bay front has central doorway with classical pedimented surround, and flanking bay windows with canted sides,

which rise to a continuous moulded cornice. Inside, some panelling of varying types survives on both floors.

(146) HOUSE, No. 37, on a corner site, two storeys, ashlar walls, is early 18th-century. The upper storey has rusticated quoins on the corner, and windows with moulded architraves and sills. To the E. is a later rubble-built section. Internal features are lacking.

HOUSE and SHOP, No. 38, see mon. 249.

(147) HOUSES, Nos. 39–40 (Plate 143), three storeys, cellars, and attics in a mansard roof, reduce to two storeys and attics at rear. They are the remaining two of three houses built after 1786 and described as newly built in 1808 when the outgoing lessee was John Hames, mason (leases in Town Hall). It is possible that Hames built them.

The seven-bay street front is ashlar with windows rising from platbands. The ground-floor plans, originally conforming to class 13b, have been altered for modern shops. The adjacent entrances are now windows and the hallway of No. 40 is incorporated in No. 39. Inside No. 40 the stairhall was entered through a broad segmental arch; the stair has ramped handrail, square balusters and turned newels. Fanlights were inserted over first-floor doors in the early 19th century probably when the house was used as a bank. A fireplace has a wooden reeded surround with fluted quarter-columns, and a frieze carved with frolicking cherubs, a lion and swags. No. 39, gutted on the ground floor, has a plainer stair than No. 40 and a fireplace with fretted frieze of *c*. 1800.

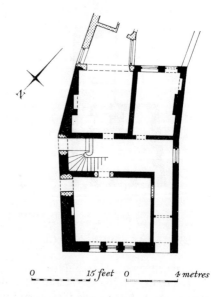

0   15 feet   0   4 metres

Fig. 97   (148) 49 Broad Street.

(148) HOUSE, No. 49 (Fig. 97), now a bank, three storeys, cellars, red brick walls in Flemish bond, hipped roof, was built in 1770 by John Truman (deeds) and bears a small slab in the S. wall inscribed 'JT 1770'. The walls have brick platbands, dentilled eaves course, and stone quoins on the W. corners. The plan approximates to class 13b but the ground-floor partitions have been largely removed. First-floor windows on the street front have stele-type over-lintels of Grecian character and are probably early 19th-century. This front is rendered.

(149) SHOPS, Nos. 50–51, a pair, two storeys, attics, rubble walls, hipped mansard roof, were built c. 1830. The rendered street front has two roundheaded doorways and the original shop windows, one with moulded surrounds, one retaining its small glass panes. Above the first-floor platband are two sash windows flanked by blind openings.

(150) HOUSE, No. 52 (Plate 111), now incorporating No. 3 Crown Street (167), two storeys, attics and cellars, has ashlar front walls; the group is mid 18th-century. Of L-shaped plan, it has hipped roof, two tall chimney stacks, one of which has been rebuilt in brick, projecting pilaster-like quoins and moulded timber eaves cornice. The street front has a central doorway with early 19th-century pedimented surround, and on both floors are large sash windows with plain architraves and keystones. With the removal of all inner walls the original plan and position of the stair have been lost. One upper room has 18th-century panelling of three heights, and a moulded cornice.

BROWNLOW STREET

Laid out in 1840 on the Blackfriars Estate and named after 1st Earl Brownlow, owner of the land. See Blackfriars Estate (119).

BURGHLEY LANE (Fig. 111)

This was formerly the only road running E. from High Street St. Martins to Pilsgate, Burghley and Barnack. After enclosure in 1796 this road was blocked by the enlargement of Burghley Park and was replaced by Barnack Road, an entirely new road cut in that year. Within the present built-up area Burghley Lane appears never to have had buildings in it until the fragmentation of the garden of 35 High Street St. Martins in the late 18th century; the first houses were built in the early 19th century in the former gardens of Nos. 35 and 36.

(151) HOUSES, Nos. 7–13, a row of dwellings built as reflecting pairs each of class 14b plan, of two storeys,

have coursed rubble walls, flush dressings and openings with projecting keystones. The row was built by John de Merveilleux between 1834, when the land was bought from the widow of George vander Neunberg, and 1842, the year of de Merveilleux's death (deeds). In 1850 the Borough Surveyor was ordered to lay five steps in front of five new houses in Burghley Lane; these steps survive outside Nos. 9–13.

CASTERTON ROAD (Fig. 206)

(152) CLOCK HOUSE, No. 1 (Plate 162), two storeys, coursed rubble walls with flush ashlar quoins, class 10 plan, is in the Tudor style. It was built on manorial waste in 1839 by Richard Newcomb who was granted a 33-year lease from March 1840 (Ex. MS, 77/5; survey of encroachments 190). The central bay projects slightly and is gabled. The windows have labels, central mullions, and gothic glazing bars; over the central window is a circular frame for a clock face.

CASTLE STREET (Fig. 138)

(153) HOUSE, Nos. 1–2, consists of a long 17th-century range of two storeys at right-angles to the street; it is built on sloping ground, with the cellar at the street end at the same level as the ground floor of the rear wing. A corbel and door jamb indicate a late medieval date for the cellar. The building on the street front was almost completely rebuilt in c. 1830 on a class 9 plan of three bays. The rear wing, the upper part timber-framed, has a continuous first-floor jetty on the W., now underbuilt in stone; the rounded ends of jetty joists are visible. A blocked window has wooden chamfered mullions. The main house, of two storeys and attics, was built c. 1830 of rubble with flush freestone dressings, and contains contemporary fittings including a reeded fireplace surround; in the attic is a 17th-century panelled door.

(154) Former INN, No. 5, two storeys, has coursed rubble walls partly rendered. It was built as the Shepherd and Shepherdess Inn between c. 1825 and 1835 (Mercury, 15 May 1835) and later became the Castle Inn. The four-bay street front has large sash windows on the first floor, and two smaller below flanked by elliptically-headed arches, the wider leading to a carriage-entry, the narrower framing a doorway.

(155) WAREHOUSE, at S. end of Cooch's Court, two storeys and attic, hipped roof, walls of rubble with freestone dressings, was still unfinished in 1835 when it was for sale (Mercury, 15 May). A wing formerly stood on the W. The wide entrance has a cambered head.

CHURCH LANE (Fig. 111)

(156) HOUSES, Nos. 1, 3 Church Lane and 6, 8 Church Street, three storeys, coursed rubble walls with freestone dressings, red brick chimney stacks, comprise four houses of c. 1830; they are probably those shown on Knipe's map of 1833. The doorway and sash windows on the rounded corner are all curved. Nos. 1 and 3 Church Lane are of class 14a, and 6, 8 Church Street of class 15.

(157) Former RED COW INN, No. 2, two storeys, coursed rubble walls, class 10 plan but much altered; early 19th-century.

(158) HOUSE, No. 4, two storeys and attics, coursed rubble walls, class 15 plan but the rebuilt E. gable may indicate truncation in the early 19th century; 18th-century.

(159) HOUSE, Nos. 9–11, two storeys and attics, coursed rubble walls, mansard roof, has an L-shaped plan. The main range, class 10 plan, bears a date-panel inscribed 'RB 1823'. The short rear wing, built slightly later, has recently been partly demolished.

(160) HOUSE, No. 13, two storeys with attics, coursed rubble walls, mansard roof, brick chimney stack, class 8a plan with side passage, ovolo-moulded mullioned windows of two or three lights; probably built in c. 1845.

(161) HOUSE, No. 21, two storeys, rubble walls, dressed plinth, class 10 plan with slightly later wing at rear, timber lintels over doors and windows; early 19th-century.

(162) HOUSE, No. 23, three storeys, coursed rubble walls, class 15 plan, single windows on each floor, sash and casement; after 1833 (not on Knipe's map).

CHURCH STREET (Fig. 111)

The road from Easton-on-the-Hill formerly ran along Church Street, and thence along Church Lane to High Street St. Martins. In 1796 the present Kettering Road was created, forming a more direct route.

(163) HOUSE, No. 1, three storeys, coursed rubble walls, originally comprised two houses, the W. having a class 15 plan and the E. a class 10. The end room of the latter unit has been removed. The building-date is given on a panel, 'JB 1828'.

(164) CHURCH COURT, a row of class 15 dwellings, one storey and attics, coursed rubble walls, red brick chimney stacks, converted to garages, is now derelict. The row may have consisted of three or four units, and was built in the 18th century.

(165) WAREHOUSE, two storeys and attics, coursed rubble walls, mansard roof, is early 19th-century. On the E. are four oval openings for ventilation with red brick surrounds and iron-barred wooden frames. Above are tall windows, many blocked. The original function of the building is unknown but the ground floor was used for storage.

(166) Former MALTING, Nos. 2–4, coursed rubble walls, was originally of three storeys extending to the rear wing of mon. (235). Demolition of a central section has left the W. part detached and this has become two houses and a store. Originally there were small square openings on each floor. The site was bought by Moses Lumby in 1813; he cleared four houses and built the maltings before his death in 1838 (deeds).

Nos. 6 and 8 Church Street, see mon. 156.

CROWN STREET (Fig. 86)

Named after an adjacent inn, this narrow street runs on one side of the infilled W. end of Broad Street.

(167) HOUSE, Nos. 3–4 (Plate 111), formerly one dwelling, is mid 18th-century. At the rear it incorporates a timber-framed wing giving on to Red Lion Street, but this may be a later acquisition. It is of two storeys, attics and cellars and the walls are ashlar. A wooden eaves cornice is heavily moulded. The street elevation is designed with the lower stage different from the upper. The ground floor, originally of three unequal bays, is plainer than the upper, without quoins or surrounds to openings; above the platband the wall has quoins (Plate 121), and the four windows, two of which are now blocked, have moulded surrounds and triple keystones. The arrangement of rooms probably conformed to class 10 but only one partition remains. One room contains 18th-century fielded panelling in two heights.

(168) MARSH HARRIER INN, No. 7, three storeys, cellars, and attics in a mansard roof, has coursed rubble walls and freestone dressings. It was constructed as one building on two plots between 1791 and 1798. The E. plot was owned by William Baker, schoolmaster, who in 1791 leased the W. plot from Browne's Hospital; in 1798 a lease from the Hospital states that Baker had built over both sections (Browne's Hospital Muniment Room, All Saints' leases, March 1791 and 1798).

The street front has sash windows with platbands at sill level. Recently the W. end wall was completely rebuilt. Reset in the S. wall is a panel inscribed, 'FBA 1671'. On the first-floor is a late 18th-century plaster ceiling with circular pattern enriched with swags in the Adam manner.

EIGHT ACRES

A short road encroaching on the former open fields, is named after an adjoining field. Houses were built along one side in the early 19th century. (See New Town and mon. 262.)

ELM STREET (Fig. 187)

This section of the extramural road was given the name Elm Road in 1868.

(169) ELM COTTAGE (Fig. 98), two storeys, cellar and attics, stone walls, plan approximating to class 10, is probably the house referred to in 1822 as being newly built (*Mercury*, 3 May). It contains a stone fireplace with angle-roundels.

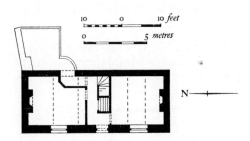

Fig. 98   (169) Elm Cottage, Elm Street.

EMPINGHAM ROAD
See New Town and mons. 263–267.

FOUNDRY ROAD

This road forms the S.W. side of the early 19th-century development known as the New Town (see mons. 268–270).

GAS LANE (Fig. 143)

(170) HOUSES in Cecil Court, row of three dwellings now of one storey and attics with stone walls raised recently in brick, comprise a pair of dwellings, probably converted from a single 18th-century house of class 10 plan, to which a third room was added to the E. in the early 19th century.

GAS STREET (Fig. 85)

This street runs along the E. side of Tenter Meadow adjacent to the site of the Blackfriars, and takes its name from the gas works established next to it in 1825 (452).

(171) HOUSES, Nos. 5–9 (Fig. 99), consist of two pairs and a single class 15 dwelling, each with coursed rubble walls. Nos. 5 and 6 have ashlar quoins and dressings, and rebuilt outshuts; on the front is a date-panel, 'W.R. 1819'. Nos. 7 and 8, without quoins, were built soon after Nos. 5 and 6; No. 9 is set back and was the last to be erected.

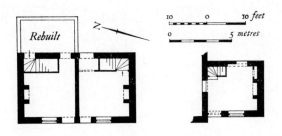

Fig. 99   (171) 5–6 and 9 Gas Street.

HIGH STREET (Fig. 100)

High Street was the axial road of the Danish burh. In the Middle Ages the Butcher Row was in the middle of the road, at its E. end, and almost opposite St. Michael's Church; there was a conduit which shared the same supply as that in St. Paul's Street. A booth in Butcher Row was given to St. Michael's nunnery before 1250 (PRO, SC 11/426). The Shambles was rebuilt in 1751 at a cost of £176 (Chamberlains' Accounts) and a drawing by Nattes shows the new building to have had a long roof supported on posts and to have been open along the sides. In 1720 there were also 'drystandings and stalls' against the neighbouring shops (Ex. MS, 87/12). A new shambles and market was begun in 1804 and completed in 1808 on an adjacent site (61). High Street has always been of importance, and since at least the 18th century it has been the principal commercial street in the town. All buildings have been more or less drastically altered to suit them to the needs of the 19th and 20th-century shopkeepers.

Former HOUSES and SHOPS, No. 1, see mon. 279.

Fig. 100   Map showing monuments in High Street, Ironmonger Street and Wellington Lane.

(172) SHOP, No. 3 (Fig. 101), three storeys, plastered red brick, comprises two blocks, running back from the street, now linked on the ground floor. It may be identified as the draper's shop, counting house and warehouse sold by Edward Thorpe to Garmston Chapman in 1824 (*Mercury*, 8 Oct. and 10 Dec.) and was probably built shortly before that date. The two-bay street block, with upper sash window, was formerly separated from the rear block by a narrow yard. This rear block has a timber-framed S. wall and the remainder is built of brick or stone. A fireplace has fluted surround and corner paterae.

(173) HOUSES and SHOPS, Nos. 6–7 (Plate 106), two storeys and attics, have a rear range on the E., probably originally timber-framed, of the 17th century. The seven-bay main range was remodelled or rebuilt in the mid 18th century; the ashlar street front with separated quoins and first-floor sash windows, having moulded surrounds and stepped keystones, the central one fluted, was built at this time. A wooden moulded and bracketed cornice remains only over No. 7. The early 19th-century shop front to No. 7 (Plate 138) has a central doorway integral with flanking bow windows and entrances to side passages, one of which is now blocked; the cornice is concave over the doorways and convex over the windows. The E. passage served the house at the rear of the shop, and the W. is a public footpath known as

Wellington Lane. The ground floor of No. 6 is gutted, but at the rear a timber-framed turret contains part of an early 19th-century stair. A first-floor room in No. 6 has

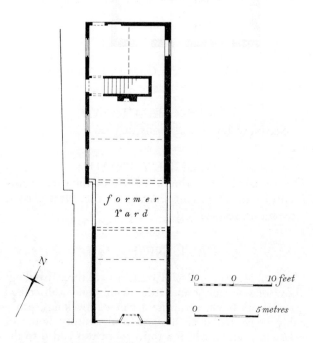

Fig. 101   (172) 3 High Street.

early 19th-century beaded and panelled window reveals. A substantial moulded wooden bracket in a rear room of No. 7 has ornamental guttae, early 18th-century.

(174) HOUSE, No. 8 (Plate 110), three storeys and attics, red brick, gabled mansard roof, interior gutted, consists of two parallel ranges and a central linking block running back from the street. The rear range dates from the first half of the 18th century and the remainder was built in the 1760s. In 1768 the building, then the Globe Inn, was described as recently built (*Mercury*, 21 July), but the linking block appears to have been altered after that date.

The mid 18th-century street front of three bays breaking forward in the centre has two platbands, first-floor sash windows with lowered sills and modern iron balconies; the central window was originally wider and scars suggest it was of triple, possibly Venetian, form. The top-floor sash windows have moulded sills and shaped brick keyblocks; the central opening is a lunette, apparently original, with moulded brick architrave, key block and apron. The mansard roof and a wooden dentilled eaves cornice are early 19th-century. In each gable is a blind window with aprons and sills. The corresponding wing at the rear, also of three storeys and attics, is built of coursed rubble with freestone quoins, and has a gabled roof. The N. elevation (Plate 110) of three bays has platband, moulded string-course, coved eaves decorated with three demon masks and attenuated swags in plaster (Plate 122), and later sash windows with freestone dressings, perhaps of *c.* 1768. The attic floors are of plaster.

(175) HOUSE, No. 9, front block of three storeys, ashlar walls, is early 19th-century. The ground floor is gutted except for a side passage. The three-bay street front has sash windows and a plain rebuilt parapet. Inside, is an early 19th-century fireplace with corner-bosses. At rear is an 18th-century block with sash windows and 19th-century staircase; it was later extended at the rear to form a two-storey wing. In *c.* 1840 a narrow two-storey stone wing with attics was added beyond; its function is unknown.

(176) GOTHIC HOUSE, No. 10 (Fig. 102), mostly two storeys, comprises a long range running back from the street. It incorporates the rear wing of a large, probably 16th-century, house of which the S. end was replaced by the present mock-gothic building in 1849. At the rear of the early house is a block of the same date, formerly detached, but now joined to it by a small structure possibly of the late 16th century. The street front of 1849 (Plate 163)

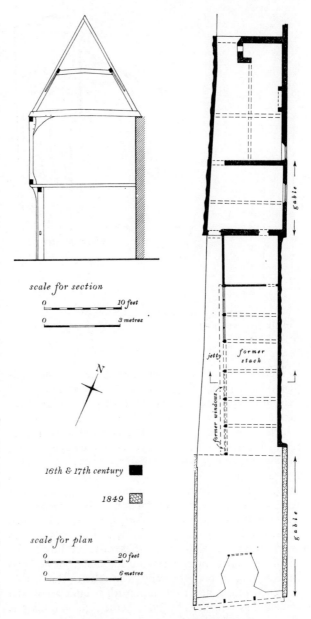

scale for section

0   10 *feet*

0   3 *metres*

N

16th & 17th century ▮

1849 ▨

scale for plan

0   20 *feet*

0   6 *metres*

Fig. 102   (176) Gothic House, 10 High Street.

was described at the time as a 'fine specimen of the revived Tudor style' (*Mercury*, 22 June).

The early house is of timber-frame two storeys high and is jettied on the W. where there is a narrow passage. Six bays remain but, except for the principal posts, the W. wall below the jetty has been removed from the four S. bays. Originally the plan consisted of two rooms, of three and two bays, separated by a chimney stack now removed. Cross beams have double-ogee mouldings which continue along the wall-plate but some mouldings have been hacked back as chamfers. Each room was lit by a continuous range of windows, with four lights

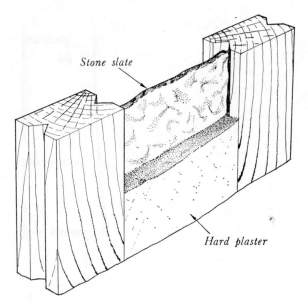

Fig. 103   (176) Gothic House. Detail of infilling in timber-frame.

to each bay; mortices for mullions remain in the wall-plate. Each principal post has an external square rib expanding to a bracket below the jetty; in the sides are grooves to receive the infill of stone slates, several of which survive in the N. gable, covered with plaster (Fig. 103). The roof, originally open to the upper rooms, has braced and cambered tie beams, collars clasping purlins, and wind braces; half-bays are marked by collars only. A collar, inserted when the chimney stack was removed, bears a painted inscription 'T. Rayment 1788'. Thomas Rayment, a clockmaker, is recorded between 1764, his marriage-date, and 1792, and in 1775 he was working in the High Street (*Mercury*, 13 July). The small late 16th-century structure adjoining on the N. is timber-framed but generally featureless. The earlier detached block, also timber-framed, is built across the site and has evidence of a jetty on the S.; the infilling is of stone slates covered with plaster. The two-bay roof has collars clasping windbraced purlins. Adjoining on the N. is another building probably of 17th-century date; the walls are of stone and the single room has intersecting beams.

The S. section giving onto the street is of three storeys and attics and the walls are probably brick but the front is rendered to imitate timber-framing (Plate 163). Twin bay windows and gables with carved barge-boards face the street. Between the bays is the date 'MDCCCXLIX' but this is now obscured. The interior has been gutted.

(177) HOUSE, Nos. 11–12 (Plate 141), two storeys and attics, timber-framed with later stone end wall, comprises a front range of the 16th or early 17th century

(class 2 plan), and a slightly later parallel rear range; the main front was jettied, now only traceable in the E. end wall. In the 18th century two three-storey bay windows were added; they rise above the eaves and have canted sides and semi-octagonal hipped roofs. The rear wall, slightly jettied, has exposed timber studs marked with Roman numbers. In the E. end wall is a four-light wooden ovolo-moulded window. Inside, on the first floor, the absence of mortices in some studs implies former, smaller, windows in the positions of the 18th-century bays. In the rear wall are two rectangular oriel windows carried on brackets; they are probably replacements.

(178) HOUSE, No. 14 (Plate 92), three storeys, cellar and attics, has dressed stone walls and some timber-framing now mostly internal. The earliest, perhaps late medieval, structure of which there is evidence is a rear wing, of timber-frame with a stone stack on the E. side; its roof has a pair of collared rafters. In *c.* 1700 the S. range next to the street was rebuilt in stone; it extended back as far as the early stack. At about the same time a two-storey block with full-height bay window, now demolished, was built N. of the stack. The ashlared street front of *c.* 1700 is decorated with bolection-moulded framework defining panels and windows. The wide eaves are supported on shaped brackets (Plate 123). Inside, a staircase of *c.* 1700 exists on the first and second floors of the S. range, the scar of its lower flight being traceable against the S. face of the chimney stack; it has a continuous mast-like newel, square end-newels, heavy moulded hand rail, turned balusters and closed string (Plate 132). The first-floor room had until recently bolection-moulded panelling in two heights with elaborately moulded cornice and pulvinated frieze. Some early 19th-century wall-paper with a coffered pattern was noted. In the rear range there was formerly a bolection-moulded fireplace surround of *c.* 1700; the stone jambs of another surround with recessed mouldings survive.

Parallel to the main house and facing Silver Lane is a

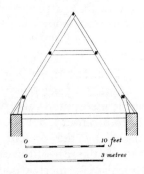

Fig. 104   (178) Range behind 14 High Street. Section of roof of middle block, *c.* 1700.

long range of three dates: the larger and central block of *c.* 1700 has two storeys and attics, stone walls, and is undivided internally; the roof has principal rafters with curved feet, and collars (Fig. 104). The S. block, of ashlar with moulded window surrounds, linked with the main house, is early 18th-century and of two storeys; an upper room has fielded panelling of two heights. The small block on the N. is two-storey and late 18th-century.

(179) Houses and Shops, Nos. 15–17 (Plate 92), three storeys and attics, ashlar front and coursed rubble rear walls, timber-framed stair turrets, were built *c.* 1700. The street fronts conform generally to the design of No. 14 but the deep bracketed eaves are lower (Plates 122, 123). The segmental-headed dormers are 19th-century. The houses originally had class 15 plans but the ground floor has been entirely gutted for modern shops, and at the rear various later additions have been made. The upper stages of the street elevations are ornamented by moulded ribs which form architraves to the windows and string-courses at lintel level; vertical ribs denote the tenements which are each of three bays. No. 17 is elaborated by further vertical ribbing; the triple window with cornice and pediment on the first floor replaces a bow window shown in this position in 1804 by Nattes. No. 15, seen before the present shop front was installed, had the jambs of tall ground-floor openings probably implying that the row was originally designed for shops; the ashlar jambs were rebated, and framed by bolection-moulded ribs.

Behind each house was a square timber-framed stair turret. That behind No. 15 was removed in 1970–1; the stair in No. 16, with splat balusters, moulded string and handrail and square newels, alone survives (Fig. 15). Between the turrets of Nos. 16–17 a timber-framed gallery, of two storeys, the upper jettied, was added in the 18th century. At the rear are a number of ranges dating from the 18th and early 19th centuries.

(180) Houses and Shops, Nos. 18–19, three storeys, attics and cellar, ashlar front and rubble rear walls, were built between 1719 and 1736; side walls are partly timber-framed but no earlier structure is traceable. This is probably the building described by Stukeley in 1736 as 'entirely new built, pulled down by Mr. Moore father of the present owner' (Stanfordia Illustrata ii, 102); a Thomas Moore bought two houses in High Street in 1719 (Court Rolls). Later in the 18th century a pair of dignified shop fronts was added, possibly replacing earlier shop windows of which four ovolo-moulded jambs survive; an apothecary's workshop was also built in the yard. The E. shop remained a chemist's until *c.* 1968 (Pl. 93). The building demolished after 1719

had 'a room wainscoted, upon every panel the monogram . . . IHS painted and inlayd with gold, very thick and splendid', and a chimney-piece with arms said to be of Edward III (Stanfordia Illustrata ii, 102, 116).

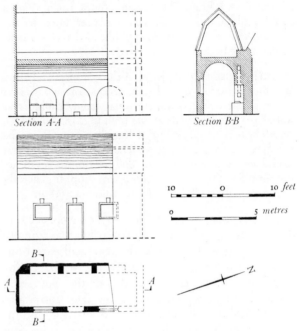

Fig. 105   (180) Apothecary's workshop behind 18–19 High Street. Plan, sections and elevation.

The five-bay street front has upper windows with moulded architraves and fluted keystones, spaced rusticated quoins, platband, and plain parapet with pilasters rising above a shallow moulded cornice; one surviving lead rainwater head is inscribed 'T^{M}M' for Thomas Mills, druggist (died 1839). The shop fronts, separated by a central passage, have eight wooden fluted Corinthian columns supporting an architrave with panelled soffit, frieze fluted over the doorways, and cornice; the smaller front on the W. has been removed except for the end columns, and the window and door arrangement of the E. front recently altered. The rear elevation has windows with wooden lintels and the doorways have freestone lintels with keystones. The ground-floor plan, originally consisting of two dwellings of classes 9 and 13, has been destroyed except for a central passage, probably an original feature, which separated them; the stair, rebuilt in the 19th century, has modern lower flights. The first-floor rooms are arranged in double depth. Original fielded panelling remains in some upper rooms in one of which is an internal porch; beaded-panelled window reveals and a mahogany glazed cupboard in an alcove are early 19th-century. On the second floor fireplaces have wooden bolection-moulded surrounds of the early 18th century. The attic floors are of plaster laid on reeds or straw.

A four-bay rear wing of two storeys and attics, with brick walls, is early 19th-century. The recently-destroyed late 18th-century apothecary's workshop of three bays, of one storey and attic in mansard roof, was of ashlar and brick. The main compartment had a barrel-vault above which was a plaster floor to the attic; in the rear wall were roundheaded recesses containing later boilers etc. (Fig. 105).

(181) HOUSE, No. 20, front of three storeys and attics in a hipped mansard roof, rear section of two storeys under pitched roof, parapet, ashlar front, rubble rear wall, has a class 13b plan. It was built in c. 1820 in which year Thomas Mills, druggist, leased the site from the Marquess of Exeter (Ex. MS). The two-bay street front has upper windows with moulded surrounds, keystones and moulded sills; below is a modern shop. It generally conforms with Mills' own house adjoining (180).

(182) HOUSE, No. 21 (Plate 101), on a corner site, three storeys and attics, ashlar-fronted, originally class 10 plan with stacks in the rear wall, was built in 1732. This date with initials 'HI', probably for Humphry Iliffe, is inscribed on the surviving chimney stack, together with the date '1793' and initials 'T$_S$E' for Thomas Snow, upholsterer, and his wife Elizabeth. Snow bought the property in 1792 having leased it for several years, and dated rainwater heads bear his initials 'TS 1801' (deeds at No. 3 St. Leonard's Street).

The main front, in Ironmonger Street, has a central roundheaded doorway set in horizontally rusticated walling almost totally removed by later shop fronts. The upper storeys on both elevations exhibit an elaborate design articulated by fluted pilasters which accentuate the central entrance bay on the E. The pilasters with bases at first-floor level carry separate architraves, friezes with triglyphs, and a continuous moulded cornice below a plain parapet. The five-bay E. front and two-bay S. front have platbands at sill level; the windows have exaggerated voussoirs and moulded surrounds interrupted by rusticated blocks (Fig. 10). Interior fittings are limited to windows with moulded architraves and beaded side panelling of the early 19th century. The ground floor had become a shop by 1804 (Nattes' drawing), but in 1836 the present shop front was installed by the proprietor Richard Knight who is recorded as adding 'several elegant windows' (Mercury, 6 May 1836). These shop windows are on both elevations and have classical columns, some round, some square, and modern plate glass.

(183) UNDERCROFT (Fig. 106; Plate 59), beneath No. 23, with coursed rubble walls, and quadripartite vault

of segmental section, is of medieval date. The diagonal ribs run down to the modern floor level, the remainder die into the wall; all are heavily projecting and chamfered. The S.W. diagonal rib divides in order to accommodate a doorway in the S. wall. This S. doorway, approached by a flight of steps, although much restored retains some part of the original internally rebated and externally chamfered jambs. The web of the vault on the N. rises higher than elsewhere so as to avoid an opening in the N. wall; this opening is now a doorway but doubtless replaces an original feature, probably a window. To the E. is a segmentally-vaulted compartment opening off the main undercroft with which it is apparently contemporary. The axial rib of the main vault is carried on the keystone of the outer arch of the compartment. In the back wall is a recess of uncertain date.

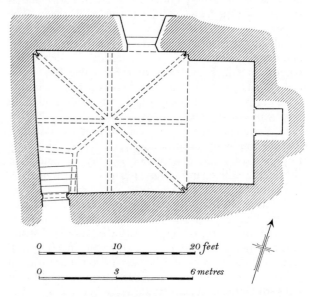

Fig. 106   (183) 23 High Street. Plan of undercroft.

(184) HOUSE, Nos. 25–26 (Fig. 107; Plate 99), originated as a timber-framed structure of the early 17th century, probably comprising three rooms with continuous jetty facing the street. In 1645 a stone-built wing was added at the rear and at sometime in the 17th century the back wall of the main range was replaced in stone. Early in the 18th century the street front was heightened and encased and a further wing, jettied on the E., was added at the rear; this resulted in a pair of houses of classes 9 and 13. Refitting in the early 19th century included a central staircase and shop fronts.

The front elevation, of three storeys and attics, has ashlar wall above the shop fronts. The windows, arranged as three pairs, have eared surrounds which step

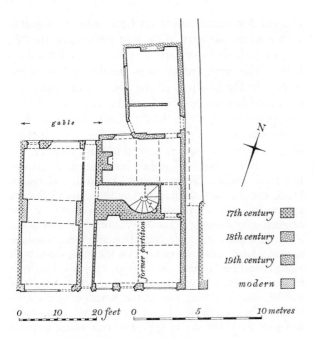

former partition

17th century ▦
18th century ▨
19th century ▦
modern ▦

0   10   20 *feet*   0   5   10 *metres*

Fig. 107 (184) 25–26 High Street.

up at the centre of the head (Fig. 10); single-sheet glazing recently replaced sash windows. A platband and continuous sills stop short of the rusticated quoins. A moulded cornice is independent of the quoins. Early 19th-century shop fronts largely survive and consist of two doorways with classical columns between shop windows; in the end bay is a plain opening to a public footpath. Inside, ceiling beams in the front range indicate former axial and cross partitions; in the former back wall is a 17th-century ovolo-moulded window. In the N. gable of the rear wing is a stone inscribed '1645'; the windows, originally mullioned, have hood-moulds. Fittings of the 18th century include a staircase in No. 25 with shaped splat balusters and a fireplace with a stone eared surround now containing an early 19th-century cast-iron grate with rococo decoration. Two rooms with fielded panelling have quarter-octagonal corner porches. The stair in No. 26 of the early 19th-century has turned balusters and is set in a circular well having roundheaded niches at intervals.

(185) HOUSE, Nos. 28–30 (Plate 112), two storeys and attics, originated as a single, probably timber-framed, structure of unknown date. Early in the 18th century Nos. 28 and 29 were refronted in ashlar. No. 30 became a shop, and shortly before 1876 it was refronted with terracotta details of extravagant design by Blashfield (*Mercury*, 3 Mar.). The five-bay front of Nos. 28 and 29 has moulded plinth, platband, and a boldly projecting cornice with plain frieze; surrounds to the windows and to the central doorway have ovolo mouldings and keystones (Fig. 11). Shop fronts of *c*. 1830 have panelled

pilasters, capitals with roundel decoration, and later glazing.

(186) HOUSE, No. 31 (Plate 111), two storeys, attics and cellar, ashlar front and coursed rubble rear walls, is stylistically of *c*. 1740. The ground stage of the street front has been removed for a shop, but above, the wall has quoins alternately rusticated and beaded on the arris. The windows have rounded surrounds of unusual but doubtless original profile. The widely projecting eaves are carried on a heavy modillion cornice. On the ground floor the quoins have been reset further E. beyond the modern shop front. Inside, the plan probably conformed to class 13b with the present modern stairs in the position of the original. In an upper room is 18th-century panelling in two heights with bolection-type moulding, dado rail and wooden cornice.

(187) HOUSE, No. 40, originally one storey and attics, raised to two storeys and attics in the later 19th century, has stone walls and is probably 17th-century. It consists of a single ground-floor room and a side passage, the 17th-century doorway to which has four-centred head and chamfered jambs in a rectangular wave-moulded surround.

(188) HOUSE, No. 41 (Plate 105), two storeys, ashlar walls, large and small unchamfered quoins (Plate 121), was totally reconstructed as a shop in recent years. It was built in the mid 18th century and some architectural elements of this date have been reset in the present building the upper storey of which bears a superficial resemblance to the original. The ground floor is completely modern. The main front is on the W.; the three upper windows have moulded surrounds, eared at head and foot, and triple keystones (Fig. 10). The centre part of the wall extends above a renewed wooden dentilled cornice as a decorative frontispiece with shaped cheeks and a pediment enclosing branch-sprays; on the face is a cartouche with scrolled surround, formerly bearing the letters 'JˢL' and crest (*demi eagle with wings displayed*). Before the recent rebuilding, there was an early 19th-century shop front occupying two bays, and an adjacent window with plain surround and triple keystone, all below a platband; the parapeted gables terminated with central chimney stacks, and there were dormer windows. The N. elevation now has a first-floor window uniform with those on the W. but with a pediment. No early features survive internally. At the N.E. corner of the modern E. range is a one-stage buttress with weathered top, of uncertain antiquity.

HOUSE, Nos. 46–47, demolished in 1966. Medieval doorway reset at (253) Maiden Lane (q.v.).

(189) HOUSE, No. 51 (Fig. 108), was demolished in 1966. It originated as a three-storey late medieval

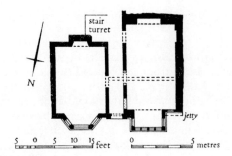

Fig. 108   (189) 51 High Street (demolished).

timber-framed house with an L-shaped plan and first-floor jetty (class 3); the compartment W. of the central passage was originally divided into two rooms. In the 17th century a rectangular bay window was added, and later the jetty was largely underbuilt. A second bay window with canted sides was added in the 18th century, and a new roof constructed, lower on the E. than on the W. The N. elevation (Plate 82) had an 18th-century central stone doorway with moulded architrave and cornice, and pulvinated frieze. The rectangular bay window had stone mullions on the lower two floors, but the top storey was an 18th-century addition of timber. On the extension of the rear wing was a plaster panel dated 1690 and a representation of a windmill in the pargetting. Inside, the E. room had an original stack in the rear wall. In the 18th century the ceiling was raised and the room fitted with a plaster cornice containing heads in roundels, and urns, linked by swags; a chair rail with rosettes and a mahogany veneered door with decorative inlay and enriched architrave were also added. The W. room was subdivided until c. 1600 when the E. wall was painted with floral decoration (Plate 85). Built into the chimney was a limestone panel (Plate 33), now in Stamford Museum, inscribed:

'Vous qen ceste mesoun entrez
pur Blau(n)che fem(m)e al seign(eur) Wake p(ri)ez
file al counte de Lancastre Henri
as queux dieux face vraye merci'

Lady Wake, daughter of Henry, Earl of Lancaster, died in 1380 and was buried in the Greyfriars, Stamford.

(190) HOUSE, No. 53, two storeys and cellar, class 4, almost entirely rebuilt in recent years using some earlier materials. A jetty on the N. is preserved (see Stamford Report I, no. 66, p. 48).

(191) HOUSES, Nos. 54-55 (Fig. 109; Plate 93), originated as a two-storey timber-framed building of the early 16th century. It comprises two ranges: one, of class 2 plan, faces High Street and is jettied on that side; the other, slightly later, is parallel to

Cheyne Lane and jettied on both sides. In the late 17th century the jetty of the street range, on the N., was underbuilt in masonry, apparently with a shop front. The same range was heightened to three storeys in the first half of the 18th century, given a new roof having principal rafters with curved feet, and provided with an ashlar front elevation. The lower part of a large chimney stack at the junction of the two ranges was removed in this century.

The street front, of ashlar, has rusticated quoins, moulded window surrounds with keystones, platband, block cornice and a parapet. On the ground floor a section of the 17th-century under-building of the original jetty remains in the N.W. corner; it consists of a moulded pilaster with vertical ribs, and there is indication of a large window opening on the main front with a horizontal rib beneath the sill (Fig. 110); the feature is repeated midway along the front. The whole length of the W. side is jettied, but at the junction of the two blocks the overhang varies suggesting marginally different dates for the ranges. The rear range remains two-storeyed, but no original openings survive.

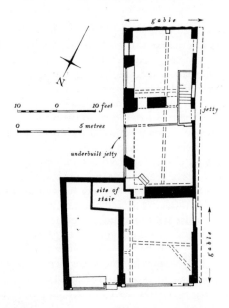

Fig. 109   (191) 54-55 High Street.

Internally, the main range has wave-moulded axial beams and a dragon beam at the N.W. corner. In the angle of the two ranges was a timber-framed 18th-century stair turret, now surviving only on the upper floors; the stair has turned balusters with square knops. One room retains a fireplace with eared surround and moulded shelf. In the rear range are axial beams with mouldings similar to those in the main range, but other beams are encased. The original arrangement of rooms in this range is not clear but it may have consisted only of two rooms on the ground floor. The roof, of three bays, has tie beams with arch braces to swell-headed posts.

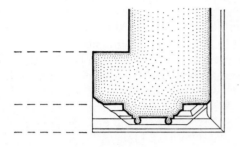

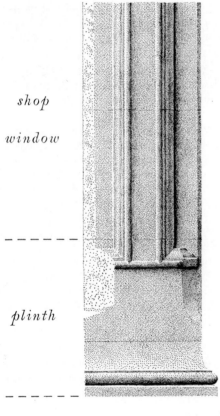

shop

window

plinth

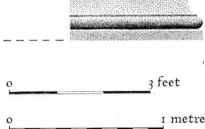

0   3 feet

0   1 metre

Fig. 110   (191) 54–55 High Street.
Remains of 17th-century shop front.

(192) HOUSE, No. 56, three-storey main range, two-storey rear wing, resembling class 5; originally timber-framed throughout but the street front was cased in stone in the early 19th century. It is probably 16th-century but has had a number of later alterations. The main building is L-shaped with a jetty along the full length of its E. side, facing Cheyne Lane, and the remains of a second jetty on the W. side of the rear wing. The long jetty is carried on six unchamfered brackets and stops at its S. end against a corbelled-out masonry wall, originally the S. gable wall of the wing; the W. jetty is largely hidden by a long 19th-century bay window. The wing was extended first in coursed rubble in the 17th century, then in brick in the early 19th. The roof of the front range is asymmetrical; the ridge is centred over the front part and the eaves on the street side are higher than those at the rear. The street front has a long early 19th-century shop front with pilasters; the upper part of the wall is in three bays with sash windows and continuous sills. Inside, the front range has an axial, cased beam placed off-centre, perhaps suggesting a former passage at the rear of the front room; on the third floor such a passage exists. The rear range has a thick S. gable wall incorporating a chimney stack, but this has been removed on the ground floor. The ceiling has intersecting beams with wave-and-hollow mouldings. On the first floor, the wing has a central and two terminal tie beams supported by arch braces from swell-headed posts; the roof has clasped purlins and windbraces. In the W. wall the absence of peg-holes in the wall plate indicates two former windows. Later fittings include an early 18th-century bolection-moulded overmantel in three panels.

(193) HOUSE, No. 57, of two and three storeys, cellars, with ashlar walls, consists of an early 18th-century street block and a rear wing, possibly contemporary, with small projecting closet at its far end. The front elevation is late 19th-century in a mid 18th-century style. The windows of the rear wing have moulded architraves and fluted keystones. The ground floor has been gutted for a shop, but on the first floor an early 18th-century wooden cornice remains (Plate 123). In the rear wing is a mid 18th-century cupboard with rounded head, key block and semi-dome painted with scene of frolicking cupids with bunches of grapes.

(194) HOUSE, No. 59 (Plate 92), formerly the Pineapple Inn, three storeys and attics, has a wide eaves cornice supported on moulded brackets (Plate 123), ashlar front wall with bold quoins, platband, and windows with moulded architraves; it was built in the early 18th century. The roof with clasped purlins remains.

(195) HOUSE, No. 63, three storeys, ashlar front, class 14b, probably dates from 1819 when the freehold was sold (*Mercury*, 15th Oct.). It was then described as good

and substantial and having a shop, counting house, two good parlours and four bedrooms. The ground floor has been gutted for a modern shop.

(196) HOUSE, No. 64, two storeys and attics, ashlar front and rubble rear walls, has a class 12 plan; ground floor partitions have since been removed. It was built in the first half of the 18th century but the plain two-bay front wall is early 19th-century. The rear wing has windows with emphasized keystones and heavy glazing bars. Inside, the first-floor rooms have fielded panelling of two heights and wooden cornices; off the front room is an original closet. The stair, of which only the upper flights survive, has turned balusters, cut string with scrolls decorated with rosettes, and ramped and moulded hand rail.

(197) HOUSE, Nos. 68–69, two storeys, is 18th-century. The ashlar front wall has bold quoins, platband, two pairs of first-floor windows with moulded architraves and plain keystones. The remainder is much altered and rebuilt.

(198) HOUSE, No. 70, two storeys, attics and cellar, stone walls, is 18th-century. The ground floor, originally conforming to class 14b, has been entirely gutted except for an internal side passage. One room has an 18th-century wooden cornice. The house was extended at the rear twice in the early 19th century, first in brick then in stone.

(199) HOUSE, No. 71, three storeys and cellar, with ashlar front elevation having platband between upper storeys, was built c. 1820–30; soon afterwards two warehouses each of two storeys were added at the rear. The house, comprising a single room on each floor and a kitchen in the cellar (class 15), has a plain but elegant semicircular staircase behind a chimney stack. The first-floor room contains a fireplace with angle-roundels and a plaster ceiling with Greek key pattern. The first warehouse has brick walls, the second stone, and both have mansard roofs.

(200) HOUSE, No. 72, two storeys and attics, ashlar front and rubble rear walls, class 10 plan, is mid 18th-century. The front has rusticated quoins, and four upper windows with continuous sills, moulded architraves and keystones; the ground floor has been gutted for modern shop. Rooms on the first floor, originally arranged in double depth, contain 18th-century moulded door architraves.

(201) HOUSE AND SHOP, No. 74, three storeys and attics, coursed rubble with freestone dressings, class 10 plan, sash windows, moulded stone cornice to gabled roof, was described as being newly built and having a large shop when it was sold in 1840 by St. John's Rectory (Ex. MS, 63/2 1–7). The present shop front is modern.

HIGH STREET ST. MARTINS (Fig. 111)

High Street St. Martins is the successor of the axial road through Edward the Elder's burh of 918; it was a diversion from the early Great North Road which lay to the W. Since then, and the subsequent building of the bridge, this street has formed the approach to Stamford from the S. (Plate 3). During the Middle Ages it was called Highgate (Peck XI 51; PRO, E 210/482). Fragments of a few medieval houses survive (214, 232, 238); a large 12th-century building on the site of No. 27 has been demolished, but a drawing of it by Buckler exists (Plate 61; BM Add. MS. 24434, no. 79). There were several inns, notably the George (239), but also the Bull and Swan (216), Coach and Horses (209), and Ram.

The distinction made in 1722 between 'the upper end of the town' and 'the trading part' to the N. (Mercury, 12 April) appears to have been of long standing and, despite the decrease in shops at the N. end, remains true today. In the Middle Ages most institutions, such as the hospital of St. Thomas and St. John, and the majority of shops were in the N. part of the street (Ex. MS, 53/4). During the 18th and 19th centuries the 'upper end' was occupied mainly by professional or more affluent people.

(202) ANCHOR INN, No. 1, coursed rubble walls, ashlar quoins and dressings, slated roof, comprises a main block of three storeys and a contemporary range on the N. of two storeys, and attics in a mansard roof. It was described as 'newly erected' in 1821 when Joseph Kilbourn, ostler at the George, became tenant (Mercury, 12 Jan.). The main block of class 10 plan, three-bay elevation, has sash windows with triple keystones in low relief, and platband sills. The two-bay range has similar features but on the N. is a large bow window at first-floor level. The interior has been much altered and a large room on the first floor subdivided. Fittings of the early 19th century include a plain stair and a plaster ceiling cornice with angle-paterae.

(203) HOUSE, No. 4, two storeys, attics, mansard roof, coursed rubble walls, flush dressings, class 13b plan, two-bay street front, ground floor gutted for shop; early 19th-century.

(204) HOUSE, Nos. 5–6, two storeys, coursed rubble walls, class 8a plan, front wall removed on ground floor to provide two shop fronts with pentice roof, interior gutted; possibly 17th-century in origin but now mostly 19th-century.

(205) HOUSE AND SHOP, No. 7, two storeys and attics, coursed rubble walls, consists of a class 12 building with

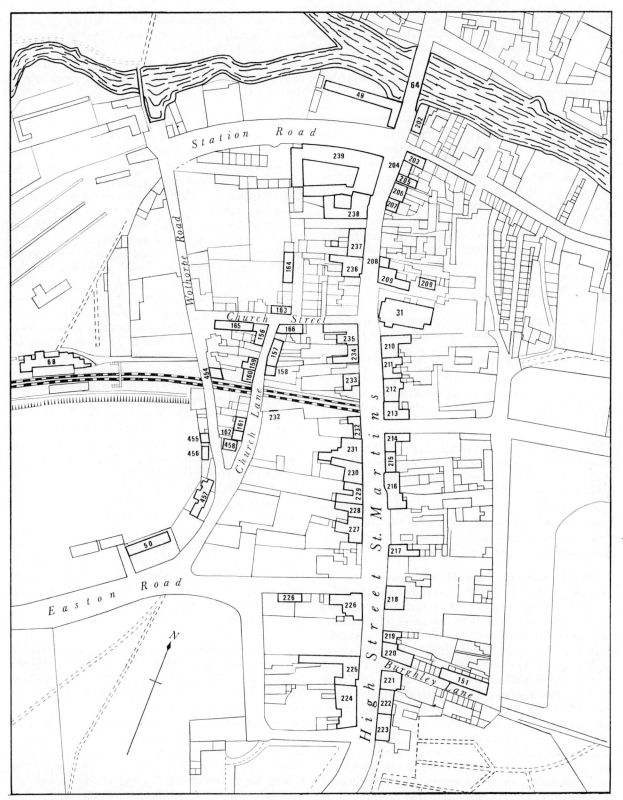

Fig. 111 Map showing monuments in Burghley Lane, Church Lane, Church Street, High Street St. Martins and Wothorpe Road.

the stair in the rear wing and a shop at the street end; early 19th-century, much altered. The present shop front with pilasters and continuous cornice over windows and central door is a recent rearrangement incorporating original woodwork; a former side passage has been removed.

(206) HOUSE, Nos. 8–10 (Plate 112), two storeys and attics, ashlar front wall, coursed rubble rear walls, dates from the early 18th century. It comprises three tenements each of class 13a plan. The front elevation has five upper windows with plain surrounds, the central window being larger than the flanking pair. Later shops have destroyed the ground floor except for the party walls. The wooden eaves cornice has square brackets and returns short of the corners of the building. Inside, there are remains of corner fireplaces to internal stacks but otherwise there are few early fittings. Since the 18th century the house has carried one end of the George Inn sign which spans the road.

(207) HOUSE, No. 11 (Plate 73), two storeys, coursed rubble walls, is a two-room class 6 house of the 17th century. The N. room, rebuilt or refaced in ashlar in the 19th century, has a wide opening for a later shop; the S. room has a two-storey bay window of the 17th century with canted sides, ovolo-moulded mullions, moulded string-courses at lintel-height, and gable with shaped kneelers.

(208) HOUSE, No. 18, three storeys, ashlar front, plaster rear wall, probably over rubble, approximately class 12 plan, was built late in the 18th century. The street front is exceptionally plain, the cyma eaves-cornice being the only moulding. The stair hall has two hipped roofs at right angles to the gabled main roof. Internally, there remain some lengths of skirting board and dado, both moulded and decorated with fluting.

(209) Former COACH AND HORSES INN, No. 19, now class 9b, originated as a 17th-century L-shaped building of one storey and attic. In 1797 the Earl of Exeter leased the property to George Betts, victualler, on condition that specified alterations were carried out (EX. MS, 88/51). Stone was made available from the Earl's quarry at Wothorpe. The street front of three storeys with coursed rubble walls and flush quoins and dressings is the result of these alterations; some internal work was also undertaken. The S. gable of the pre-1797 house can be seen externally. The street front, in three symmetrical bays, has triple sash windows on two floors and plain sashes on the top floor. The rear range contained stables and a kitchen in 1797 but it was raised in height and made domestic in the 19th century. In the entrant angle is a two-storey block which received its present appearance in c. 1798. The front range has a deep plan with a central through-passage and an internal chimney stack

but some of the partitions are later. The two cellars are vaulted in ashlar, one being mentioned in the 1797 lease. Inside, a first-floor room has a plaster floor.

A four-bay stable with half-hipped mansard roof, built in c. 1798 under the terms of the lease, stands behind the inn.

(210) HOUSE, No. 20 (Plate 74), class 3, two storeys, has coursed rubble walls, rendered on the W., and some timber-framing. It has a late medieval origin, possibly 16th-century, and consisted of a main range and cross wing originally of two rooms. In the late 18th century it was considerably altered by the addition of a stone casing on the street front, and wings at the rear, but the position of the original entry was preserved towards the S. end. The main range has a thick ground-floor wall on the W. implying the under-building of a former jetty; the roof-pitch is not symmetrical, indicating that the front wall has been raised. The cross wing on the N. has a timber-framed first-floor jetty continuous with that suggested for the main range, and almost entirely under-built. The street front of the main range has sash windows with plain surrounds and triple keystones and a wooden porch in the Roman Doric style with free-standing columns and open pediment, of the late 18th century (Plate 124); the cross wing has twin roundheaded windows, probably early 19th-century, and above are sash windows with wooden surrounds. The N. wall of coursed rubble encasing timber-framing conforms with the early structure at the N.W. corner. The N. rear wing encroaches on the back section of the cross wing.

Inside, the principal feature is an area of late 16th-century painting on a timber-framed wall in the cross wing; it comprises polychrome floral decoration within a regular fret pattern and an upper frieze in red and white (Plate 85). Further areas of painting were recorded before subsequent covering (M. Barley, *House and Home* (1963), Plate 57). In an upper room there is panelling in four heights with miniature mouldings, early 17th-century. The remaining fittings are early 19th-century and include a simple stair and reeded plaster cornices.

(211) HOUSE, Nos. 21–22, two storeys, coursed rubble walls, probably has a 17th-century origin, but only the rectangular outline of the building of this date survives. The street front of No. 21 was refaced or rebuilt in ashlar with two platband sills in the late 18th century; the work included the doorway with emphasized keystone, and a bay window with canted sides. A broader bay window on No. 22 has a hipped roof which continues as a pentise over the door. A single-storey wing behind No. 21 is 18th-century, and another behind No. 22 is later still. A 17th-century chamfered axial beam in No. 22 and cross beam in No. 21 may indicate the two-room arrangement of the original house; one has a

splayed scarf joint held by pegs. Fittings include a wooden ventilator grille of wavy splats, 18th-century.

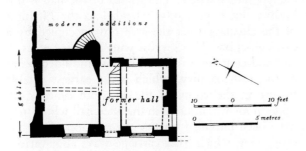

Fig. 112   (212) 23 High Street St. Martins.

(212) HOUSE, No. 23 (Fig. 112), two storeys, coursed rubble walls, has a 17th-century or earlier origin but the present street elevation has an early 19th-century appearance. Report was made in about 1940 of a stone pier of the 13th century but this has not since been traced; the report may in fact relate to No. 53 (mon. 232). In December 1797 this and buildings to the S., No. 23A, were leased by the Earl of Exeter on condition that alterations, chiefly to internal partitions, were carried out (Ex. MS, 88/52). The alterations involved the conversion of the house from class 2 or 6 to class 10. The document implies that the house then had two rooms of unequal size with a near-central entrance at one end of the larger, S., room. A cross beam in the larger room and axial beam in the smaller are now cased but the arrangement is probably original. At the rear is a large wing, probably mid 19th-century. Internal fittings include an 18th-century stone fireplace with panelled facing, said to be reused, and panelling in two heights in the entrance passage, probably of 1798.

(213) Former HOUSE AND WORKSHOP, No. 23A, two storeys, part with attics, coursed rubble walls, comprise the scant remains of a coachmaker's shop of the late 18th century, and an adjacent house which followed the construction of the railway tunnel below the site in 1846–7. It is recorded that repairs were carried out at a cost of £111 in 1793–4 (Exeter Day Books). In 1797, the coachmaker's shop was occupied by Thomas Chamberlayne who took out a lease, conditional on repairs, from the Earl of Exeter, not only for the house to the N. (212) but also for a shop. He extended the shop front to a new building on the S. where the later house now stands. The street elevation of the shop originally consisted of four pilasters with square pinnacles above eaves level, but the whole of the front wall has since been removed. The end pinnacles survive on spur walls which retain short lengths of platband; the two central pinnacles are now in the garden of No. 23.
The house has two large sash windows originally both

triple, hipped roof, and coursed rubble walls with flush quoins and dressings.

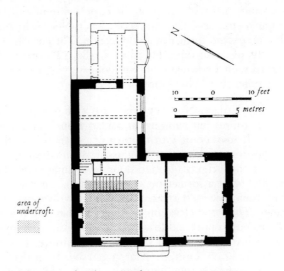

Fig. 113   (214) 24 High Street St. Martins.

(214) HOUSE, No. 24 (Fig. 113; Plate 143), two storeys, attics in a mansard roof, well-coursed rubble walls with flush dressings and quoins, consists of an early 19th-century house of L-shaped plan of class 11a with a medieval vaulted undercroft beneath the N.W. angle of the building. The house has a three-bay elevation with continuous sills to upper and lower sash windows; the central doorway has a wide surround with rounded head and rusticated jambs and voussoirs. The wooden eaves cornice is simply moulded. Interior fittings of the early 19th century are austere with reeding providing the decorative theme.
The undercroft (Fig. 114; Plate 60) is, on the evidence of the corbel decoration, 13th-century. It has a quadripartite vault with transverse and diagonal ribs springing

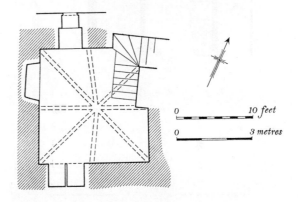

Fig. 114   (214) 24 High Street St. Martins.
Plan of undercroft.

from corbels (Plate 63); the diagonals spring from a lower level than the transverse. The present entrance in the N.E. corner is later and breaks through the web of the vault. A late blocking on the E. probably marks the original entrance. The undercroft has rubble walls and did not extend further in any direction. The corbels are mostly of mask-type, but that in the S.E. corner is carved with a bearded head with long waving hair, and two others have cloud motifs.

(215) HOUSE, No. 24A, class 10, two storeys, the upper rooms in semi-attics, ashlar front wall, and cellar. It may be of 17th-century or earlier origin, the proportions and relative heights of ceiling beams, tie beams and original ground-floor level suggesting the possibility of a former open hall (class 1). Later wings have been added at the rear of the original two-room front range. The street elevation in three bays has continuous sills to both upper and lower windows, plain openings, and a low parapet with simple coved cornice. Inside, there are heavy beams, one arranged axially in the N. section, others across the range in the S. The ground-floor level has been lowered several feet.

(216) BULL AND SWAN INN, No. 25 (Fig. 115; Plate 75), two storeys, cellar, coursed rubble walls, some timber-framing, originated as a medieval open hall parallel with the street, possibly with a cross wing on the S. (class 1b); part of the smoke-

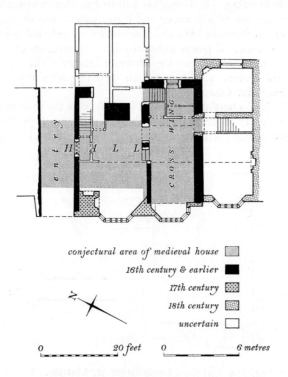

conjectural area of medieval house ▨
16th century & earlier ■
17th century ▨
18th century ▨
uncertain ☐

0   20 feet   0   6 metres

Fig. 115   (216) Bull and Swan Inn.

blackened roof over the hall is the principal feature to survive of this period, the walls having been much altered subsequently. The length of the hall is not known but it probably extended to the N. limit of the curtilage over the area now occupied by a carriage-entry. The S. cross wing is jettied at its E. end and contains a roll-and-hollow moulded beam of the 16th century, which is the earliest datable feature in the wing. In the late 16th century, an upper floor was inserted in the open hall which may have been curtailed by the construction of the N. cross wing which has a carriage-way; also, various thick walls on the rear side of the hall range, probably added at this time, may indicate a chimney stack and staircase necessary after the flooring of the hall. Early in the 17th century both hall and S. cross wing received semi-octagonal bay windows of two storeys on the street side; they have ovolo-moulded mullions, transoms in the upper windows, kneelers and gables. In the 19th century the front wall was advanced outwards so infilling the side lights of the bay windows and providing space for two chimney stacks. A small 18th-century house on the S. was added to the inn during the early 19th century and access was made from the cross wing.

The three-gabled street front gives the building an early 17th-century appearance. The timber-framed carriage-entry has a partially underbuilt overhang at first-floor level. Applied against the gable over the entry is a reset end truss with its pargetting, until 1899 at the E. gable end of the S. cross wing (*Mercury*, 2 June 1899); depicted in the plaster is the crest of Cecil (*garb supported by two lions*), probably 17th-century. Part of the roof over the former hall comprises eight pairs of rafters with collars, notched, halved and pegged, suggesting an early, possibly 14th-century, date. Below the collars this roof is destroyed. The three-bay roof over the carriage-entry consists of cambered and braced tie beams, clasped purlins and curved windbraces; 16th-century.

(217) HOUSE, No. 30 (Plate 147), now part of Stamford High School, three storeys, cellar, has ashlar front elevation and coursed rubble rear walls with flush ashlar dressings. It was built by William Redifer early in the 19th century, and was described in 1821 as newly built (*Mercury*, 20 April).

The three-bay street front is elegantly enriched with a cast-iron first-floor balcony which is supported on three unevenly spaced wooden Doric columns with entablatures; two columns combine to form a porch, and the balcony is carried over a bay window with canted sides and gothic glazing bars. The frieze of the porch contains a glass panel which lights the hall through a second fan-light over the door. The upper windows have plain surrounds and continuous sills. The plan conforms to class 12. Internally, the early 19th-century decoration includes reeded door surrounds with angle-roundels, reeded plaster cornices, and a plaster cornice in the hall enriched with lions' heads.

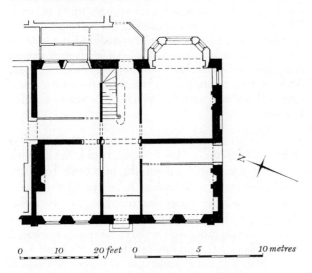

Fig. 116 (218) 33 High Street St. Martins.

(218) HOUSE, No. 33 (Fig. 116; Plate 113) now part of Stamford High School, two storeys, cellars and attic, ashlar front, coursed rubble rear and side walls, has a class 9a plan of early 18th-century origin; it was considerably modernized in the early 19th century and few internal fittings of the original period survive. The street front on the W. includes two-light ovolo-moulded mullioned basement windows below a moulded plinth (Fig. 13); the five bays above are unevenly spaced but have some symmetry due to a spur wall on the N., which masks the adjacent property boundary. The front has emphasized quoins on the spur wall and the S.W. corner, moulded platband, moulded window surrounds (Figs. 10, 11, 12), sills, ornamental key-stones and pilasters of two debased Orders, the lower derived from the Ionic (Plate 119), the upper from the Corinthian (Fig. 14). Additions of the early 19th century include the stone surround to the doorway, which has narrow pilasters and scroll brackets support-ing a flat hood, and a bracketed, widely-overhanging eaves cornice. The ashlar stacks on the gable walls in each range have double rectangular shafts, the front pair having rusticated bands and moulded bases and cornices; the rear pair are plainer. The rear wall has some original windows with plain ashlar surrounds, a central round-headed landing window, and a central doorway with moulded architrave and keystone, but the elevation is dominated by a large 19th-century bay window and

other more recent additions. Windows on the S. eleva-tion have plain architraves and keystones; some are blind and perhaps were always so. Inside, the central entrance hall is divided by an early 19th-century arch with elliptical head; the stair, set in a compartment with rounded ends and a roundheaded niche, is an addition of this date. Modern partitions to provide passages have curtailed one front and one rear room. Reeded or beaded shutters, moulded plaster cornices, and a door surround incised with modified Greek key pattern form the principal early 19th-century decoration. In an attic room is a moulded stone fireplace surround, the only fitting of the early 18th-century house to survive.

(219) HOUSE, No. 34, two storeys, attics and cellar, coursed rubble walls with flush dressings, has an early 18th-century origin but extensive alterations were made in the early 19th century when it was converted from class 10 to approximately class 12 plan. It originally comprised a central entrance flanked by single rooms, and a stair hall, which survives, beyond; the stair has turned balusters. The timber-framed rear wall of the stair hall may indicate that the wing originally ex-tended further to E.; the whole of the E. side of the house is now obscured by later buildings.

(220) HOUSE, No. 35 and Nos. 1–2 Burghley Lane (Plate 113), two storeys, attics and cellar, ashlar front wall, remainder of coursed rubble, was built in the second quarter of the 18th century; shortly afterwards a wing was added at the rear. The main range, with plan approximating to class 9a, is notable for the amount of rustication with which the street front is ornamented. All openings of the five-bay front have rusticated sur-rounds with exaggerated keystones (Figs. 11, 117); the quoins are also rusticated. The design of the doorway (Fig. 118), elaborated with a pediment and pulvinated frieze, may be compared with that of mons. (72) and

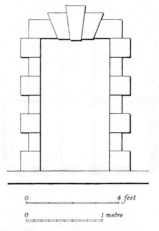

Fig. 117 (220) 35 High Street St. Martins. Ground-floor window.

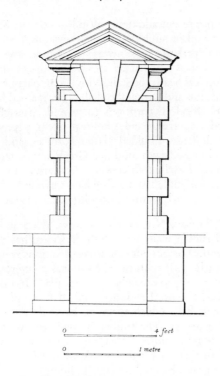

Fig. 118   (220) 35 High Street St. Martins. Doorway.

(357). The eaves have a wooden modillioned cornice (Plate 123). On the S., window-surrounds on the main block and on the wing are of the same design; they have triple keystones and flush dressings, and are linked by a platband at lintel level. Inside, the central passage leads

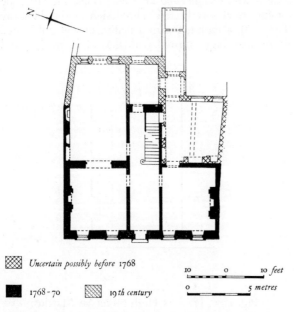

Uncertain possibly before 1768

1768-70   19th century

Fig. 119   (221) 36 High Street St. Martins.

to a wider stair hall, from which the lower flight of the stair has been removed. The upper flight has turned balusters, square newels and square tread-ends; mid 18th-century. The stair is contained in a turret with hipped roof. The main roof has principals with curved feet and clasped purlins.

The rear wing, now Nos. 1 and 2 Burghley Lane, comprises a class 10 house with a single room beyond. The fittings include plain panelling in two heights, and a fireplace flanked by semicircular roundheaded cupboard recesses and shaped shelves. The stair has turned newels and square balusters; late 18th-century, reset. The main door of No. 1 Burghley Lane formerly had a semicircular hood with enriched brackets, the scars of which remain.

(221) HOUSE, No. 36 (Fig. 119; Plate 142), two storeys, attics and cellar, coursed rubble walls with freestone dressings, and plinth, was built by John Clarke between 1767, when he acquired the lease, and 1771, when it was described as 'newly built' (*Mercury*, 25 June 1767; Court Rolls).

The street elevation of five bays comprises rusticated quoins (Plate 121), window surrounds with triple keystones, platband, parapet and shallow cornice with small brackets (Fig. 120; Plate 120), and central doorway with pediment, scroll brackets and semicircular fanlight encroaching on the pediment. The design of the cornice resembles those on the houses built in the following two decades by the Earl of Exeter; John Clarke was employed as a clerk by the Earl at this time. The date of the S.E. room, the kitchen, is uncertain; if later than *c.* 1770 it represents the conversion of the house from class 11 to class 9. The N.E. room was extended at the rear in the late 19th century. The interior fittings are limited to plaster cornices and ovolo-moulded architraves of *c.* 1770. The roof has square-set, staggered, butt-purlins. Attic floors are of plaster.

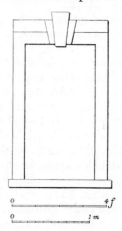

Fig. 120   (221) 36 High Street St. Martins. Ground-floor window.

(222) HOUSE, No. 37, part of Stamford High School, two storeys, consists of an early 19th-century building on the N., of which few internal features survive, a mid 19th-century S. extension, perhaps c. 1840–50, and a rear wing. The earlier section has coursed rubble walls and the extension has an ashlared front. The interior has been largely gutted. The street elevation comprises four bays, the second, originally the doorway, is now a window; the S. two bays are of the later period. Inside, the main room has a reeded plaster cornice; a square space beyond has elliptical arches on each side. In the S. section is a marble fireplace with reeded surround and on the first floor is a stone fireplace with incised Greek fret, both c. 1840.

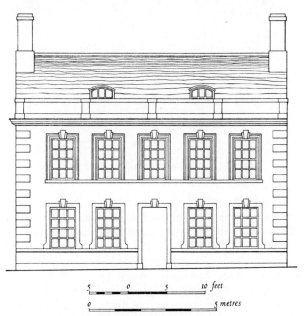

5　　0　　5　　10 feet
0　　　5 metres

Fig. 121　(223) 38 High Street St. Martins. Reconstruction of front elevation.

(223) LADY ANNE'S HOUSE, No. 38 (Plate 115), now part of Stamford High School, two storeys, attics and cellar, ashlar front wall, coursed rubble rear wall partly rebuilt in modern brick, dates from the early 18th century when it comprised a class 10 house with a five-bay elevation (Fig. 121). The former central doorway was at some date before 1794 (*Mercury*, 20 June) exchanged with the window in the fourth bay; internally, the hall and N. room were united and the S. room became the new hall. Later, the reset doorway was itself adapted as a window. The front has spaced rusticated quoins (Plate 121), continuous sills, lower windows with plain surrounds, upper windows with moulded surrounds, all with triple keystones; below the parapet is a moulded cornice. Inside, the ground floor retains some bolection panelling and an early 18th-century stone fireplace.

Attached to this house on the S. is a large two-storey wing of some pretension. The street front has terminal pilasters composed of two superimposed Tuscan orders (Fig. 14) supporting a moulded cornice across the parapet. This architectural treatment suggests a building-date in the first half of the 18th century, but the pairs of large sash windows, each with projecting architraves, fluted imposts and keystones, indicate considerable alteration in the early 19th century. The detail of the upper pilaster also suggests alteration at this time. The continuous sills of the upper windows, interrupted by the pilasters, may be of the first period. The interior, redecorated in the early 19th century, contains reeded architraves, marble fireplace surrounds and enriched plaster cornices.

(224) HOUSES, Nos. 39–41 (Plate 81), mostly two storeys and attics, rendered rubble walls, have been formed out of two houses of the 17th century. The larger, on the S., had three heated ground-floor rooms (class 8b) (Fig. 7), and the N. house had a class 8a plan. The street front of the S. house (now No. 39 and S. half of No. 40) is dominated by three tall bay windows with canted sides, each with ovolo-moulded mullions. Early in the 18th century the bays were increased in height, the additions having hipped roofs, ashlar walls and plastered timber cheeks; some mullions have been removed from the earlier windows. Between the second and third bay is an original doorway with moulded surround, keystone block, and an early 18th-century semicircular hood carried on richly carved console brackets. The original N. house (No. 41 and the N. half of No. 40) has an ashlar and rendered front wall and a three-storey ashlar bay window with canted sides, hipped roof, and ovolo-moulded mullions, of the 17th century. Entrance to No. 41 is through a projecting porch of Tudoresque design; this is a reset section of the Corn Market built in 1839 in front of Browne's Hospital and removed in 1862 (see introduction to Broad Street). The original central entrance to the N. house has chamfered jambs and head and now contains a two-light stone mullioned window within the blocking.

Inside, the three rooms of the S. house all have later partitions and original chamfered axial beams; later fittings include 18th-century door architraves and a fireplace with bolection-moulded fireplace surround. The roof is 18th-century and has staggered purlins. The interior of the entrance of No. 41 now has a mid 19th-century character with a raised ceiling to conform with the ceiling heights of a later rear range added in c. 1830–40 when the whole building was in single occupation. A second rear wing was added at the S. end a few years later in the Tudor style and is now the entrance to No. 39.

(225) HOUSE, No. 42, (Fig. 122; Plate 142), two storeys, attics and cellar, ashlar front wall, coursed

rubble rear walls with quoins and plain window surrounds, was built shortly before *c.* 1796 (map, Burghley Estate Office). It now includes an earlier two-storey range on the S., approximating to class 5, possibly of the early 18th century but with a mid 19th-century street-front. The principal house comprises a main range of class 9b plan and a short kitchen wing beyond which is a long single-storey wing. In 1813 it was described as a modern house with two kitchens, breakfast, eating and drawing rooms, with a drawing room and nine bedrooms above (*Mercury*, 11 June). The front elevation of three bays with platband, parapet and slight cornice, consists of a central doorway with fluted stone pilasters and steeply-pitched pediment, triple sash windows with stone mullions on the ground floor and plain sashes on the first floor. Slit windows flanking the door and the triple windows are probably early alterations. Reset in the rear wall is a rectangular panel with oval cartouche inscribed 'H^Ws 1674' (Plate 129). The internal decoration of the early 19th century is extensive, reeding being the dominant motif in both window surrounds and plaster cornices. The stair is original but plain. The kitchen has a wide, segmental-headed fireplace flanked by round-headed openings, all with keystones.

The subsidiary house on the S. was refitted internally in the late 19th century.

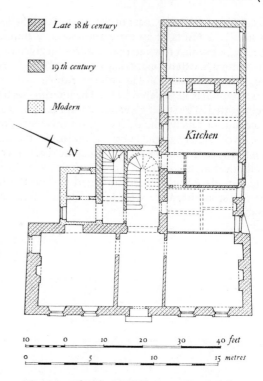

Fig. 123   (226) 43 High Street St. Martins.

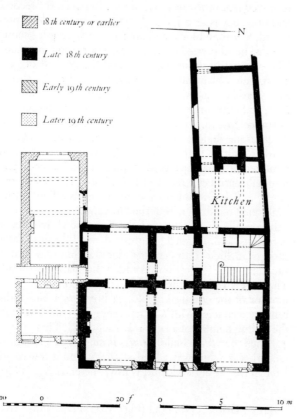

Fig. 122   (225) 42 High Street St. Martins.

(226) HOUSE, No. 43 (Fig. 123; Plate 114), two storeys, attics and cellar, ashlar front wall, remainder coursed rubble with freestone dressings, originated as a class 11b house shortly before 1788 when it was described as newly built (*Mercury*, 28 Mar.). In the early 19th century a large stair turret, replacing an original one, was built in the entrant angle, and the rear wing was extended, both additions having hipped roofs. The street elevation in five bays, widely spaced in the centre, has a platband, parapet, slight cornice, and chimney stacks with moulded cornices. The outer pairs of windows are plain, the centre has a moulded architrave, and the doorway a moulded stone surround and flat hood. Inside, the central hall is wide and leads through a segmental-headed arch of the 19th century to the later stair hall containing a round-ended stair of plain design. The main rooms have shutters with beaded decoration, and plaster cornices, one with key pattern and rosettes. The 18th-century kitchen fireplace has segmental head, and is flanked by roundheaded recesses. In attics, are two stone fireplace surrounds, early 18th-century presumably reset. Heavily moulded beams and joists of *c.* 1600 are reused in the cellar.

Built into the stable wall is a doorway with depressed head in square frame, and a three-light ovolo-moulded window, both of *c.* 1600.

(227) HOUSE, No. 45 (Plate 114), two storeys, attics and cellar, coursed rubble walls, rendered on the front,

has a 17th-century origin as indicated by the carpentry of an attic partition, beams and floor joists. The early plan, approximating to class 8a, consisted of a range with adjacent corner fireplaces on the rear wall, but the cross wall has been removed; to the S. is a carriage-entry. In the mid 18th century the street front was given a contemporary appearance by the addition of plain projecting window-surrounds, ashlar quoins and wide platband, and rendering to the wall face. The 18th-century wooden doorcase has moulded jambs and open pediment. Early in the 19th century, the carriage-entry became a room; the camber-headed arch was blocked and a doorway, now a window, was incorporated in the blocking, and the platband was made up in plaster. Inside, in addition to the chamfered beams and joists is a cross partition of 18th-century fielded panelling in two heights.

(228) HOUSE, No. 46 (Fig. 124; Plate 147), three storeys, cellar under part, fine ashlar walls, single-storey rear wing in red brick, was built in the second quarter of the 19th century. The rear wing was designed to be of two storeys and would have masked exposed brickwork in the N. part of the back wall of the main range. The street front is of restrained design of three slightly unsymmetrical bays with sash windows having platband sills and plain openings, except for slightly raised keystones. The central doorway has reeded jambs and truncated pediment, and the windows above are blind. Below the parapet is a cornice. Inside, the rooms are arranged on a class 9b plan with the stair at right angles to the central passage. The principal fittings comprise four stone fireplace surrounds, each carved with lions' masks or human heads, and door architraves of refined design.

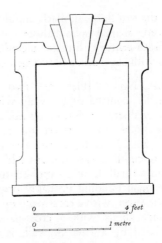

Fig. 125　(229) 47–50 High Street St. Martins. Ground-floor window.

(229) HOUSE, Nos. 47–50 (Plate 97), two storeys and attics, ashlar front wall, coursed rubble rear walls, dates from the first half of the 18th century. At one time it was the Marquis of Granby Inn. The building is remarkable for the design of the window surrounds. The front elevation is symmetrical: three ground-floor windows have shaped surrounds extending to ground level, exaggerated quintuple keystones and continuous sills (Figs. 10, 125); between the windows are two round-headed doorways with plain surrounds, the N. opening serving a through passage. The upper windows have moulded eared surrounds, quintuple keystones and continuous sills. The cornice is dentilled. At the rear are two wings, one of 17th-century origin, containing a chamfered wave-stopped beam, the other of the early 19th century. (Inside partly seen.)

(230) HOUSE, No. 51, two storeys, cellar and attics, coursed rubble walls, freestone dressings, was built at the end of the 17th century on an L-shaped plan approximating to class 10, with a rear wing containing the kitchen. In the early 18th century the plan became U-shaped with the building of a second small rear wing at the S., but in c. 1825 the area between the wings was infilled by a two-storey structure with flat lead-covered roof. The kitchen wing was also extended in the early 19th century. The street front of five bays has 18th-century windows with modern lintels; over a side passage is an oval window in rectangular surround. The gable of the kitchen wing has been rebuilt in brick. The early 18th-century wing has a timber-framed S. wall with a jetty partially underbuilt in brick. Flues in the rear wall unite to form a massive chimney stack. Inside, the front range has a late 17th-century staircase with turned balusters, square newels, plain handrail and closed string. Amongst the fittings of the late 17th or early 18th century are bolection-moulded fireplace

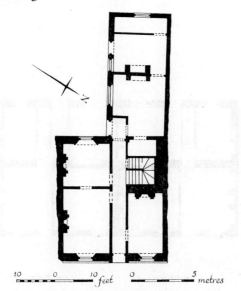

Fig. 124　(228) 46 High Street St. Martins.

surrounds on the first floor, similarly moulded panelled doors, and some shaped splat balusters on a service stair. Later 18th-century fittings include a fielded panelled dado with chair rail, and wooden cornices.

(231) HOUSE, No. 52 (Plate 82), two storeys and attics, small cellar, coursed rubble walls with freestone dressings, rendered street front, comprises an L-shaped building (class 3) of the early 17th century; a subsequent infilling in the angle, possibly in the 18th century, has given a plan resembling class 9b. An additional short rear wing joins a small detached 17th-century range at the rear. The main building probably originated as a hall, next to the street, with a cross wing on the N.; the present entrance aligns with a cross-passage which, although enclosed by a later S. wall, is an original feature. The street front on the E. is dominated by twin parapeted gables, that to the cross wing being slightly in advance of the main range. Against the gables are three-storey bay windows with canted sides except for the top stages which are square-set. Although these bays are early 19th-century they may replace 17th-century predecessors. The doorway with depressed head in square surround, and a window above with mullion and label, are 17th-century but restored; a similar doorway has been reset at the far end of the lengthened cross-passage. On the rear elevation are further stone mullioned windows of the 17th century. Inside, the former hall has a large chimney stack in the end gable wall; the cross wing, probably always with two rooms, appears to have had fireplaces in the S. wall, one backing on to the cross-passage. In an attic in the wing is a fireplace with depressed four-centred head. Early 19th-century fittings are of high quality and include a round-ended stair with moulded oak handrail, and reeded or fluted plaster cornices of elaborate and varied designs.

Beyond an early 19th-century kitchen wing at the rear is a two-storey rubble-walled building of 17th-century date. It has an ovolo-moulded window but its original use is unknown.

(232) HOUSE, No. 53 (Plate 114), two storeys, coursed rubble walls, front rendered, class 10 plan, is mostly mid 18th-century. The N. gable and a single-storey kitchen wing were added c. 1846 when the adjacent railway cutting was dug. The five-bay street front is symmetrical. Window architraves are plain and projecting, with triple keystones. Internal fittings of the early 19th century include the stair and a reeded fireplace surround.

In the N.W. angle of the house is a circular column or respond; it is about 1 ft. in diam. and a height of 5 ft. 6 ins. is visible. Loose in garden is an early 13th-century tympanum-shaped window head of two lights, pointed and chamfered externally but with round-headed openings; the back face is without rebates (Plate 62). Incorporated in the garden wall is a semi-circular chamfered arch, now springing from ground

level, with hood mould and responds, probably 12th-century.

(233) HOUSE, No. 55, two storeys and attics, comprises two parallel ranges, the rear extending further S. than the front; the small remaining area was the site of the Cage as shown on Knipe's map of 1833. The front range, of class 6 plan, has one original cross-wall, and appears to have a 17th-century or even late medieval origin, but no datable features survive. A drawing of 1827 by Twopeny shows the front elevation with two three-storey gabled bay windows with mullions of 17th-century date; between the bays was a pentice and another was N. of the N. bay, over a door. The present front in the Jacobean taste was added in 1868. The rear range, with class 10 plan, was added in c. 1840; the walls are of ashlar and the openings plain. Fittings, almost entirely of c. 1840, include marble and stone fireplaces with angle-roundels or rosettes.

(234) HOUSE, No. 58, two storeys, attics and cellar, coursed rubble walls, is probably of 17th-century origin. A rear wing is early 19th-century. The street front has 18th-century sash windows on the first floor, each with wooden lintels; bay windows, one a shop-window, on the ground floor, are 19th-century or later. The original plan consisted of three rooms in line, each with a pair of axial beams; the cross partitions are apparently all later. Beams on the E. are supported by posts, one of iron, the other of square timber with cap and base mouldings. Beneath the W. beam is a length of partition with vertical ovolo-moulded planks; probably 18th-century. Fittings include a chair-rail with nail-head ornament of c. 1800 (cf. mon. (97)). On the first floor the pairs of axial beams are repeated. The roof has

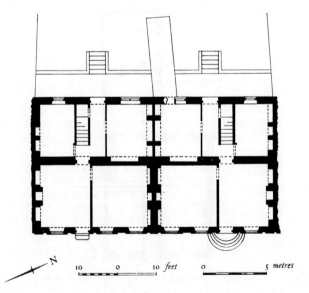

Fig. 126   (237) 66–67 High Street St. Martins.

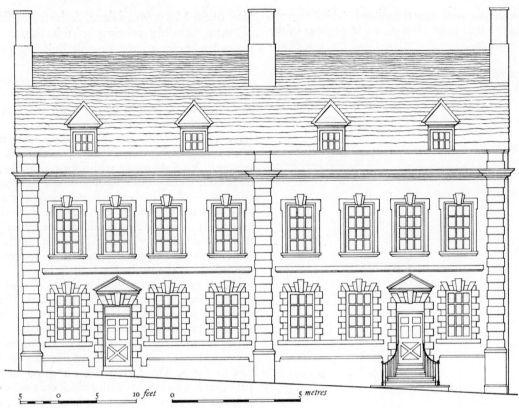

Fig. 127 (237) 66–67 High Street St. Martins. Front elevation.

heavily cambered collars, purlins, but no ridge-piece. The single-storey rear wing contains two two-light chamfered mullioned windows, probably reused.

(235) HOUSES, Nos. 59–60 (Plate 143), a pair each of three storeys and cellars, with two-storey rear wings, have coursed rubble walls, the main E. front being of carefully squared blocks with ashlar dressings. They date from the first quarter of the 19th century. Behind No. 60 is part of an early 19th-century malting (see mon. 166) now incorporated in the house. Each house of three bays has continuous sills, sash windows with single keystones and moulded wooden doorcases with angle-roundels, open pediments, and lattice fanlights. The plans conform to class 12. The rear wing of No. 60 has been raised to three storeys. Inside, reeding of architraves and cornices is the predominant decoration. Roof construction comprises square-set staggered purlins pegged to the principals.

(236) HOUSE, No. 65 (Plate 83), two storeys, coursed rubble walls, has a front range of class 6, probably of the early 17th century, behind which a timber-framed range was added at a slightly later date. The street elevation consists of two full-height rectangular bay windows with stone mullions, gables with finials, and a wooden doorway with ovolo-moulded frame of the early 17th

century. The later addition has three gables on its W. wall. Inside, against the S. wall is a stone fireplace with four-centred inner and square outer head; in 1861 it was uncovered and found to have a painted black-letter inscription consisting of verses 4 and 5 of Psalm 116 (*Mercury*, 19 April). A corner fireplace, with early 19th-century gothic-style iron grate, is in the rear range. Trusses of the original roof over the front range have collars and straight braces, all lap-jointed to the principals, and formed the base for the waggon-shaped ceilings of the upper rooms.

(237) HOUSES, Nos. 66–67 (Figs. 126, 127; Plate 102), a reflecting pair, two storeys, cellars and attics, coursed rubble with ashlar front walls, were built in the second quarter of the 18th century. Both houses are remarkable in being almost entirely unaltered internally and externally, and are unusually complete examples of better-class houses of their period.

Each house is in four slightly unequal bays with the entrance in the penultimate bay. Rustication to the doorways, ground-floor windows and pilasters dominates the design (Figs. 10, 13, 128). The pedimented doorways and the lower windows have exaggerated keystones and voussoirs, and the upper windows have eared surrounds with triple keystones. The moulded cornice breaks forward over the pilasters which separate and terminate the houses. A platband stops short of the pilasters. Contrasting with the front wall, the rear elevation has a rough rubble wall with large flush quoins; the sash windows have timber lintels of small size and are arranged arbitrarily. Each house is of class 9 with one room serving as an entrance hall. The lower part of the stair is enclosed but the upper flights have oak balusters with square knops and carved tread-brackets. Fittings include timber dentil cornices with fretwork friezes in each house, and stone fireplaces with broken pediments (Plate 128) flanked by recesses with segmental heads and triple keyblocks.

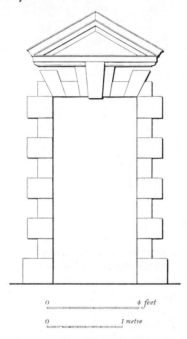

0   4 feet

0   1 metre

Fig. 128   (237) 66 High Street St. Martins. Doorway.

(238) THE HERMITAGE, Nos. 68–69 (Fig. 130; Plate 72), now part of the George Hotel. The building, which is two storeys high with squared freestone and rubble walls, consists of three ranges round a yard which is closed on the N. by the George Hotel (239). It dates from the late 15th century, but an interpretation of the building has proved difficult. The E. range resembles a three-cell house. The W. range has an open hall, an abnormal arrangement of screens passages with parlour above, and probably a cross wing to the S.; it perhaps constituted a second house. The S. range may have contained kitchen and lodgings. A 19th-century description (*Gent's Mag. Lib. Eng. Top.* VII, 158–9; *Mercury*, 15 Aug. 1862) originated the erroneous assumption that the structure incorporates the hos-

pital of St. Mary Magdalene. A draft building lease of 1484, possibly relating to this site, cannot be proved to refer to the present building (Ex. MS, 53/4).

The *E. Range*, with attics and cellars, was originally a three-cell structure, that on the N. probably being a parlour. The S. section of the street front, rebuilt in *c.* 1700 in coursed rubble, has contemporary windows (Fig. 11) but with modern mullions and transoms reproducing earlier ones. The N. section, of squared masonry, has a doorway with four-centred head, continuous moulding and a label with one head stop. The adjacent window replaces a former doorway and window, and the two-storey bay window is modern. An external stack in the S. gable blocks an earlier ground-floor window. The interior has been much altered. Beneath the N. room is a vaulted undercroft (access not possible); the room has intersecting, double-wave moulded beams with a modern boss. A small round-headed window in the W. wall is blocked. The central room has a number of later partitions, one enclosing an early 18th-century stair with turned balusters, cut string and square newels (Plate 133). The room's S. wall is early 19th-century and replaces one that stood a few feet to the S. The S. room has 18th-century fielded panelling in two heights with a block cornice; the panelling has been reset against the later N. wall. Round-headed recesses in the S. wall are *c.* 1800. On the first floor, attic stairs have splat balusters of the early 18th century (Plate 132). Over the S. room is a double-wave moulded tie beam with scar from a former central boss, but the roof appears to have been rebuilt in the post-medieval period.

The *S. Range* has window openings on the N. of *c.* 1700 with plain architraves; some have original wooden mullions and transoms, with iron casements and lead cames. The W. wall is timber-framed and was formerly jettied. Inside, the E. room has three moulded beams, two carved with running vine ornament (Fig. 129). Above the fireplace is a length of early 17th-century run-through panelling. The central room has a wide blocked fireplace with flanking recesses having broad architraves and triple keystones, dating from the time when the room was a kitchen in the early 18th century. The roof, of *c.* 1500, over the E. and central sections of the S. range, of five bays, with original close-studded partition below the second truss from the W.,

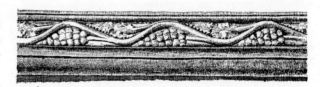

Fig. 129   (238) The Hermitage. Beam in S. range.

has tie beams, braces to the principals which diminish above a clasped purlin, and curved windbraces; there were thus two upper rooms of unequal size open to the roof. The W. section, slightly narrower than the E., is probably contemporaneous with the W. range. It has a four-centred doorway in the N. wall opening into the passage of the W. range; the upper floor level was lowered 2½ ft. in 1927.

to the roof, was floored over when the range was widened. The principal external features are a post-medieval four-light hollow-moulded mullion window on the W., and first-floor windows on the E. with wooden mullions and transoms of c. 1700. Inside, on the ground floor there is first, to the S., the cross-passage referred to above; in its S. wall is an internal stone doorway uniform with those at the ends of the passage.

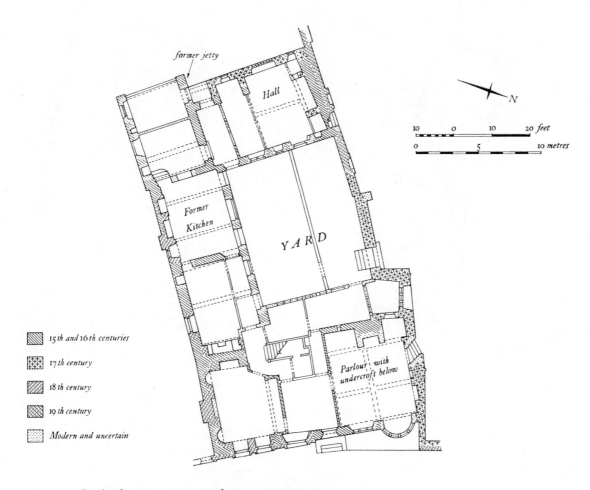

Fig. 130 (238) The Hermitage, High Street St. Martins.

The *W. Range* has at the S. end two parallel cross-passages, the southernmost having stone doorways at each end, both with chamfered jambs, four-centred heads and hood moulds. A third door leads into the S. range. The E. part of the S. range appears to have been built against the E. of the first two doorways, showing that the W. range is earlier than the S. Probably early in the 17th century the range was widened on the W.; the large chimney stack on this side impinges against the W. doorway implying that it too is later than the main structure. The N. room of the range, originally open

In the timber-framed, close-studded, N. partition are two blocked doorways with four-centred heads. The studwork is filled with stone slates let into grooves, and plastered. The second passage or area has a similar N. partition and two doorways of the same design but somewhat repaired (Plate 77). This partition is continued on the first floor below a moulded tie beam. The inserted ceiling beam in the main room has stepped stops to the chamfers. On the first floor, along the line of the former W. wall is an original roll-and-hollow moulded cornice.

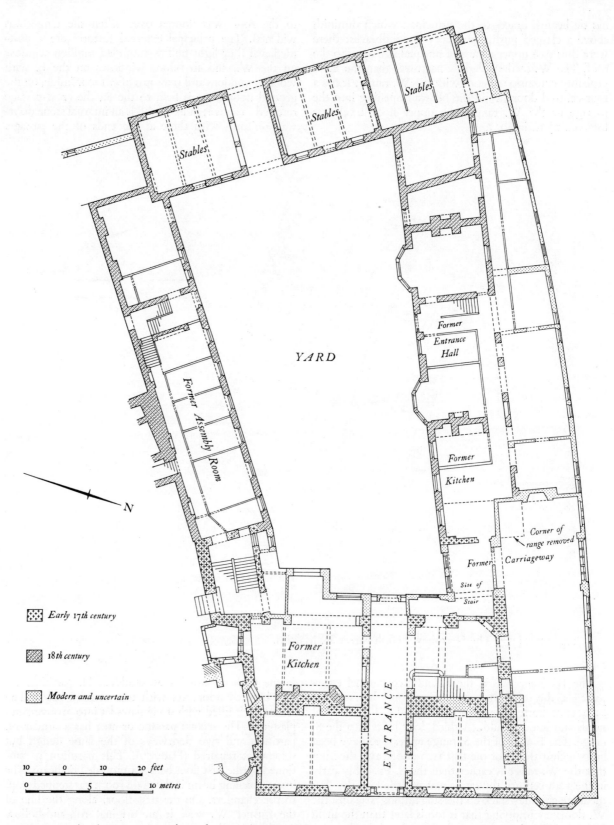

Stables

Stables

Stables

Former
Entrance
Hall

YARD

Former
Kitchen

Former Assembly Room

Corner of
range removed

Former Carriageway

N

Site of
Stair

Former
Kitchen

Early 17th century

18th century

Modern and uncertain

ENTRANCE

10   0   10   20 *feet*

0   5   10 *metres*

Fig. 131   (239) George Hotel, High Street St. Martins.

(239) GEORGE HOTEL, No. 70 (Figs. 131, 132; Plates 94, 119). The George Inn was in existence by 1568 when Andrew Scarre was given licence to sell wine there (*Cal. Pat.* (1566–9) no. 1919, 330), and the same family continued to hold it until the end of the century (PRO, PCC Prob. 11/84, William Scarre; NRO, Fitzwilliam Misc. 433, Widow Scarre, 1595). The earliest part of the present building, the E. range, comprises an almost entire inn of *c.* 1600. It was refronted in 1724 by George Portwood, mason, whose account for stonework was for £59. Other alterations and repairs carried out between then and 1726 by Portwood and Robert Pilkington, joiner, included work on three galleries which probably existed in wings flanking the yard; the cost amounted to £165 (Ex. MS, 51/21/23). Between 1785 and 1792 the Earl of Exeter carried out many improvements costing over £1,830 (Exeter Day Books). New stables were constructed during this period under Thomas Manton, mason. The N. range was built in 1787–8; Manton was again the mason, and £815. 2. 6. is recorded as having been spent. The S. range was rebuilt in 1791–2, John Hames being the mason, and Alice Pilkington the carpenter and joiner; the sum of £214. 4. 6. only is listed but the accounts are probably incomplete. In 1815 the inn had 38 bedrooms, 10 sitting rooms, a bar, and stabling for 86 horses. It is recorded that in 1839 one room of the main range, probably the N.E. room,

was called The Exeter 'to which coach passengers are ushered'; it was damaged by fire in that year (*Mercury*, 12 May 1815, 15 Feb. 1839). In 1849 Station Road was cut, involving the demolition of an octagonal cockpit, constructed by Portwood in *c.* 1725 (Ex. MS, 51/21/23, 24); alterations in 1850 by Moses Peal included the construction of a new carriage entry through the N. wing (*Mercury*, 26 July). Later in the century new kitchens and service rooms were built on the N., but since then work has been limited to alterations.

The inn consists of four ranges grouped round an irregular-shaped yard. The *Main Range* on the E. is of three storeys, coursed rubble back and side walls, and two parallel gabled roofs; the E. front, encased in ashlar in 1724 by Portwood with the carpentry by Pilkington, is in five bays with central roundheaded entry and sash windows having moulded sills and architraves, and triple keystones (Figs. 10, 11, 12). Placed centrally on the parapet is a stone panel with side scrolls, bearing the arms of Cecil with crest and supporters (Plate 119). One lead rainwater head bears the arms of Cecil and date 1728, and on brackets of both downpipes are the same arms. A large beam with lattice work braces, bearing the inn sign, and spanning the High Street, closely resembles that shown by Nattes in 1804 but it is probably a 19th-century replacement. The N. and S. gable ends each have 17th-century transomed windows, some with labels, of varying numbers of lights. At the rear N.W. and S.W. corners two original stair turrets survive in part, together with mullioned and transomed windows. The W.

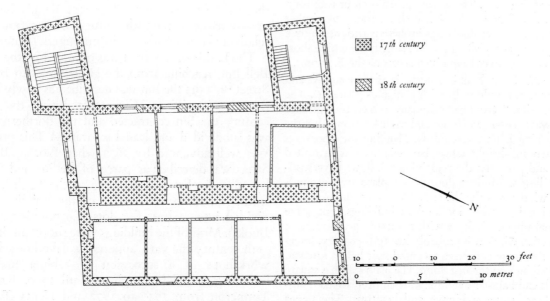

17th century

18th century

N

| 10 | 0 | 10 | 20 | 30 *feet* |

| 0 | | 5 | | 10 *metres* |

Fig. 132　(239) George Hotel. Plan of second floor of front range.

elevation, much altered at ground-floor level, contains early 19th-century sash windows, and has indications of earlier openings in the upper storeys; a moulded string-course of *c.* 1600 remains. The eaves course is hollow-moulded. Inside, the range comprises four ground-floor rooms separated by a wide through passage, formerly a carriage entry. The lofty rooms are spanned by chamfered beams with wave stops, the front rooms by one beam, the rear by two. The N.E. room has fielded panelled shutters; the N.W. room, now a stair hall with modern stair, has in a corner a reset early 18th-century stone fireplace with eared surround and pedimented and panelled entablature (Plate 128). The S.W. room, formerly the kitchen, has a wide 18th-century fireplace now mutilated, a blocked window formerly opening onto the central passage, and a three-light mullioned window in the S. wall. The S.E. room, probably the dining room in the early 18th century, is lined with modern panelling. Spanning the central passage is a roundheaded arch carrying the upper walls. In the S.W. stair turret is a stair (Plate 133) with square newels, turned balusters and closed string, which was installed in 1726 by Pilkington for £18. 2. 10. (Ex. MS, 51/21/23, 24); it is approached by an early 18th-century doorway, originally external, with round head, stone architrave and moulded capitals. The N.W. turret was drastically altered in 1850 when a carriage entry was cut through the ground floor to give access to Station Road; a new roundheaded rusticated arch was constructed, but this entry is now blocked at both ends. The upper floors (Fig. 132) of the E. range are divided into two rows of lodging rooms on either side of a spine wall. Several rooms retain early 17th-century stone fireplaces with chamfered jambs, four-centred heads and moulded shelves (Plate 128). There were probably four rooms on the E. and four on the W., each separated by timber partitions. Former doorways in these partitions imply a passage or gallery along the W. side, from which short cross passages may have given access to the E. rooms.

The *N. Range*, built in 1787–8, is of three storeys and has coursed rubble walls with platbands (Plate 94). The symmetrical S. front had originally two central entrance doorways with round heads and triple keystones, but the E. opening is now a window. Flanking the doorways are two full-height ashlar bay windows with canted sides and parapets; the remaining windows have rusticated lintels. Modern doorways replace two ground-floor windows at the W. end. The lower part of the N. elevation is masked by modern buildings, but some original upper windows with rusticated heads remain; a Venetian window is probably late 19th-century. Internally the range comprises a central stair hall, a kitchen, and lodgings on the first floor. The plain stair has square newels and balusters, and the kitchen fireplace has elliptical head, stone architrave and keystone. The upper rooms were reached by a passage on the N. side as at

present. Several 18th-century doors with fielded panels and architraves survive.

The *W. Range* consists of three stables with a wide entrance to the yard. They may be the stables for which payment was made to Thomas Manton, mason, in 1785 and 1788 (Exeter Day Books). The range, two storeys high, has coursed rubble walls; the windows have rusticated heads and continuous sills. Internally, each stable has a central passage with three bays on either side defined by shallow roundheaded recesses. The stalls have been removed and the N. stable made into a garage. The first floor was converted into a ballroom in the late 19th century but has since been subdivided.

The *S. Range*, rebuilt in 1791, of two storeys with large cellar, has coursed rubble walls, stone dressings, broad platband and moulded eaves course. The N. elevation is of nine bays with two doorways towards the W. end, one of which led into a stairhall. The upper floor, now lodging rooms, was formerly an assembly room occupying four bays with an anteroom at the E. end. The assembly room was subdivided in 1924. The roof has square-set tusk-tenoned purlins, and collars.

The *Stable Yard* to the W. consists of two parallel ranges. The late 18th-century N. range, partly demolished at the E. end, now comprises six double loose boxes each with a single door and circular window; above is a hayloft. The walls are of coursed rubble. The single-storey S. range is early 19th-century and much altered to form garages.

IRONMONGER STREET (Fig. 100)

This straight street has every appearance of having been deliberately laid out, but evidence for this has not been found; it was certainly in existence in the early 17th century. The street already had its present name by the 18th century, when it housed a relatively large number of ironmongers. (Plate 145.)

The E. side of the street was occupied by the Blue Bell Inn, reaching from the High Street to Broad Street. In 1595 the Inn was described as newly built (NRO, Fitzwilliam Misc. 433); during the 17th century the Inn contracted and the northern part was subdivided and leased separately. This process was well advanced by 1677 when No. 36 Broad Street was described as 'parcel of the Sun and Bell'; by 1684 the Inn was confined to the High Street frontage and the remainder of the building was divided into at least five lots (Corporation Lease Books). Most of the buildings were shops, but in the 18th century the yard appears to have housed the workshops of a succession of cabinet makers, including Saunders Laughton until 1750, Robert Timperon from 1750 to 1772 and Henry Tatam after 1772 (Court Rolls).

(240) HOUSE, No. 1 (Fig. 133; Plate 73), two storeys, cellar and attics, ashlar walls, class 10, probably dates from the late 17th century. In the early 18th century windows with moulded surrounds and sills were inserted on the street front on the first floor, in the position of former, taller windows; above the earlier lintels is scroll ornament in relief. Leaf-decorated wooden eaves brackets, and quoins with raised margins (Plate 121), are of the first period. The rear wall is stone on the ground floor and timber-framed above; the coved eaves are widely projecting. Inside, partitions to a former, almost central, passage have been largely removed, but the early 18th-century stair at the back, with turned balusters and square knops, remains. Early 19th-century fittings include ceiling cornices with acanthus decoration and an elliptically-headed recess with keyblock.

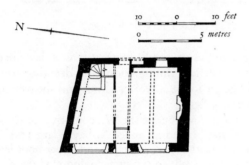

Fig. 133   (240) 1 Ironmonger Street.

(241) SHOP, No. 2, two storeys with attics in mansard roof, red brick walls, is early 19th-century; it was built as a shop and has a side entrance serving a dwelling on the first floor. Early 19th-century pilasters to the shop front remain; the fascia is applied against a vestigial platband which is traceable on either side. One sash window has triple lights.

(242) HOUSE, No. 3 (Plate 107), two storeys and attics, ashlar front wall, class 10 plan, was built in the first half of the 18th century. The door and window openings on the street front have plain projecting surrounds with keystones; the elevation is enriched with rusticated quoins, platband and deeply projecting wooden cornice with shaped brackets. A shop front with flat bay window, occupying the N. bay, may be early 19th-century. A rear window has ovolo-moulded mullions. The interior is largely gutted except for a stair against the back wall. For plan see Fig. 7.

(243) HOUSE, Nos. 4-5 (Plate 145), two storeys and attics, mostly timber-framed, has a late 16th-century origin; a central carriageway is an original feature but has been narrowed on the S. The building formed part of the Blue Bell Inn. A first-floor room, adjacent to the carriageway, overhangs on the street side, has a hipped

roof, and is perhaps 18th-century. A two-storey rear wing with cellar was added in the 18th century; the lower walls are of stone, the upper, jettied at the gable end, are timber-framed. The interior walls are almost entirely early 19th-century, when a second rear wing with mansard roof was also added. The two shop fronts give the street elevation, with the exception of the jetty, an early 19th-century appearance; the smaller shop window, beneath the jetty, is bow-fronted, the larger has a central entrance, rounded ends to each window and later glazing bars. The upper window in the jetty is a triple sash. Inside, ceiling beams in the S. room are stop-chamfered and the joists are laid flat. The N. room, now subdivided, has intersecting beams. In the S. rear wing is a fireplace with eared surround of the 18th century.

At the rear of No. 5 is a stone *Warehouse* of the early 19th century; the wide openings are modern. At right angles is a two-storey range with attics in a mansard roof, and walls partly of dressed stone and partly of timber-frame; it is perhaps mid 19th-century.

(244) SHOP, No. 6, three storeys and cellar, coursed rubble walls with freestone dressings and quoins, red brick N. gable, was built c. 1840. The L-shaped plan provides for a shop, and a side hallway with staircase which serve accommodation on the upper floors; the entrance is late 19th-century. Inside, the main rooms have plaster cornices with Greek meander pattern.

(245) HOUSE, No. 8, three storeys and attics, ashlar front wall, mansard roof, was probably built c. 1800. The front of three bays has upper sash windows with continuous sills; the ground floor has a late shop front but the main door and a roundheaded passage-entry are retained. The plan is narrow, only one room deep.

(246) HOUSE, Nos. 9-10 (Plate 99), three storeys and cellar, ashlar front and rubble rear walls, was built in the early 18th century by Henry Butcher (died 1736), upholsterer, who bought the site in 1706 for £70 (deeds).

This large building comprises two houses of classes 13 and 9. The seven-bay street elevation has rusticated quoins and continuous platbands at sill level; all windows have eared architraves but the lower also have flat hoods above pulvinated friezes (Fig. 10). A plain parapet rises off a moulded cornice which breaks forward above the quoins. In the early 19th century shop fronts were installed but that in No. 9 alone remains; this has a central doorway with semicircular fanlight flanked by large windows surmounted by segmental fanlights (Plate 138). The interiors have been much altered. In the main house (No. 10) the stair has turned balusters and rises past an arch with keyblock. One upper room has double-height fielded panelling with wooden cornice; other fittings include plain panelling, doorcases and a stone fireplace, all of the late 18th century. The fittings in No. 9 are mainly late 18th-century. For plan of No. 10 see Fig. 7.

(247) HOUSE, No. 11, three storeys, coursed rubble with ashlar dressings and quoins, was built between April 1796 and February 1798, when it was described as newly erected by Thomas Harper, ironmonger (indentures of 1819, in deeds of 3 All Saints' Place, and of 1798 in deeds of 10 Ironmonger Street).

The plan approximates to class 10 with a rear block housing stairway and lesser rooms. The three-bay street front has modern shop front, upper sash windows with lintels and keystones in relief, and third-floor platband at sill level. A rainwater head is dated 1802. Fittings include a moulded fireplace surround between roundheaded recesses, and moulded doorcases.

(248) HOUSE AND SHOP, No. 12, three storeys and attics, coursed rubble with flush ashlar quoins and dressings, double roofs with central valley, class 14b, is late 18th-century. The absence of a door between hall and front room implies its use as a shop from the beginning. The stair, in the rear block, has square balusters and turned newels. An upper room has fluted plaster cornice.

(249) TERRACE, Nos. 13–14, and 38 Broad Street, two storeys, attics and cellar, walls of coursed rubble with ashlar dressings, is late 18th-century. Before alteration to modern shops, each house consisted of an L-shaped plan of three rooms with a stair in the angle. The staircase in No. 13 has splat balusters with shaped profiles (Fig. 15).

KING'S MILL LANE (Fig. 201)

(250) THE VALE HOUSE, No. 2 (Fig. 134), two storeys, attics and basement, three storeys on garden side, has coursed rubble walls with flush dressings, squared stones on the W. closely resembling ashlar, and hipped roofs. In July 1784 the site, apparently vacant, was bought by Joseph Robinson, miller, from William Gooude, for £100. The present house was completed for Robinson by 1788 to designs by William Legg; in that year a carpenter advertised that he had been employed on the house under Legg (*Mercury*, 25 Jan.). At Robinson's death in January 1823, the house was bought by Thomas Gilchrist who appears to have effected the early 19th-century refitting (deeds). The house has an unconventional plan and its building-sequence is obscure. It seems to have originated as a simple range on the garden side with an entrance hall and stair on the street side. Slightly later, possibly before the completion of the first building, a wing was added

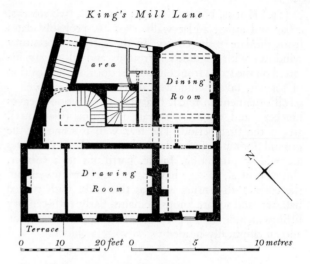

Fig. 134 (250) The Vale House.

at right angles on the S. In 1823 it was described as having 'excellent dining room and drawing rooms, breakfast parlour . . . water closet and shower bath' (*Mercury*, 5 Sept.).

The main elevation, on the W., comprises a three-bay front on the N. and an added S. bay (Plate 150). The former has platbands at principal and upper floor levels, and continuous sills to the upper windows; the sills of the two main S. windows have been lowered and the N. window provides access to a garden terrace. The central upper window is emphasized by a balustrade below the sill, probably a 19th-century enrichment. A straight joint and a slight setting-back separate the S. bay from the main block which is of different character. This bay has a tall shallow roundheaded recess rising from a platband continuous with that on the N. The plain impost moulding of the recess ignores the horizontal elements of the main block. The upper window in the recess is segmental-headed. A bracketed cornice continues over both sections and is apparently of one date. The E. elevation of the main range is set back from the road and is reached by a passage which bridges the basement-area on a two-bay loggia; the doorway has a segmental head with lunette. The street end of the S. wing consists of a cantilevered two-storey wooden bow window with triple sashes on each floor. The roof of this range is half-hipped.

Inside, the entrance-passage with barrel-vaulted ceiling leads into the corner of the main stair hall which is perhaps entirely early 19th-century; the plain wooden stair is cantilevered and has a ramped handrail. A roundheaded window with panelled reveals and decorative arrises lights the stair. An axial passage leading off the stair hall has a heavy dentilled cornice of *c.* 1785. The principal room has early 19th-century decoration with a fireplace having moulded surround and angle-paterae.

The adjacent room has plaster cornice with husk-and-swag pattern. Rooms in the S. bay have heavy wooden cornices of *c.* 1785 or slight plaster cornices of the early 19th century. Upper rooms contain wooden fireplaces; one of *c.* 1785 is enriched with fluting, repetitive leaves, and carved motifs (Plate 130). Plaster ceilings are in the same vein. In the basement, the kitchen has a hearth flanked by elliptical-headed recesses. In garden, reset in red brick wall, is a 15th-century doorway with four-centred crocketed head the outer order having small capitals (Plate 65). At the S. end of garden is a single span bridge of freestone and coursed rubble with ashlar abutments carved with large roundels (Plate 150). Near-by walls and piers carry carved urns.

(251) HOUSE, No. 3, two storeys, attics, coursed rubble walls, mansard roof, originally comprised a pair of class 15 cottages. It was built by James Brown, fellmonger, before 1811 and possibly before 1802 (deeds).

LUMBY'S TERRACE, see 22 Water Street (447).

MAIDEN LANE (Fig. 143)

Perhaps known as Cornwansty in the Middle Ages, this street seems always to have been of relatively little importance, particularly in the post-medieval period. Digby House (255) is the only substantial early house in the street, and the unimpressive nature of its alterations typifies the undistinguished character of the later houses.

(252) HOUSE AND SHOP, Nos. 2–3, of three storeys, red brick walls, Welsh slate roof, was built in the early 19th century possibly as a shop with one large and one small room flanking a passage to a court behind. Around this court are three single-storey stone-built ranges built at different times in the 17th century.

(253) HOUSE, Nos. 5–6, two storeys, stone walls, is the surviving portion of a 17th-century house. Two-storey gabled stone-mullioned bay windows flank a modern doorway. A former room on the N. with a similar bay window has been demolished (NMR). A 15th-century two-centred doorway, removed from 46–47 High Street in 1966, is reset in the E. wall (Plate 65).

(254) HOUSE AND SHOP, No. 8, class 10, two storeys and attics with stone-slated mansard roof, was built in the early 19th century, partly on the site of a possible N. wing of Digby House (255). The ashlar elevation has sash windows and a modern shop front. Behind, to the N., is an earlier two-storey stone wing, and to the S. is a small timber-framed block which, with a passage, may have formed part of a service wing to Digby House (q.v.).

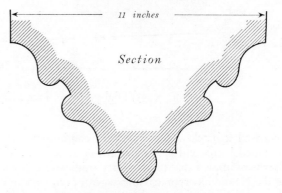

11 inches

Section

Fig. 135　(255) Digby House. Carved boss and section of beam, 16th-century.

(255) DIGBY HOUSE, Nos. 9–10 (Figs. 136, 137), two storeys and attics, stone walls rendered on the W., has a main range, probably of the early 16th century, and a slightly later rear wing. At the N. end of the street front are the remains of an early 16th-century tripartite window; the central light has a central mullion and transom below which is a modern door; one side light is partly blocked, the other replaced by a sash window, but a label with returns extends over the whole window. On the first floor is a rebuilt oriel window with an original base carved with the arms and supporters of Digby(?) (*a crown held by two beasts rampant, one crowned, and fleur de lis in base*; supporters: two beasts, rampant sejant, one collared) with modern colouring (Plate 76). The two-storey rear wing has a full-height rectangular bay window largely reconstructed in brick but with an original chamfered stone plinth. A later outshut at the rear of the main block provides access to the wing. Inside, there is a large internal chimney stack, probably original. The N. room, subdivided in the 19th century, has a heavy stop-chamfered cross beam, and in the N.

Fig. 136　(255) Digby House. Front elevation.

end wall a blocked doorway with continuous wave-moulded jambs and depressed four-centred head. This doorway implies that the property originally extended to the N. and incorporated a passage or even a room on that side. A later fireplace has an 18th-century wooden surround and overmantel. The rear wing has inter-secting roll-moulded beams (Plate 76) and foliated boss (Fig. 135) of the first half of the 16th century; in the N. wall is an original wooden door frame.

HOUSE, No. 13, see mon. 359.

(256) HOUSE, Nos. 15, 16, two-storey rubble front wall, timber-framed rear wall, is 17th-century in origin. It has a three-room plan and cross passage. In the front wall, rebuilt in the 19th century, are reset two medieval head-corbels.

(257) KING'S HEAD INN, No. 19, two storeys and attics, originally timber-framed, has a 17th-century or earlier origin. It was later cased in coursed rubble, and in the early 19th century the street front was replaced by a wall of squared stone. The interior, now unified, has a reused cross beam, probably replacing a cross wall; it supports a heavy stop-chamfered axial beam which per-haps defines the length of a former hall. Whether this hall was originally open to the roof or whether the ceiling beams and floor are original features of the 17th century is uncertain.

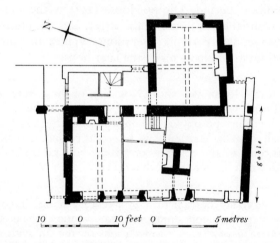

Fig. 137　(255) Digby House.

MALLORY LANE (Fig. 138)

As late as 1729 this lane was called Mallory Bridge (Browne's Hospital leases), identifying it with the Maleroye or Maleroie Bridge of the early 14th century (Cambridge University Library, Add. MS. 3021). The culvert from Scotgate runs along its length.

(258) DOORWAY, on W. side of lane, two-centred, with chamfered and rebated jambs, formerly taller and

wider, but incorrectly rebuilt; probably medieval, provenance unknown.

MALTINGS YARD (Fig. 209)

(259) Former HOUSE, now house and parish reading room, two storeys, basement and attics, coursed rubble walls, flush dressings, class 10 plan, dates from the mid 18th century. The main elevation is of three bays with central doorway now blocked, platband, moulded wooden eaves cornice on two sides, parapets on the other. Interior considerably altered for its present use.

(260) Former MALTINGS, group of four ranges, two dating from the first quarter of the 19th century, and two from the second quarter. Mostly three storeys, coursed rubble or squared stone walls. The floors are supported on rows of cast-iron columns.

MELANCHOLY WALK (Fig. 201)

(261) FREEMAN'S COTTAGES, two storeys, coursed rubble walls, mansard roof, comprise seven dwellings of class 14a plan; two dwellings at the E. end were formed out of an 18th-century building which had a central entrance. The present row was built in 1838 but was recently gutted and altered externally. Set in the wall is a panel inscribed 'N^NE 1838' for Noah Norton, the owner and presumably builder (Improvement Commissioners' minutes).

NEW TOWN (Fig. 206)

New Town is situated on a triangular plot of land bounded by Empingham Road, Rock Road, Foundry Road and Eight Acres. It was developed piecemeal in the early 19th century, encroaching on land S. of the Oakham Turnpike road. By 1845 the number of houses probably reached 45. They had gardens and yards but were generally small, and were constructed either by speculators or future occupiers.

EIGHT ACRES

(262) HOUSE, No. 11, two storeys, coursed rubble walls, freestone quoins and dressings, hipped roof, originally comprises a row of three dwellings; before 1833 (Knipe's map).

EMPINGHAM ROAD

(263) HOUSE, No. 10, two storeys, rubble walls, yellow brick chimney stacks, comprises the surviving pair of dwellings, with class 14a plans, in a former terrace of six. A stone panel bears the date '1849'. Interior altered to make one house.

(264) MOUNT PLEASANT, Nos. 20–34, a terrace of eight houses, of two storeys with coursed rubble walls, freestone quoins, cambered lintels with keystones, stone ball finials on each gable apex; class 14a, mid 19th-century.

(265) HOUSES, Nos. 36 and 38, a pair, two storeys, yellow brick; class 14, mid 19th-century.

(266) HOUSE, No. 40, two storeys, yellow brick, slated roof, class 10 plan, lattice-work fan light; first half 19th-century.

(267) HOUSE, No. 50, two storeys, coursed rubble walls with freestone quoins, was built in two stages in the early 19th century; the N. range (class 8a) had been built by 1833 (Knipe's map), and the S. wing, containing the stair, was built soon afterwards.

FOUNDRY ROAD

(268) HOUSE, No. 12, two storeys, rubble walls, freestone quoins and dressings, class 15, formerly with single-storey rear wing, now heightened; early 19th-century.

(269) HIT AND MISS INN, two storeys, rubble walls, freestone quoins and dressings, originally comprised an early 19th-century class 10 dwelling at the E. end and a large barn or workshop on the W., under a continuous roof. Soon afterwards the barn was converted into two two-storey dwellings at slightly different dates; later it was converted to its present use. To the E. of the house are attached two single-storey outbuildings with rubble walls.

(270) HOUSE, No. 27, two storeys, rubble walls, freestone quoins and dressings, originally comprised two class 15 dwellings; mid 19th-century, altered to make one house.

ROCK ROAD

(271) HOUSES, Nos. 7 and 8, a pair, two storeys, coursed rubble walls, freestone quoins, brick stacks, have class 14 plans. A date-stone is inscribed '1817'.

(272) HOUSE, No. 9, two storeys, rubble walls, freestone quoins, sash windows, class 14 plan; first half 19th-century.

(273) HOUSE, No. 10, two storeys, rubble walls, freestone quoins and dressings, casement windows, approximating to class 15 plan, was built after 1833 (Knipe's map).

NORTH STREET (Fig. 70)

A continuous road runs from St. Peter's Street to St. Paul's Street, for the greater part immediately outside the town walls. In 1868 it was split into West Street, North Street, and East Street. Elm Street is a southerly branch of the same road, closely following the actual line of the wall. During the early 19th century almost the whole length of this road was built up with small houses and cottages, all of which encroached on the manorial waste. The dwellings were generally mean and included brothels in North Street to which the railway navvies resorted in the 1840s (*Mercury*, 1 Jan. 1847). Almost all of the early 19th-century houses were demolished before 1970.

(274) HOUSE, No. 2, class 15, three storeys, ashlar front wall, has a three-bay symmetrical front with sash windows under cambered heads; *c.* 1820 and now derelict. The first-floor room has a plaster floor.

(275) Row of four houses, two storeys and attics, rubble walls, mansard roof, each with class 14a plan, was described as newly built in 1812 (*Mercury*, 16 July). They are probably later than Stukeley House (97), completed 1801, in whose grounds they stand. The ground floor has been gutted and the entrances altered. Back-to-back fireplaces in each house have segmental heads.

PRIORY ROAD

(276) PRIORY HOUSE (TF 03930735) was built following a lease from the Earl of Exeter to Messrs. Treen and Lely in 1771, in which an expenditure of £200 was stipulated (Ex. MS, 77/1/13). Joseph Treen, tea dealer of the High Street, died in 1780 when his widow sold the lease (*Mercury*, 6 Apr. 1780). The house stands on the scarp above the Welland flood plain, and the sloping site resulted in a building of two storeys, attics and cellars on the N. and three full storeys on the S. The walls are of coursed rubble. The house of *c.* 1771 has a class 10 plan; on the S. a slightly later wing perhaps followed the sale of 1780. The three-bay N. front has two blocked windows and an early 19th-century Tuscan porch with cast-iron columns. On the S. the main features are early 19th-century curved bay windows on the principal floor. The cellar has wooden mullion-and-transom windows. The internal fittings, entirely of the early 19th century, include a stair with terminal scroll, and richly moulded architraves to doors and windows. The roof has staggered square-set purlins.

The *Garden*, flanked by ditches and with central gravel path, survives largely as it was described in 1780 (*Mercury*, 6 Apr.).

RED LION SQUARE (Fig. 138)

The Square derives its name from the former Red Lion Inn, at No. 2 (278), which ceased to exist sometime before *c.* 1720. During the 18th century it was also known as the White Meat Market. Originally it probably extended further to the W. and S., but has been curtailed by early encroachments. By the 14th century the stalls which occupied open space had been rebuilt in more permanent form; these replacements were arranged in rows, called Butchers Street, Wollerowe and Byhindback. One tenement in Byhindback, described in 1340 as consisting solely of shop and loft (Peck XI, 35), was probably typical. These encroachments were progressively cleared during the later 18th century, the last ones being removed *c.* 1800.

The most notable building is No. 6–7 (280) occupying the S. side of the Square. Of considerable importance, its original status is uncertain but it is tempting to regard it as a possible guildhall.

(277) HOUSE, No. 1, two storeys and attics, timber-framed, rendered, dates from the second half of the 17th century. The two-bay collared roof has heavy timbering. The ground floor is gutted for a shop.

(278) HOUSE, No. 2, two storeys, comprises a range placed end on to the street; the central part has a medieval origin as suggested by the roof pitch. The section next to the street was rebuilt with an ashlar front in the 18th century; it originally extended further S. on the site of No. 3, as shown by a single jamb of a destroyed window on the first floor. The rear section was rebuilt in red brick in the early 19th century and at the same time a shop front with central doorway was installed. Also, space for a small office was acquired from the adjacent property. Inside, the staircase has a fretted balustrade in the Chinese taste, somewhat repaired. At the E. end of the yard stands a stone building of two storeys and attics, *c.* 1700; it was probably built as kitchens and servants' quarters. Wooden transom-and-mullion windows remain with original iron casements.

(279) Former HOUSES and SHOPS, now mostly offices; a corner site with Nos. 4 and 5 in the Square and No. 1 in High Street (Plate 161). In 1843 the Marquess of Exeter renounced part of No. 1 High Street in order to allow the Improvement Commissioners to widen the road provided the Comissioners built a 'new and respectable front' (*Mercury*, 28 April 1843). In 1846 the Corporation sold to the Marquess Nos. 4 and 5 Red Lion Square, already partly demolished by the Commissioners, on con-

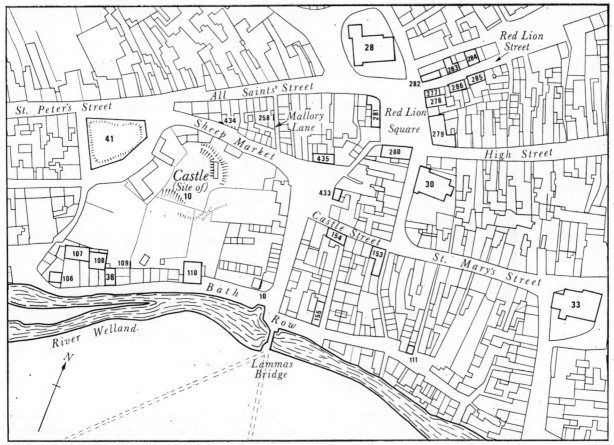

Fig. 138   Map showing monuments in Bath Row, Castle Street, Mallory Lane, Red Lion Square, Red Lion Street and Sheepmarket.

dition that he rebuilt them (Ex. MS. 46/3). The architect was one of the Brownings, probably Bryan, and the contractor was Moses Peal who submitted a tender for £2,750. The building was roofed by December 1848 (*Mercury*, 31 March, 14 April, 7 July, 14 July, 22 December 1848).

The building was designed to include three houses and shops but the ground floor has been totally altered. It is of three storeys with attics and cellars, and the walls are of squared and coursed rubble with freestone quoins and dressings. Its architectural style combines Jacobean and Dutch motifs, the windows being mullioned, some transomed, and the attic dormers having shaped gables. The corner between two streets is obtuse. Rainwater heads feed into a heavy cornice-like timber gutter.

(280) HOUSE, Nos. 6 and 7 (Fig. 139), two storeys, attics and cellar, timber-framed, is a 15th-century building of some size. A stone front was added on the E. in the 18th century. It is jettied at the front (N.) and originally at the back (S.), where it has been underbuilt. Later shop fronts replace much of the N. wall; that belonging to No. 6 was installed in 1848 (*Mercury*, 22 Sept.).

The medieval structure incorporates large timbers; on the upper floor are slightly curved parallel braces arranged in herringbone fashion between widely spaced posts and studs (Fig. 139). The plaster infilling was secured by wooden pegs projecting from the sides of the studs and braces. The wall plates have splayed scarfs. In the centre of the S. wall, on the first floor, are the remains of a three-light wooden window with cusped and traceried head (Plate 76). The roof is divided into six unequal bays. The two W. bays may have formed a separate room, at least on the first floor; the dividing truss has the same technique of plaster infilling as occurs externally and is therefore probably original. There are no other indications of the original plan. The upper rooms were open to the roof which is of crown post construction with braced tie beams; the crown posts are braced upwards to the collar purlin and downwards to the tie beam (Fig. 139). A second, higher, collar may be a later but still early insertion.

In the cellar three large recesses, each with flat, two-centred, chamfered heads are of late medieval date. Later

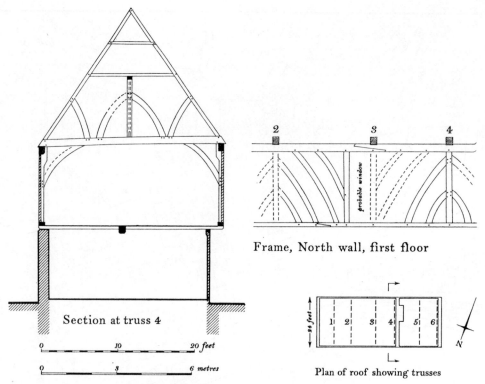

Section at truss 4

0   10   20 feet

0   3   6 metres

Frame, North wall, first floor

Plan of roof showing trusses

Fig. 139   (280) 6–7 Red Lion Square.

features include a large glazed lantern on the roof; it contains seats and dates from *c.* 1830.

(281) HOUSES AND SHOPS, Nos. 8–10 (Plate 140), three storeys, cellars, ashlar front wall, coursed rubble rear wall, comprise three original shops with living accommodation above. The row follows the curve of the street at its N. end. It was built in 1818 by the second Marquess of Exeter on land which had been leased to the Earl of Exeter in 1797 on condition that the buildings then standing were rebuilt according to plans by Legg (Blore, 207, 208). Rebuilding however did not take place until 1818 (*Mercury*, 2 April). The cost of the present row was £1,120 (Drakard, 349). A clock in the wall of the N. tenement is signed 'Haynes, Stamford'; Thomas Haynes, clockmaker and silversmith, occupied the corner property of the former building in 1804 and continued business on the same site after the premises had been rebuilt (Nattes' drawing).

The three shop fronts are early 19th-century; No. 10, the more pretentious, has a central entrance flanked by Doric columns, and Nos. 8 and 9 have side entrances with attenuated columns, and each have separate doorways to the dwellings on the upper floors. Inside, early 19th-century doors and architraves survive, but the stair in the central tenement is modern.

(282) HOUSE, No. 11, a corner building, three storeys and attics, coursed rubble walls, freestone dressings, mansard roof, is late 18th-century. Sash windows on the upper floors have continuous sills.

RED LION STREET (Fig. 138)

Named after the adjacent inn (278), this narrow street runs on one side of the infilled W. end of Broad Street.

(283) HOUSE, No. 1, three storeys and attics, coursed rubble walls, freestone dressings, and hipped mansard roof. Its building-date is inscribed on a panel over the S. door: 'W P E 1793'. The S. street elevation has three sash windows with continuous sills, and lintels with projecting keystones on each upper floor. The four ground-floor openings originally comprised doors and windows alternately but the E. pair is now amalgamated. The arrangement implies a dwelling and shop with separate doors to each. Interior gutted.

(284) Former LORD NELSON INN, No. 3 (Plate 111), two storeys, attics and cellar, ashlar walls, overhanging eaves, originally approximating to class 10 plan, is 18th-century. One of the additions at the rear, including a mutilated shop front with flanking doors, may date from *c.* 1838 when improvements to the premises were made by William Baker, wine and coal merchant (*Mer-*

cury, 12 Jan. 1838). The street front of three bays has separated quoins, central door with stone pediment carried on brackets, and first-floor sash windows with plain wide surrounds; ground-floor windows are modern. Interior gutted except for stairs.

(285) HOUSE, Nos. 7–9, class 3, two storeys and cellar, has wide eaves and gabled dormers. The timber-framed and jettied cross wing may be 16th-century; in the 17th century the two-room main range was entirely rebuilt in stone and the whole building reroofed. The street elevation has modern shop fronts; the upper windows are sashes and include one triple sash of the early 19th century. Seventeenth-century features include two-light ovolo-mullioned windows in the end wall of the main range, and one with wooden mullion and transom in the rear wall. Wooden and stone fireplaces have bolection-moulded surrounds. The E. bay of the four-bay roof, over the cross wing, is higher than the rest but the ridge is in line. The roof has principal rafters with curved feet and two pairs of purlins, the upper pair being staggered, probably late 17th-century.

(286) HOUSE, No. 10, two storeys and attics, timber-frame, replaced in stone at sides and rear, is probably early 17th-century. The gabled street front has a first-floor jetty, now encased, and a modern shop front below. Later tie beams above the original ones imply a replacement roof. Interior gutted.

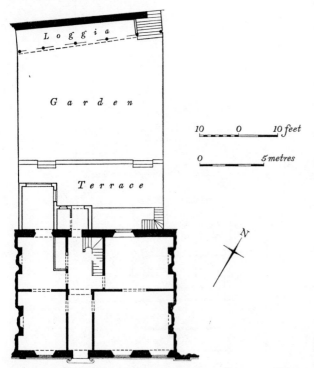

Fig. 140   (288) 8 Rutland Terrace.

ROCK ROAD (Fig. 206)
This lane forms a back lane to the S. of Scotgate.

(287) TERRACE, Nos. 12–15, two storeys, coursed rubble, slated roofs, comprising four class 15 houses in two reflecting pairs, was built between 1844 and 1845 for R. Newcomb (*Mercury*, 20 Sept. 1844; survey of 1845). They are situated on top of warehouses (mon. 425). The front, with roundheaded first-floor windows and keystones above a platband, has some architectural pretension for otherwise modest dwellings.

HOUSES, Nos. 7–8, 9, 10, see mons. (271, 272, 273).

RUTLAND TERRACE (Fig. 201)

(288) TERRACE, Nos. 1–20 (Figs. 140, 141; Plate 154), three storeys, front walls of ashlar or rubble, partly stuccoed, rear walls of coursed rubble, consists of 20 houses with low-pitched slated roof; Nos. 1–12 have transverse roofs at the rear. The terrace was built on two early enclosures, one of which had been a bowling green at least as early as 1712 (Court Rolls). In 1827 the bowling green and adjoining paddock were bought by J. C. Wallis, veterinary surgeon (*Mercury*, 2 Feb. and 30 Nov. 1827). Building of all 20 houses started in 1829 and by August of that year seven at the E. end were advertised for letting (*Mercury*, 9 April and 21 Aug. 1829). These seven have stuccoed fronts whereas the remainder are ashlared. Wallis occupied one of them. In 1830 tenders were invited for the completion of nine more houses, probably those at the W. end. Advertisements for various houses show that the terrace had been completed by 1831 (*Mercury*, 30 April 1830 and 11 March 1831). By 1831 Wallis had mortgaged the houses for a total of £6,000 (deeds); his finances were so stretched that he probably became bankrupt, and the freeholds were subsequently sold.

Although the terrace has an overall appearance of uniformity, minor variations between groups of houses reflect the interrupted history of its construction. Four giant pilasters divide the façade into a central group of five houses, with side groups of equal length but comprising seven houses on the E. and eight on the W.; the pilasters are incised with margins terminating as Greek key patterns, the central pair having capitals enriched with anthemion ornament, the outer being plain. The ground-floor windows and doorways have round heads; those in the central bay have rusticated quoins. The first-floor french windows give onto balconies with wrought-iron balustrades of varying designs; the hooded balcony

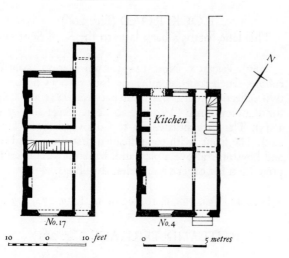

Fig. 141   (288) 17 and 4 Rutland Terrace.

with trellis balustrade to No. 8, though differing in style, appears to be original (*Mercury*, 11 March 1831).

The plans of the houses fall into two main groups with the exception of Nos. 8 and 20 which are of individual size and plan. Houses Nos. 1 to 7 and 9 to 12 conform to class 14b plan and houses Nos. 13 to 19, which have narrower fronts but deeper plans, to class 13b. The rooms may be generally identified with those mentioned in the early advertisements; No. 8, of four bays, class 9a plan, had in 1831 a first-floor drawing room 40 ft. long; it has since been divided. The W. house, No. 20, has a three-bay entrance front on the W.; roundheaded recesses and a window on the S. simulate the arrangement of openings in adjacent houses. Some internal alterations were made to this house in about 1870 in order to give access to a new wing on the N. Throughout the terrace the interior fittings are uniform and of chaste design but some plaster cornices in No. 8 are more elaborately enriched with classical motifs. Advertisements show that this house contained water closets from the start. At the rear of the E. houses are contemporary stables and coach houses. Until recently, at the rear of No. 8, there stood a loggia with wooden Doric columns.

RYHALL ROAD

(289) TERRACE, Nos. 1, 3, 5, 7 and 9, two storeys, coursed rubble walls, slated hipped roof, comprises four dwellings of class 14 plan and one, formerly the Parting Pot Inn (1845 survey), which is larger. The sash windows have flat arches of pindle on edge. It was built in the early 19th century and before 1833 (Knipe's map).

(290) HOUSES, Nos. 11 and 13, a pair, two storeys, coursed rubble walls, sash windows with flat arches of pindle, were built in the early 19th century and later extended at each end, all before 1833 (Knipe's map).

ST. GEORGE'S SQUARE (Fig. 143)

St. George's church and the surrounding Square lie on the S.E. edge of the Danish burh. Since the 18th century, if not earlier, the square has been residential, with business or professional practices carried on from the houses. The S. side has large plots reaching almost to the river, which have encouraged the building of large houses and the establishment of trading concerns, such as Thomas Smith, timber merchants, at No. 19 in the early 19th century. Nos. 17, 14 and 19 are outstanding houses of the 13th to 17th centuries. In the early 18th century the building of the Assembly Rooms emphasized the social importance of the Square, and later in the century the Theatre was built near by in St. Mary's Street.

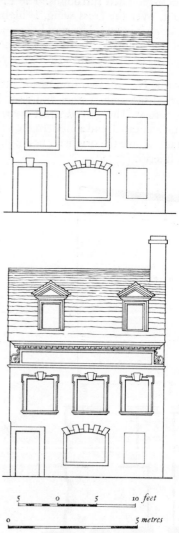

Fig. 142   (291) 1 St. George's Square. Elevation before and after mid 18th-century alterations.

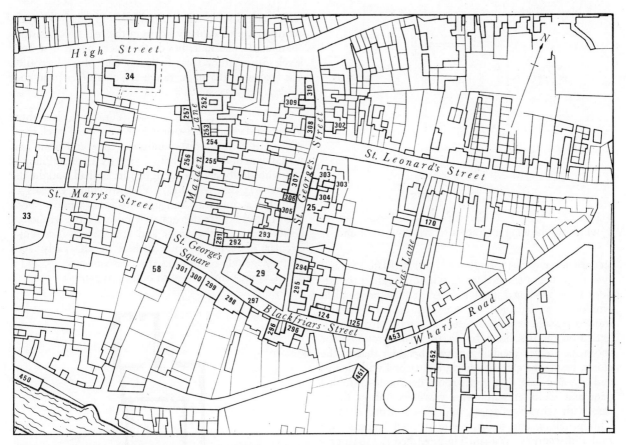

Fig. 143   Map showing monuments in Blackfriars Street, Maiden Lane, St. George's Square, St. George's Street and Wharf Road.

(291) HOUSE, No. 1 (Fig. 145; Plate 107), class 15, two storeys and attics, was built in the early 18th century with an ashlar front wall and side walls of stone, brick and timber-frame. The street front at that time had a side doorway with plain surround and keystone, now cut back, a central ground-floor window with a segmental head, spaced voussoirs and plain surround; above these openings were two windows also with plain sur-

rounds and single keystones (Figs. 144, 146). There were probably two small windows in the E. bay. In the mid 18th century the front was much altered: the small E. window on the first floor was enlarged and all three upper windows were given wooden eared architraves with stepped key blocks; the wall was raised to receive a long sunk panel with wooden terminal consoles, presumably for a trade-name (Fig. 142). The new roof has

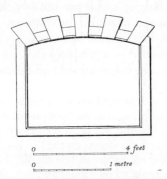

Fig. 144   (291) 1 St. George's Square. Ground-floor window.

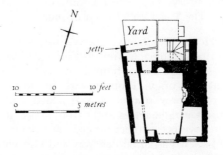

Fig. 145   (291) 1 St. George's Square.

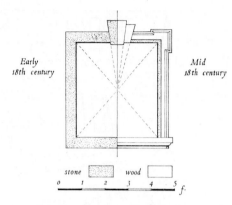

Fig. 146   (291) 1 St. George's Square. First-floor window, showing alteration to window surround.

an enriched wooden modillioned cornice (Plate 122) and two large pedimented dormer windows. The ground-floor stage remained unaltered except that the small E. window was enlarged. A late 18th-century timber-framed passage at the rear leads to a stair turret and is jettied on the first floor. Inside, the main ground-floor room has fielded panelling in two heights; that in the closet, beside the chimney stack, is enriched with dentils and egg-and-dart. The upper room has ovolo-moulded panelling, dado rail with Greek wave decoration, door-case with pulvinated frieze, and plaster dentil cornice. This panelling and staircase with turned balusters are mid 18th-century. William Lindsey (died c. 1763), carpenter, owned this house and is presumably responsible for altering and refitting it in the middle of the century (deeds and will).

(292) HOUSES, Nos. 2–4 (Plate 108), two storeys and attics, coursed rubble walls, were built in the mid 18th century, probably as a pair of class 10 houses; the E. house, is now a pair of class 15 dwellings (Nos. 3 and 4). The door and window openings have plain architraves and stepped keystones.

(293) HOUSES, Nos. 5–7, two storeys and attics, coursed rubble walls, were built in the second half of the 18th century. They had the same development as mon. 292. The S. elevation has a platband.

(294) HOUSE, No. 9, two storeys, has stone rubble walls perhaps replacing timber-framing. The main range, class 2, has a timber-framed rear wall and may be 16th-century in origin. Probably early in the 17th century, a two-storey rear block was added with twin gabled roofs at right angles to the front range; its walls appear to have been timber-framed. The present front of three bays has a central doorway and sash windows of the early 19th century. Inside, the N. room was originally the hall; a substantial chimney stack between this and the rear room is original. Cross beams in the front

range are double-ogee moulded and may be 16th-century; a 17th-century beam in the rear block is stop-chamfered. The stair, beside the stack, has at first-floor level 18th-century splat balusters with shaped profiles. Tie beams in the main range are chamfered; the roof space is not accessible.

(295) TERRACE, Nos. 10–12 (Fig. 147), has three storeys and cellar, two-storey rear wings, red brick front wall with yellow brick window arches, and stone rear wall. It was built shortly before 1829 by Thomas Pilkington who doubtless also designed it; he had bought the site in 1813 (Ex. MS, 84/7). Each dwelling, of class 12 plan, has a doorway and ground-floor window, both with round heads; the upper windows have segmental heads. Between the front and rear rooms is a semi-circular staircase. Interior fittings of the early 19th century include roundheaded arches and recesses, and a dentil cornice enriched with lion-head paterae.

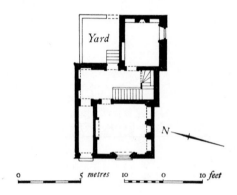

Fig. 147   (295) 12 St. George's Square.

(296) HOUSE, Nos. 14–15, two storeys, attics and basements, has rubble walls, partly rendered. It is said to be the house of David Cyssell who died in 1536 (PRO, PCC Prob. 11/29), and is still owned by the Cecils. In the early 17th century it was lived in by Alice Balguy and is presumably therefore the capital messuage occupied by Thomas Balgaye in 1595 (NRO, Fitzwilliam Misc. vol. 433). Peck says it was demolished in 1720 (Peck XI, 26) but in fact the old structure was retained and drastic remodelling carried out.

The building is ranged round three sides of an open court. The main range on the S. is probably early 16th-century. It had E. and W. cross wings which have been extended towards the street; on the E. a lower range was built against the old gable, and on the W. the cross wing was probably replaced by a longer wing in the early 17th century. This latter wing contains a large blocked window with cut-back label and returned ends, possibly of

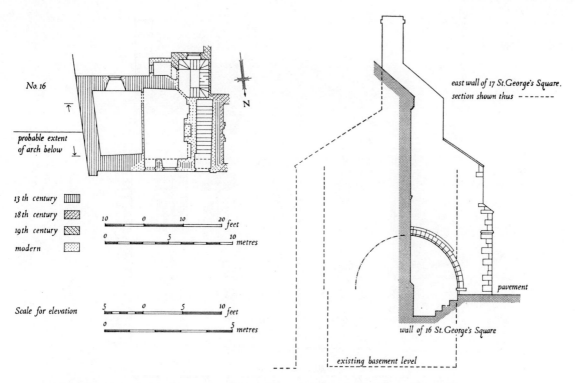

No. 16

probable extent
of arch below ↓

13th century
18th century
19th century
modern

10   0   10   20 feet
0   5   10 metres

Scale for elevation

5   0   5   10 feet
0   5 metres

east wall of 17 St. George's Square.
section shown thus - - - - - -

pavement

wall of 16 St. George's Square

existing basement level

Fig. 148   (297) 17 St. George's Square. Ground-floor plan and elevation of E. wall.

the early 17th century. The roofs of the cross wings continue to gables on the S. wall of the house. In the S. wall is a wooden mullion-and-transom window, perhaps c. 1720. In the N. gable wall of the E. cross wing is a small upper projecting window, triangular on plan, perhaps c. 1600. A number of blocked window openings are 17th or 18th-century, and on the N. and S. are early 19th-century two-storey bay windows.

The interior has been much altered and the original arrangement cannot be detected. The E. wing has in its N. gable a massive fireplace; reset in this stack is a stone bracket with embattled top, of unknown use, c. 1500. In the S. wing are various reset roll-moulded beams, possibly early 16th-century. The early 18th-century stair has closed string, turned balusters with square knops, and square panelled newels. Some rooms have early 19th-century plaster cornices and shutter panels.

(297) HOUSE, No. 17 (Fig. 148; Plate 61), two storeys and basement, stone walls, incorporates three walls of a building probably of the 13th century. At the N.E. corner is a large single-stage buttress with weathered top of medieval date; in E. wall is a blocked arch with chamfered voussoirs, cut-back label and chamfered imposts; it is semicircular and approximately half is visible externally. The street elevation has been largely refaced but a length of medieval moulded string-course returns round the buttress at present first-floor level. These early features cannot be easily explained but the

blocked arch may belong to a former undercroft which was partly below ground level. Two cambered tie beams are possibly medieval. A drawing of the N. side of the building before its alteration and refacing was made by Twopeny in 1831 (Plate 61; Twopeny, 290/b.2, p. 4).

In the 19th century a stair turret was added at the rear. A 13th-century two-light window (Plate 62) revealed in the 19th century was removed to the vestry of St. Mary's church (q.v.; Mercury, 29 April 1881).

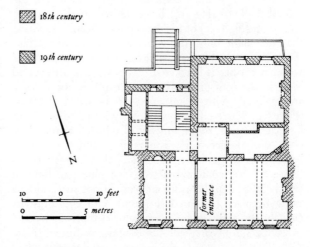

18th century

19th century

N

10   0   10 feet
0   5 metres

former entrance

Fig. 149   (298) 18 St. George's Square.

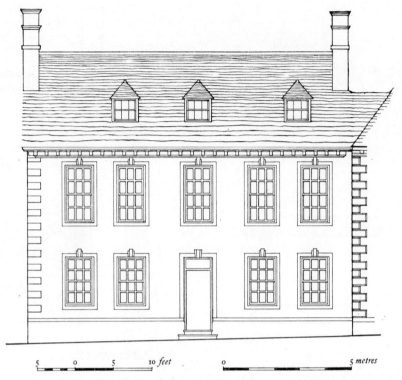

Fig. 150   (298) 18 St. George's Square. Reconstruction of front elevation.

(298) HOUSE, No. 18 (Fig. 149; Plate 115), two storeys, attics and cellar, ashlar front wall, was built in the second quarter of the 18th century. Remaining of that date is the front range of class 10 plan, but Knipe's map of 1833 shows that another wing then stood at the rear suggesting a class 11 arrangement. Soon after 1833 additions in coursed rubble with freestone dressings replaced this wing; they comprise a large room and a staircase. At the same time the formerly central front doorway and the windows in the second bay were exchanged, the moulded plinth (Fig. 13) being resited in the process. The front (Fig. 150) of five bays has rusticated quoins at the N.E. angle only; the windows have narrow architraves (Fig. 11) and small triple keystones. The moulded wooden cornice is bracketed. Eaves soffit boards found loose in the roof probably came from this house; they are painted with floral patterns between brackets (Plate 85). Three tall sash windows with marginal panes light the large S. room, in front of which is a stone balcony with lattice-work iron railings which return as balustrades to garden steps. Inside, the E. front room (Plate 89) has contemporary fielded pine panelling in two heights, dentil cornice and eared door surrounds; a stone fireplace has eared surround with egg-and-dart enrichment, and wooden overmantel comprising a panel of carved scrollwork, side-scrolls and a pediment (Plate 130). Two doorways to the former central entrance hall are blocked but the doors remain on the E. The W.

room has an early 19th-century plaster ceiling cornice elaborated with acanthus and lions' heads. The staircase, lit by a Venetian window, rises from basement to first floor; it has reset 18th-century turned balusters with square knops.

Fig. 151   (299) 19 St. George's Square. Date-panel formerly on chimney stack.

(299) HOUSE, No. 19 (Fig. 152; Plate 88), has a basement and two main storeys with two storeys in the attics. The front wall is of ashlar with rusticated quoins, and the rear wall of coursed rubble with freestone dressings. The rooms are arranged in double depth (class 9a). It was built in 1674, the date being recorded on a panel formerly on a chimney stack. With the exception of a blocked opening on

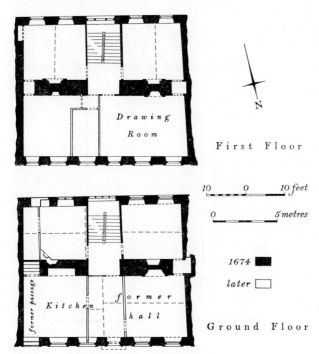

Fig. 152   (299) 19 St. George's Square.

First Floor

10   0   10 feet

0   5 metres

1674 ■

later □

Ground Floor

piece at first-floor level; this patching is inscribed 'J I 1779'. The doorway has a broken scroll pediment supported on consoles; it is of small scale, scarcely reaching the platband (Fig. 153). At eaves level is a wooden bracketed cornice; two tiers of attic windows have hipped roofs. Twin chimney stacks have rusticated quoins, arches on each face and cornices (Fig. 154). One stack was formerly inscribed 'October 17 MDCLXXIV'; the panel is now detached (Fig. 151).

The rear elevation (Plate 88) is less orderly than the front, and has a cellular arrangement of platbands, continuous sill-bands and window surrounds. The central bay has large windows with wooden mullions and transoms, lighting the stair at half-landing levels; the upper window with a Venetian arrangement of lights in a square surround impinges on the underside of the eaves, at which point the cornice brackets are omitted. Flanking windows mostly have early 18th-century sashes with heavy glazing bars. Two basement windows have ovolo-moulded mullions.

Fig. 153   (299) 19 St. George's Square. Main doorway.

0   4 feet

0   1 metre

the main front, and the introduction of sashes to most of the windows, the exterior of the house has been little altered; the ground-floor rooms on the street side were subdivided in the early 19th century to provide a central entrance-hall flanked by equal-sized rooms. It is unquestionably the most distinguished house of its time in the town. The stylistic affinity between it and Lyndon Hall, Rutland, is noticeable. Lyndon, the masonry for which was completed in 1673, was probably designed by the owner Sir Abel Barker in conjunction with John Sturges, and the contractor for the masonry was John Sutton of Stamford (*Country Life*, 10 Nov. 1966).

The main elevation on the N. is in six bays with the entrance in the fourth; it departs from symmetry on the ground floor in order to accommodate a doorway, now blocked, in the E. bay. This doorway appears to have lacked architectural emphasis. The windows have moulded side architraves (Figs. 10, 11, 12, 13) which rise to meet similarly moulded platbands; keystones are carved with grape and cabochon ornament. The windows now have sashes but the kitchen windows retained wooden mullion-and-transom frames until early in this century (survey in house). The slightly narrower window over the central doorway has been altered, and its architrave, together with an area of ashlar below it, is of different limestone, perhaps implying a former centre-

Inside, the fittings are of 1674 unless otherwise stated. Rooms on the street side originally comprised a hall (Plate 89) occupying three bays on the W., a two-bay room probably always a kitchen, and a side passage on the E. which led to a stair and the basement. There was also access direct to the basement from the street by a doorway, now blocked, partly below pavement level; the weathering of the plinth rises slightly over its head. Bolection-moulded panelling in the former hall is in three heights; it was somewhat altered when partitions were introduced to form the present entrance hall. Original panelled shutters survive. A limestone fireplace (Plate 126) has side pilasters with Ionic capitals, pulvinated frieze and dentilled cornice; inset in a central panel is a black lozenge. To one side is a small closet. In the S. range, the central stair which rises to the attics has shaped splat balusters (Fig. 15), square newels and moulded rail (Plate 132). The W. room has a heavily moulded plaster cornice and the E. room panelling of various dates and provenances.

On the first floor two doors with 17th-century surrounds lead to rooms on the N. side of the house. The present drawing room occupies the three W. bays but the 17th-century bolection-moulded panelling and enriched cornices continue beyond the present E. partition, suggesting that the room originally extended further. The E. door would, in this event, have served a small room by way of a lobby or internal porch in the corner of the larger room. The drawing room has a mid 18th-century wooden fireplace surround, eared and elaborately carved with rococo decoration (Plate 130). The E. room, now subdivided, has an early 19th-century plaster cornice. Three upper rooms have 17th-century doors and surrounds, and moulded stone fireplaces (Plate 126).

Fig. 155 (300) 20 St. George's Square. Doorway.

(300) HOUSE, No. 20 (Plate 109), of two storeys with attics and cellar, ashlar walls, class 9a, is early 18th-century. The rooms are arranged in double depth. The rear elevation was altered in the early 19th century when a full-height bay window with canted sides replaced two former windows the outermost jambs of which survive. Otherwise, the house has been little altered. The main elevation of five bays has sash windows without architraves, and a central pilastered and pedimented doorway (Fig. 155) which projects only slightly from the wall face. The moulded eaves are bracketed, and the three dormers have alternate gabled and semicircular roofs. Inside, a number of rooms have 18th-century wooden cornices; the stair in the rear range has turned balusters and newels. In the basement the kitchen has a corner fireplace with segmental head and fluted keystone.

(301) HOUSE, No. 21 (Plate 109), two storeys, attics and cellar, has walls of ashlar at the front and coursed rubble at the rear. The front range was refaced in c. 1768 and is of four unequal bays with the wall extending over an internal passage in a fifth bay. In 1768 the Earl of Exeter leased the house to Robert Miller conditional on his rebuilding the front in freestone for at least £100; the lease was renewed in 1772 after the work was completed (Ex. MS, uncatalogued). A description in 1773 suggests a class 11 plan (*Mercury*, 5 Aug.). In 1847 a deep range was added at the rear possibly as a replace-

Fig. 154 (299) 19 St. George's Square. Chimney stack.

ment, and the street entrance was moved from the third to the first bay; Mr Grant was then given permission to move the 'portico' (*Mercury*, 5 March 1847). The front elevation has windows with plain surrounds and triple keystones. The present entrance has an early 19th-century cast-iron porch with Doric columns, frieze with triglyphs and an open pediment; it was moved from the third bay where its scars are visible. The rear elevation which includes a basement has windows with segmental heads. Inside, the early 19th-century stair has plain balusters and newels. The two front rooms each have a cased cross beam, that in the W. room probably being on the line of a former side wall of a central entrance passage.

ST. GEORGE'S STREET (Fig. 143)

This street seems never to have been occupied by men of more than average affluence, and consequently contains rather small houses. These date from the Middle Ages onwards.

(302) HOUSE, No. 6, two storeys, cellar and attics, class 6, originated as a timber-framed structure to which an ashlar front wall was added in the 18th century. Two posts of the early building survive in the rear wall. The three-bay front wall has sash windows with plain architraves and continuous platband-sills; a cross partition on the first floor shows that the window over the central door had been blocked by the late 18th century.

(303) HOUSE, Reedman's Court (Fig. 156), two storeys and attics, rubble walls, contains evidence of a late medieval structure which was open to the roof (class 1a). Features of this date include several smoke-blackened rafters, each pair being pegged at the apex and

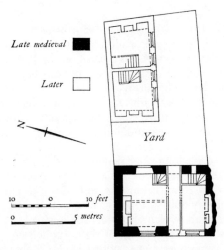

Fig. 156   (303) Reedman's Court, St. George's Street.

halved for collars; the splayed jambs of the N.W. window continue into the attics where they are blocked; a stop-chamfered tie beam bisects the building equally.

In yard of the foregoing is a pair of class 15 dwellings, of two storeys and attics, coursed rubble walls, and mansard roof; it was built in *c.* 1830 and is shown on Knipe's map of 1833.

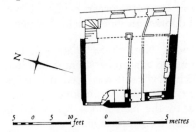

Fig. 157   (304) 11 St. George's Street.

(304) HOUSE, No. 11 (Fig. 157), one storey and attics, rubble walls, retains the outline and some of the structure of a medieval house; it was later extended at the rear. The main external feature is an external chimney stack, which projects slightly beyond the wall face on the street side; it is weathered in two stages and surmounted by a circular ashlar flue, presumably of medieval date (Plate 61; drawing by Twopeny, 290/b. 13, p. 68). There are sills and jambs of blocked windows at the upper floor level. Inside, a timber cross partition is the only early survival.

(305) HOUSE, No. 17 (Plate 115), former White Hart Inn, two storeys, cellar and attics, originated as an L-shaped timber-framed building of the 17th century; the rear wing with stone gable wall survives. Early in the 18th century the main range was cased in stone; it has an ashlar E. wall with rusticated S. quoins, plain window and door architraves with stepped keystones, and moulded timber cornice. Later in the 18th century a plain coved hood was added to the central doorway; the two flanking windows have been widened.

(306) HOUSE, No. 18 (Plate 115), two storeys and attics, class 10, was built in stone with stone-slated roof in the 18th century, perhaps in the first half, on a two-room plan with central doorway and a timber-framed stair turret at the rear. The front elevation in bands of ashlar and coursed rubble has rusticated quoins, platband, uninscribed panel and flat arches with channelled masonry joints over doorway and windows. Inside, a reset late 18th-century panel is painted in Chinese style with pavilion, birds and figures.

(307) HOUSES, Nos. 20–21, two storeys, stone rubble walls, probably originated as a three-cell house of the 17th century (class 8b), but is disguised by the rebuilding of the street front. Openings on the street side have

wooden lintels. Inside, the N. room is entered from a through-passage; the doorway has a wooden four-centred head. On the S. of the passage are two rooms, the larger having a chamfered cross beam; the partition between them is of timber. Behind is a wing of uncertain date, the upper room of which is separated from the front range by a timber partition. Later fittings include an early 19th-century corner cupboard with shaped shelves and doors with shaped fielded-panels.

(308) HOUSE, Nos. 23–24 (Plate 83), two storeys, class 7, originated as a timber-framed building, the rear wall of which survives. It was cased in stone early in the 17th century; a two-storey mullioned bay window was then added to the hall which has a chimney stack backing against a cross passage.

(309) HOUSE, No. 26, class 15, two storeys, with stone walls, was built in the 17th century; a two-storey timber-framed bay window with plaster cornice was added in the 18th century.

(310) HOUSE, No. 27, two storeys and attics, with stone walls and mansard roof, was built in *c.* 1800 on a three-room plan (class 8b). The first floor retains its small-paned iron window-frames; the ground floor is a modern shop.

ST. JOHN'S STREET (Fig. 169)

Forming part of the Great North Road in the Middle Ages, this street lies on the line of the W. side of the Danish burh.

(311) HOUSES, Nos. 1, 2 and 3, two storeys and attics, stone walls partly encasing the timber-framing of No. 1, have an irregular plan conforming with the curve of the street. The exterior of No. 1 was refaced soon after 1822 when Nos. 2 and 3 were rebuilt after the corner house had been demolished by the Turnpike Trustees for road improvement (LRO, Terrier of St. John's church, 1822). The two new houses share a central stack and have stairs along the back wall. A fireplace with angle-roundels survives on the first floor.

(312) HOUSE, Nos. 11, 12, two storeys and attics, rendered front walls, has an 18th-century or earlier origin. The ground floor is gutted for shops. In the slate-hung, timber-framed rear wing of No. 12 there is an 18th-century kitchen fireplace with elliptical head and keystone.

(313) HOUSE, No. 14, three storeys, coursed rubble and freestone dressings, is the pair of houses built by the Earl of Exeter in 1795–6 at a cost in excess of £378. The mason was Robert Hames and the carpenter Thomas Pilkington (Exeter Day Books). Demolished 1973.

ST. LEONARD'S STREET (Fig. 187)

Called Cornstall in the Middle Ages and St. George's Street in the 18th century, this street only acquired its present name in about 1830. The medieval name implies a market function for which there is no other evidence. The street is an early extension of settlement E. of the Danish burh; by the 12th century this had become a parish with a church, St. Michael in Cornstall, on the N. side. The street declined in the late Middle Ages, the church became redundant, and some house sites were vacant by 1570, but by 1650 recovery was taking place and new houses were being built (Blore, 285–90). The long frontages of surviving 17th-century buildings indicate that there was no shortage of land. The extramural part of the street was mainly built in the 19th century, and part of it forms the N. boundary of the Blackfriars Estate laid out in 1840. (See also Blackfriars Estate.)

(314) HOUSE, No. 1, on a corner site, three storeys, rubble side wall, ashlar front wall, originally comprised two class 15 dwellings of the early 19th century. The almost symmetrical ashlar elevation on to St. Leonard's Street misleadingly unifies the two dwellings; a large fixed ground-floor window suggests that the corner building, entered from St. George's Street, was designed as a shop.

(315) HOUSE, No. 2, three storeys, rubble side walls, ashlar front wall, is of class 14b, but the original stair position is unknown. It is early 19th-century; slightly later a stair turret was added at the side. All the openings on the front elevation are plain. Inside, two rooms have moulded plaster cornices; window surrounds have angle-roundels.

(316) HOUSE, No. 3 (Plate 82), formerly the Olive Branch Inn, two storeys and attics, timber-framed rear wall, ashlar front wall, has a panel on the E. face of the chimney stack inscribed '1666', presumably the construction date. The surviving 17th-century work comprises a single room with a staircase against the back wall. On the front is a three-storey bay window with canted sides, ovolo-moulded mullions and a gable. On the first floor is a late 17th-century bolection-moulded fireplace. At the rear is a long stone range formerly of two storeys and attics; the first floor and attics were united to form an assembly room in the late 19th century. The range was probably built in 1749, the date inscribed on a panel in the E. wall, which also bears the initials '$_H^W{}_E$', presumably those of Henry Wright, upholsterer, who bought the property in 1740 (deeds). He built a row of four class 15 cottages with corner flues beyond the rear

wing; they are now in ruins. The inn was extended at the side in the late 19th century.

(317) HOUSE, No. 4 (Fig. 159), two storeys, coursed rubble front wall, remainder orange-coloured brick, class 12, was built in 1845 by Moses Peal on the site of a former house (plan in St. George's vestry, survey of property, 1837); the frontage was brought forward 15 ins. to line with its neighbours (*Mercury*, 9 May 1845). The street front is of two bays with sash windows. Built into the side wall of the rear room is a 17th-century two-light ovolo-moulded window.

(318) HOUSE, No. 5, two storeys and cellar, late 19th-century stone walls partly encasing timber-framing, now of class 13b plan, has a 17th-century origin. A gable wall on the E. and the upper part of the rear gable on the N. are timber-framed.

(319) HOUSE, Nos. 6–7, two storeys, originally timber-framed, now cased in stone, is probably 16th-century or early 17th-century. In the E. gable a tie beam and rafters are exposed. The plan, of class 8b, and the steeply-pitched roof indicate the early origin of the house. (Inside not seen.)

(320) HOUSE, No. 10, timber-framed, two storeys with continuous jetty on the street front, the ground stage underbuilt in stone, may have a late 16th-century origin. The roof is now slated. The original plan comprised three main rooms (class 8b); the centre room has a later raised ceiling despite the jetty, and an end room has a stop-chamfered axial beam. A tie beam is archbraced to a swell-headed post.

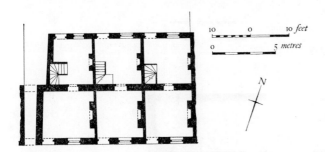

Fig. 158   (321) 15–17 St. Leonard's Street.

(321) TERRACE, Nos. 15–17 (Fig. 158; Plate 141), three storeys and cellar, coursed rubble walls; class 14a, early 19th-century. The doorways have rounded heads, and the windows have sashes.

(322) HOUSES, Nos. 18–19 (Fig. 160; Plate 141), two storeys, cellars and attics, brick walls; class 13a plan, early 19th-century. Doorways and entrance to side passage have round heads.

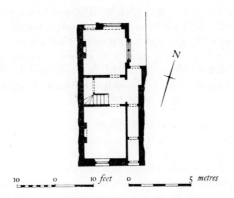

Fig. 159   (317) 4 St. Leonard's Street.

(323) REINDEER INN, No. 20 (Plate 141), three storeys at front, two at rear, cellars, coursed rubble walls, is early 19th-century; class 9 plan, with roundheaded central doorway and sash windows.

TERRACE, Nos. 29–31, see mon. (121)
HOUSES, Nos. 32 and 33, see mon. (122)
HOUSES, Nos. 34–38, see mon. (123)

(324) TERRACE, Nos. 42–45, two storeys and attics, coursed rubble walls, freestone dressings, consists of four class 15 dwellings; built by William Gregory in the early 19th-century (Ex. MS, 84/10).

(325) TERRACE, Nos. 47–52, three storeys and basement, coursed rubble walls, orange brick chimney stacks, comprises six class 15 dwellings of the early 19th century. They are probably the new and substantial houses which Mr. Gregory, builder, was selling in 1835 (*Mercury*, 20 Mar.). There are no living-room windows in the rear elevation which overlooks a school.

(326) Former CARPENTER'S ARMS, No. 54, two storeys and cellar, ashlar front wall, remainder rubble, consists of an 18th-century main range of class 10 plan; a rear wing containing a club room and staircase is described as recently built in 1855 (*Mercury*, 27 April). The house was probably built by one of the Kidson family of carpenters who lived here from 1702 to 1772; it was a

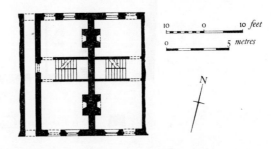

Fig. 160   (322) 18–19 St. Leonard's Street.

public house by 1801 (deeds). The front elevation was originally of four bays with an asymmetrically placed doorway; the ground floor is now lit by two rectangular bay windows of the early 19th century, and two of the first-floor windows have had their sills raised. The rear wing has a mansard roof and the club room is approached by an external stair on the W.

(327) HOUSE, No. 59 (Plate 72), two storeys, now class 10 plan, ashlar front and rubble rear walls, is probably 17th-century; the 18th-century front has a full-width bay window with canted sides. This projection, incorporating a central doorway, has a substantial platband at lintel level and narrow platbands at sill level. Scars of a former building survive in the E. gable; the W. party wall is timber-framed. An axial beam has wave stops, and the roof has collars clasping purlins; the interior is otherwise modern.

(328) HOUSE, No. 60 (Plate 72), two storeys and attics, now class 10 plan, timber-framed rear wall partly replaced in brick, coursed rubble side walls, has a 17th-century origin as indicated by a hollow-stopped chamfered axial beam. The front wall, entirely of the 18th century, stands forward of the old line as a full-width two-storey bay window with canted sides; the lower part of the wall is of ashlar, the upper of timber-frame. A central doorcase has flat hood with shaped brackets. At the rear a stair turret, probably early 19th-century, has coursed rubble walls and hipped roof. Inside are some early 19th-century door architraves with angle-roundels.

(329) HOUSE, No. 61 (Plate 72), two storeys, class 6, coursed rubble walls, has a panel inscribed '1685', presumably the building date; the panel has diamond-pattern border and hood mould. The front elevation has on each floor two windows with large dressed jamb stones, and to the E. a narrow blocked window. To one side is a broad cross passage, open at the ends, from which access to the house is gained.

(330) HOUSE, Nos. 62–63 (Plate 72), one storey and attics, stone walls, has a date panel on No. 62 inscribed '1662'. This date relates to the main structure, but the rear wall of No. 62 is medieval and has a stone buttress with mutilated weathered top, and possibly a second buttress to the E.; both wall and buttress were originally higher. The 17th-century front consists of a two-storey bay window with ovolo-moulded mullions, canted sides and a parapeted gable. No. 63 has a two-storey bay window with rendered stone walls, wooden mullions and hipped roof, and an enveloping pentice, all of the 18th or early 19th century.

ST. MARY'S HILL (Fig. 169)

St. Mary's Hill leads from the bridge over the Welland towards the town centre. Until recently it formed part of the Great North Road. Surviving buildings of the 12th and 13th centuries (336 and 338) indicate its early importance; besides shops an undercroft is mentioned in the 14th century (PRO, C14/147). The 'great inn called Kyngesin' of 1388

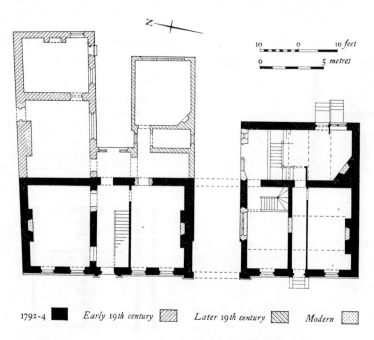

1792-4 ■   Early 19th century ▨   Later 19th century ▧   Modern ▦

Fig. 161   (331) 1–2 St. Mary's Hill.

may have been in St. Mary's Hill (*Cal. Inq. Misc.* 5 (1387–93) no. 93); alternatively it could have been in St. Martin's parish. Dominated by St. Mary's church, the street owes much of its present character to the decision of the Council to have their new Town Hall here in 1777, and to the 9th Earl of Exeter's building activities in the late 18th century.

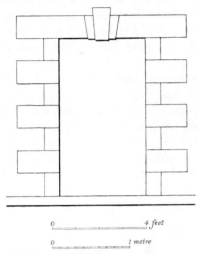

Fig. 162　(331) 1–2 St. Mary's Hill. Ground-floor window.

(331) HOUSES now Municipal Offices, Nos. 1–2 (Fig. 161; Plate 116), were built as a pair of houses by the Earl of Exeter in 1792–4 at a cost in excess of £800 (Exeter Day Books), perhaps to designs by Thomas Lumby.

Three storeys high, of coursed rubble, they comprise a five-bay house on the N. and a three-bay house on the S., each with a central doorway. Between them is a slightly projecting carriage-entry with segmental head, and rooms above belonging to the N. house; the lower windows are of Venetian design, the upper semicircular. The other windows have flush dressings and continuous sills (Fig. 162). The mean cornice beneath a low parapet has shaped brackets. The N. house, of class 10 plan, was altered in the early 19th century when a two-storey wing was added at the rear; later in the century another, lower, wing was added to the S. of this wing. The S. house, of class 9 plan, is less altered but some partitions have been moved. Interior fittings are mostly early 19th-century and without distinction. The roof has square-set tusk-tenoned purlins.

(332) Former BOAT AND RAILWAY INN, No. 3, is referred to in the Exeter Day Books for 1779: 'repairs to John Granger's warehouse which was taken down when the Sign of the Boat was built, £6'. The greater part of the 18th-century inn,

known as the Boat, survives but the present Tudor-esque appearance is the result of alterations made in 1849 by Edward Browning in connection with the rebuilding of the bridge and adjacent toll-house ((64), (333), (450)).

It has a class 10 plan, is of two storeys with attics and has coursed rubble walls with freestone dressings. The 1849 alterations included a central dormer with Dutch profile, rising from the wall, two moulded string-courses inserted at first-floor level, and an oriel with shaped cresting dated '1849', built out on brackets over the central doorway; wooden mullion-and-transom windows were inserted at the same time. A reset mid 18th-century stair leads to the attics; it has turned newels and bracketed treads but the balusters are missing. A two-storey rear wing of coursed rubble with freestone dressings is late 18th-century, and in the angle a three-storey timber-framed block with red brick infill is probably *c.* 1800.

(333) HOUSES, Nos. 4–5, originated as a 17th-century house, the S. half of which was largely rebuilt in 1849. The early house may have been built in 1658, the date inscribed on a panel reset in the E. wall; it has walls of coursed rubble. The plan is almost square, two rooms deep, and with a central chimney stack. In the rear wall are two first-floor mullioned windows each of three lights; the rebuilt front wall has a modern shop front and parapet. Except for a cross wall enclosing a passage, possibly original, the internal walls have been removed. A number of 17th-century ceiling beams remain, one of which bears evidence of a door opening. The roof, containing two tiers of attics and spanning the whole building, consists of heavy collared rafters. In an upper room is a 17th-century plaster frieze, the design based on brattishing (Fig. 163).

Fig. 163　(333) 4–5 St. Mary's Hill. Plaster frieze, 17th-century.

The S. house of 1849 was designed by Edward Browning as a result of the Improvement Commissioners granting to the Marquess of Exeter 'a small corner of ground adjoining the west parapet of the bridge, that the harmony of the structure should be preserved' (*Mercury*, 30 Mar. 1849). Besides encroaching on the 17th-century house on the N., it also incorporates in its S. wall the gable wall of a former house, probably of 18th-century origin, the quoins of which survive. The building (Plate 163), in the Jacobean idiom, has two storeys and attics, mansard roof and walls of alternate ashlar and pindle courses. The street front, in three bays with mullioned windows and moulded string-course and cornice, has flush dormers with ornate profiles and central doorway with panel inscribed '1849' and the Exeter monogram 'ᴴᴱ' within a Garter.

(334) HOUSE, No. 8, class 2, two storeys and attics, timber-framed with a jetty partly underbuilt in stone, is 16th or early 17th-century. The street front (Plate 78), on the E., has an early 19th-century shop front comprising two sash windows with flush panels below the sills. Above are sash windows and a modillion cornice of the 18th century. The jetty joists have rounded ends. Two larger joists divide the plan into unequal bays: the narrowest on the N. was probably originally a passage and the centre and S. bays may have contained a single room, heated by a stack in the rear wall. A rear wing may be contemporary with the front range but is at a lower level. It is in three bays, timber-framed, partly rebuilt in stone. Joists are heavy and laid flat. In the E. bay is an early 19th-century stair of plain design. The roof has clasped purlins and curved windbraces.

(335) HOUSE, No. 9, class 2, two storeys and attics, timber-framed, rubble chimney stack, is probably 16th-century. The street front (Plate 78), on the E., is jettied; one brace to the jetty remains and the bressummer is moulded although partly hidden by plaster. The eaves are carried on a moulded beam above a plaster cove. Reeded pilasters, sill and corner-roundels of an early 19th-century shop front remain at the S. end. The upper windows have leaded casements. The chimney stack on the W. is very broad at the base and sets back in stages. The interior walls have been removed except for one at the N. end enclosing an entry; beams, now cased, indicate that a former cross-wall divided the space unequally into a larger central room with fireplace in the rear wall, and a small, unheated room on the S. An original close-studded cross-partition, reaching to the ridge, exists on the first floor.

(336) HOUSE, No. 10 (Fig. 164), two storeys, stone and timber-framed, comprises the N. half of a 12th-century house of stone which was partially rebuilt in the late Middle Ages and again altered in the 19th

century. The building incorporates at one side of the street front a 12th-century doorway of two orders, the inner roll-moulded, the outer zig-zag, with rebated inner jamb; it is *in situ* (Plate 65). In the rubble side wall beyond this doorway is part of a half-round arch which springs from a mutilated chamfered capital just above ground-floor level. The arch is now blocked but during demolition of the adjacent house on the S. (No. 9A) in 1885 it was seen to be of two chamfered orders, semicircular, 14 ft. span, and springing from chamfered jamb and column. Parts of other corresponding imposts were found on the site, showing that at least one other arch stood near (*Mercury*, 15 Jan., 12 Mar. 1886). The 12th-century house measured therefore at least 36 ft. from front to rear, and perhaps about 40 ft. wide, this being the combined widths of Nos. 9A and 10; the ground stage was clearly an unvaulted undercroft, domestic accommodation being on the first floor.

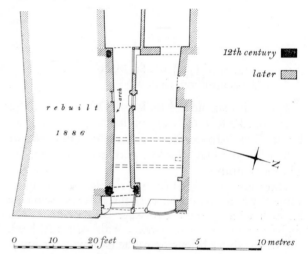

Fig. 164   (336) 9A–10 St. Mary's Hill.
Plan showing possible extent of 12th-century house.

The surviving late medieval structure (Plate 78; drawing by Twopeny, 1829, 290/d. 9, p. 34) is a rebuilding of the first floor of the N. part of the original house. It has a close-studded gable wall facing the street, heavily plastered in imitation of patterned timbering in 1881 (*Mercury*, 2 Jan. 1882). The first floor was originally open to the roof; this roof has collars which clasp purlins, and straight windbraces to the principals, and was originally three bays long but only the E. bay and a tie-beam survive. At the W. end alterations in the late 19th century have removed most early features.

(337) HOUSES, Nos. 11 and 12, a pair, built in 1790 for the Earl of Exeter by John Pearson, mason, at a cost

above £387 (Exeter Day Books, 1791). The houses are three storeys high with coursed rubble walls, freestone dressings and quoins. Below the low stone parapet is a bracketed cornice. The building is in six bays with sash windows and continuous sills (Fig. 10); a shop front on the S. obliterates three bays, but the N. house retains its openings including, in the outer bay, a doorway with gothic glazing bars in the fanlight. The elevation is symmetrical and the plan of each house conforms to class 13b, but the S. house is wider than that on the N. Interior fittings are plain and mostly early 19th-century; fireplaces have angle-roundels.

(338) HOUSE, No. 13 (Figs. 165, 166), has an under-croft, and some features in the upper walls, of the early 13th century. It now has two storeys and attics above the undercroft, and the walls are of coursed rubble. The main range was considerably altered in the 17th century. A rear range in timber-framing with brick infilling may date from the early 18th century.

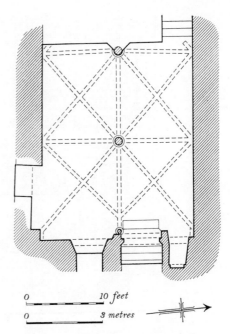

Fig. 166　(338) 13 St. Mary's Hill. Plan of undercroft.

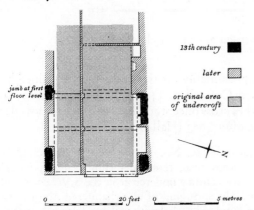

Fig. 165　(338) 13 St. Mary's Hill. Ground-floor plan showing probable original area of undercroft.

The undercroft is two bays wide (N.-S.) and now two bays long (E.-W.), but it was originally at least one bay longer (Plate 58). It has a quadripartite vault of round arches, chamfered ribs and a central row of circular columns with capitals and simple bases. The W. column is partly embedded in the later W. wall and a rib for the third bay survives in the N.W. corner. One wall corbel is carved with a male head, the rest are mask-shaped. The E. wall, largely unaltered, contains a large and a small window flanking a doorway with steps leading up to street level. The diagonal ribs meet the central transverse rib above the springing, so allowing the vault-web to avoid the segmental rear-arches of the door and windows (Plate 58). The doorway is flanked by an attached shaft carrying the vault-ribs and by a rectangular pier of freestone. In the S. wall is a blocked roundheaded doorway of the 18th century.

Above ground, the main range occupies the area over the E. half of the undercroft. Although basically of the 17th century, the range contains, on the N. at ground-floor level, almost two bays of early 13th-century wall-arcading (Plate 62). It was discovered and rebuilt in 1890 (Mercury, 14 Mar.), and consists of shafts with bell-shaped capitals, standing on a ledge; the roundheaded arches are chamfered at the springing with broach stops, but the heads are plain. The rear wall appears remodelled. Other 13th-century features occur at the S.W. corner of the front range, and comprise a voussoir for an opening in a former N.-S. wall and, immediately above it on the first floor, a chamfered door jamb (at least 7 ft. tall) with a rebate on its E. side. It may therefore be conjectured that the 13th-century house consisted of an undercroft two bays wide and at least three bays long, entered and lit from the street side. It was probably used as a shop. The ground-floor rooms appear to have been ceiled slightly above the head of the wall-arcading and, to judge from the assumed length of the undercroft, they comprised a front and rear room extending to the full width of the property. A similar arrangement of two rooms probably existed on the first floor, and the size of the door between them would suggest that they were the principal rooms.

The general appearance, both inside and out, is now due to alterations since the 17th century. A chamfered tie beam has stepped stops. The three-storey rear wing contains a wooden mullion-and-transom window of the early 18th century; one room has reset 17th-century panelling of unknown provenance.

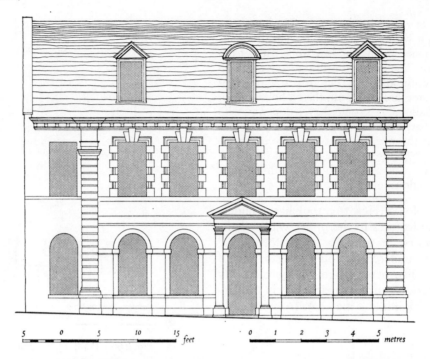

Fig. 167   (341) 2 St. Mary's Place. Reconstruction of front elevation.

(339) HOUSES, Nos. 14–16, and Nos. 31–32 St. Mary's Street, a row of five, each of three storeys, attics and cellars, have walls of coursed rubble with freestone dressings. Payments of £380 to Thomas Manton, mason, and £914 to George Pilkington, carpenter, are recorded in the Exeter Day Book for 1780–1; the total cost was £1,799. Nos. 14–15 were begun in 1780 and the other three in the following year.

The row has a roof parallel with the street, and each house has two short hipped roofs at right angles at the rear. The street elevations have sash windows and continuous sills but the rear windows have wooden mullions and transoms with leaded lights and iron casements, all of the same date. The houses conform to class 14b in plan. Fittings are uniform and generally plain. In the basement are cupboards with ventilation grilles of shaped wooden slats.

ST. MARY'S PLACE (Fig. 169)

The early importance of St. Mary's Place is demonstrated by the fragment of a 13th-century undercroft (340) and the undercroft possibly of the guildhall of the guild of Corpus Christi (342); it is now dominated by the Town Hall (57) and the large house (341). It was formerly called Monday Market, the name appearing in the 16th century, and

was presumably the site of the market gained by the Town Council in 1481 (Cal. Chart. VI, 253–4). A market cross once stood here and was removed some time after 1683 (Hall Book 2, 103).

(340) HOUSE, No. 1, two storeys, attics and cellar, ashlar front wall, remainder rubble, incorporates part of a 13th-century undercroft in the S.W. corner of the cellar. The springing of one chamfered rib of the vault and a moulded corbel with nail-head decoration survive. The main range, next to the street, of class 10 plan, has a 17th-century roof with cambered tie beam and a windbrace; the ashlar refronting, with large sash windows, is early 19th-century. The rear wing may also be 17th-century, and was further extended at a later date. Interior fittings in the front range include bolection-moulded panelling on both floors, a fireplace surround with egg-and-dart enrichment, of the early 18th century, and panelling and fireplace of c. 1840. The early 18th-century stair has square newel and turned balusters. The later rear wing has a roof with reused blackened timbers. All the attic floors are plastered.

(341) HOUSE, Nos. 2–3 (Plates 100, 103), two storeys and attics, ashlar front wall, was built in the early 18th century. In the early 19th century it was largely rebuilt and greatly extended at the rear by the addition of three-storey rubble-walled wings.

The early range (Fig. 167; Plate 103), on the W., is of six bays, and to the S. is a slightly later extension of two bays (Plate 100). The main house has an asymmetrical street front, the S. five bays forming a symmetrical elevation defined by rusticated Tuscan pilasters; all the openings on the ground floor have round heads, plain architraves and continuous sills (Fig. 12) and imposts; the central door is further elaborated with pilasters, pulvinated frieze and triangular pediment. Above a broad platband, the first-floor windows have continuous sills, rusticated architraves and triple keystones; there are three pedimented dormers. The windows in the N. bay have the same form as the others but have single keystones and no architraves. The whole elevation is united by a wooden dentilled eaves cornice. The S. window was made a doorway when the house was subdivided shortly before 1833. The slightly later two-bay addition on the S. is marked by superimposed Tuscan pilasters (Fig. 14) rising from a plinth and supporting a cornice at both first floor and eaves level. The windows have eared architraves and triple keystones; the segmental dormers are early 19th-century.

Sometime in the early 19th century, but before 1833 (Knipe's map), the front part of the house was refitted and the rear entirely rebuilt and enlarged. Three rear wings with hipped roofs were built, each of three storeys and of coursed rubble with flush dressings. Also four single-storey rooms were added further to the E. Of these last the S., in ashlar of three bays with hipped roof, may have been a library; above the tall sash windows are blind rectangular panels and a moulded eaves cornice. To the N. was a kitchen, in coursed rubble. Further N. are two detached ashlar out-buildings, also with hipped roofs.

Inside, the main stair and most fittings, including plaster friezes with Greek key and other decoration, are early 19th-century. On the ground floor the N. room retains 18th-century fielded panelling in two heights. The S. room, of grand proportions, has similar panelling with dentil cornice, and a coved and moulded plaster ceiling, all perhaps early 18th-century but restored in the early 19th century (Plate 131). The plaster decoration is probably of the latter date. The former library has a plaster ceiling in early 18th-century style (Plate 131).

(342) HOUSE, No. 4, incorporates a single room of early 18th-century date in the angle between the later front range and rear wing. The main building, of class IIa plan, was constructed in 1790–1 by John Hames, mason; he received £344. 10. o. and John Boyfield was paid £477 for work by carpenters, joiners, painters and glaziers (Exeter Day Book).

Beneath the E. end of the main range is a vaulted undercroft, comprising one complete bay and part of a second; the carved detail suggests a late 14th or 15th-century date (Fig. 168; Plate 63). The quadripartite vault

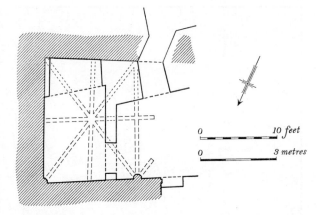

Fig. 168　(342) 4 St. Mary's Place. Plan of undercroft.

springs from semi-octagonal corner shafts and has deeply chamfered ribs with central boss carved with an angel holding a shield. To the W. there is also a foliated boss at the intersection of the ridge and transverse ribs. Part of a rebated door jamb in the N. wall of the second bay is all that remains of a doorway to the street. Various walls, perhaps of c. 1790, now support the vault and form partitions. In 1674 this undercroft was described as 'the cellar under the guild hall' (Ex. MS, 86/5). Of the two guilds associated with St. Mary's church, that of Corpus Christi had a guildhall which in the 15th century was used by the Town Council (Hall Books). The surviving undercroft may have formed part of this guildhall.

The front range, of three storeys, attics and cellar, is in five bays with central doorway; all windows have continuous sills and there is a stone eaves cornice. A small doorway leads to a curved passage across the N.E. corner of the building. The distorted rear wall possibly conforms with the alignment of an earlier structure. The rear wing of two storeys and attics, under a mansard roof, has ashlar W. wall, the remainder of rubble; on the E. are large chimney stacks. The staircase of 1791, in the rear wing, is plain in design.

ST. MARY'S STREET (Fig. 169)

This street marks the S. limit of the Danish burh. The W. half became part of the Great North Road after the building of the bridge. Shops are recorded in the 14th century (PRO, C 14/147) and a building lease of 1434 specifies a shop with solar (PRO, E 315/31 p. 3). The George and Angel (350) was an important inn in the late Middle Ages, and No. 19 (355) was probably also an inn. In the early 19th century the Black Bull Inn was rebuilt as the Stamford Hotel (352). By the 18th century the present distinction between the commercial W. half of the

Fig. 169　Map showing monuments in St. John's Street, St. Mary's Hill, St. Mary's Place and St. Mary's Street.

street and the professional E. half was emerging; however the Earl of Exeter built several large private houses in the W. half in 1785 and 1791 and the distinction only crystalized in the early 19th century. The long sequence of high-quality houses from the 12th to 18th centuries indicates the importance which this street has always enjoyed (Plate 98).

In the early 19th century there were several proposals to link the top of St. Mary's Hill with High Street (*Stamford News*, 16 Dec. 1834) which resulted in 1849 in the abortive scheme represented by mon. 350.

(343) HOUSE, Nos. 1–2, three storeys, attics, cellar, red brick walls, with hipped roof, was built in *c.* 1830–40 as an unequal pair of dwellings, later united. The ground floor is now a shop. In the larger house part of the staircase in the centre of the block and a fireplace with angle-roundels survive.

(344) HOUSE AND SHOP, No. 4 (Plate 139), class 11a,

has two storeys, stone walls and mansard roof with attics. It was built *c.* 1791–2 as the rectory for St. John's church, the former parsonage being unfit for habitation (LAO, 3/32). In 1792 the Earl of Exeter gave £100 towards its cost (Exeter Day Books). At the rear is an earlier wing of the mid 18th century which has iron casement windows. In the early 19th century a shop front with two bow windows was added together with a single-storey rear extension on the E. Inside, the former central passage has been removed. In the earlier rear wing is a plain early 19th-century stair. On the first floor is an imported late 18th-century fireplace with wooden surround enriched with paterae, foliage swags and a central pineapple.

(345) HOUSE, Nos. 5–6, two storeys and attics with stone walls, comprises a late medieval house of class 1 or 2, with two later rear wings, the E. of the 16th century and the W. of the late 18th century. In 1604 the house formed part of the endowment of Snowden's Hospital (52). The street elevation, largely rebuilt in the 18th century, has two modern or rebuilt shop fronts with bow windows; a doorway with one double hollow-

chamfered jamb survives at No. 6 (E. house), and at the S.E. corner is a tall buttress with weathered top, both of medieval date. Inside, the W. house (No. 5), formerly the hall, has a fireplace at the W. end of the rear wall and a heavy axial beam, both possibly secondary. To the E. of the original entrance, a heavy chamfered cross beam and an axial beam define a smaller, probably service, room. Two tie beams with double hollow-chamfers and formerly with hollow-chamfered braces survive on the first floor. The rear wing behind No. 6 consists of two rooms, the N. having a 16th-century ovolo-and-hollow moulded beam, a three-light window with chamfered mullions, and 18th-century panelling in two heights. The S. room, once possibly open to the roof, has floor joists of reused 16th-century timbers. Both the front range and this wing were reroofed, using ancient material, probably in the 17th century. Behind No. 5, another rear wing of two-room plan with hipped roof was added in the late 18th century.

(346) HOUSE, No. 8, class 5, two storeys and attics, with stone walls, has mansard roofs. Chamfered beams in the S. part imply a 17th-century origin but the house was largely rebuilt in the early 19th century; the interior is mostly gutted.

(347) HOUSE, No. 9 (Fig. 171), two storeys, timber-framed, with gable walls of stone, incorporates part of a late 12th or early 13th-century structure. This early work (Fig. 170) consists of two and a half bays of arcading, now blocked and forming the side, or W., wall of the house. The arches are chamfered, the columns octagonal, and one chamfered capital survives. The half arch, at the N. end, terminates on a chamfered jamb and appears to be an original feature; the central arch has been largely removed, and the S. arch is partly obscured.
The present house dates from the 16th or 17th century

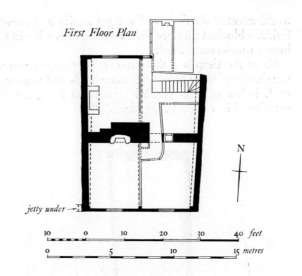

Fig. 171   (347) 9 St. Mary's Street.

and comprises two parallel ranges, jettied on the S. and underbuilt in stone on the N. A two-light window in the rear wall implies a 17th-century date for the underbuilding. Pargetting on the W. gable simulates scalloped barge-boarding. Inside, on the first floor, the ranges each contain one large room; the two-bay roofs have arch-braced tie beams, coupled rafters and clasped purlins. Heavy close-studding has down-braces.

(348) HOUSE AND SHOP, No. 10 (Fig. 172; Plate 141), two storeys and attics, class 5, with walls partly stone and partly timber-framed, has a 16th or 17th-century origin; a shop front with two bow windows flanking the door, and single bow above, were added in the early 19th century. The front wall is timber-framed and jettied. In the stone rear wall are the remains of an ovolo-moulded mullioned window of five lights. The roof is parallel

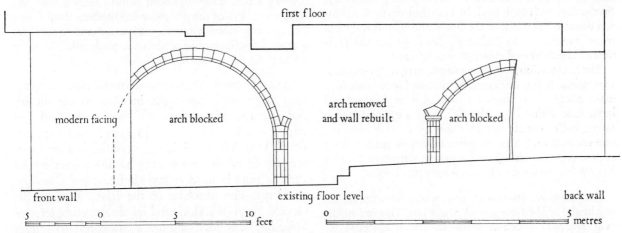

Fig. 170   (347) 9 St. Mary's Street. Remains of late 12th-century arcade.

to the street at the front and at right angles at the rear. Inside, a blocked fireplace on the ground floor is said to have a four-centred head.

N. of the shop is a three-storey early 19th-century warehouse of three bays with stone walls and mansard roof. It has an iron-wheeled winch and hoist, and is mentioned in a sale of 1845 (deeds).

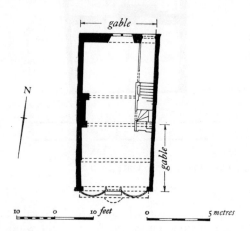

Fig. 172   (348) 10 St. Mary's Street.

(349) HOUSE, Nos. 11–12, originated as a stone building of class 1a plan and was built in the 14th or early 15th century, parallel to the street with the hall at the W. end. In the early 16th century the E. section was rebuilt as a two-storied, timber-framed and jettied range with blind tracery on each storey between the windows; a central timber-framed jettied porch was also added to the hall entrance. The building was illustrated by Stukeley in 1735 (Plate 70; Designs, p. 20). Of this building only two windbraced roof trusses, one closed with studding, survive. Stukeley described the hall as having a large stone window full of painted glass, and a gilded ceiling. In the early 18th century, the hall was altered by Boniface Bywater, whitesmith, to make a shop (Stukeley, *Surtees Soc.* 76 (1863), 324). In 1748 Alderman Williamson demolished much of the house and rebuilt the main front (annotation on Stukeley's drawing) but the position of the medieval entrance was retained.

The S. elevation, two storeys and attics, is symmetrical with ashlar front, rusticated quoins, and stone moulded eaves course. The windows have plain architraves and keystones. Behind, on the W., is a long two-storey range, built possibly in two stages in the 17th century; one encased roof truss, its principals apparently having curved feet, remains. The lower and narrower N. part has ovolo-moulded and chamfered cross beams.

(350) HOUSES, SHOPS AND BUILDINGS, Nos. 13–14, are on the site of the George and Angel Inn. This late medieval inn was acquired from Browne's Hospital by Richard Newcomb in 1843 (LAO, AT/40) with the intention of creating a new street between St. Mary's Hill and High Street, but only two shops were built. The remaining part of the George and Angel, on the E. side of a narrow yard, of two storeys, stone rubble walls, freestone dressings, in two sections of different heights, is late 18th-century. The ground floor, formerly a kitchen, has heavy chamfered cross beams. The first floor was fitted out as an assembly room in the early 19th century. It was lit by two large windows and has a projecting closet carried on brackets. A separate parallel range on the W. consists of a smithy, open to the roof, and is early 19th-century.

As part of the proposed street between St. Mary's Hill and High Street two matching three-storey buildings with curved corners (Nos. 14 and 15) were built at the S. entrance in about 1849 (Plate 158). An advertisement for tenants for the completed buildings appeared in 1849 (*Mercury*, 26 Sept.). Each has elegant shop fronts on both streets, composed of five Ionic columns, entablature with a frieze having anthemion enrichment; a decorative iron lamp bracket is over the corner entrance (Plate 139).

(351) HOUSE AND SHOPS, No. 15 (Plate 108), two storeys, attics and cellar, now in five bays, with ashlar front and rubble rear walls, was built in the early 18th century. In 1775–6 the E. section was rebuilt as a separate shop and house with an elevation consisting of two closely spaced shop windows, a doorway and a window to a parlour, all beneath a pentice. The design and arrangement of the upper windows, then numbering six for the whole front, was retained; an estimate for £206. 3. 7. for rebuilding, excluding the cost of dismantling, was received from Pilkington, Pearson and Burton on 9 October 1775 (Ex. MS, 89/24) (Fig. 173). By 1822 (Drakard, opp. p. 336) a bow window had replaced the former shop windows, and the doorway had been moved to the W.; at about the same time the E. first-floor window was blocked. Also in the early 19th century a rear wing was built behind both E. and W. tenements. W. of the doorway are modern shop fronts but five first-floor windows with eared architraves and double keystones remain above a platband. No early features remain internally.

(352) Former STAMFORD HOTEL, No. 16 (Fig. 174; Plate 152), was begun in 1810 on the site of, and incorporating parts of, the Black Bull Inn which was first mentioned in 1546 (LAO 1545/6 i, 17; ii, 137). The surviving parts of this inn are 18th-century or earlier; some may be those described in 1786 as 'built in modern style in freestone' (*Mercury*, 26 May). The purchase of the Black Bull by Sir Gerard Noel of Exton, and its almost complete rebuilding, was part of Noel's campaign to attract political and electoral support against the Exeter

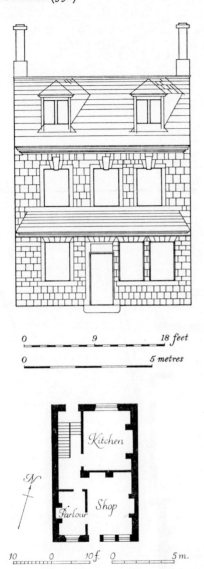

0   9   18 feet

0   5 metres

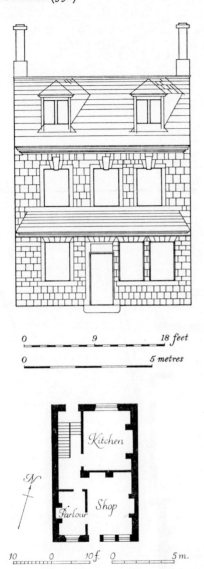

Kitchen

N

Parlour   *Shop*

10   0   10 f.   0   5 m.

Fig. 173 (351) 15 St. Mary's Street. Copy of plan and elevation accompanying estimate for rebuilding in 1775.

interest in Stamford. Work began in 1810 to designs by J. L. Bond of London, who was at the same time engaged on Exton Hall for Noel. Most of the ashlar came from Noel's own quarries near Ketton, and Roche Stone from near Leeds was also used (Drakard, 376). By 1813 the S. range was sufficiently advanced for Noel to give a dinner for his election committee (*Mercury*, 10 Dec.). Work ceased about this time following Noel's defeat at the election of 1812, and the hotel remained empty until 1825 when it was leased to Thomas Standwell. It was reopened 'to accommodate families of highest distinction in superior style' (*Mercury*, 12 Aug. and 1 Oct. 1825). Some minor additions at the rear were

made at this date. In 1845 the hotel was sold and further improvements were carried out (Burton, 194; *Mercury*, 9 Oct. 1846).

The street front is a noble example of neo-Classical architecture although insensitive in size and scale for such a constricted site. Much external and internal decoration is closely derived from Hellenistic originals.

The building consists of a main block, almost square in plan and practically all of 1810, and a rear wing of various earlier dates. The street front, of three storeys with fine ashlar walls, has horizontal rustication to the lowest stage, and above, the centre seven of nine bays are articulated by a giant Corinthian Order composed of engaged unfluted columns and capitals supporting an architrave, plain frieze and cornice enriched with anthemion decoration and lions' heads. The outer bays balance except for the segmental-headed carriage entry on the W. which is reflected as a windowed recess on the E. The lower windows have sashes but the two upper tiers have casements. Above the attic parapet (Plate 152), ornamented only with rinceau decoration over the outer bays, is a stepped podium enriched with wreaths and palmettes, and carrying a seated classical figure of Justice in artificial stone, by John Rossi according to Gunnis (*Dictionary*, 328). The lintel of the main entrance has scroll decoration, and above is a long balcony with iron balustrade composed of classical and gothic motifs. The rear of the building by contrast is in coursed rubble and is without architectural distinction save that many of the corners are rounded.

The N. wing, partly early 18th-century, consists of two adjoining parallel ranges, and the roof returns to the W. at the far end. The W. of the ranges, possibly incorporating a pre-18th-century structure in the N. half, is of two storeys and attics, with mostly ashlared walls, windows with moulded stone surrounds, and a wooden heavily dentilled eaves cornice (Plate 118). An early 19th-century elliptically-headed carriageway is now blocked on the W., but the upper four windows of the 18th century remain. The E. wall of the range, of two storeys, has sections in ashlar, coursed rubble and later brick; the range is 18th-century and later.

Inside the main block the entrance hall has elliptical arches with scrollwork decoration on the soffits, elliptical wall-arches, and a circular central panel supported on pendentives which are decorated with circles containing lions' heads (Plate 137). Capitals and dado rails are enriched with classical decoration, and a doorway has eared architrave with battered sides. Beyond, the round-ended stair hall has a stone cantilever stair with plain balustrade, and is lit from a large circular lantern having windows in the drum and an oculus in the dome, all decorated with bands of palmette and other classical patterns. The lofty main ground-floor rooms are grouped in double depth around the entrance and stair

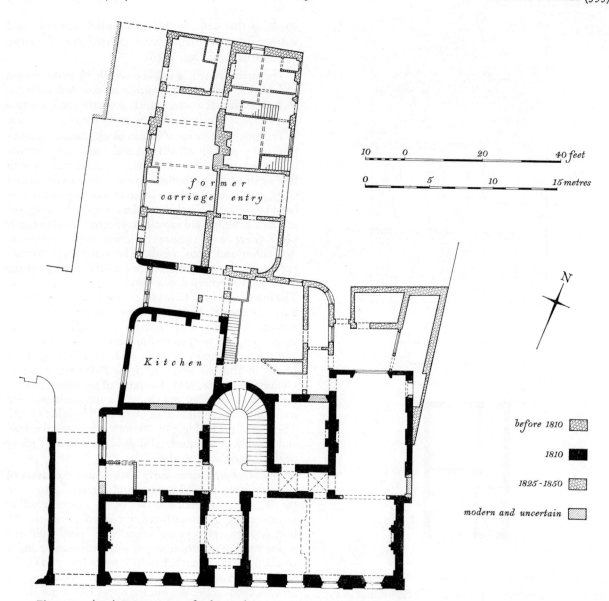

Fig. 174   (352) Former Stamford Hotel.

hall, but the arbitrary plan of the rear rooms may reflect the slow growth of the building. The room E. of the entrance originally comprised two unequally sized rooms, and is now amalgamated with a third on the N.E. Leading off the stair hall is a passage with groined vaulting. Most of the rooms have plaster cornices enriched with classical ornament. Stone fireplace surrounds are individually designed with rounded pilasters with palmette and other decoration (Plate 153). Doorcases are finely moulded (Fig. 175). In the stair hall is a projecting sashed bay window with curved corners, forming an office counter, perhaps dating from the improvements of 1845. On the first floor are a number of large rooms, the principal being the ballroom. This room of five

bays was originally two storeys high with a gallery at the W. end and a segmental ceiling; a floor was inserted at gallery level in 1926 by Traylen. Tall wall pilasters with capitals and anthemion enrichment are cut by the modern ceiling (Plate 153). The lower windows on the E. have eared architraves and battered sides, and on the N. are shallow roundheaded wall-recesses. The fireplace has a Tudor head but the surround is of Egyptian character with pilasters and capitals of exaggerated proportions.

(353) HOUSE, No. 17 (Fig. 7), two storeys with attics, class 4, timber-framed, has hipped roof end-on to the street; it is perhaps 17th-century. The formerly jettied front has been underbuilt in ashlar and the W.

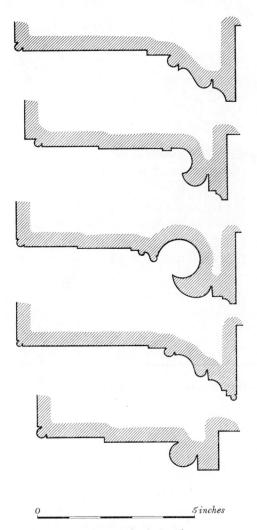

0   5 inches

Fig. 175 (352) Stamford Hotel.
Profiles of internal door surrounds.

wall totally rebuilt in rubble. Inside, heavy roughly chamfered beams define four bays on each floor; the two N. bays are an early addition. The roof has staggered purlins.

(354) HOUSE AND SHOP, No. 18, three storeys and attics, ashlar front wall and mansard roof, now class 13, is early 19th-century. At the rear is a late medieval two-storey range, originally timber-framed but partly replaced in stone or brick; it was curtailed on the S. by the later house. The 19th-century block has a contemporary shop front consisting of a central door flanked by bow windows; the ground floor of the interior has been gutted. The early range has a smoke-blackened crown-post roof with ogee-shaped braces between tie beam and crown post and originally straight braces between crown post and collar purlin (Plate 76). Two trusses survive defining an 8 ft. bay; the distance from the N.

wall to the street allows for a five-bay roof. The medieval roof has been strengthened by purlins and struts, possibly in the 17th century.

(355) THE VAULTS, former Eagle and Child Inn, No. 19, includes buildings from the late Middle Ages to the 19th century, ranged on three, originally four, sides of a courtyard. The front range is largely medieval but alterations in the 18th and 19th centuries to the part W. of the carriage entrance have obscured early features. The two rear ranges are probably 17th-century. The two-storey E. part of the front range consists of two rooms, and a gabled and jettied carriageway; it is timber-framed with stone underbuilding. A formerly external stair on the yard side serves the upper rooms. Inside, on the first floor, is a fireplace with stone jambs and moulded timber bressummer, possibly late 16th-century. The roof has windbraces and clasped purlins. The central beam of the carriageway is moulded and on the jetty bressummer is a carved wooden head on a diamond of foliage. The rear ranges have stone walls except for the ultimate two-storey compartment on the W. which was originally timber-framed but is now largely of stone; this latter has a three-bay roof with two tiers of collars clasping purlins, and two windows with ovolo-moulded mullions. The remainder of the range, comprising service rooms, has divisions and chimney stacks of the 18th century. The two-storey E. range, probably also 17th-century, has heavy chamfered cross beams.

(356) HOUSE, No. 20 (Plate 147), three storeys and attics, stone walls, has a two-storey rear wing on the N. It incorporates a late medieval L-shaped house of class 5 partly rebuilt and enlarged to form a house approximating to class 12 in the 18th and 19th centuries. The jettied street front was underbuilt and refaced in the mid 18th century and further heightened in c. 1800; the rear wing was extended in the 18th century. The doorway has lattice fanlight and a porch (Plate 124) composed of free-standing columns, frieze enriched with fleurs-de-lis, and a cornice and open pediment both with mutules, probably c. 1800. To one side is a two-storey bay window with canted sides.

(357) HOUSE AND OFFICE, Nos. 21–22 (Fig. 178; Plates 106, 147), comprise a class 9a house (No. 22) of the second quarter of the 18th century on the E., and an office block (No. 21) built shortly after 1827 on the W. The house may be that in St. Mary's parish which Leonard Stevenson bought from William Lindsey in 1748 (Court Rolls); it was stated to be new in 1773 when Stevenson insured it with the Sun Company (Policy 3129757) although this description cannot be taken too precisely. In 1827 the owner, Thomas Hippisley Jackson, solicitor, obtained the site of No. 21 by exchange from

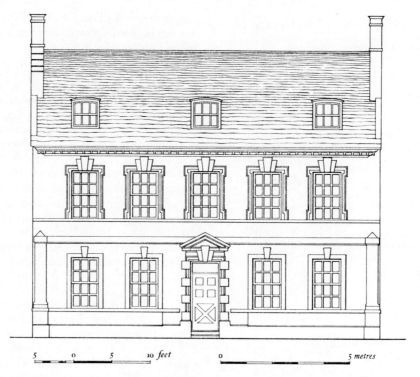

Fig. 176 (357) 22 St. Mary's Street. Reconstruction of front elevation.

the Marquess of Exeter, and afterwards built the present offices for his own use (deeds).

At the rear of the class 9 house there is a 17th-century wing. The large chimney stack in its N. wall suggests that this was a kitchen of a former house of which there are no other remains.

The *House*, of two storeys and attics, ashlar front and coursed rubble rear walls, has at the front a roof parallel with the street, and twin roofs at right angles at the rear. The street front of five bays has a central doorway with moulded surround, rustication, triple keystone and pediment (Figs. 176, 177). The lower windows have plain surrounds, continuous sills and keystones, but the upper have eared and moulded surrounds, shaped at the foot, and triple keystones. The sills of the four outer windows have been lowered to the level of a wide platband in the late 19th century, and the formerly continuous sill now returns to the platband. The ground stage terminates with two pilasters around which the lower sills and the platband are continued. The gable chimney stack has five flues linked by arcading (Plate 120). Inside, two upper rooms have panelling in two heights; one has a fireplace with eared surround and overmantel with pediment and pilasters, 18th-century (Plate 127). The staircase, also 18th-century, has turned balusters. The main roof has principals with curved feet.

The *Office* of c. 1827 has red brick walls and a front of Wittering Pindle with freestone dressings and quoins

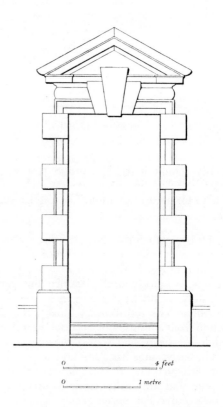

Fig. 177 (357) 22 St. Mary's Street. Doorway.

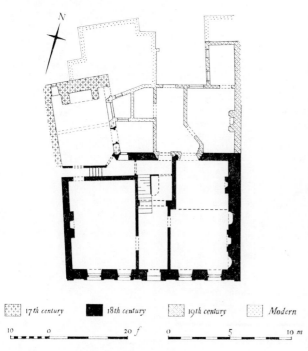

17th century   18th century   19th century   Modern

10   0   20 f   0   5   10 m

Fig. 178   (357) 22 St. Mary's Street.

(Plate 120); it is designed in the Gothic style and comprises two rooms, back to back. The street elevation comprises a central roundheaded window with intersecting glazing bars, flanked by two pointed-headed doorways, one leading to a through passage giving access to the office, garden and house; the other formerly served the cellars which were in separate occupation, but a later passage now leads to the rear room. The upper windows have pointed heads, moulded labels and Gothic glazing bars. At the rear is a small wing containing a strongroom. Fittings include a fireplace with reeded surround and angle-roundels.

(358) HOUSE AND OFFICE, Nos. 23–24 (Plates 100, 107), are now united. No. 23, the house on the W., was described in 1753 as having been built by Edward Seabrook, wool stapler, on ground where a tenement previously stood (deeds). No. 24 was built by James Bellaers, merchant, sometime after 1754, when the land was described as void, but well before 1779 when it was described as an 'accompting house' having domestic accommodation on the upper floors with access to No. 23 (deeds of 1779, and marriage agreement). In the 19th century the houses were separated, and are now again in single occupation.

No. 23, of two storeys and attics, has ashlar walls and five-bay street front. The windows have plain architraves on the ground floor and eared above, all with keystones in relief; the two outer bays are linked by continuous sills. The central doorway has a pedimented surround with Ionic pilasters (Fig. 179), and the door has fielded panelling arranged as quadrants. The moulded cornice has dentils (Plate 122), and the three dormers have straight and curved pediments. The interior, of class 11b plan, is entirely of the mid 18th century and includes fielded panelling and eared surrounds to doorways. Access to the stair hall is through a round-headed archway with key block and spandrel foliage, and to the far room through a pedimented doorway with fluted pilasters and Doric frieze (Plate 135). The staircase has moulded balusters, open string with scroll brackets, and panelled dado. The five-bay roof has principal rafters, curved at the feet. Beyond the rear wing is a small late 18th-century bath wing with quadripartite vault on each level.

No. 24, of two storeys and attics, has ashlar walls. The three-bay street elevation had a central entrance, as shown by the scars of a door-pediment, but in the early 19th century it was transposed with the W. window; the interior was consequently altered with a stair placed axially to the new entrance. These alterations were probably carried out after 1814 when the firm of Bellaers went bankrupt (*Mercury*, 5 Aug.). The ground-floor openings have plain surrounds, the upper being moulded, all with keystones in relief; the panelling of the door repeats that of No. 23. The wooden cornice has shaped brackets. One of the two original offices has fielded panelling.

0   4 feet
0   1 metre

Fig. 179   (358) 23 St. Mary's Street. Doorway.

Fig. 180 (360) 26 St. Mary's Street. Front elevation of N. range.

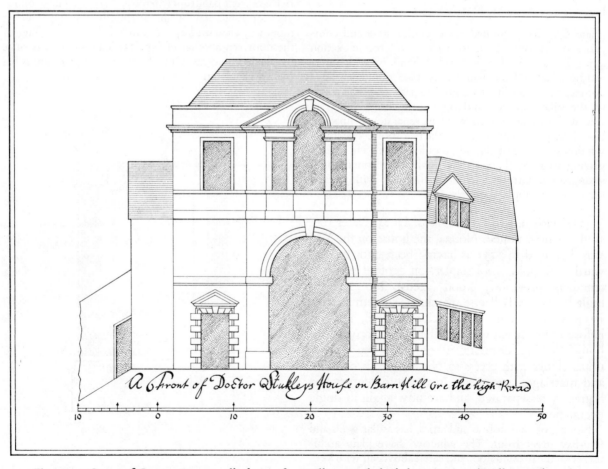

A Front of Doctor Stukleys House on Barn Hill ore the high Road

Fig. 181 Copy of George Portwood's design for William Stukeley's house, 1741. (Bodleian Library)

(359) HOUSES, No. 25 St. Mary's Street and No. 13 Maiden Lane (Plate 109), a pair each of class 12 plan, with cellar, attics, mansard roof, and ashlar front wall. The S. house (No. 25) was built *c.* 1766 by John Hopkins on a building lease from the Earl of Exeter. In 1772 Hopkins was accused of encroaching on the street with a bay window (Ex. MS, 90/54); in the following year he bought the site of the N. house (No. 13) and built the present house forthwith.

No. 25 has a canted bay window of two storeys between two pilasters and pedimented doorways (Fig. 182). The parapet has a moulded cornice and terminal urns. The rear wall of rubble has a timber-framed jettied upper storey. Inside, the entrance hall of No. 25 has fluted and marbled half columns supporting round arches, and the W. room has a plaster dentil cornice. No. 13 has similar decoration internally.

(360) HOUSE, No. 26 (Plate 109), two storeys and attics, ashlar walls, class 11a, consists of three ranges on the N., E. and W. sides of a small garden. The W. range was built in the second quarter of the 18th century, and the N. range was added towards the middle of the century. Perhaps *c.* 1766, when the owner John Hopkins built the adjoining house on the N. (359), the W. elevation of the W. range was heightened to match its neighbour. The E. range, formerly a coach house, was rebuilt in the early 19th century. The S. elevation of the N. wing has affinities with an unexecuted design by George Portwood (probably senior) for a house for Dr. Stukeley, but this design was for a building of considerably larger scale (Fig. 181; Harris in Rogers, 84, 85).

The three-bay W. elevation of the W. range has a pedimented doorcase with semicircular fanlight. The heightening of the façade in 1766 is marked by blind panels above the windows, a block cornice, and a parapet formerly surmounted by urns. This heightening is also visible on the S. gable. The S. elevation of the N. range (Fig. 180; Plate 104) has a central Venetian window below a pediment; on the ground stage are two round-headed recesses, the E. containing a door and the W. originally an open porch. Inside, the W. range has a stone fireplace of individual design (Plate 128), and a staircase with turned balusters (Plate 133), all second quarter of the 18th century. The first-floor room in the N. range has an enriched plaster ceiling of the mid 18th century (Plate 136).

(361) HOUSE, No. 27 (Plate 116), was built in 1794–6 at a cost of over £728 (Exeter Day Books). At the same time a two-storey link with the Assembly Rooms was built on the S., comprising a lobby

Fig. 182   (359) 25 St. Mary's Street. Doorway.

and formerly a kitchen. The masonry was undertaken by William Pearson for about £270; two marble fireplaces supplied by Edward Bingham for £20 do not remain.

The house is of three storeys with cellar, and the walls are of coursed rubble with ashlar quoins and dressings (Plate 121). The symmetrical main front on the N. is in five bays with plain parapets and moulded and bracketed cornice; all openings have stepped keystones and the upper windows all have continuous sills (Fig. 10). The four-bay E. front and the two-bay link block continues the same treatment. Inside, fittings of 1794–6 include an elliptical-headed recess with panelled reveals, cupboard-recesses arranged to balance doorways, staircase with plain balusters and turned newels, and moulded stone fireplace surrounds of simple design. Reset in cellar are sections of bolection-moulded panelling of the early 18th century.

(362) ST. MARY'S RECTORY, No. 28 (Fig. 183; Plate 71), of two storeys with stone walls, probably retains much of a medieval open hall with a single cross wing (class 1b). The walls have been periodically rebuilt and in the front, N., wall is (1) the reset head of a two-light roundheaded window of the 12th-century, the concealed face said to be moulded (*Mercury*, 13 Sept. 1895), (2) a low blocked window with chamfered reveals, perhaps once of two lights, probably medieval, and (3) a vertical straight joint of uncertain significance. Inside, the former open hall, on the W., has an inserted floor with two moulded cross beams of the 16th century.

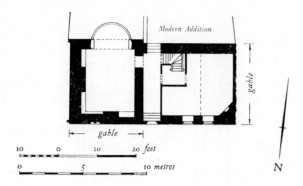

Fig. 183   (362) 28 St. Mary's Street.

The cross wing is entirely panelled in 19th-century woodwork of Gothic design, said to have been removed from the church. Fittings include a 16th-century linen-fold panelled door, a late 17th-century bolection-moulded fireplace and an early 18th-century staircase with closed string and turned balusters. The first-floor rooms are mostly open to the roof-collars. The roof over the hall has clasped purlins and is probably 17th-century.

(363) HOUSES, now warehouses, between Nos. 28 and 29, two storeys with squared rubble front wall, may on evidence of the roof have a 17th or early 18th-century origin. They comprise two buildings. That on the E., which is taller, has an 18th-century stable incorporated at the rear; the three stalls have roundheaded wooden arches with key blocks. The W. building, probably later, has a roof with tusked tenoned purlins. The lower part of the front wall is modern and the upper part featureless.

(364) HOUSE, No. 30 (Fig. 184; Plate 79), on a corner site with L-shaped plan resembling class 3, timber-framed, is late medieval; an early 19th-century room fills the angle. It has a first-floor jetty on the N. and most of the W.; a room at the S. end has a lower roof and no jetty and is probably later. The N.W. room, incorporating a chamfered dragon beam, was originally

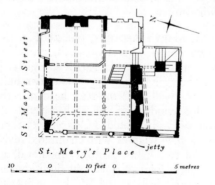

Fig. 184   (364) 30 St. Mary's Street.

of two bays with intersecting ceiling beams; it has been extended to the S. to include a third bay, perhaps a passage. A much rebuilt chimney stack on the S. has a brick quatrefoil on the W. face. Scratched in the plaster on the W. gable is the date 1605.

HOUSES, Nos. 31 and 32, see mon. 339.

(365) HOUSE, No. 33, originally two storeys, timber-framed, has a 17th-century origin. In 1784 the N. half was heightened and refronted in coursed rubble by Robert Hames at a recorded cost of £14. 2. 6. (Exeter Day Books); the new front matches the design of the adjoining houses. Scars of the roof of the original house are visible internally. The ground floor has been gutted for a shop.

(366) TERRACE, Nos. 34–36, three storeys and cellars, has coursed rubble walls with flush freestone dressings and continuous sills. The ground floor is occupied by later shops. The property was leased for 61 years by Stamford Corporation to the Earl of Exeter in January 1784 on a building lease stipulating an expenditure of £1,000. By August 1786 the Earl had spent £2,000 on the present building (Ex. MS, 47/31/26; Burton, appdx. 58). The two E. houses, Nos. 34, 35, were begun in 1784, followed by the W. house, which was built slightly forward, in 1785. The Exeter Day Books record payments of about £1,200 on these houses. John Hames received £520 for masonry, and other payments include £160 to Robert Pilkington for work on one end house, and £4. 4. 0. to John Booth for two carved chimney-pieces; a third chimney-piece was installed in No. 35 in 1786. Alterations were made to No. 35 in 1787 including a fireplace by Edward Bingham at a cost of £8. 11. 6. A coachhouse and stables were built by Thomas Manton in 1785, and in 1790 John Hames built a stable for No. 36. The houses correspond in style with others, built by the 9th Earl, with characteristic dentilled cornices. In 1784 Thomas Lumby was paid for surveying these houses.

Nos. 34 and 35 are each of class 14b but No. 36 is five bays and of class 9a plan. At the rear of No. 35 is a full-height bay window, perhaps part of the alterations of 1787. The *Stables* of No. 34, now single-storey, have coursed rubble walls, and a roundheaded doorway flanked by lunette windows now blocked; late 18th-century. Behind No. 36 are two-storey *Stables* built in 1790 (see above); the N. elevation has a low-pitched gable containing a lunette with triple keystone, above a moulded string-course at eaves level, and three round-headed ground-floor openings with keystones. The lower part of the elevation is masked by a lean-to.

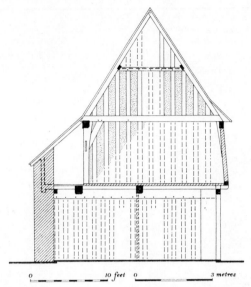

Section through front range looking West

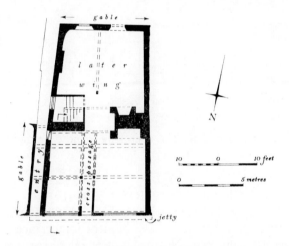

Fig. 185   (368) 40 St. Mary's Street.

(367) TERRACE, Nos. 37–39, has a street elevation similar to the adjoining terrace (Nos. 34–36) and was also built for the 9th Earl of Exeter. It was begun in 1791 and completed the following year at a total cost of £1253. 14. 6. Some of the stone was supplied to John Cole, mason, by William Legg, and carpentry was by Alice Pilkington; payments to other trades are recorded (Exeter Day Books, 1791–3). The plan of each house conforms to class 14b. In the basements are pantries with ventilation grilles formed of pierced and shaped slats.

(368) HOUSE, No. 40 (Fig. 185; Plate 79), two storeys, attics and cellar, timber-framed walls, class 2, is probably 16th-century. A rear wing may be 17th-century. The street front has a first-floor jetty but the ground stage is entirely modern; the upper stage with recently exposed and heavily restored close-studding has modern windows. The house extends over a narrow entry at the E. end. Internally, the main range is gutted but the pattern of beams, with mortices for former partitions, shows that the ground-floor plan originally consisted of a cross passage with the main room on the W. and two smaller rooms on the E. The first floor consists of two large rooms. The house was built and roofed asymmetrically with lower eaves at the rear. The chimney is set partly within this lower part. One beam on the ground floor is wave-moulded. The five-bay roof, with clasped purlins and wind braces, is ceiled at the collars, and an attic floor has been inserted at eaves level. A late medieval green-glazed ridge tile was discovered in the roof space in 1974 (Fig. 186); it has a housing for a finial. Later fittings include an 18th-century stair with splat balusters of shaped profile.

(369) HOUSE, No. 42, class 6, two storeys, timber-framed, is 16th or early 17th-century. A tie beam with arch brace to a swell-headed post divides the structure into two bays, but the roof itself is in four bays. Collars clasp the purlins, and the tie beam is morticed for a former partition.

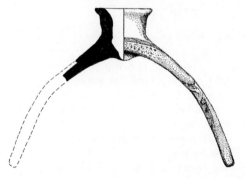

Fig. 186   (368) 40 St. Mary's Street. Medieval ridge tile.
(Scale 1 : 4)

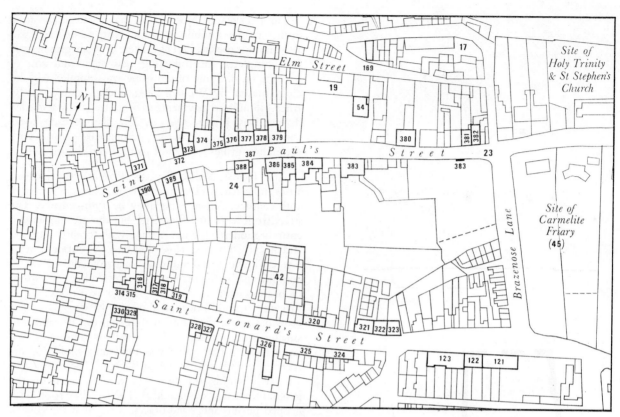

Fig. 187 Map showing monuments in Elm Street, St. Leonard's Street and St. Paul's Street.

To the rear is a range of buildings, running N. and S., in separate occupation. The range was mainly timber-framed but the ground stage is now of stone. The N. section, now used as kitchens, is a two-storey two-bay timber-framed structure of c. 1600; a large fireplace in the N. gable wall is the only original internal feature. The S. section, perhaps 18th-century but much rebuilt, has a half-cellar in the slope of the ground; the ground-floor walls are of stone, but the upper part is in timber-framing of small scantling with brick nogging. At the S. end of the range is a small stone-built two-storey dwelling of the early 19th century.

(370) Houses, Nos. 43–44, originated as a single timber-framed class 3 house of two storeys, probably of late medieval date; No. 43 and the present through passage (Brooks Court) formed the main range, and No. 44 the cross wing. Behind No. 43 a timber-framed two-storey wing has been added. The through passage may have an early origin. The cross wing is jettied on the front and side, and part of the dragon beam is visible externally. The wing is now two and a half bays long, the S. end having been rebuilt or extended in brick and stone in the late 19th century. In 1656 a new two-storey bay window with ovolo mullions was added to the N. wall of the cross wing (Plate 83); a date panel in the

gable bears this date. The main range is now fronted in stone.

ST. PAUL'S STREET (Fig. 187)

Forming the main road to the E. of the Danish burh, this street must have been of importance at an early date. Saxo-Norman pottery kilns have been found on the N. side. The parish church of St. Paul was founded by the early 12th century, and Holy Trinity, which lay in an extramural suburb, came later but before 1154. The medieval prosperity of this street is demonstrated by two 13th-century houses, Nos. 14 and 16–17, and by the long-demolished Brazenose House. This house, reputed to be the scene of the secession from Oxford University in 1333, appears to have been a large stone building around a courtyard; the surviving gateway indicates a 13th-century date.

The E. part of the street declined in the late Middle Ages, and Holy Trinity parish was united with St. Michael's in 1559 and by the 18th century was totally depopulated. St. Paul's parish was joined to St. George's in the 16th century, and its church became a school. The W. part of the street was occupied during the 17th and early 18th centuries by relatively prosperous craftsmen like the Norris family (bellfounders, at No. 12) and William Clarke (mason, at No. 13). The street subsequently retained a modest level of prosperity. A conduit stood in the centre of the road until its removal to the S. side in 1797.

(371) HOUSE, No. 4, three storeys, coursed rubble walls and freestone dressings, modern tiles, was built *c.* 1830–40. It has a central doorway, a single room on the W., now a shop, and formerly had a carriage-entry on the E.; the latter with elliptical arches formed in brick has been blocked.

(372) HOUSE, No. 7 (Plate 72), one storey and attics, two-storey cross-wing, timber-framed wall partly replaced in stone, originated as a medieval hall and cross-wing house of class 1 or 3. The through-passage was probably always in the cross wing which has a wider frontage than the hall. The height of the hall might imply that it was originally open to the roof. On the street front the cross wing has first-floor and eaves-level jetties, and below the latter is a small oriel, restored and plastered but probably original. Other bay windows are 18th-century. Inside, in the N.W. corner of the hall and against the end wall, is the springing of a chamfered stone arch. There is no indication of original chimney stacks. The cross wing contains no medieval features. Later fittings include 18th-century fielded panelled dados, and wooden cornices.

(373) HOUSES, Nos. 8–9 (Plate 72), two storeys and attics, stone walls, comprise a front range of class 2 plan, probably of the 17th century, a lean-to extension at the rear of the 18th century and a further two-storey wing beyond of the early 19th century. The front range has been gutted but a modern masonry pillar supports chamfered axial beams which formerly held partitions. The roof has clasped purlins.

(374) HOUSES, Nos. 10–11 (Plate 74), class 3, two storeys, attics and cellar, timber-framed walls partly replaced or underbuilt in stone, originated as a single late medieval house consisting of a hall with chamber over (No. 11) and a cross wing (No. 10) containing the service rooms. A two-storey range was added behind the hall in the 17th century, filling the angle between hall and cross wing. There is a long cross passage in the cross wing which was originally jettied on the street end. The cross wing has a five-bay roof with tie beams and purlins morticed to principals. A wide fireplace in the N. gable wall, and one cross partition, may be original. The hall, now and perhaps always with stone walls, has in the back wall an original chimney stack, and a ceiling

of intersecting bracket-moulded beams. The street front is now largely occupied by an early 17th-century bay window, with canted sides and ovolo-moulded mullions, roofed with a pentice which is continued over a doorway to one side. Above is a smaller timber-framed bay window with hipped roof, of the 18th century. Alongside is a stone plaque bearing the arms of the Bakers' Company above the names Joseph and Jane Caldecott, 1716 (Plate 129); Joseph Caldecott bought the house in March 1716 and lived there until his death in 1750 (Deeds; Ex. MS, 87/13/22, 23, 26). The jetty to the cross wing was underbuilt in the present century.

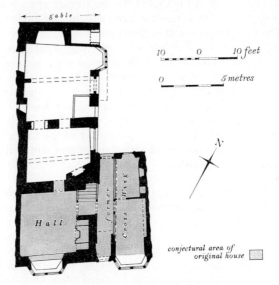

Fig. 188   (375) 12 St. Paul's Street.

(375) HOUSE, No. 12 (Fig. 188; Plate 75), class 3, two storeys, part with attics, stone walls, originated as a hall-and-cross wing house of *c.* 1500. In *c.* 1600 a wing was added behind the hall. A new ashlar front, destroying the cross-wing roof, was built in two phases starting in 1663, by Toby Norris the younger, bellfounder, who lived and worked here. The hall, now with a higher ceiling than elsewhere, was probably originally open, but it had been ceiled by 1626 when the house was described as having a 'chamber over the hall', in the probate inventory of Toby Norris the elder (LAO 131/443).

The street front comprises two two-storey gabled bay windows with canted sides, ovolo-moulded mullioned windows, bolection-moulded doorway (Plate 120), and string-course. On the gable-kneelers are remains of finials, and on the E. gable is a lozenge-panel inscribed 'T N S 1663' for Toby and Susannah Norris (Plate 129). This date refers only to the E. bay window, the W. part of the front being marginally later but in the same style. The E. elevation of the two-storey rear wing is of coursed rubble; a single-storey bay window with ovolo-moulded mullions is covered by a pentice which continues over the adjacent doorway.

Inside, the plan still reflects the late medieval hall on the W., and the cross wing on the E. The screens passage is within the cross wing, and the hall has its chimney stack backing against it. The former hall is lined with 17th-century run-through panelling with fluted pilasters; in the 18th century a new cornice was added. The original fireplace has plain stone jambs and roll-moulded wooden bressummer; within it is a smaller opening with 18th-century wooden surround with winged cherub's head in high relief. In the former cross wing both the axial and cross partitions may be late medieval. The rear wing consists of two main rooms, and fittings include a stone fireplace surround with four-centred head, and a cross beam with pyramid stop, both of c. 1600, late 17th-century bolection-moulded panelling in two heights. On the first floor are bolection-moulded doors and fireplace surrounds, and a plaster floor. Over the cross wing is the lower part of a roll-and-hollow moulded brace, presumably a remnant of the medieval roof. The main range has a 17th-century roof with collars clasping the purlins.

(376) HOUSE, No. 13 (Plate 112), two storeys, ashlar front wall, has an L-shaped plan, the front range of class 6 plan with a side-passage on the E.; this and the first part of the rear wing are of 17th-century origin. The house was remodelled in the mid 18th century, probably by William Clarke, mason, who bought the premises in 1743 as occupying tenant and resided there until 1786 (deeds). The street front has projecting window surrounds with single keystones. The three, unevenly spaced, upper windows remain, but a modern shop front now occupies two ground-floor bays. On the E. a passage entrance has reeded pilasters, roundels on the caps, and thin projecting pediment. A stair turret in the entrant angle is 18th-century. Inside, the first room in the rear wing has a 17th-century cross beam with wave-moulded stops. Other rooms have a variety of 18th-century fittings: panelling in two heights, arched recesses with keyblocks, and iron casements in wooden mullion-and-transom frames.

(377) CONDUIT HOUSE, No. 14 (Fig. 189), two storeys, walls mainly of stone, incorporates a pier and part of a wall-arcade of the 13th century (Plates 62, 63).

The plan of the building to which these features belong can only be conjectured: a hall, parallel with the street, with an aisle on the N. and a wall-arcade at the 'high' end, on the E., may be suggested. A transverse gable occupying the E. half of the rear wall may have an early origin. The ridge of the main roof is centred over the suggested 'nave' of the hall, implying an early arrange-

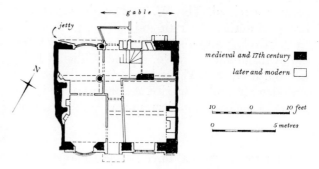

Fig. 189   (377) 14 St. Paul's Street.

ment, but the roof construction is not visible. The W. half of the rear wall has a timber-framed first-floor jetty, probably of late medieval date. The house was considerably altered in the 18th and 19th centuries. Inside, the 13th-century pier, 8 ft. high, has a chamfered base and moulded capital. The surviving section of wall-arcading, at present first-floor level, comprises a head corbel supporting a foliated capital, the springing of an arch of one chamfered order, and a hollow-moulded hood-mould enriched with floral paterae. If the conjecture of an aisled hall is accepted this survival of the wall-arcade would have been a half-arch at the E. end of the aisle.

Later features in the house include a wooden fireplace surround with eared architrave and carving of a female figure in a chariot; also a roundheaded corner cupboard with shaped shelves, reeded pilasters and triple-fluted key block, both 18th-century, and a fireplace with reeded surround, early 19th-century.

(378) HOUSE, No. 15, two storeys, stone walls now rendered. A plan and elevation of 1787 (Sidney Sussex College, Cambridge) shows the building as having a doorway with a two-centred head, slightly to the E. of the present entrance (Fig. 190). The plan suggests a medieval house of class 1 with a two-bay hall on the W. and a single-bay service compartment on the E. Although a later note says that the building had since been rebuilt and subdivided, the present wall-height may indicate the survival of much of the medieval wall. The house, class 10, has an appearance, both inside and out, of c. 1800. The street front has a central doorway with moulded architrave, pediment and fanlight. Flanking bay windows have vertical sashes; first-floor sashes are horizontal sliding.

(379) HOUSE, Nos. 16–17 (Fig. 192), now two storeys, rubble walls, modern roof, includes a considerable part of an open hall of the late 13th century. A wall-arcade (Plate 60), and a window above in the W. gable, a braced tie beam and possibly a window jamb in the S. wall, remain from this period. The

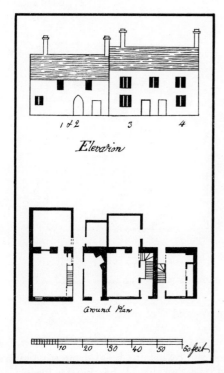

Fig. 190 (378, 379) 15, 16–17 St. Paul's Street. Copy of survey of 1787. (*Sidney Sussex College, Cambridge*)

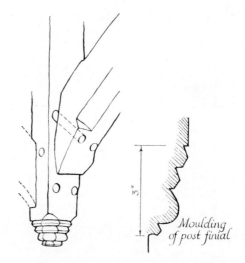

Fig. 191 (379) 16–17 St. Paul's Street. Detail of wall-post showing face-pegging.

surviving features show that the house originally comprised an open hall at the W. end, apparently of two bays, and a section, probably two-storeyed and containing the service rooms, at the E. end. Later in the Middle Ages much of the exterior walling was rebuilt and an upper floor was inserted in the hall; new windows, an external chimney stack, and a doorway in the N. wall reusing 13th-century mouldings, were added at the same time. A survey of 1787 (Sidney Sussex College, Cambridge) shows that the house had by then been subdivided into two cottages (Fig. 190). A rear wing was added before 1787, but this was rebuilt in the late 19th century, and another wing, of the early 19th century, has recently been removed. The 13th-century features of the house came to light in 1970 during alterations, and have since been preserved in the rearrangement of the interior.

The street front now has an early 19th-century character with vertical and horizontal sash windows beneath thin wooden lintels; the W. and central upper windows have medieval jambs. The W. gable wall of the open hall, presumably the high end, includes a wall-arcade of two bays (Plate 60) with moulded two-centred arches springing from a central head-corbel and side corbel, that on the S. being foliated, that on the N.

missing (Plate 63). The lower part of the window above has splayed sill and jambs, and is also late 13th-century (Fig. 193). The added chimney stack in the N. wall has a ground-floor fireplace with roll-moulded jambs and wooden lintel, recently restored; the fireplace on the first floor has chamfered jambs. The inserted floor in the hall is carried on three heavy chamfered beams.

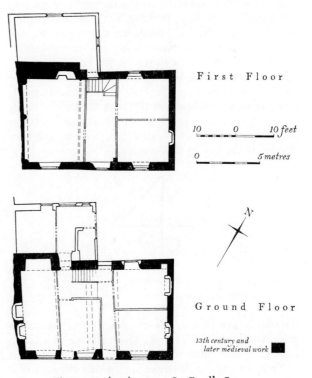

First Floor

10   0   10 feet

0   5 metres

N

Ground Floor

13th century and later medieval work

Fig. 192 (379) 16–17 St. Paul's Street.

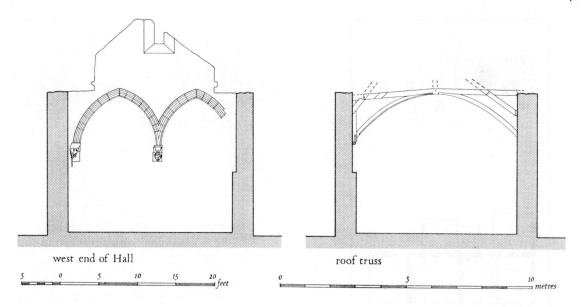

west end of Hall   roof truss

Fig. 193 (379) 16–17 St. Paul's Street. 13th-century wall-arcading and roof truss.

Of the late 13th-century roof (Fig. 193) a tie beam with arch braces, wall-post with moulded terminal and two asymmetrical passing braces have survived. The square-section but slender, chamfered, arch braces are face-pegged to the tie beam and the wall-post (Fig. 191). Mortices in the sides of the surviving wall-post received axial braces to a wall plate. Above the tie beam the roof structure is modern. A housing in the tie beam for a passing brace on the N., balancing that on the S., was apparently not used, there being no corresponding mortice in the wall-post to receive the brace.

The house contains few later features of note. On the jamb of the central upper S. window is scratched a mark, presumably a merchant's rather than a mason's, in the form of a reversed 4 and a scroll; it is probably 15th or 16th-century and may indicate that a floor had been inserted in the hall by that time (194).

Fig. 194 (379) 16–17 St. Paul's Street. Merchant's mark.

(380) BYARD HOUSE, No. 19, two storeys with ashlar walls, was built in 1851. It stands on the site of a building which was dated 1666. In 1848 an application was made by one of the Brownings, probably Bryan, to the Improvement Commissioners on behalf of the Marquess

of Exeter, the owner, to build a new house with an elevation repeating that of the old one. Permission was initially refused on the grounds of its encroachment on the street (*Mercury*, 24 Mar., 7 April 1848). The present building, of class 9, has two bay windows with canted sides and gables, and follows the 17th-century style of its predecessor (BM, Twopeny drawings).

(381) HOUSE, No. 24, two storeys and attics, has a red brick front wall of the mid 18th century probably encasing timber frame of the 17th century; the rear wall and an internal beam with stepped stop are indications of the earlier house. The front elevation (Plate 110) has ashlar quoins, flush except on the first floor where they stand proud, continuous sills, moulded string-course and a parapet with ashlar pilasters rising from a shallow moulded cornice. The attic masks the two gables of an M-shaped roof. The ground floor and attic storey are in Flemish bond and the second storey is in stretcher bond. The doorway has a flat stone hood, repeating the moulding on the string-course, but the brackets are modern. On the ground floor, window surrounds are plain with single keystones but on the first and second floors they have fasciae and single or triple keystones. The plan, conforming to class 13b, is an 18th-century adaptation but except for some panelled doors the fittings are 19th-century and modern.

(382) O'BRIEN ARMS, No. 25, two storeys, attics and cellar, with front wall of ashlar and side walls of coursed rubble, was built as an inn. The single front room may date from the late 18th century; a rear wing is marginally later.

(383) BRAZENOSE HOUSE, No. 28 (Figs. 195, 196; Plate 95), two storeys, attics and cellars, street front of ashlar, other walls of coursed rubble, dates from the early 18th century. It comprises two parallel ranges, the rear one being shorter than the front. In the S.E. angle of the two ranges is a rainwater head inscribed 'EP 1723' possibly for Elizabeth Lepla who bought the property in 1722. Extensive alterations were made in the early 19th century, probably by R. S. Hurst Whitworth (died 1831) who bought the house in 1822 (deeds). The work included the enlargement of the S.W. rooms and the addition of a two-storey bay window.

The street front of six bays has the main entrance in the wider fourth bay and, originally, a minor doorway in the first bay. All openings have moulded architraves (Figs. 10/11/12, 13) and fluted keystones of uniform design; the entrance is accentuated by a flat hood, and the doorway (Fig. 197) has a glazed fanlight. The stone eaves cornice is bracketed. The rear elevation has a single-light ovolo-moulded window lighting the cellar; the principal windows have architraves with beaded arrises, proud of the wall face, and above each is a narrow relieving arch. The early 19th-century extension has sash

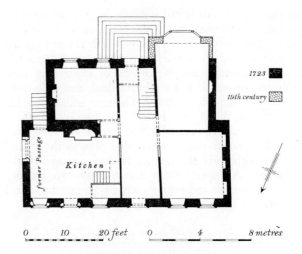

Fig. 196 (383) Brazenose House.

windows with gothic glazing bars. A garden doorway is approached by a wide flight of steps which return at the sides, probably also c. 1825.

Inside, the plan of the rooms conforms to class 9. The hallway retains an early 18th-century egg-and-dart cornice. Fielded wall-panels are of plaster. Interruptions

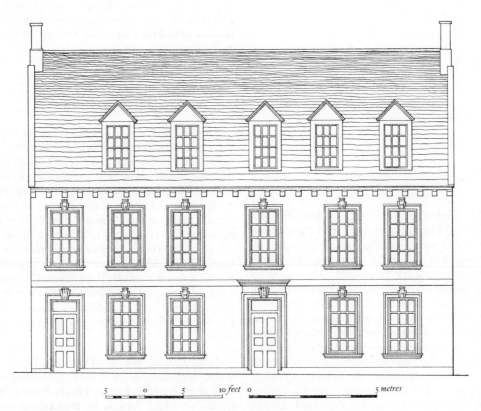

Fig. 195 (383) Brazenose House. Reconstruction of front elevation.

in the moulded dado rail indicate the original position of doors to the side rooms, now entered by doors of *c.* 1825. The early 18th-century oak stair (Plate 134) has heavily carved scroll-brackets to the treads (Plate 130), turned balusters, newels formed of clusters of four balusters, moulded and swept handrail, and bolection-moulded dado-rail of plaster. The stair hall, which has a modillioned cornice, is lit by a window, roundheaded internally, square externally. The front E. room, originally the kitchen, now entered by a door in the second bay, incorporates the former through-passage in the first bay. An upper room has an early 18th-century wooden cornice and plaster ceiling with fret and scroll decoration apparently of *c.* 1800 (Plate 136).

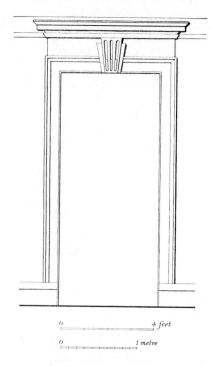

Fig. 197 (383) Brazenose House. Doorway.

The *Stables,* single storey with attics, ashlar N. wall, rest of coursed rubble, mansard roof, are 19th-century. There are two decorative openings of omega shape.

Into the N. wall of the garden is built the 'Brazenose Gate' of the 13th century (Plate 65). The medieval house to which the doorway belonged survived until the late 17th century when the Corporation attempted by means of leases to secure its replacement by a new building. In 1673 a lease specified that Anthony Markham was to spend £300 on a new building within three years, and also to affix 'the Brazenose upon the court gate next the street or elsewhere the mayor and aldermen shall appoint' (Hall Book 2, 63). This may imply that the surviving gate is *in situ,* but Peck says that the gate was rebuilt in a new position by the Corporation

in 1688 (Peck, XI, 24). Stukeley in 1735 shows the gate next to the road, with a five-bay late 17th-century house immediately to its W. (Designs, 18). There is no structural indication of it having been rebuilt. The gateway and building have for long been associated in popular imagination with the secession from Oxford University in 1333.

The gateway has a two-centred head with numerous roll-and-hollow mouldings which rests on attached and detached shafts with stiff-leaf capitals and moulded bases; first half 13th-century. The original 'brazenose' door handle referred to in 1673 was removed by Brazenose College, Oxford, on their purchase of the house in 1890 (*Mercury,* 11 July; RCHM *Oxford,* 26).

(384) CLAPTON HOUSE, No. 30, two storeys and attics, coursed rubble walls, freestone dressings, comprises a class 10 house of the early 18th century to which a taller single-room block was added at the W. end late in the century; behind this addition a wing was built in *c.* 1840. The original house has a five-bay street front, the central three bays having been doorways at one time or another. The W. section, of three bays, projects slightly in front of the older building, and has an entrance in the E. bay leading to a passage between the two sections; it is probably the house for which John Dixon was paid £113. 18. 6., and Clarke and Hames £75. 6. 6., in 1781 (Exeter Day Books). Inside, the earlier house has chamfered cross beams, and fittings elsewhere include a late 18th-century fireplace surround, and cornices of *c.* 1840.

A survey of 1787 (Sidney Sussex College, Cambridge) shows this house, and also a medieval or late medieval house adjoining to the E. approximating to class 2, with a side-entry (Fig. 198).

(385) HOUSE, No. 31 (Plate 110), of class 14b plan, three storeys and cellar, has ashlar front and rubble rear walls. On a cellar-arch is scratched 'GS 1747', a possible date for the building. The street front, in three slightly uneven bays, has a side entrance and uniform windows with eared architraves (Figs. 11, 12) and stepped keystones; below a plain parapet is a classical cornice. An asymmetrical rear wing is an addition, presumably of 1763, the date on a rainwater head. Inside, the front room has fielded-panelled dado and a plaster dentilled cornice; the back room is similar but plainer; the intercommunicating doorway is roundheaded and early 19th-century. Upper rooms have moulded wooden cornices. The stair has turned balusters, square knops, and ramped rail and dado.

(386) HOUSE, No. 32 (Plate 73), two storeys, stone walls, originated as an L-shaped building of the early 17th century, with a central four-centred doorway in a square surround flanked by two two-storey bay windows and a continuous moulded string-course at first-

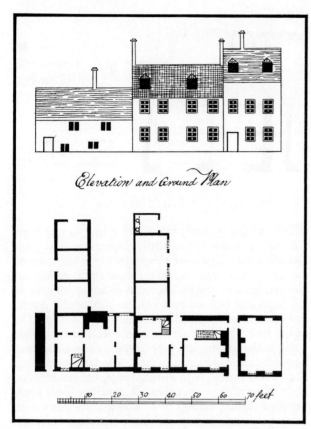

Fig. 198 (384) 30 St. Paul's Street. Copy of survey of 1787. (*Sidney Sussex College, Cambridge*)

floor level. Disturbed masonry suggests a former window over the door. The entrant angle was infilled, perhaps in the 18th century, in timber-framing with later brick nogging, and was finally extended in stone. The roof is apparently a 19th-century renewal at a lower pitch. A small doorway adjacent to the W. bay is blocked. Inside, the 17th-century partitions are timber-framed. An upper fireplace has a reused 15th-century roll-mounted beam as a lintel. Other rooms have various panelling of the 17th and 18th centuries, some reset, and stone panelled fireplace surrounds.

(387) CONDUIT (Plate 119). A conduit formerly in the middle of St. Paul's Street was fed by a piped supply from a spring at Conduit Head. By 1639 responsibility for maintenance was in the hands of St. George's parish, and a house, called Conduit House (mon. 377), was set aside to help cover the costs. In 1797 the Commissioners of the Deeping St. John to Norcote Turnpike agreed to pay an annual sum of £1 10s. as compensation for demolishing the old conduit in the middle of the road and building a new one on the present site (Blore, 269). The storage tank was later rebuilt at a higher level than the conduit, but both the tank and its roof have since been demolished. Iron pipes were laid from the spring in 1847 under Browning's supervision (*Mercury*, 27 Aug.).

The late 18th-century conduit consists of a wall of rusticated masonry with two roundheaded recesses flanking a small recess which once held the conduit spout. Behind are later walls surrounding steps down to a cistern or settling tank, now filled in. One recess has been mutilated by the insertion of a door.

(388) HOUSE, No. 37, two storeys and attics, coursed rubble walls, timber lintels, was built as a pair of class 15 houses in the late 18th or early 19th century. The ground floor has been gutted.

(389) HOUSE, Nos. 41–42 (Plate 112), two storeys and attics, ashlar front wall, remainder of rubble, retains a large chimney stack at the rear, possibly of medieval date. Although now ostensibly of the early 18th century, the shape may reflect that of a medieval house. The 18th-century rebuilding provided a pair of dwellings of dissimilar plans: one has a pair of rooms in line with a stair turret, partly timber-framed, at the rear; the other has rooms arranged in depth with a staircase between them (class 13b). The street front in seven uniform bays has separated quoins, moulded cornice, plain platband, and window and door openings with moulded surrounds; the three dormers with sashes have alternate triangular and semicircular pediments. Two ground-floor windows have been recently united to form a shop window. Inside, early 18th-century fittings include moulded cornices and chair-rails, fielded panelling in one room, and a stone fireplace with central fluted keystone and panelled surround.

(390) HOUSES, Nos. 45–46, two storeys, attics and cellar, front wall of ashlar, rear walls of coursed rubble, are late 18th-century. Both houses are of class 13b. The ground floor has been gutted to form a single shop, but a fielded-panelled door and upper windows, one with triple sashes, survive. A turned stair newel of the late 18th century remains in an attic. An early 19th-century double-fronted shop front with patterned glazed fanlight has been removed (photograph in shop).

ST. PETER'S HILL (Fig. 201)

This area derives its character from the open space formerly occupied by St. Peter's Church (41). Being nearer to the centre of the town its social status was marginally higher than that of St. Peter's Street.

(391) HOUSE, No. 3, two storeys, cellar and attic, mansard roof, is 17th-century although much rebuilt in the 19th century. The street front has a wide single-storey mullioned bay window with later pentice roof

and ovolo-moulded doorway. The interior, of single-room plan, class 15, has been gutted.

(392) HOUSE, No. 4, two storeys, basement and attics, rubble and ashlar walls, is early 19th-century. Until recently it had a bay window to the street. The interior is gutted but a stair probably existed against the back wall.

(393) HOUSE, No. 5, is ostensibly a 17th-century single-room building of two low storeys with stone walls, class 15, but the steeply pitched roof perhaps indicates an earlier structure. Of the 17th century is a two-storey mullioned bay window with canted sides, gable towards the street, and a two-light mullioned window in the party wall on the S.

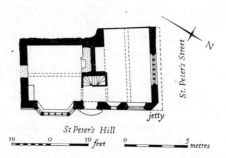

St Peter's Hill
10　　0　　10 feet　0　　　　5 metres

Fig. 199　(394) 6 St. Peter's Hill.

(394) HOUSE, No. 6 (Fig. 199, Plate 79), two storeys, attics, originally timber-framed, slate roof, was built in c. 1600 to a class 3 plan. Early in the 17th century the E. elevation was cased in stone and the jettied N. end underbuilt in reused masonry, the overhang being retained. The house comprises two rooms at right angles with a chimney stack between. The S. room has a two-storey bay window with canted sides and chamfered mullions. The doorway, opposite the stack, has a moulded stone architrave and pulvinated frieze; to the N. is a blocked window. The N. room has an E. window with ovolo-moulded surround, now with sashes but originally with mullions in uniformity with the upper windows. In the stone underbuilding of the N. wall is a window composed of miscellaneous fragments including part of a 14th-century string-course. Above, in the timber-framed wall which extends W. beyond the gabled roof is a blocked four-light window. The present roof is a replacement, in heavy squared timbers, of the 17th or early 18th century; the N. room was originally roofed as a cross wing. A short section of the earlier roof survives on the W.

(395) HOUSE, No. 7 (Fig. 200), two storeys, rendered stone walls, ashlar plinth, was probably built c. 1600 with a plan comprising two rooms and an end-passage,

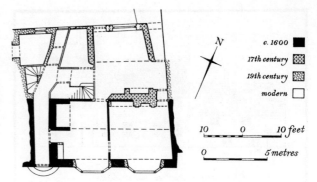

N
c. 1600
17th century
19th century
modern

10　　0　　10 feet
0　　　　5 metres

Fig. 200　(395) 7 St. Peter's Hill.

all in line (class 7). Early in the 17th century a rear wing was built, and in c. 1800 extensive alterations were made including the addition of a second wing at the rear and two canted bay windows on the street front, which was also increased in height. The main doorway, of c. 1600, has depressed four-centred head in rectangular frame, and continuous moulded jambs with shaped stops. The earlier rear wing is of two storeys with coursed rubble walls, ashlar quoins, and hipped roof; the walling may be partly a rebuilding in c. 1800. The later rear wing, also of two storeys with mansard roof, has ashlar walls; in its N. wall is a roundheaded doorway with triple keystone. Inside, fittings of c. 1600 and the early 17th century include a stop-chamfered fireplace bressummer, and panelling with reeded pilasters. Other fittings are of c. 1800: white marble fireplace with fluted sides, paterae, and quarter-columns at sides; arch with fluted columns and elliptical head; simple curving staircase, recently altered; first-floor fireplace with wooden surround having fluted pilasters, central panel carved with paterae and swags, and shelf enriched with dentils and leaves.

ST. PETER'S STREET (Fig. 201)

St. Peter's Street is part of an E. to W. road which is at least as early as the earliest settlement at Stamford and takes its name from one of the oldest churches in the town. As Stamford expanded a new parish of St. Mary Bynnewerk was formed at the W. end of the street, perhaps in the early 12th century. The church, and by implication the parish, was not very rich and it was one of the first to become redundant in the 15th century. The W. section of the street declined, but during the 17th and 18th centuries the E. part maintained a modest respectability, being occupied mainly by craftsmen and tradesmen.

(396) HOUSE, No. 1, two storeys and attics with first-floor jetty to the street, class 5 plan, originally timber-

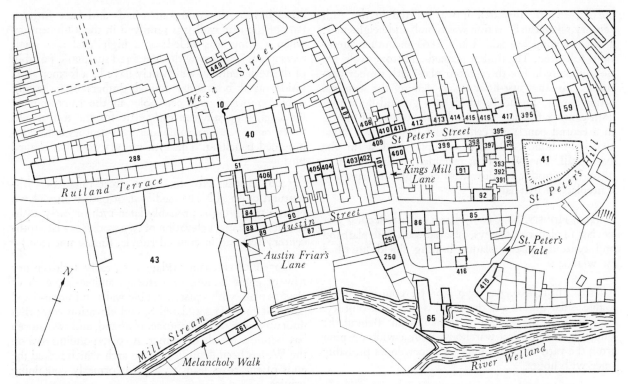

Fig. 201   Map showing monuments in Austin Street, King's Mill Lane, Rutland Terrace, St. Peter's Hill, St. Peter's Street, St. Peter's Vale and West Street.

framed but partly rebuilt in stone, has a late medieval origin. Early 19th-century modernization included a two-storey timber-framed rear wing. The rear of the original building is traceable; the lower stage of the timber-framing has been replaced in brick and stone. Beneath the encased jetty is a bay window of *c.* 1830 with canted sides and slender mullions; a reeded doorcase shaped to the jetty supports an open pediment. Inside, the fittings are mostly early 19th-century.

(397) HOUSE, No. 2, three storeys and cellar, four storeys at rear, walls of coursed rubble, was built *c.* 1830. The plan, class 14b, comprises single front and rear rooms, each with slightly projecting bay windows. Inside, heavily ornamented ceiling plasterwork of *c.* 1830 survives.

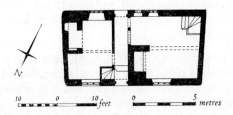

Fig. 202   (398) Former Williamson's Almshouses.

(398) Former WILLIAMSON'S ALMSHOUSES, now No. 3 (Fig. 202), one storey and semi-attics, has stone rubble walls; the street front has casements with wooden lintels and leaded lights, and hipped-roofed dormers. It was probably built in the early 17th century. The first-floor E. room contains decorative plasterwork of elaborate but provincial character (Plate 84), also early 17th-century. The ceiling is divided by ribs into quatrefoils and diamonds, each compartment being filled with conventional patterns including foliage, scrolls, cherubs, human and animal heads, and hippocampi; the wall decoration includes vine trails, goose between foxes, mouse between cats, and woman between men, possibly Susannah and the Elders.

Behind the almshouses is a two-storey building in coursed rubble except for the plastered timber N. wall. It was built in two stages in the 18th century and originally comprised two dwellings, probably to provide further almshouse accommodation. Most of the windows retain their wooden casements with leaded lights.

(399) WELLS HOUSE, No. 4, two storeys and attics, originally timber-framed, may have an early 17th-century origin but subsequent alterations have obscured its development. A building described throughout the 17th century as having a hall, parlour and chambers presumably survives in the present structure (LAO,

99/102, 165/91, 165/202). It was refitted in the 18th century when the E. section was rebuilt and heightened; a kitchen wing was added in *c.* 1800 and other alterations followed. The timber-framed and stone walls are now plastered. The three-room plan with timber partitions on the first-floor may denote the original arrangement. In the E. block is a ground-floor mid 18th-century fireplace surround with swags and figures in a central panel; the central part was lit by a stone two-light hollow-moulded mullion window in the back wall. The W. block, extended to the rear in *c.* 1830, has a gothic window with ogee glazing bars, and a fireplace of that date.

(400) HOUSES, Nos. 8–9 (Plate 142), a reflecting pair of class 14 plan, two storeys, ashlared walls with platband and centrally placed plaque bearing shield inscribed 'w w 1804'.

(401) SHOP, No. 9A, two storeys, coursed rubble walls, ashlar quoins and dressings, is mid 19th-century. Surrounds to the wide shop front remain. Behind the single-room shop is a warehouse with a wide opening from the yard and two opposing upper doors probably once with hoists.

(402) HOUSE, No. 10, two storeys and attics, rubble walls rendered on N., originally class 2 plan, may be late 17th-century. On the street front a two-storey bay window with canted sides and hipped roof was added in the 18th century. Inside, the central passage has been widened to take a new stair; the former stair was probably sited against the rear wall.

(403) HOUSE, No. 11, formerly The Greyhound Inn, of two storeys, coursed rubble walls, class 10 plan, freestone quoins, mansard roof, is late 18th or early 19th-century. Interior now gutted, the stairs being in a new wing.

(404) HOUSE, No. 14, two storeys, attics and vaulted cellar, rubble walls, class 6 plan, is probably 18th-century. The windows, mostly with sliding sashes, and the central doorway have wooden lintels. An upper room contains an early 19th-century reeded fireplace surround with angle-roundels.

(405) HOUSE, No. 15 (Plate 83), class 6 plan, two storeys and attics, coursed rubble walls, containing two features of the late 12th century, is ostensibly of the 17th century, probably *c.* 1663. The street elevation comprises: a 12th-century roundheaded doorway with chamfered jambs and arch, abacus, and hood-mould, and heavy keystone of the 17th-century; a two-storey bay window with canted sides, ovolo mullions, and lozenge panel inscribed 'AM 1663' set in the gable; other win-

dows have 17th-century surrounds and later fittings. Part of the rear wall was removed in the 17th century when a wing was added; at a high level is a small rectangular window with chamfered surround, possibly of the 12th century, which may have lit a former stair. Inside, axial beams are reused timbers each having sloping mortices and peg holes in the soffit, not in the sides, suggesting an early date for the timbers. In the entrance passage is some later 17th-century bolection-moulded panelling. The 17th-century roof has clasped purlins.

(406) HOUSE, No. 19, has a street range of 17th-century, or possibly late medieval, origin having a class 2 plan; a rear wing is probably later 17th or early 18th-century. The street elevation of two storeys is a late 19th-century refacing in coursed rubble. (Inside not seen.)

(407) EXETER COURT (Plate 155), early 19th-century row of eight houses, two storeys and attics, each of class 15 plan, with squared-rubble walls and stone-slated mansard roof. The ashlared S. end elevation comprises doorway with triple keystone, platband, and two-storey bay window mostly of timber. A corresponding row on the W. has been demolished. An arch which linked the ends of the rows leads to a yard formerly containing privies.

(408) Former CHEQUERS INN, No. 27, two storeys and attics, dressed rubble walls, and mansard roof, class 15 plan, is late 18th or early 19th-century. The inn was recorded in 1813 (Blore, 256). Openings in the front wall have wooden lintels.

(409) HOUSE, No. 28, two storeys, stone and brick walls, class 13a plan, is early 19th-century.

(410) HOUSE, No. 29, two storeys, coursed rubble outer wall, large freestone quoins and dressings, class 6 plan, is probably 17th century in origin. The E. chimney stack may be 18th-century. The present shop windows are later; the building had become a grocer's shop and dwelling before 1858 (*Mercury*, 21 May). The rear wall of the house is apparently timber-framed, and beyond is a continuous outshut, perhaps an original feature. Inside, is a later 17th-century door with scratch mouldings.
In yard, a stone barn with rubble walls may be late 18th-century; it was occupied in 1813 by Charles Reesby, miller (Blore, 256), and may be associated with the industry of sack-making, carried on here before 1799 (*Mercury*, 21 June).

(411) HOUSE, No. 30 (Fig. 203), two storeys with barrel-vaulted cellar, stone walls, class 10, is mid 17th-century; it has a central entrance and one original end chimney stack. The street front has two secondary, slightly projecting, two-storey bay windows with canted sides. In the rear wall, a doorway has chamfered

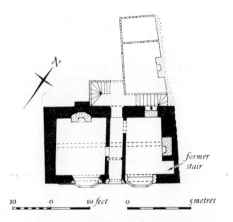

Fig. 203   (411) 30 St. Peter's Street.

jambs and wave-stops, and a blocked two-light window has ovolo-moulded mullion. An original winding stair survives in the cellar beside the E. stack.

(412) HOUSE, Nos. 31–32, two storeys, timber-framed and plastered, may be 15th-century; there are two rear wings. A photograph of c. 1900 (NMR) shows the house with a stone front wall, now entirely removed; openings then visible suggest that this is the building drawn by Stukeley in 1735 as 'Sempringham Hall' (Plate 70; Designs, 75; Stanfordia Illustrata II, 73). The main range, of four bays with carriageway in the third bay, has a roof with clasped purlins and windbraces. In the W. rear wing of two half bays length, one arch brace is visible; the end of the wing has been curtailed by a 17th-century stone range which continues beyond. The wing is timber-framed except for the lower stage on the E. and probably 15th-century. Reset in the E. wing are two 15th-century stone doorways with continuous moulded jambs, depressed heads and head-stops; until the late 19th century at least one doorway was within the carriageway. In the yard is a lead pump of c. 1800.

(413) HOUSE, No. 33, two storeys with attic and cellar, dressed coursed rubble walls, mansard roof, is late 18th-century. In the S. wall is a reset date slab, '1660'. The symmetrical street front has two bay windows, with canted sides and sashes, flanking a central plain roundheaded doorway. The plan, of class 11a, comprises two front rooms, central passage and staircase, and kitchen in a rear wing.

(414) HOUSE, No. 34 (Fig. 204), two storeys, coursed rubble walls, incorporates part of a roof of an open hall at right angles to the street, possibly of the 15th century. The present appearance of the house is due to extensive alterations by the Dixon family in the last quarter of the 18th century. This house is probably that leased by the Corporation to Joseph Dixon, carpenter, and after his death to John Dixon his son, also a carpenter, in 1778. In 1783 'Mr Dixon' was presented at the Court Leet for two bay windows which were encroaching on the street (Ex. MS, 90/27).

The house now has an L-shaped plan with timber-framed stair turret in the entrant angle (class 11b). The main range was originally timber-framed but has been partly refaced in stone. The street front has a central doorway with reeded surround, and another doorway above, presumably replacing a window. The two two-storey canted bay windows, mostly of timber, and the wooden eaves cornices are doubtless carpentry work by the Dixons. The medieval roof, which extends over the S. end of the rear wing, comprises nine pairs of rafters, all heavily smoke-blackened, with a straight, lap-jointed collar at every third pair of rafters, and clasped purlins. The four-bay roof over the front range is probably 16th or 17th-century and cuts the S. end of the earlier roof; it has clasped purlins and incorporates two cambered tie beams. The late 18th-century alterations include an extension to the rear wing, and internally, a fireplace with wooden fluted sides and central panel.

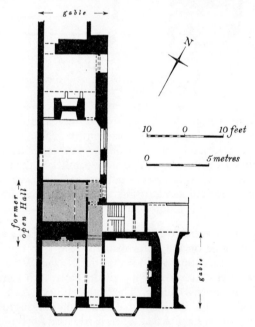

Fig. 204   (414) 34 St. Peter's Street.

(415) HOUSE, Nos. 35–36 (Fig. 205; Plate 71), two storeys, is a late medieval timber-framed house of class 1b plan, partly encased in stone in the 17th century. The original house has a two-cell cross wing; part of the rear wall of the hall remains, showing that the chimney stack was external. The hall roof has braced crown posts (Fig. 205). In the 17th century the hall was floored over and the front wall replaced in stone on the same front line.

There is a two-storey gabled bay window in stone with mullions and canted sides. In the early 18th century a stone-walled rear wing was added behind the hall. A shop front with central door and flanking roundheaded windows was added to the cross wing in the early 19th century.

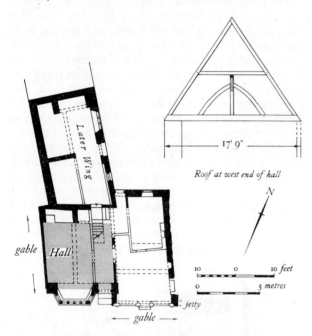

Fig. 205   (415) 35–36 St. Peter's Street.

(416) HOUSE, No. 37, two storeys, stone rubble walls, class 10 plan, has an early 19th-century appearance, but the inserted jambs of the windows, and other features, imply an earlier origin; it is built parallel to the street. The W. window has a triple sash and the upper windows have segmental heads rising above the eaves. Inside, some early 19th-century architraves survive.

(417) TORKINGTON HOUSE, No. 38, comprises a two-storey range on the S., probably of the 17th century, lesser 18th-century additions on the N. and W., and a large three-storey rear wing of the early 19th century built in coursed rubble. The 19th-century work was carried out for the influential family of Torkington; a strong-room suggest that it was partly used for business. The rendered street range has two-storey timber bay windows with canted sides, and a mansard roof of c. 1800. The early range consisted of two rooms and central passage. The interior has some early 19th-century fittings including reeded architraves and reset panelling. In garden, a terrace contrived out of the former *Town Walls* (11) has a reset four-centred doorway of the 17th century, now blocked, and two roundheaded recesses in the thickness of the wall and two in the retaining wall of the terrace. Visible masonry is early 19th-century.

ST. PETER'S VALE (Fig. 201)

(418) HOUSE, No. 1 (Plate 144), two storeys and attics, rubble walls, mansard roof, has a class 10 plan. The sash windows have wooden lintels. It is early 19th-century and is shown in Knipe's map of 1833.

(419) HOUSE, No. 2, formerly terrace of three class 15 dwellings, two storeys, rubble walls, slated gabled roof, is early 19th-century and before 1833 (Knipe's map). Some openings have been altered; the interior has been gutted.

SCOTGATE (Fig. 206)

Scotgate forms part of the old Great North Road and runs along the bottom of a small valley the sides of which have been extensively quarried, especially at the N. end. The quarry behind Rock House was used as a romantic setting for an early 19th-century house; the quarry on the other side of the road is incorporated into warehouses.

The fact that most of the street formed the parish of St. Clement suggests that settlement along the road had reached a sufficient size to warrant creation of a separate parish at an early date. The parish declined in the Middle Ages and was amalgamated with St. John's in 1554. It remained a poor street until the present day. In it are two early almshouses (52, 53) and, although these were originally the homes of relatively affluent men, it is significant that Scotgate was the site chosen for Corporation Buildings (422), an attempt by the council to provide cheap accommodation for the poor of the borough. In the early 19th century the N. end of the street was transformed by the building activities of Richard Newcomb who put much money and effort into raising the social and architectural level of the street.

(420) BREWERY HOUSE, No. 4, three storeys at front, two-storey rear wing, coursed rubble walls, slate hipped roofs, is early 19th-century. The front range, of class 10 plan, has chimney stacks in the rear wall.

(421) HOUSE, Nos. 22–23, two storeys and attics, coursed rubble walls with ashlar quoins and dressings, was built c. 1700, approximately to a class 10 plan but with a single-storey rear wing which was rebuilt in brick in the 19th century. Alterations to some openings were made when the house was divided, but two original wooden mullion-and-transom windows remain on the first floor. Inside, a stone fireplace with shelf of c. 1800 is reset in the rear wing.

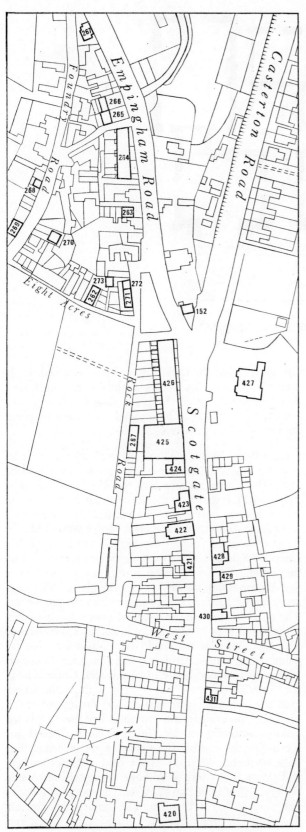

Fig. 206 Map showing monuments in Casterton Road, New Town, Rock Road and Scotgate.

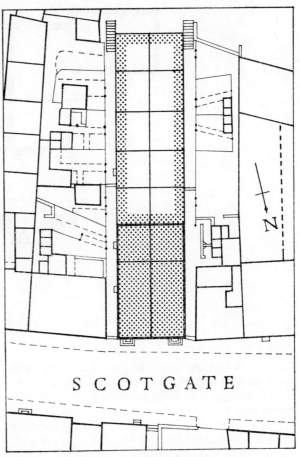

Fig. 207 (422) Corporation Buildings. Southern part now demolished (1:500).

(422) HOUSES, Nos. 25–26, a pair, three storeys and vaulted cellar, have coursed rubble walls with ashlar dressings, and half-hipped mansard roof. Ground-floor bow windows are early 19th-century additions. The upper windows each consist of three leaded casements. The houses, known as Corporation Buildings, are survivals of a layout which included sixteen single-room tenements arranged in two back-to-back rows (Fig. 207). In March 1794 the Town Council approved the plans, and in 1796 building was progressing under John Boyfield who received a final total sum of £1178. 18. 6. in that year (Hall Book IV, 257; Chamberlains' Accounts for 1793–6).

(423) HOUSE, No. 28, of one storey and attics with stone walls, wooden ovolo-moulded windows with mullions and transoms, was built shortly before 1850 to a class 11 plan in a deliberately vernacular style.

(424) GREEN MAN INN, No. 29, two storeys and attics, ashlar front and rubble side walls, has vaulted cellars. The E. section of the main range was built in the early 18th century and the W. section followed soon after.

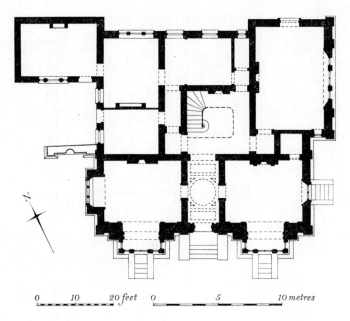

Fig. 208   (427) Rock House, Scotgate.

Two rear wings are later. The three-bay front has six windows with keystones and an original but arbitrarily-placed doorway with hood mould and blank panel for inscription. The wooden cornice is moulded. Formerly of class 8b plan, it has, inside, chamfered axial beams and a bolection-moulded door to the cellar, of *c.* 1700.

(425) HOUSES AND SHOPS, Nos. 30–31 (Plate 158), were built in *c.* 1844 by Richard Newcomb; stables and warehouses were added at the rear shortly afterwards (*Mercury*, 20 Sept. 1844). The houses, of two storeys, coursed rubble walls, ashlar dressings and slated hipped roofs, have projecting shop fronts with large sash windows divided by columns. Between the houses is a pedimented archway and, beyond, two parallel two-storey stable ranges facing into a yard. The ends of the ranges are linked by a wide segmental arch behind which are four parallel vaulted warehouses built into the side of rising ground and apparently on the site of a quarry; above these vaulted chambers are four cottages (see mon. 287).

(426) ROCK TERRACE (Plate 154), comprising ten dwellings each of two storeys and cellar except for the central pair which is of three storeys, was built in 1841 by Richard Newcomb (Burton, 247). The contractor was Robert Woolston (*Mercury*, 1 June 1934). The two central and the terminal houses break forward, emphasis being given to the centre by a balcony over the entrances and by the initials 'RN' in the decorative frieze. The lower windows have original cast-iron balconies. Gate piers to the front gardens are in the neo-Greek style, but the railings have been removed. Each house is of class 14b with a slightly later rear wing; double doors between the main rooms slide into the thickness of the wall. The internal decoration is sparse compared with the external.

(427) ROCK HOUSE (Fig. 208; Plate 159) was built in 1842 by Richard Newcomb for his own use (Burton, 247). The contractor was Robert Woolston (*Mercury*, 1 June 1934). It stands on the site of an earlier house built within a stone quarry which gave the house its name. It is of two storeys, with the main part of ashlar and rear wing of coursed rubble; the hipped roofs are Welsh slated. The design of the main elevations is classical but the eclectic use of differing motifs has resulted in a florid composition usually associated with mid Victorian architecture; the interior decoration is in the same vein. The entrance front has a recessed centre and flanking pedimented bays of which the lower part is rusticated and the upper is enriched with miniature classical columns; ground-floor bay windows have elaborate friezes. At each corner are giant pilasters, Corinthian at the front, Tuscan at the rear. Finials, with pediments on each face, serve as acroteria. Inside, the main rooms are profusely decorated: the entrance hall has a plaster ceiling consisting of an enriched circle flanked by rectangles; the stair hall has a coved and panelled ceiling with lay light; doorcases either have console brackets and decorative cornices or have segmental surrounds with tympana carried on brackets. The stair, rising without newels, has a cast-iron balustrade with rinceau decoration. A fireplace in grey marble has a Greek key

pattern edging, sloping sides in the Egyptian manner and a shield of arms for Newcomb.

(428) HOUSE, No. 51, formerly Crown and Wool-pack Inn, two storeys and attics, has coursed rubble walls, ashlar quoins, and mansard roof. It originated as a class 10 house of *c.* 1800, received two additional rear wings during the early 19th century and was refronted in the later 19th century. Inside, fittings of the early 19th century include a fireplace surround with dentil cornice, in an upper room.

(429) HOUSE, No. 52, one storey and attic, with stone walls, was originally an open structure of three bays, perhaps a 17th or 18th-century barn.

(430) HOUSE, No. 58, of class 5, two storeys, has stone walls, plastered on the front. The main part, on the S., is 17th-century and a rear wing 18th-century. In garden, a stone bakehouse with brick oven, 19th-century.

(431) HOUSE, No. 66, two storeys, coursed rubble walls, hipped roof with modern tiles, has L-shaped plan of class 11; *c.* 1840. The three-bay front has central door and blind window above; other windows are sashes.

(432) TERRACE of six houses, Nos. 70–73 and Nos. 14 and 15 All Saints' Place, two storeys and attics, coursed rubble walls, mansard roofs half-hipped at the W. end, was described as 'newly and substantially built adjoining together' when offered for sale in 1793 (*Mercury*, 15 July 1793). The terrace, following the curve of the street, has a carriageway at the W. end and triple sash windows with wooden lintels. The interiors have been gutted but there is some indication of an earlier building at the E. end.

SHEEPMARKET (Fig. 138)

The name Sheepmarket is given to a long triangular area N. of the site of the castle (10) and partly overlying its outer defences. In the 18th century the sheep market was held at the top of Barn Hill (Ex. MS, 63/66) but in 1777 the inconvenience of this site caused the Council to seek a new one. A part of Castle Dyke was leased from the Earl of Exeter; it was levelled by William Clarke, and both Henry Tatam and John Dixon were asked to provide plans and estimates for the sheep pens, which were finally made by Dixon in 1781 (Hall Book 4, p. 62, 64, 99). Later in the same year the market was transferred to the new site from Barn Hill (*Mercury*, 25 Oct. 1781). In 1782 the Earl gave £100 towards the costs incurred (Exeter Day Books). The houses formerly on the N. side, being built in the yards of All Saints' Street tenements, were of low quality.

(433) HOUSE, No. 4, three storeys and cellar, coursed rubble walls with freestone quoins and dressings, is early 19th-century. The symmetrical three-bay front has narrow blind central window recesses. The entrance and staircase are central.

(434) DOORWAY, reset in wall of No. 9, two-centred, with moulded jambs and label, probably late 14th-century, provenance unknown.

(435) GOLDEN FLEECE INN, No. 18, one storey and attics, coursed rubble walls with ashlar quoins and dressings, mansard roof, is late 18th or early 19th-century. The building has a class 8b plan and four-bay front elevation, triple-sash windows and wooden pedimented doorway.

TINWELL ROAD
(TF 023078)

(436) HOUSE, No. 1, two storeys in coursed rubble with flush dressings, was built *c.* 1830, and in 1845 was occupied by Daniel Gilbert, stonemason (1845 Survey). The W. half has been rebuilt. To the E. and now incorporated in the house is a former coach house with granary over, which in 1845 was owned by Isaac Lumby. Three shallow segmental-head openings on the N. are now partly blocked and contain windows.

(437) WINDMILL COTTAGE, No. 8, two storeys and attics, stone walls plastered on front, mansard roof, class 10 plan, is early 19th-century. A single-storey rear outshut, probably contemporary, was later increased to two storeys. Two two-storey bay windows were added by the tenant who claimed compensation for the improvement in 1854 (St. Mary's Vestry Book).

WATER STREET (Fig. 209)

Known in the 14th century as Estebythewater (Peck, XII. 2, 30), the street ran eastwards by the river to Hudd's Mill. During the Middle Ages the street included several high-quality stone houses, one of which, dating from the 13th century, survived until the 19th century (Plate 61; Twopeny, 290/b.2, pp. 42, 43). By the 18th century the street had a very mixed population; at the W. end Bucks Farm Yard was subdivided and later became the present Maltings Yard. At enclosure in 1796 the rural part of the road was abandoned.

The river frontage was in part used as a wharf, and in 1740 James Bellaers was unloading coal and loading grain and malt opposite his house (deeds, 16 Water Street). This use of river transport led to the establishment of several maltings along Water

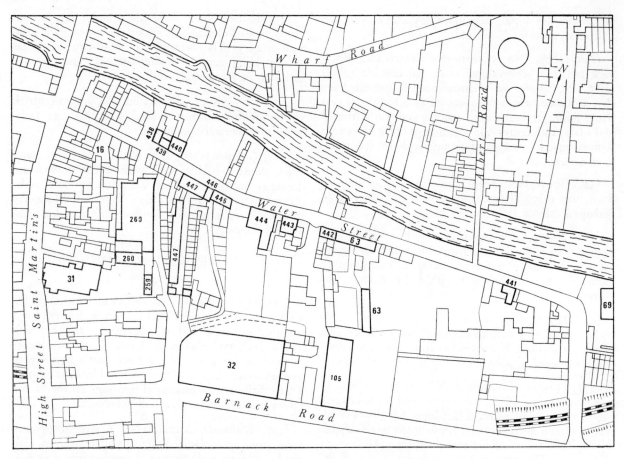

Fig. 209   Map showing monuments in Barnack Road and Water Street.

Street, and by the end of the 18th century there was also a brewery. The street is now almost de-populated.

(438) HOUSE, No. 2, two storeys, attics, coursed rubble walls, flush quoins, mansard roof, narrow street front, class 14; early 19th-century.

(439) HOUSE, No. 3, three storeys, coursed rubble walls, casement windows with wooden lintels, originally two class 15 dwellings each with a single window on each floor, slated roof; early 19th-century.

(440) Former FOX AND HOUNDS INN, No. 4, two storeys, attics, coursed rubble walls, flush quoins, brick chimney stacks, class 10 plan; early 19th-century.

(441) HOUSE, No. 9, two storeys and attics, coursed rubble walls, class 11a plan, was probably built in the second half of the 18th century. The rear wing has a mansard roof. The three-bay street front has timber lintels, absence of quoins, and a small central upper window with leaded lights. The plain 18th-century stair has closed string, square newels and balusters.

(442) HOUSE, No. 12 (Fig. 210; Plate 107), of two storeys with coursed rubble side wall and ashlar front wall, was probably built in the early 17th century to a class 2 plan. Shortly before 1745 it was refronted, encased and partly remodelled by Thomas Lindsey, joiner. He had inherited the property in 1721, mortgaged it in 1745 for £60, when it was described as 'newly built', and sold it to his son William in 1757. William's widow sold it in 1771 to William Clarke, mason, of 13 St. Paul's Street (deeds).

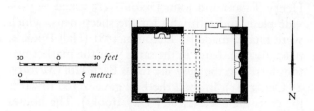

Fig. 210   (442) 12 Water Street.

The main front on the N., of three bays, has a plain chamfered plinth, possibly of the 17th century, a central pedimented stone doorcase with side pilasters and windows with plain projecting architraves and single keystones. The lower windows have sashes and the upper have modern casements below transoms, possibly reproducing the original arrangement. Inside, a cross beam indicating the position of a former partition, and an axial beam defining the length of the original main room, are both features of the early 17th century. In c. 1745 a hallway was made by adding a second cross partition; a rear wing with staircase, added at the same time, has since been removed. On the first floor, the W. room, made larger in the 18th century, has fielded panelling in three heights with chair-rail, and a fireplace surround composed of full-height fluted Doric columns and entablature with triglyphs, all of c. 1745; a fielded panel with scroll-shaped top enriches the overmantel. In the E. room is a smaller fireplace with panelled overmantel having side consoles and formerly a pediment, also of c. 1745.

(443) House, No. 15, main building of two storeys and attics, front elevation with alternate thick and thin courses of ashlar, remainder rubble, class 10 plan, was built in the first half of the 18th century. A rear range with mansard roof and a wing on the E., both of one storey and attics, were added in the early 19th century. The street front, rebuilt in the late 18th century, of three bays with central doorway, all placed off-centre in the wall, has sash windows with keystones, and moulded wooden eaves cornice. The E. wing formerly contained two cottages.

The main building may be that occupied in c. 1740 by James Bellaers, saddler and coal-merchant (deeds at Messrs. Pope, Evans and Dalton). (Inside not seen.)

(444) Welland House, No. 16 (Fig. 211; Plate 143), main range of two storeys, attics in mansard roof, has coursed rubble walls with flush dressings. It was built by Joseph Phillips, brewer, in 1834 on land partly bought in that year and partly acquired by his father between 1790 and 1796 (deeds). The street front, of five uneven but symmetrical bays with central doorway, has windows with triple keystones and continuous sills. A rear range of three storeys also parallel to the street has single and triple sashes; windows of the latter type also follow the curve of the wall at the S.E. corner of the range. A two-storey wing on the E. side of the garden has a W. elevation, partly with blind windows and partly with screen in the form of a two-storey timber trellis. Both have slate roofs and are of c. 1835–45. Interior fittings of c. 1834–45 survive throughout and include pilasters with incised Greek key pattern, enriched plaster cornices, one with roundels linked by rinceaux, fireplace surrounds, one reeded another with Doric half-columns,

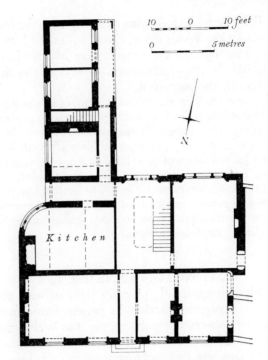

Fig. 211   (444) Welland House, Water Street.

beaded-panel shutters, and a staircase in the rear range with cantilevered wooden treads and turned balusters. At the head of the stairs is a screen formed by two Doric columns and pilasters ornamented with a Greek fret.

Reset in the wall of the adjacent brewery is a panel inscribed 'J P J 1791' for Joseph and Judith Phillips, parents of the builder of the house (Plate 129).

(445) House, No. 17, one storey and attics, coursed rubble, originated as a malting and was so described in 1835 (deeds of adjacent property). It consists of a street range with wide entry on the W., and a rear wing. Internal partitions date from the conversion to a house, but heavy floor beams of the malting survive.

(446) House, No. 18, two storeys, rubble walls, flush quoins, early 19th-century, has on front wall reset panel inscribed 'IL 1674' in relief within a sunken lozenge.

(447) Lumby's Terrace (Plate 155), consisted of two rows of dwellings of which only the W. row (Terrace Nos. 1–13) remains; at right angles is a group of four incorporating an entrance passage (Nos. 19–22 Water Street), and at the S. end is a pair of freestanding houses. The group was built piecemeal as the land was gradually acquired by Moses Lumby, a butcher of St. Martin's parish, who died in 1838, and by his son (deeds). Date-panels which include the initials 'M.L.' show that the W. house of the freestanding pair was built in 1826 and

the E. house in the following year. By 1839 the four houses facing Water Street (Nos. 19–22) had been completed but not the terrace (map by Dewhurst and Nichols, 1839); the census of 1851 shows that all were by then occupied.

The main row on the W., of c. 1840, of two storeys, coursed rubble walls, has dwellings with class 14a plans. Openings have cambered heads without dressings. Nos. 19–22, of two storeys, coursed rubble walls with flush dressings, and slate roofs, also have class 14a plans; in the centre is a wide access passage. The upper windows are sash, the lower altered or enlarged. The freestanding pair, three storeys with semi-basements in the sloping ground, sash windows, hipped roofs on the S., gables on the N., has class 15 single-room plans.

WELLINGTON LANE (Fig. 100)

Although apparently an early right of way, this narrow passageway derives its present name from an early 19th-century public house, the Wellington Tavern (*Mercury*, 21 Dec. 1827). The few buildings in the lane are encroachments on the gardens of adjoining houses.

(448) TERRACE, Nos. 4, 5, 7, three storeys and cellars, red brick, hipped and gabled roof, is early 19th-century. Two dwellings are uniform, the third extends at the rear; each has a class 15 plan with a staircase against the back wall. The windows have sliding sashes and cambered rubbed brick arches.

WEST STREET (Fig. 201)

(449) TERRACE, Nos. 10–12, two storeys, ashlar front and rubble rear walls, each with class 14a plans; mid 19th-century.

WHARF ROAD (Fig. 143)

This road follows the line of the town walls and takes its name from the wharves that formerly existed along the river at this point.

(450) Former TOLL HOUSE and WAREHOUSES are mainly of two storeys. The Toll House at the W. end was built in 1849 when the bridge was rebuilt to the designs of E. Browning (*Mercury*, 13 April). The walls are in bands of pindle and freestone, and the windows have ovolo-moulded mullions. The style is Tudoresque. On a corbelled chimney stack on the S. is a slab bearing the arms of Cecil. This house and that opposite, and the partially rebuilt Boat Inn on the N. (332, 333), provided an approach to the new bridge in uniform architectural styles.

The gabled *Warehouses* (Plate 162) on the E. are in coursed rubble and date from c. 1756. In 1755 Henry Ward, ironmonger, took a building lease of the site stipulating an expenditure of at least £300 (Ex. MS, uncat.). The early openings have wooden lintels, and two tall blocked openings on the S. formerly gave access from the river. The interior has no early features except heavy chamfered beams.

(451) PORTAL (Plate 162), consists of a large semi-circular headed arch with rusticated voussoirs and key-stone set in a wall of narrow coursed rubble divided by a moulded string and framed with ashlar quoins and a heavy dentil cornice with plain frieze and block parapet. It was built in 1845 to designs by Bryan Browning as the entrance to Grant's iron foundry; Gregory and Tinkler were the contractors (*Mercury*, 5 Sept. 1845; Burghley Account Book, 15 Nov. 1845). Blashfield set up his terracotta works here in 1858. In 1937 it was re-built several feet to the S., and parallel with the road, under supervision of H. F. Traylen.

(452) GAS WORKS. A range in red brick with yellow brick arches and slate hipped roof survives; it probably dates from 1824 when the Gas Company was formed (*Mercury*, 16 July). It comprises two former dwellings, that on the N. approximating to class 10, presumably for the foreman, the other of one-room plan. The doorways have rounded heads and the upper windows are con-spicuously tall. The front is articulated by shallowly recessed window bays.

(453) HOUSE, No. 5, two storeys, rubble walls, stands on the acute angle formed between Gas Lane and the line of the medieval wall, here represented by Wharf Road. No part of the walls appear to be medieval. The N. range, against Gas Lane, is not shown on Knipe's map of 1833; the S. range may be 18th-century but contains no early features.

WOTHORPE ROAD (Fig. 111)

This road is on the line of an early route leading to a crossing of the Welland, which pre-dates the Town Bridge.

(454) TIVOLI COTTAGE, class 14b, three storeys, ashlar front wall, remainder coursed rubble, was built as a house and shop in 1849. The street front has a round-headed doorway, plain window openings and continu-ous platband sills. A sash window has replaced the wider shop window. Between the top windows is a panel inscribed 'WB AM 1849' within a wreath. The house was advertised for letting in 1850 as having a good view and being near the station (*Mercury*, 27 Sept.).

(455) HOUSE, No. 2, two storeys, coursed rubble walls, dressed quoins, brick chimney stacks, class 15 plan with lean-to against gable end, casement windows with timber lintels; after 1833 (not on Knipe's map).

(456) HOUSE, No. 4, two storeys, ashlar walls, red brick chimney stacks, class 10 plan, sash windows with keystones; before 1833 (on Knipe's map).

(457) HOUSE, No. 6, formerly three houses arbitrarily arranged, has coursed rubble walls and brick chimney stacks. The S. dwelling of two storeys, class 15 plan, with later extension on the S. was built after 1833; the central dwelling, originally single-storey and class 15 plan, was built before 1833 and has been extended S. to meet the foregoing house; the N. dwelling, of one storey, now a garage, is after 1833 (Knipe's map). The windows have vertical and horizontal sashes, or casements, with wooden lintels.

(458) HOUSE, No. 7, coursed rubble walls, red brick chimney stacks, class 10 plan with outshut at rear, three-bay front with sash windows, timber lintels, bears date-panel 'R.B. 1820', possibly for Robert Bell who was fined for erecting a dwelling, enclosing waste land and making a garden (Stamford Baron, Court Rolls, April 1830).

Fig. 212   Seal of Browne's Hospital (48).

GLOSSARY

OF THE MEANING ATTACHED TO THE TECHNICAL TERMS USED IN THE INVENTORY
Terms for which a sufficient interpretation is given in the *Concise Oxford Dictionary*, 4th ed. (1951), reprinted with revised *addenda* (1954), have not been included.

ACHIEVEMENT—In heraldry, the shield with helm, crest, mantling, supporters, etc.

APRON—A panel, plain or decorative, below an architectural feature or composition.

ARCH—*Depressed*—struck from a centre or centres well below the line of springing.
Flat—having a horizontal soffit.
Nodding—curved forward in advance of the plane of the springing.

ARCHITRAVE—*Eared*—having the framing mouldings extended laterally at the head and returned.

BARNACK—A hard shelly building stone from the Upper Lincolnshire Limestone; used widely in the 12th and 13th centuries and deriving its name from the village of Barnack.

BAY—The main vertical divisions of a building or feature defined by recurring structural members as in an arcade, a fenestrated elevation or a timber frame.

BEAM—*Axial*—in a ceiling, placed centrally on the main axis of the related structure.
Cross—in a ceiling, placed on the short axis of the related structure.
Dragon—in a ceiling, placed diagonally in a corner of a building to carry jetties (q.v.) on the adjacent sides.
Intersecting—in a ceiling, combined axial and cross beams.

BENEFACTOR'S TABLE—Tablet or panel recording a benefaction.

BLIND—Unpierced by any openings.

BRACE—Diagonal timber strengthening a framework.
Arch—curved, usually between wall and roof timbers, and often being one of a pair.
Passing—of considerable length, passing across other members in the roof truss.

BRACKET-MOULDING—Double-ogee moulding.

BRATTISHING—Upstanding ornamental cresting, particularly of repetitive leaf form.

BRICKS—*Rubbed*—of soft fabric, abraded to special shapes after firing.

BUTTRESS-ES—Projecting support to a wall.
Angle—two meeting, or nearly meeting, at right angles at the corner of a building.
Clasping—clasping or encasing the angle.
Diagonal—projecting diagonally at the corner of a building.
Lateral—at the corner of a building and axial with one wall.

CAP—A capital.

CAPITAL—*Cushion*—cut from a cube with its lower angles rounded off to adapt it to a circular shaft.
Stiff-leaf—formed by a number of stylised leaves of lobed form.
Water-leaf—enriched with broad tapering leaves of sinuous form.

CASEMENT—A wide concave moulding in window jambs, etc. Also the hinged opening part of a window.

CONSOLE—Scroll-shaped ornamental bracket.

CONTINUOUS SILLS—Window sills continued across the elevation to form a platband.

CROP-MARK—Visible variation in vegetation caused by buried or levelled features.

CROSS WING—In a house, a wing at the end of, and at right angles to, the main range.

CROWN POST—In a roof truss, a central post between tie beam and collar.

CUT-OUT PANELLING—Carved in low relief, the raised surface remaining flat.

DIAMOND MULLION—Of square section, set diagonally.

DOUBLE DEPTH—Of a house the plan of which consists of two parallel ranges of rooms; also known as DOUBLE PILE.

ENGAGED SHAFT—A column partly attached in its circumference to an adjacent feature.

FIELDED PANEL—A panel with bevelled margins.

FLUSH DORMER—A dormer window the front of which is flush with the wall face below.

FOIL—A leaf-shaped space defined by the cusping in an opening or panel.

GARDEROBE—A small room containing a latrine.

HALL—In a medieval house, the principal room which was often open to the roof.

HEAD—*Flat*—having a rectangular head.
Four-centred—struck from four centres.

HOLLOW CHAMFER—A shallow concave moulding.

IMPOST—The projection, often moulded, at the springing of an arch.

INDENT—Sinking, usually for a brass plate.

JETTY—The projection of the upper storey of a building beyond the plane of the wall face below.

JEWELLED—Prism-like decoration in relief.

KEEL MOULDING—A moulding, with profile resembling the section through the hull and keel of a boat.

KEY-BLOCK—Simulated keystone, often of wood.

KNEELER—A corbel or bonding-stone strengthening a gable parapet or coping.

LUCARNE—Small gabled window.

LOMBARDIC CAPITALS—Letters based on medieval manuscript alphabets of N. Italy.

MOUCHETTE—In window tracery, a curved dagger-shaped opening.

NAIL-HEAD—Ornament, of pyramid form, resembling a nail head.

NOOK-SHAFT—A column shaft in a recess in a jamb, splay or reveal.

OFFSET—The ledge where one vertical plane of a wall sets back above another.

ORDERS—In arches, concentric rings of voussoirs receding towards the opening.
Roman Doric—an architectural Order comprising a column, sometimes fluted, moulded capital and base, architrave, frieze with triglyphs, and cornice.
Tuscan—a simple Order, comprising an unfluted column, moulded capital and base, architrave, plain frieze, and cornice.

ORIEL WINDOW—A projecting window, usually carried upon corbels or brackets; also the large projecting window lighting a hall.

OUTSHUT—A subsidiary range parallel and contiguous to the main range of a building, and with a roof of single pitch.

OVERDOOR—Decorative panel above a doorway.

OVERMANTEL—Decorative feature or panel above a fireplace surround.

OVERTHROW—Decorative panelling or ironwork spanning an opening.

PARGETTING—Plasterwork with relief or incised decoration.

PATERA-AE—In Classical architecture, a dish-like ornament. In Gothic architecture, a flower or lobed-leaf ornament, often square.

PEDIMENT—*Broken*—in which the centre part of the raking cornice and the tympanum are omitted.

PEGGING—In a timber-framed structure, dowelling with headless wooden pegs; hence pegholes.
Face-pegging—method of securing timbers by pegs alone, without the use of mortices and tenons.

PINDLE—A fissile sandy limestone, used in the early 19th century as a facing material.

PLANK-AND-MUNTIN—Timber wall construction consisting of vertical planks grooved into stout uprights.

PLATBAND—A projecting flat horizontal band of masonry or brickwork, as distinct from a moulded string.

POST—*Haunched*—in timber-framed construction, a post with a bracket-like swelling on one face to carry a beam.

PURLIN—*Clasped*—one that is held in notches between the collar beam and the principal rafter.
Collar—in a trussed roof, a horizontal beam running longitudinally beneath the collar beams.
Staggered—one which does not align with its neighbour.

RAIL—In carpentry and joinery, the horizontal member of a framed construction.

REEDING—Decoration formed by parallel and adjacent convex mouldings.

REREDORTER—Monastic latrine.

RETICULATED—Net-like; in tracery, a net pattern composed of circular, ogee or other shapes.

RIDGE AND FURROW—Remains of former cultivation; initially strips of tilled land, with furrows on either side, raised by the action of ploughing.

ROLL MOULDING—A prominent continuous convex moulding, also called a Bowtell.

SASH WINDOW—*Hung*—in which the movement of the glazed frames is vertical.
Sliding—in which the movement of the glazed frames is horizontal.

SCRATCH-MOULDED PANELLING—Panelling having small plain panels with shallow incised mouldings on the framing.

SCREEN—In secular buildings, a partition separating the main space of a hall from the service end.
Screens Passage—the space at the service end of a hall between the screen and the end wall.

SERVICE END or WING—In a medieval house, that part at one end of the hall containing the butteries, larders, etc.

SHOULDERS—Of an arch, the corbels supporting a lintel.

STAGES—Divisions of a structure marked by distinct horizontal features.

STAIRCASE—*Closed string*—with the raking supporting member(s) parallel-sided and housing the treads and risers.
Open or cut-string—with the raking supporting member(s) cut to the shape of the treads and risers.

STAMFORD WARE—Type of pottery made in Stamford dating from the late Saxon period to the 12th century.

STAND PATEN—A paten with a foot.

STIFF-LEAF—See CAPITAL.

STOP—1. Block, often shaped or carved, terminating a projecting moulding such as a string or label.
Head—carved in the form of a human, animal or grotesque head.
Mask—with a pointed profile and chamfered sides.
2. The feature, at the end of a chamfer or moulding, shaped to transfer the latter to a square section, hence stop-chamfered.
Broach—half-pyramidal.
Leaf—of foliate form.
Run-out—dying out gradually.

STRAIGHT-JOINT—An unbonded junction between two structures.

STRAPWORK—Decoration consisting of interlaced strap-like bands.

STRING, STRING-COURSE—A projecting continuous horizontal course or moulding.

STUDS—The common uprights in timber-framed walls.

STUDWORK—Timber framework consisting largely of studs.

SWAG—In architectural ornament, a festoon suspended from two points and carved to represent cloth or flowers and fruit.

TRACERY—*Flowing*—comprising compound curves.
Geometrical—comprising simple curves.
Net—see RETICULATED.
Vertical—with predominantly vertical mullions.

TRUSS—An open structural framework, especially of a roof.
Closed—having the framework filled, so as to form a partition.

TUSKED TENON—Tenon passing through mortice and secured by a peg on farther side of beam or rafter.

UNDERBUILT—Addition of a wall beneath a jetty (q.v.).

WALL-POST—An upright against, or partly in, a wall and supporting a beam.

WATER-HOLDING BASE—A base having a concave moulding, or mouldings, in its upper surface.

WAVE MOULDING—A compound moulding comprising a convex curve between two concave curves.

WEATHERING—A sloping surface for casting off water.

Plates

From west, showing St. Mary's Place, the Town Bridge and High Street St. Martins.

From west, showing Broad Street, High Street and St. Mary's Street.

PLATE 2

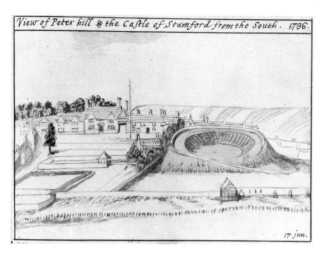

(10) THE CASTLE. Drawing by W. Stukeley, 1736.
(Stamford Archaeological Society)

(6) ROMAN ROAD. Crop-mark of road between Stamford and its meeting with the Great North Road;
recorded before destruction. (CUAP)

PLATE 3

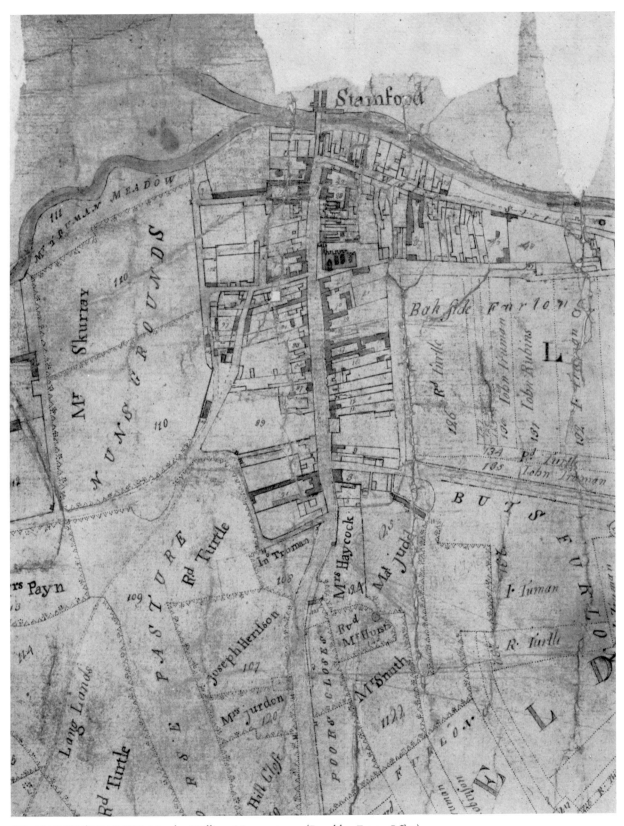

ST. MARTIN'S PARISH. Map by William Murray, 1773. (Burghley Estate Office)

From west. Drawing by William Twopeny, 1826. (BM)

12th-century bridge and culvert under hospital.

(64) TOWN BRIDGE and (49) LORD BURGHLEY'S HOSPITAL.

Arches from S.W., before destruction.   E. arch from S.

(44) NUNNERY OF ST. MICHAEL. Arches below reredorter.

(47) PRIORY OF ST. LEONARD. Drain and arch below reredorter, from N.

From south west, before alteration in 1930.

From south east, after alteration.

(54) STAMFORD SCHOOL CHAPEL, formerly church of St. Paul.

Church from north west.

Nave arcade from north.

(47) PRIORY OF ST. LEONARD.

PLATE 8   CAPITALS: 12TH AND EARLY 13TH-CENTURY

(47) St. Leonard's Priory. N. arcade,
     late 12th-century.

(47) St. Leonard's Priory. N. arcade,
     mid 12th-century.

(47) St. Leonard's Priory. N. arcade, W. respond,
     late 12th-century.

(28) Church of All Saints. S. arcade, E. respond,
     early 13th-century.

(28) Church of All Saints. S. arcade,
     early 13th-century.

(54) Former Church of St. Paul. N. arcade,
     early 13th-century.

(54) Former Church of St. Paul. N. arcade,
     early 13th-century.

(54) Former Church of
St. Paul. Corbel.

(28) Church of All Saints. Piscina in South Chapel.

(33) Church of St. Mary. West doorway, detail.

(47) St. Leonard's Priory. West front, detail.

PLATE 10 CHURCHES: EARLY 13TH-CENTURY

(33) CHURCH OF ST. MARY. West tower.

South chapel from east.

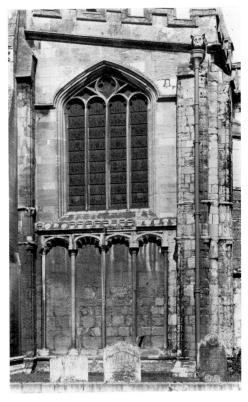

South aisle from west.

South aisle from south east.

(28) CHURCH OF ALL SAINTS.

PLATE 12　　　　　　　CHURCHES: 13TH AND 14TH-CENTURY

(33) CHURCH OF ST. MARY. West tower from south.

From south west.

Nave and south aisle, looking north west.

(28) CHURCH OF ALL SAINTS.

PLATE 14   CHURCHES: 13TH-CENTURY AND LATER

(29) CHURCH OF ST. GEORGE. Nave, looking south east.

(33) CHURCH OF ST. MARY. Nave, looking west.

(33) CHURCH OF ST. MARY. North Chapel, looking north east.

Statue on spire, probably of
St. William of Norwich.

Tomb recess in North Chapel.

Statue on spire.

(33) CHURCH OF ST. MARY.

South porch.

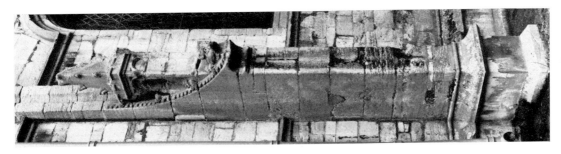

Buttress, N. wall.

North porch.

(28) CHURCH OF ALL SAINTS.

(31) Church of St. Martin. Boss in porch,
showing shield with arms of See of Lincoln.

(28) Church of All Saints.
Figure at springing of tower vault.

(28) CHURCH OF ALL SAINTS. Tower vault.

Decoration below tower parapet.

Vestry doorway.   Clock face on tower.

(28) CHURCH OF ALL SAINTS.

PLATE 20   CHURCHES: 15TH-CENTURY

(31) CHURCH OF ST. MARTIN. Nave, looking west.

Chancel roof.

Nave and south aisle, looking north west.

(30) CHURCH OF ST. JOHN BAPTIST.

PLATE 22   CHURCH ROOFS: 15TH-CENTURY

(30) CHURCH OF ST. JOHN BAPTIST. Nave roof, looking west.

(28) CHURCH OF ALL SAINTS. Roof of South Chapel.

North side; 3rd and 2nd angels.

South side; 6th and 7th angels.

(30) CHURCH OF ST. JOHN BAPTIST. Roof of nave.

PLATE 24   CEILINGS: 15TH-CENTURY

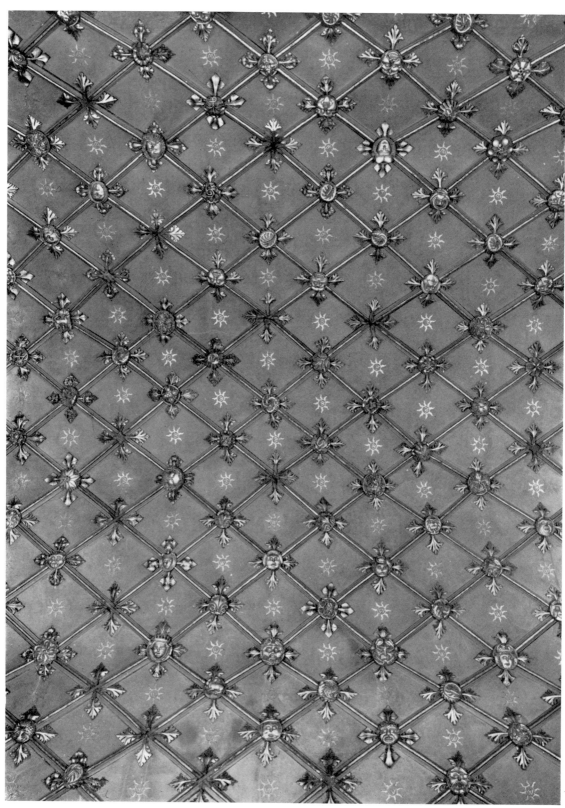

(33) CHURCH OF ST. MARY. Ceiling of North Chapel; shortly before 1484.

Central boss carved with the badge of York.

(33) CHURCH OF ST. MARY. Ceiling bosses in North Chapel; shortly before 1484.

PLATE 26   CHURCH TOWERS: 15TH-CENTURY

(31) CHURCH OF ST. MARTIN, from south.

(30) CHURCH OF ST. JOHN BAPTIST, from south east.

(34) CHURCH OF ST. MICHAEL, from north, 1835.

(29) CHURCH OF ST. GEORGE, from south west; tower partly rebuilt in 17th century.

PLATE 28   CHURCHES: EARLY 19TH-CENTURY

Exterior from east.

Interior, looking east.

(34) CHURCH OF ST. MICHAEL, 1835.

(37) METHODIST CHAPEL, BARN HILL.
    South front, reconstructed in 1863 from the original front of 1803.

(36) CONGREGATIONAL CHURCH, STAR LANE, 1819.

PLATE 30   BRASSES: 15TH-CENTURY

(28) CHURCH OF ALL SAINTS.
  Brass (8), possibly of John Browne, 1442, and wife Margery, 1460.

(28) CHURCH OF ALL SAINTS.
   Brass (9), possibly of John Brown, 1475, and wife Agnes.

PLATE 32   BRASSES: 15TH-CENTURY

(28) CHURCH OF ALL SAINTS.
  Brass (1), probably of William and Margaret Browne, 1489.

(54) Former Church of St. Paul. Detail of
monument (3), early 14th-century.

(189) 51 High Street. Inscribed slab
now in Stamford Museum, late 14th-century.

(54) Former Church of St. Paul. Coffin lid (1), c. 1400.

(33) Church of St. Mary. Statue, 14th-century.

PLATE 34 GLASS: 15TH-CENTURY

Glass (3):
(a) St. Giles; (b) St. Botolph.

Glass (3):
(e) St. Leonard; (f) St. Peter Martyr.

Glass (3):
(c) St. Blaize; (d) mitred saint.

Glass (4):
(c) The Virgin of the Mantle; (d) God the Father.

(30) CHURCH OF ST. JOHN BAPTIST. Glass in north aisle, probably 1451.

E. window (1): demi-angel.   E. window (1): The Annunciation.

S. aisle window (5): Moses striking the rock; Samson and the gates of Gaza; David and Goliath.

S. aisle window (5): Crucifixion; Three Maries at the Tomb; Resurrection.

(31) CHURCH OF ST. MARTIN.

PLATE 36   GLASS: 15TH-CENTURY

St. James the Great.

The Trinity.

Royal Saint.

The Virgin.

St. John Baptist.

Possibly the Virgin.

(48) BROWNE'S HOSPITAL. Glass (1) in Chapel.

Glass (7), head of male saint, in doctor's cap.

Glass (7), King Solomon.   Glass (5), King David.   Glass (6), St. Paul.

(48) BROWNE'S HOSPITAL. Glass in Audit Room windows.

PLATE 38   GLASS: 15TH-CENTURY

(29) CHURCH OF ST. GEORGE. Glass (2) in chancel.

(48) Browne's Hospital.
Glass (7) in Audit Room, device of Browne (Stokke) family.

(48) Browne's Hospital.
Glass (2) in chapel, St. Michael.

(48) Browne's Hospital. Glass (3) in
passage, arms of Browne and Elmes.

(31) Church of St. Martin. Glass in E. window
of chancel, 15th and 16th-century.

(29) Church of St. George.
Glass (2) in chancel.

PLATE 40   MEDIEVAL FONTS

(31) Church of St. Martin. 14th-century.

(34) Church of St. Michael. 15th-century.

(28) Church of All Saints. 15th-century.

(30) Church of St. John Baptist. 15th-century.

(48) BROWNE'S HOSPITAL. Screen at west end of Chapel.

(30) CHURCH OF ST. JOHN BAPTIST. Screen to South Chapel.

PLATE 42   CARVED WOODWORK: LATE 15TH-CENTURY

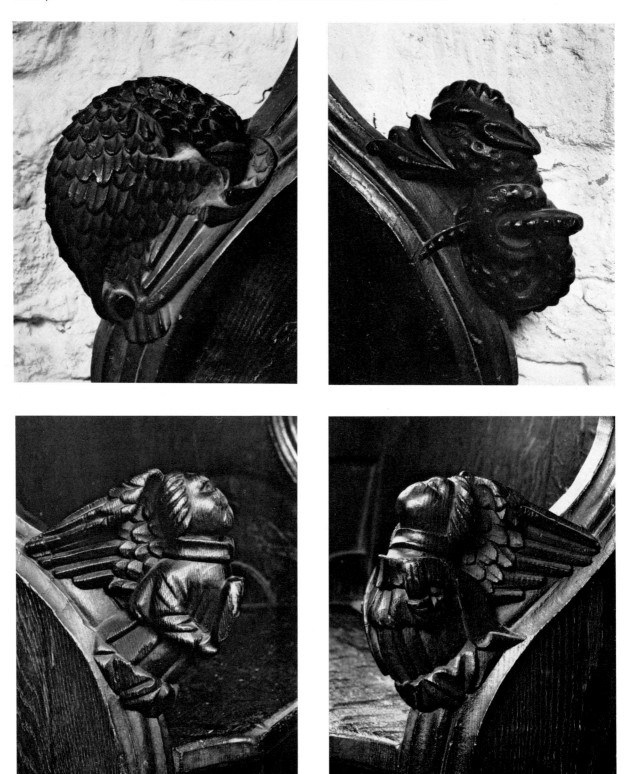

(48) BROWNE'S HOSPITAL. Stalls in chapel; carving on arm-rests.

(48) BROWNE'S HOSPITAL. Stalls in chapel; finials and misericords.

PLATE 44   LATE MEDIEVAL DETAILS

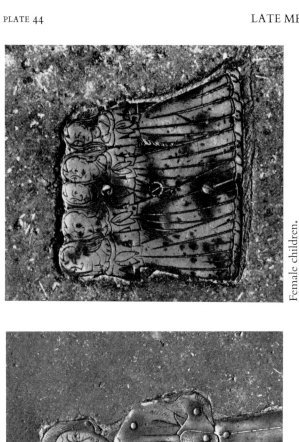

Female children.

Drawing of vault-boss by Stukeley, 1736.
(Stamford Archaeological Society)

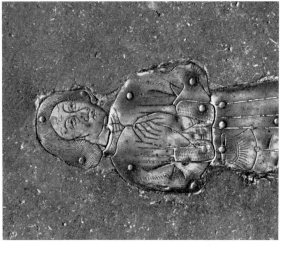

Nicholas Byldysdon.

Figure of St. Lawrence.

(30) CHURCH OF ST. JOHN BAPTIST. Brass (3) of Nicholas Byldysdon and wife Kateryn, 1489.

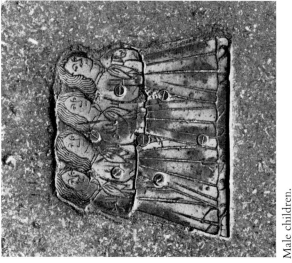

Male children.

Vault-boss, from site of Austin Friary.

(101) 14 BARN HILL. Reset carvings.

(33) CHURCH OF ST. MARY. Monument (1), probably of Sir David Phillips (d. 1506) and wife.

PLATE 46   MONUMENTS: 16TH-CENTURY AND LATER

Monument (4) of Richard Cecil, 1552, and wife Jane, 1587.

North chapel, looking west, before enlargement in 1865, showing
monuments (1), (5) and (4). (From engraving by Sharp and Ackermann)

(31) CHURCH OF ST. MARTIN.

(31) CHURCH OF ST. MARTIN. Monument (1) of William Cecil, first Lord Burghley, 1598; detail of effigy.

PLATE 48   MONUMENTS: LATE 16TH-CENTURY

(31) CHURCH OF ST. MARTIN. Monument (1) of William Cecil, first Lord Burghley, 1598.

(31) CHURCH OF ST. MARTIN. Monument (5) of John Cecil, 5th Earl of Exeter, 1700, and
     Anne his wife, 1703. Executed by Stephen Monnot in 1704 and installed by William Palmer
     in 1706.

PLATE 50   MONUMENTS: EARLY 18TH-CENTURY

(31) CHURCH OF ST. MARTIN. Monument (5) of John Cecil, 5th Earl of Exeter, 1700, and Anne his wife, 1703.

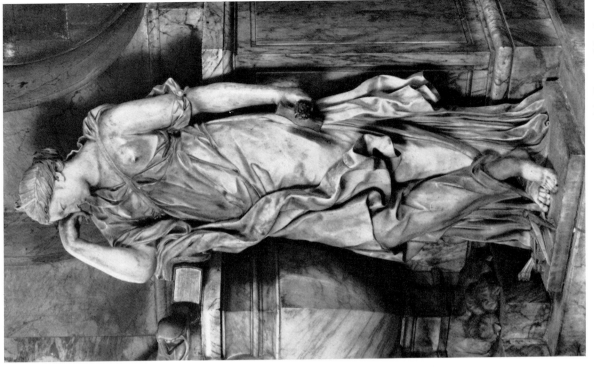

(31) CHURCH OF ST. MARTIN. Monument (5); figure of the Arts, carved in 1704 by Stephen Monnot.

(29) CHURCH OF ST. GEORGE. Monument (5) of Sir Richard Cust, 1734, and Anne his wife, 1779, by J. Bacon, 1797.

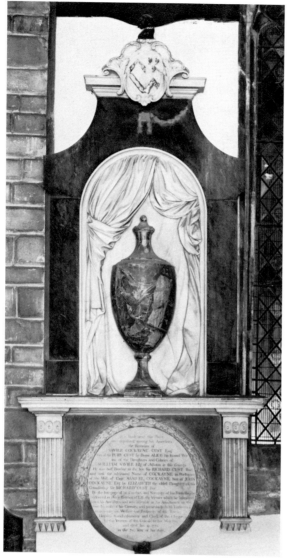

(29) Church of St. George. Monument (4) of Ursulah Cust, 1683/4, and others.

(29) Church of St. George. Monument (3) of Savile Cust, 1772, by W. Tyler.

(31) Church of St. Martin. Monument (13) of William Mackenzie, 1770; detail.

(30) Church of St. John Baptist. Monument (15) of John Booth, 1799, by Coade.

(30) Church of St. John Baptist. Altar frontal, 1718.

(29) Church of St. George.
   Monument in bell metal (17) of Tobie Norris, 1626.

(30) Church of St. John Baptist.
   Pulpit cloth, 1701; detail.

(28) Church of All Saints. Brass (3) of John Saunders, 1693.

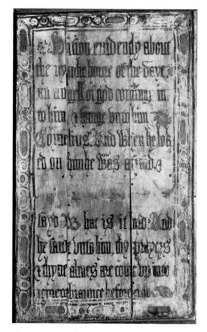

(48) Browne's Hospital.
   Painted panel in Audit Room.

PLATE 54   WOODWORK: MEDIEVAL AND LATER

(48) Browne's Hospital.
Chair in chapel, medieval.

(30) Church of St. John Baptist.
Font-cover, 17th-century.

(48) Browne's Hospital. Chest, medieval.

(48) Browne's Hospital. Chest, 1629.

(28) All Saints' Church.
Hour-glass bracket, 17th-century.

(48) Browne's Hospital.
Alms box, medieval.

(33) St. Mary's Church. 3rd bell by Tobie Norris, 1625.

(33) St. Mary's Church. 7th bell by Tobie Norris, 1626.

PLATE 56

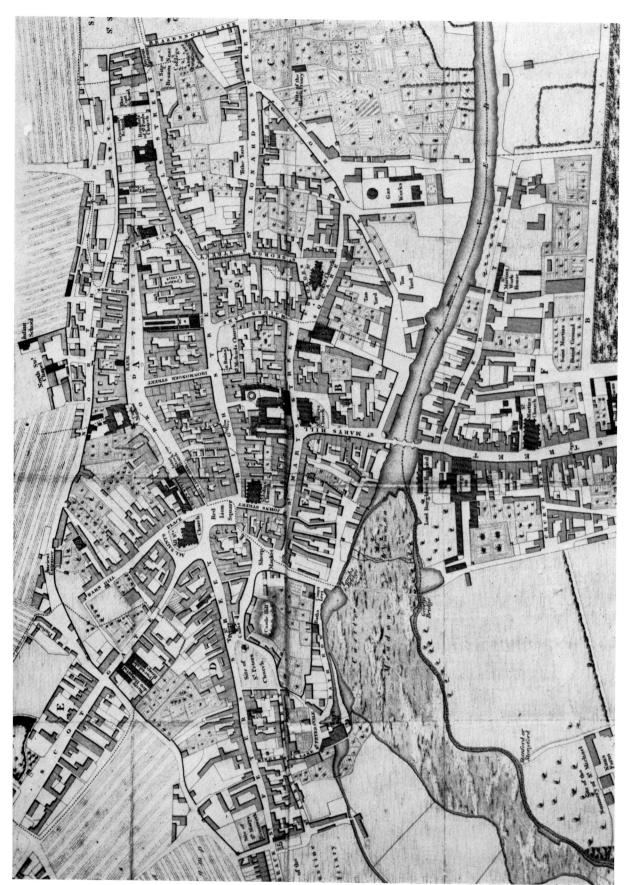

THE TOWN OF STAMFORD. Detail of map by James Knipe, 1833.

(11) TOWN WALLS. Bastion, medieval.

(46) GATEWAY OF FRANCISCAN FRIARY.
Second quarter of 14th century.

Looking east.

Looking west.

(338) 13 ST. MARY'S HILL. Undercroft, early 13th-century.

Looking east.

Looking south west.

(183) 23 HIGH STREET.

PLATE 60   MEDIEVAL VAULTS AND ARCADING

(214) 24 HIGH STREET ST. MARTINS. Undercroft, 13th-century.

(379) 16–17 ST. PAUL'S STREET. Wall-arcade in former hall, late 13th-century.

Archway formerly at 27 High Street
St. Martins. Drawing by Buckler, 1811.

(304) 11 St. George's Street. West elevation.
Drawing by Twopeny, 1825.

(297) 17 St. George's Square. North elevation.
Drawing by Twopeny, 1831.

Former house, probably in Water Street. Rear elevation.
Drawing by Twopeny, 1826.

(British Museum)

(377) 14 St. Paul's Street. Capital.

(33) St. Mary's Church. Window formerly at
(297) 17 St. George's Square.

(232) 53 High Street St. Martins. Window tympanum.

(377) 14 St. Paul's Street. Wall-arch.

(338) 13 St. Mary's Hill. Wall-arcade.

(214) 24 High Street St. Martins.
Vault-corbel, 13th-century.

(342) 4 St. Mary's Place.
Vault-boss, 14th or 15th-century.

(379) 16–17 St. Paul's Street.
Corbel, late 13th-century.

(377) 14 St. Paul's Street.
Corbel, 13th-century.

(379) 16–17 St. Paul's Street.
Corbel, late 13th-century.

PLATE 64　　　　DOMESTIC BUILDINGS: 13TH-CENTURY

East wall, west face.

Doorway in east wall.

(10) CASTLE. Hall Range, probably late 13th-century.

(336) 10 St. Mary's Hill. Doorway, 12th-century.

(383) Brazenose House. Gateway, early 13th-century.

(253) 15th-century doorway now at 5–6 Maiden Lane,
before removal from 46–47 High Street.

(250) The Vale House. Doorway, 15th-century, reset.

PLATE 66   15TH-CENTURY ALMSHOUSE

From the south east.

View of *c.* 1858 showing hospital before alterations in 1870, and Corn Market of 1839. (from old photograph)

(48) BROWNE'S HOSPITAL. Built in 1475.

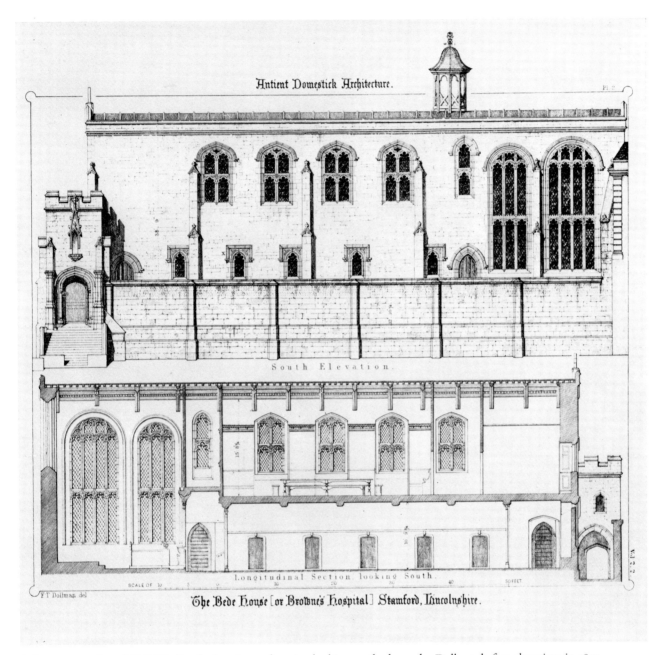

(48) BROWNE'S HOSPITAL. South elevation and section looking south, drawn by Dollman before alterations in 1870. (from *Antient Domestick Architecture*, 1858)

PLATE 68   15TH-CENTURY ALMSHOUSE

South range from north east.

Audit Room, looking east.

(48) BROWNE'S HOSPITAL.

North-east corner.

West range.

(48) BROWNE'S HOSPITAL. Courtyard before alterations of 1870. (from old photographs)

PLATE 70   MEDIEVAL HOUSES DRAWN BY WILLIAM STUKELEY IN 1735

'Peterborough Hall', All Saints' Place. Demolished.

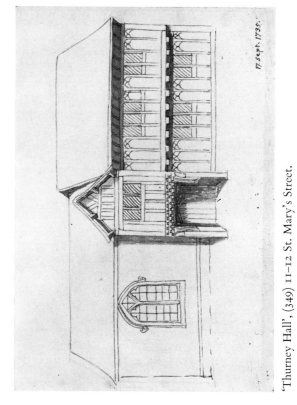

'Thurney Hall', (349) 11–12 St. Mary's Street.

'Black Hall', Red Lion Square. Demolished.

'Sempringham Hall', (412) 31–32 St. Peter's Street.

(Stamford Archaeological Society)

(362) 28 St. Mary's Street. Medieval with later alterations.

(415) 35–36 St. Peter's Street. Late medieval and 17th-century.

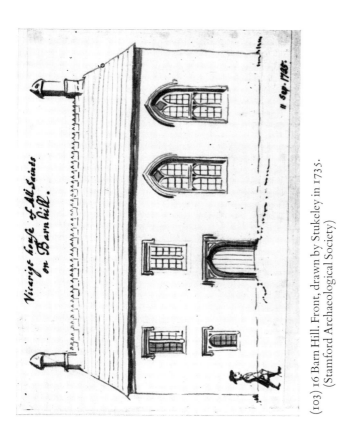

(103) 16 Barn Hill. Front, drawn by Stukeley in 1735. (Stamford Archaeological Society)

(103) 16 Barn Hill. Medieval with later alterations.

PLATE 72   EARLY HOUSES

(372, 373) 7, 8–9 St. Paul's Street. Medieval and 17th-century.

(329, 330) 61, 62–3 St. Leonard's Street. No. 61 dated 1685, nos. 62–63 dated 1662 but having medieval origin.

(238) 68–69 High Street St. Martins. Late 15th-century origin.

(327, 328) 59, 60 St. Leonard's Street. 17th-century and later.

(207) 11 High Street St. Martins. 17th-century.

(78) 13 All Saints' Street. Late 17th-century.

(386) 32 St. Paul's Street. Early 17th-century.

(240) 1 Ironmonger Street. Late 17th-century.

(374) 10–11 ST. PAUL'S STREET. Late medieval house with 17th-century front.

(210) 20 HIGH STREET ST. MARTIN'S. West front of the late 18th century disguising late medieval structure.

(216) 25 HIGH STREET ST. MARTINS. Medieval house with early 17th-century front.

(375) 12 ST. PAUL'S STREET. Medieval house with front of 1663 and later.

(255) DIGBY HOUSE, Maiden Lane. Ceiling in east wing, early 16th-century.

(280) 6 RED LION SQUARE. Window head,
15th-century.

(354) 18 ST. MARY'S STREET. Crown-post roof,
late medieval.

(255) DIGBY HOUSE. Heraldry on oriel window,
early 16th-century.

(95) 5–6 BARN HILL. Roof over rear range.

(238) THE HERMITAGE, 68–69 High Street St. Martins. Partition in west range.

(336) 10 ST. MARY'S HILL. Drawing by W. Twopeny, 1829. (BM).

(334, 335) 8, 9 ST. MARY'S HILL. Probably 16th-century.

(368) 40 ST. MARY'S STREET. Probably 16th-century.

(394) 6 ST. PETER'S HILL. From north east, c. 1600.

(364) 30 ST. MARY'S STREET. From west, late medieval.

PLATE 80   17TH-CENTURY ALMSHOUSE

North-east corner of almshouse built over
12th-century culvert.

West range from north east, probably 1616.

West range from south east, probably 1616.

(49) LORD BURGHLEY'S HOSPITAL.

(224) 39–40 HIGH STREET ST. MARTINS.

(142) 32 BROAD STREET.

PLATE 82   17TH-CENTURY HOUSES

(189) 51 HIGH STREET (demolished).

(316) 3 ST. LEONARD'S STREET. 1666.

(231) 52 HIGH STREET ST. MARTINS.

(236) 65 HIGH STREET ST. MARTINS.

(308) 24 ST. GEORGE'S STREET.

(405) 15 ST. PETER'S STREET. Mostly 1663.

(370) 44 ST. MARY'S STREET.
Bay window of 1656.

PLATE 84   17TH-CENTURY PLASTERWORK

Decoration on end wall.

Decoration on ceiling.

(398) Former WILLIAMSON'S ALMSHOUSES, now 3 St. Peter's Street.

(210) 20 HIGH STREET ST. MARTINS. Painted plaster wall,
late 16th-century.

(189) 51 HIGH STREET (demolished). Painted studwork wall, *c.* 1600.

(298) 18 ST. GEORGE'S SQUARE. Eaves soffit boards, 18th-century.

PLATE 86   17TH-CENTURY WATER MILLS

(66) HUDD'S MILL, from west.

(65) KING'S MILL, from west.

Bed of abandoned canal west of River Gwash.

Air photograph showing junction of canal (W. to E.) and River Gwash (N. to S.).

(27) CANAL.

PLATE 88   LATE 17TH-CENTURY HOUSES

Street front.

Garden front.

(299) 19 ST. GEORGE'S SQUARE. Built in 1674.

(299) 19 ST. GEORGE'S SQUARE. Ground-floor room, 1674.

(298) 18 ST. GEORGE'S SQUARE. Ground-floor room, early 18th-century.

PLATE 90

(97) 9 BARN HILL. Gateway in garden of Stukeley House, probably early 17th-century.

(58) ASSEMBLY ROOMS. Entrance front, 1727.

(60) THEATRE. Entrance front, 1768.

(194) 59 HIGH STREET. Early 18th-century.

(178, 179) 14–17 HIGH STREET. c. 1700.

(191) 54–55 HIGH STREET. Front, first half of 18th century.

(180) 18–19 HIGH STREET. Between 1719 and 1736, with later 18th-century shop fronts, now much altered. (from old photograph)

PLATE 94   18TH-CENTURY INN

Street front added by George Portwood to earlier building in 1724.

North range, south front, 1787–8.

(239) GEORGE HOTEL.

Street front.

Garden front, with alterations of *c.* 1800.

(383) BRAZENOSE HOUSE. Built in 1723.

PLATE 96   EARLY AND MID 18TH-CENTURY HOUSES

(96) BARN HILL HOUSE. West front, refaced in mid 18th century.

(72) 3 ALL SAINTS' PLACE. South front, early 18th-century.

(229) 47–50 HIGH STREET ST. MARTINS. Formerly the Marquis of Granby Inn, first half of the 18th century.

BROAD STREET from west.

ST. MARY'S STREET from east.

(184) 25–26 HIGH STREET.

(246) 9–10 IRONMONGER STREET.

(341) 3 ST. MARY'S PLACE. First half of 18th century.

(358) 23 ST. MARY'S STREET. Before 1753.

(182) 21 HIGH STREET. From south east, 1732.

PLATE 102   EARLY 18TH-CENTURY HOUSES

(237) 66–67 HIGH STREET ST. MARTINS.

(341) 2 ST. MARY'S PLACE. West front, first half of 18th century.

(100) 13 BARN HILL. Built in 1740.

PLATE 104   MID 18TH-CENTURY ARCHITECTURE

(360) 26 ST. MARY'S STREET. Rear wing from south.

(96) BARN HILL HOUSE. Summer House.

West front before recent reconstruction. (from an old photograph)

From north west.

(188) 41 HIGH STREET.

PLATE 106   MID 18TH-CENTURY HOUSES

(173) 6–7 HIGH STREET. Mid 18th-century with early 19th-century shop front.

(357) 22 ST. MARY'S STREET. Second quarter of 18th century.

(242) 3 IRONMONGER STREET.
First half of 18th century.

(442) 12 WATER STREET.
Refronted shortly before 1745.

(291) 1 ST. GEORGE'S SQUARE.
Mid 18th-century alterations to earlier front.

(358) 24 ST. MARY'S STREET.
After 1754 and before 1779.

PLATE 108   EARLY AND MID 18TH-CENTURY HOUSES

(351) 15 ST. MARY'S STREET. Early 18th-century.

(132) 11 BROAD STREET. Mid 18th-century.

(292) 2–4 ST. GEORGE'S SQUARE. Mid 18th-century.

(259, 359, 360) 13 MAIDEN LANE, 25, 26 ST. MARY'S STREET. West fronts, third quarter 18th century.

(300, 301, 58) 20, 21 ST. GEORGE'S SQUARE and ASSEMBLY ROOMS.
Early 18th-century; No. 21 refronted c. 1768.

PLATE 110   18TH-CENTURY HOUSES

(381) 24 St. Paul's Street. Mid 18th-century.

(385) 31 St. Paul's Street. Probably 1747.

(174) 8 High Street. Mid 18th-century with later
alterations to windows.

(174) 8 High Street. Rear elevation,
early 18th-century.

(167) 3–4 Crown Street.

(150) 52 Broad Street.

(284) 3 Red Lion Street.

(186) 31 High Street.

(206) 8–10 High Street St. Martins. Early 18th-century.

(376) 13 St. Paul's Street. Mid 18th-century.

(389) 41–42 St. Paul's Street. Early 18th-century.

(185) 28–29 High Street. Early 18th-century front.

(218) 33 High Street St. Martins. Early 18th-century.

(133) 14 Broad Street. Second quarter 18th century.

(134) 15 Broad Street. Second quarter 18th century.

(220) 35 High Street St. Martins. Second quarter 18th century.

PLATE 114   18TH-CENTURY HOUSES

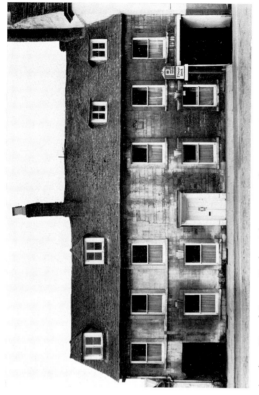

(144) 33 Broad Street. Early 18th-century front.

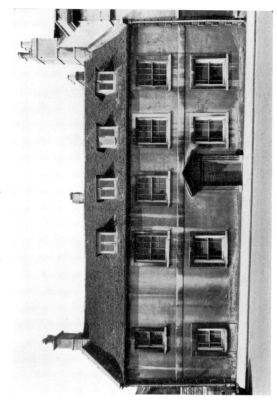

(227) 45 High Street St. Martins. Mid 18th-century front.

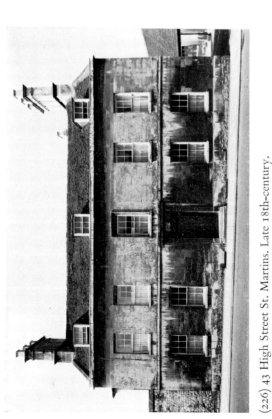

(226) 43 High Street St. Martins. Late 18th-century.

(232) 53 High Street St. Martins. Mid 18th-century.

(298) 18 St. George's Square. Second quarter 18th century.

(223) Lady Anne's House, 38 High Street St. Martins.
Early 18th-century with later alterations.

(136, 137) 19, 20–21 Broad Street. Mid and late 18th-century.

(305, 306) 17, 18 St. George's Street.
Early and mid 18th-century.

PLATE 116   LATE 18TH-CENTURY HOUSES

(331) 1–2 ST. MARY'S HILL. Built in 1792–4.

(361) 27 ST. MARY'S STREET. Built in 1794–6.

West front.

North front.

(57) TOWN HALL. Built in 1776–9.

PLATE 118   18TH AND EARLY 19TH-CENTURY BUILDINGS

(352) STAMFORD HOTEL. North wing, early 18th-century.

(126) 1 BROAD STREET. Early 19th-century front added to an early 18th-century building.

(37) Trinity Methodist Chapel. Panel representing Charity, early 19th-century.

(51) Hopkin's Hospital. Cartouche with arms of Stamford, 1770, and earlier fragments.

(57) Town Hall. Cartouche with arms of Stamford, 1776-9.

(239) George Hotel. Arms of Cecil on main front, 1724.

(218) 33 High Street St. Martins. Pilaster capital, early 18th-century.

(387) Conduit, St. Paul's Street, 1797.

(221) 36 High Street St. Martins. Cornice and
masonry details, 1767–71.

(357) 21 St. Mary's Street. Walling of
Wittering Pindle, c. 1827.

(357) 22 St. Mary's Street. Chimney stack,
second quarter of 18th century.

(375) 12 St. Paul's Street. Doorway, late 17th-century.

(97) Stukeley House, 9 Barn Hill.
Windows on main front, 1796–1801.

(57) Town Hall. 1776–9.

(361) 27 St. Mary's Street. 1794–6.

(100) 13 Barn Hill. 1740.

(188) 41 High Street. Mid 18th-
century, reconstructed.

(240) 1 Ironmonger Street.
Late 17th-century.

(98) 10 Barn Hill. 1804.

(167) 3–4 Crown Street.
Mid 18th-century.

(223) 38 High Street St. Martins.
Early 18th-century.

(221) 36 High Street St. Martins.
1767–71.

PLATE 122   EAVES-CORNICES

(174) 8 High Street. Plaster eaves-decoration. Early 18th-century.

(134) 15 Broad Street. Second quarter 18th century.

(72) 3 All Saints' Place. Early 18th-century.

(291) 1 St. George's Square. Mid 18th-century.

(358) 23–24 St. Mary's Street. Before 1753.

(179) 15 High Street. c. 1700.

(71) 2 All Saints' Place. First half 18th century.

(193) 57 High Street. Early 18th-century.

(178) 14 High Street. *c.* 1700.

(194) 59 High Street. Early 18th-century.

(179) 17 High Street. *c.* 1700.

(220) 35 High Street St. Martins. Second quarter 18th century.

PLATE 124   DOORWAYS AND PORCHES

(99) 12 Barn Hill. *c.* 1700.

(210) 20 High Street St. Martins. Late 18th-century.

(356) 20 St. Mary's Street. *c.* 1800.

(97) 9 Barn Hill. Early 19th-century.

(126) 1 Broad Street.

(100) 13 Barn Hill
(and above). 1740.

(99) 12 Barn Hill
(and above).

(127) 2 Broad Street. Front and side gates.

PLATE 126   LATE 17TH-CENTURY FIREPLACES

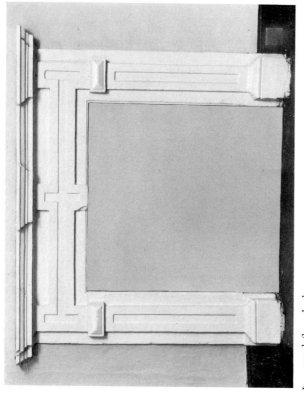

In second-floor bedroom.

In first-floor bedroom.

In former hall.

In first-floor bedroom.

(299) 19 ST. GEORGE'S SQUARE. Fireplaces of 1674.

(100) 13 Barn Hill. In first-floor room.

(96) Barn Hill House. In ground-floor room.

(357) 22 St. Mary's Street. In first-floor room.

PLATE 128   STONE FIREPLACES

(239) George Hotel. On first floor, early 17th-century.

(360) 26 St. Mary's Street. On first floor,
second quarter 18th century.

(237) 66 High Street St. Martins.
    Second quarter 18th century.

(239) George Hotel. On ground floor, reset,
    early 18th-century.

(375) 12 St. Paul's Street.

(225) 42 High Street St. Martins (reset).

Above: (144) 33 Broad Street.
Below: (444) 16 Water Street.

(374) 10–11 St. Paul's Street.

(100) 13 Barn Hill.
Stair detail, 1740.

(383) Brazenose House.
Stair detail, 1723.

(127) 2 Broad Street.
Stair detail, early 18th-century.

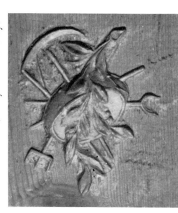

(58) Assembly Rooms. Overmantel
detail, early 19th-century.

(298) 18 St. George's Square. Carved overmantel, second quarter 18th century.

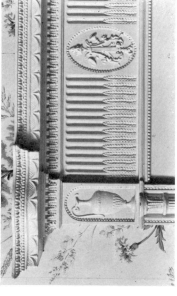

(250) The Vale House. Fireplace surround, c. 1785.

(299) 19 St. George's Square. Fireplace surround,
mid 18th-century.

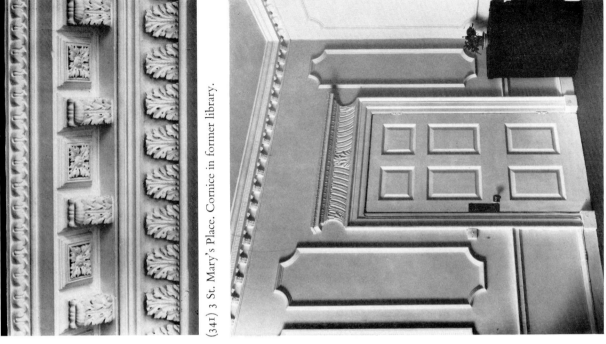

(341) 3 St. Mary's Place. Cornice in former library.

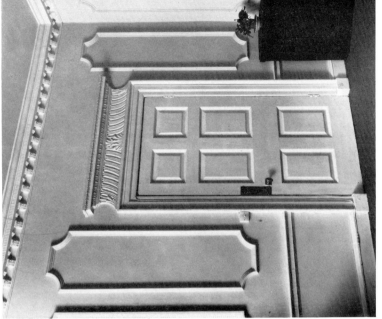

(136) 19 Broad Street. Ground-floor room, second half 18th century.

(341) 3 St. Mary's Place. Ground-floor room.

PLATE 132 STAIRCASES

(178) 14 High Street. *c.* 1700.

(127) 2 Broad Street. Early 18th-century.

(238) The Hermitage. Early 18th-century.

(299) 19 St. George's Square. 1674.

(239) George Hotel, by Robert Pilkington. 1726.

(238) The Hermitage. Early 18th-century.

(360) 26 St. Mary's Street. Second quarter 18th century.

(101) 14 Barn Hill. Second quarter 19th century.

PLATE 134 STAIRCASES

(100) 13 BARN HILL. 1740.

(383) BRAZENOSE HOUSE. 1723.

(358) 23 ST. MARY'S STREET. Mid 18th-century.

(100) 13 BARN HILL. 1740.

PLATE 136   18TH-CENTURY PLASTERWORK

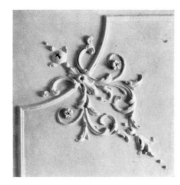

(360) 26 St. Mary's Street.
Mid 18th-century.

(383) Brazenose House. First-floor room, apparently *c.* 1800.

(100) 13 BARN HILL. Stair hall, 1740.

(136) 19 BROAD STREET. Ground-floor room, second half 18th century.

(352) STAMFORD HOTEL. Entrance hall, *c.* 1810.

PLATE 138   SHOP FRONTS

(173) 7 HIGH STREET. Early 19th-century.

(246) 9 IRONMONGER STREET. Early 19th-century.

(350) 13 ST. MARY'S STREET. 1849.

(344) 4 ST. MARY'S STREET. Early 19th-century.

PLATE 140   18TH AND EARLY 19TH-CENTURY HOUSES

(145) 34 Broad Street. Late 18th-century.

(139) 25 Broad Street. Mid 18th-century.

(281) 8–10 RED LION SQUARE. Built in 1818.

(177) 11–12 HIGH STREET. 18th-century bay windows added to earlier house.

(348) 10 ST. MARY'S STREET. Street front, early 19th-century.

(321, 322, 323) 15–17, 18–19, 20 ST. LEONARD'S STREET. Early 19th-century.

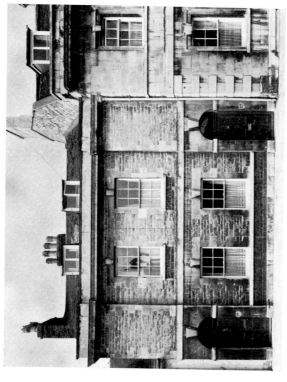

(136) 18 Broad Street. c. 1830.

(400) 8–9 St. Peter's Street. 1804.

(221) 36 High Street St. Martins. 1767–71.

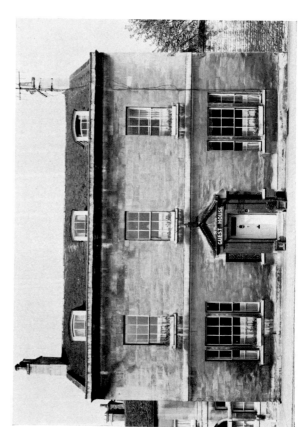

(225) 42 High Street St. Martins. Late 18th-century.

(235) 59–60 High Street St. Martins. First quarter 19th century.

(444) Welland House, 16 Water Street. 1834.

(214) 24 High Street St. Martins. Early 19th-century.

(147) 39–40 Broad Street. Soon after 1786.

PLATE 144   STREET SCENES

BARN HILL from south east.

ST. PETER'S VALE from south.

ST. PAUL'S STREET from south east.

IRONMONGER STREET from south.

PLATE 146   LATE 18TH AND EARLY 19TH-CENTURY HOUSES

(74) 16 ALL SAINTS' PLACE. Before 1793.

(93) 3 BARN HILL. Early 19th-century.

(85) AUSTIN HOUSE. Garden front, c. 1800.

(217) 30 HIGH STREET ST. MARTINS.
Before 1821.

(228) 46 HIGH STREET ST. MARTINS.
Second quarter 19th century.

(356, 357) 20, 21 ST. MARY'S STREET.
No. 20 has mid 18th-century front, heightened in *c.* 1800; No. 21 was built in *c.* 1827.

PLATE 148   LATE 18TH-CENTURY HOUSES

(71) 2 ALL SAINTS' PLACE. Second half 18th century.

(97) STUKELEY HOUSE, Barn Hill. Built between 1796 and 1801.

(85) AUSTIN HOUSE. Garden stairs, c. 1800.

(98) 10 BARN HILL. East side, 1804.

PLATE 150   LATE 18TH-CENTURY BUILDINGS

Garden front.

Bridge in Garden.

(250) THE VALE HOUSE, 2 King's Mill Lane. By William Legg, 1785.

(61) LIBRARY, formerly portico to market. By William Legg, 1804.

(110) THE BATH HOUSE. Built in 1823.

PLATE 152   EARLY 19TH-CENTURY BUILDINGS

Front from south east.

Attic storey with figure of Justice.

(352) STAMFORD HOTEL. By J. L. Bond, c. 1810.

(352) Stamford Hotel. Ballroom ceiling, detail.

Ballroom; pilaster and cornice detail.

(129) 5 Broad Street. Plaster cornice, 1846.

Fireplace surround, detail.

(352) STAMFORD HOTEL. c. 1810.

PLATE 154   EARLY 19TH-CENTURY TERRACES

(426) ROCK TERRACE, Scotgate. Built in 1841.

(288) RUTLAND TERRACE. Built in 1829–31.

(447) LUMBY'S TERRACE. West row, *c.* 1840.

(407) EXETER COURT, St. Paul's Street. East row, early 19th-century.

(447) LUMBY'S TERRACE, Water Street. Pair of houses at S. end, 1826 and 1827.

PLATE 156   BUILDINGS DESIGNED BY THE BROWNING FAMILY

(59) Former STAMFORD INSTITUTION. By Bryan Browning, 1842.

(96) BARN HILL HOUSE. North front by Bryan Browning, 1843–4.

(64) TOWN BRIDGE. By Edward Browning, 1848–9.

(96) BARN HILL HOUSE.
Doorway by Bryan Browning, 1843–4.

(59) Former STAMFORD INSTITUTION.
Doorway by Bryan Browning, 1842.

PLATE 158   MID 19TH-CENTURY BUILDINGS

(129) 5, 7, 8 BROAD STREET. By Charles Richardson, 1846.   (350) 13–14 ST. MARY'S STREET. 1849.

(425) 30–31 SCOTGATE. 1844.

(427) ROCK HOUSE. 1842.

(101, 102) 14, 15 BARN HILL. Mid 19th-century.

PLATE 160   18TH AND 19TH-CENTURY ALMSHOUSES

(50) Fryer's Hospital. By George Basevi, 1832.

(51) Hopkins' Hospital. 1770.

(53) Truesdale's Hospital. By George Basevi, 1832.

(53) Truesdale's Hospital. Courtyard by George Basevi, 1832.

(62) Stamford and Rutland Infirmary. By J. P. Gandy, 1826–8.

(69) Former Railway Station, Water Street. By William Hurst, 1855.

(68) Railway Station. By Sancton Wood, 1848.

(279) 4–5 Red Lion Square and 1 High Street. By Bryan Browning, 1848.

PLATE 162   18TH AND EARLY 19TH-CENTURY BUILDINGS

(451) Portal, Wharf Road. By Bryan Browning, 1845.

(152) Clock House, Casterton Road. 1839.

(450) Warehouses, Wharf Road. 1756.

(68) Railway Station. By Sancton Wood, 1848.

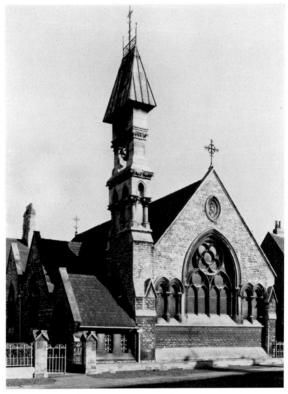

(35) Church of Our Lady and St. Augustine.
By George Goldie, 1862–4.

(176) Gothic House, High Street. 1849.

(333) 4 St. Mary's Hill. By Edward Browning, 1849.

INDEX

In this Index numbers in brackets refer to the monuments as listed in the Inventory. References to the Sectional Preface and to long accounts of monuments include page numbers but otherwise the monument numbers alone are given. The classified lists, chronologically arranged, are selective.

Printed in England for Her Majesty's Stationery Office by W. S. Cowell Ltd, 8 Butter Market, Ipswich.   Dd 505938. K24. 1/77.